SPOUSE ABUSE:

an annotated bibliography of violence between mates

by

EUGENE A. ENGELDINGER

The Scarecrow Press, Inc.
Metuchen, N.J., & London
1986

Library of Congress Cataloging-in-Publication Data

Engeldinger, Eugene A.
  Spouse abuse.

  Includes indexes.
  1. Wife abuse--Bibliography. 2. Conjugal
violence--Bibliography. I. Title.
Z5703.4.W53E53 1986   016.3641'5553   85-14546
[HV6626]
ISBN 0-8108-1838-8

FOR MY DAUGHTER, LARA ANN
may she never know the pain of an abusive relationship.

FOR MY PARENTS, CLARENCE AND HAZEL
who in over 50 years of marriage
never raised a hand in anger against each other.

CONTENTS

PREFACE

The purpose of this bibliography is to collect into one source all the important literature regarding spouse abuse and to annotate it for the use and convenience of scholars, students, helping professionals, and others who are interested in the topic. Entries found here include popular and scholarly books and articles, government publications, conference papers, master's theses, doctoral dissertations, directories, handbooks, and pamphlets published or presented in English through 1983. Virtually everything that has been annotated here has been examined firsthand.

The original hope had been to produce a complete listing of spouse abuse materials, but it seems that many publications were ephemeral and can no longer be found. It happens, too, that a few references culled from other publications are so vague, esoteric or inaccurate, they could not be verified and therefore were not included. Noninclusion, in such cases, was believed better than confusing or frustrating the user with incomplete and bibliographically suspicious entries.

Two types of material not to be found here are newspaper articles and various forms of media, such as films and recordings. These have been left for another time.

E. A. E.

ACKNOWLEDGMENTS

Rarely is a book, especially a bibliography, done without the assistance, advice and encouragement of others. That is certainly true in this case. I must, therefore, thank the many who helped with this endeavor, including the following:

> The University of Wisconsin-Eau Claire Faculty Research Grants Committee, which provided funding to begin the project;

> Steve R. Marquardt, Director of Libraries, University of Wisconsin-Eau Claire, for continued support, encouragement, goodwill and easy access to library services and resources;

> Richard Bell and Kathleen Henning, whose tolerance and patience with my frequent and huge jags of interlibrary loan requests helped me not feel all of the guilt I deserved;

> Carol Kane and Barbara Stevens, my colleagues in the University of Wisconsin-Eau Claire Reference Department, for help with database searching and general advice;

> Frada Mozenter, University of North Carolina Library, Charlotte, who provided many suggestions and much information before serious work began, and for agreeing to critique the entire manuscript;

> Sue Center and staff at the Criminal Justice Center, University of Wisconsin-Madison Law Library, for enthusiastic assistance, tolerance of my rule stretching and provision of materials not readily found elsewhere;

> William Ebbott, University of Wisconsin-Madison Law

Library for help with legal and government sources and a place to hang my hat;

Wisconsin Interlibrary Loan Services (WILS), University of Wisconsin-Madison for prompt and accurate service with my numerous and often less than complete requests;

Peg and Lara, for not complaining during the many months of living with, and eating at, a dining room table full of note cards and photocopies;

Dan Williams, my student assistant, who at first thought he was helping me work out a personal problem;

Catherine Jones, Mary Lou Albrecht and Carol Modl, who all typed portions of the manuscript;

and the many others who left their mark on this book.

INTRODUCTION

The question of family violence has until relatively recently suffered "selective inattention" from social scientists. The first domestic violence problem to attract the attention of researchers was child abuse. Only after that did adult family violence come to be recognized. As Laurie Wardell observes in the study "Science and Violence Against Wives" (The Dark Side of Families, Beverly Hills: Sage, 1983, p. 69), "O'Brien (1971) reports that the major family journal, Journal of Marriage and the Family, included not a single article with 'violence' in the title from its founding in 1939 through 1969, and Gelles (1980) adds that violence against adults in families was essentially invisible in the rarified atmosphere of social science literature. " As this bibliography shows, that is no longer the case.

The current attention on spouse abuse began in the early 1970's and received its impetus, in large measure, from Erin Pizzey's Scream Quietly or the Neighbors Will Hear. Prior to that publication, awareness seems to have been minimal with conventional "wisdom" holding that battering was rare and that, when it did exist, it stemmed from a sadomasochistic relationship between the spouses. That theory has fallen into disrepute and is found only rarely, and in modified form, in contemporary scholarly analysis.

The study of this phenomenon is still young, but already interesting patterns are evident. The several nineteenth-century articles that could be located condemned wife beating and cruelty and called for legislative reform. The examples of abuse the authors provide make clear the intensity and extensiveness of the problem. Like those who contributed to the renewed interest in the 1970's, many of the Victorian writers were feminists.

Between the turn of the century and the early 1970's little was written about wife beating per se, although a few

xi

studies of homicide provided statistics that indicate the frequency of intraspousal murder. Some evidence is also provided that such killings resulted from, or in conjunction with,
abusive behavior, sometimes of many years' standing.

The late 1960's and early 1970's saw some scholarship
and experimentation by police and law enforcement officials.
The question of the legality of wife assault, not to mention
the homicides that often occurred--the victims being husbands,
wives and the police--made this all very much a police concern. Their responses to spouse abuse were intertwined with
their concern for dealing with domestic disturbances. Early
on, there seems to have been little differentiation in police
procedures regarding family disturbances and wife battering.
In time however, pressures by enlightened law enforcement
officials and the feminist movement brought changes.

Feminists have been extremely influential in drawing
public attention to the evils of spouse abuse. They were the
primary voices of concern during the nineteenth century and
their influence is especially marked during the early days of
the public awareness and shelter establishment campaigns of
the 1970's. Their contributions continue to be important, especially at the practical day-to-day level of working with the
victims. Their impact on legislation and local government
agencies is noteworthy in the United States and abroad.

Most of the early scholarship of the 1970's was of a
sociological or psychological nature. Emphasis on the family
unit, and/or society in general, as the root cause of such
violence, or the pathology of individuals or aberrant behavior
of a few, was the norm. In many of these studies, spousal
violence is seen as one element of family violence, similar in
origin to that of child abuse, battered baby syndrome, sibling
violence, and abuse of the elderly.

With these early studies came a period of widespread
publicity. Many articles appeared in newspapers, popular
news journals and magazines of all stripes, and various news-
letters. Cases were depicted in television shows, and interviews with scholars and victims on local and national talk
shows provided the problem with much-needed exposure.

As the decade wore on, interest in the phenomenon and
feelings of responsibility spread. Gradually the helping professions were publishing awareness articles in their professional
journals with admonitions to their associates to be on the alert

for victims who needed proper assistance and referral, but
who had presented themselves ostensibly for other reasons.
Among these were social workers, nurses and physicians of
various specialities, lawyers, hospital workers, the clergy,
psychiatrists, and psychologists. Concern developed that too
often battered women were not being recognized, so their
problems were not receiving sufficient, not to mention proper,
attention, and that the helping professionals were not meeting
their responsibilities when it came to these victims.

Along with this came the realization that the abusive
personality, the characteristics of the victim, the effects of
the social and economic environment, biology, alcoholism and
many other factors associated with battering were inadequately
understood, so more research would be necessary. The same
held true for assistance and treatment programs. One could
only provide proper and effective treatment if the causes of
the problem were known and understood.

The literature of spouse abuse tends, then, to be of
several types:

1) popular books, pamphlets and articles aimed at
   bringing the problem to public attention;

2) articles and books aimed at bringing the problem
   to the attention of the helping professionals;

3) guides and directories to assistance programs for
   the abused and the abuser;

4) how-to handbooks for the establishment of treatment
   programs and shelters;

5) scholarly studies of victims, abusers, treatment
   methods and the effects on the children in the family;

6) bibliographies and literature reviews; and

7) government reports and studies of the problem for
   legislative action.

The evolution of the literature shows two major trends.
First, there has been a steady change from the more popular
writings of the early 1970's to the more scholarly studies of
the 1980's. To be sure, throughout the period popular and

scholarly books and articles have appeared. The difference
is that the majority of the early materials were populariza-
tions based on a few studies, but now the preponderance is
scholarly. More of the recent materials have been directed
at the academic and professional communities.

The second trend is the amount of information that is
being published yearly. Annual output seems to increase
geometrically. The reason, no doubt, lies in the number of
professions interested in the topic and the amount of research
and study being conducted. There have even been reviews of
the literature in recent years.

The future will see even more interest in this topic.
At present there is very little being written about psychological and emotional abuse of mates, and research regarding
husband abuse is underdeveloped. Cross-cultural comparisons
of family violence are only beginning to be done, as are
studies of premarital violence. Legal issues, such as those
surrounding marital rape and victims killing their abusers,
are yet to be settled and will provide grist for many mills.
The relationship of alcohol to battering and the effects on
children of witnessing battering parents are uncertain and deserve study.

What has been done so far is only the beginning. Most
of that beginning will be found in the following pages.

THE BIBLIOGRAPHY

1 Abood, Charles D.; Barbara Bloomfield; and Joseph D. Moran.
      "Toledo Municipal Court's Pre-Adjudication Program. "
      Court Review 18 (1980): 18-24.
      Abood, Judge, Toledo Municipal Court, and Bloomfield and
Moran, specialists in the Pre-adjudication Program, describe that
program's purpose, operation and success. Attention is aimed at
interpersonal disputes which are technically criminal, of which spouse
battering was one example. The program effectively found relief for
90% of the grievants. This program relieves the courts of a problem that can be more effectively dealt with in another manner.

2 Abrams, Susan. "The Battered Husband Bandwagon, Media Hypes
      Battered Men, Buries Battered Women. " Seven Days II
      (September 29, 1978): 20.
      The author disputes the claims by Steinmetz [1502] and Levy
and Langley [914] regarding the prevalence of husband battering. She
is especially chagrined at the attention it received from the media.
She says the "fuss" over husband battering seems to be part of a
general reaction to the women's movement and women's increasing
independence.

3 Abramson, Catherine. Spouse Abuse: An Annotated Bibliography.
      Washington, D. C. : Center for Women Policy Studies, 1977.
      20 p.
      An early bibliography with good annotations. Now dated.

4 "Abused Wives Need Treatment in Shelter, Texas MD Says. "
      American Family Physician 20 (September 1979): 203, 206.
      This news note quotes Alice A. O'Donnell, Assistant Profes-
sor, University of Texas Medical Branch, who, citing research done
at Yale, states that the family physician often does not have the resources to deal with all the needs of the victim of wife abuse. Shelters can deal with their needs, so physicians should refer them
there.

5 "Abuser Eviction Law Held Constitutional. " Response to Violence
      in the Family 3 (November 1979): 5.
      A short, newsy account of Boyle v. Boyle, which challenged
the Pennsylvania Protection from Abuse Act. This law allows the
judge to order a person who abuses another in the family to leave
the household.

1

6   Adams, David. Men Unlearning Violence. Boston: EMERGE,
        n. d.   7 p.

7   Adams, David C. , and Andrew J. McCormick. "Men Unlearn-
        ing Violence: A Group Approach Based on the Collective
        Model. " In The Abusive Partner: An Analysis of Domestic
        Battering. Ed. Maria Roy. New York: Van Nostrand Rein-
        hold, 1982, pp. 170-97.

8   Adler, Emily Stier. "The Underside of Married Life: Power,
        Influence and Violence. " In Women and Crime in America.
        Ed. Lee H. Bowker. New York: Macmillan, 1981, pp.
        300-20.
        In-depth interviews were conducted with fifty couples to de-
termine how each spouse perceived his or her own power position
within the relationship.   Equalitarian, husband-dominated, wife-
dominated and "differently perceived power structures" were the four
types which were found to exist.   In no case did battering appear to
be an element of the marriage, but several did have an ingredient
of violence or threatened violence.   Husband-dominated marriages
tend to have more violence than the others.   Equalitarian marriages
had the least.   This essay is a revised version of a paper presented
at the annual meeting of the American Sociological Association, Chicago, September 1977.

9   Adrian, Martha, and Carol Mitchell. A Study of Spouse Batter-
        ing in Montana. Helena, Mont. : Department of Community
        Affairs, 1978.   117 p.

10 Agle, Lawrence E. , and Lester Pincu. "A Casework Approach
        to Police Intervention in Family Disputes. " Social Casework
        58 (January 1977): 43-5.
        Cedar Grove, New Jersey, was experiencing an increase in
the number of family disturbances.   The authors were brought in to
train the police in proper intervention techniques, to prepare a manual of procedures and plan the interaction of various local service
agencies.   Response to the program, by public officials, was positive.

11 Ahrens, Lois. "Battered Women's Refuges. " In Fight Back!
        Feminist Resistance to Male Violence. Eds. Frederique
        Delacoste and Felice Newman. Minneapolis: Cleis Press,
        1981, pp. 104-9.
        Using the Austin, Texas, battered women's shelter as the
model, Ahrens argues that refuges for battered women, like rape
crisis centers, seem to be undergoing a transformation from feminist, nonhierarchical, community-based organizations to institutionalized social service agencies.   Feminists must be aware of such possibilities and work to prevent it from happening.

12 Ahrens, Lois. "Battered Women's Refuges: Feminist Coopera-
        tives vs Social Service Institutions. " AEGIS: Magazine on
        Ending Violence Against Women (Summer/Autumn 1980): 9-15.
        Also in Radical America 14 (May-June 1980): 41-7.

One of the original founders of the Austin shelter for battered women, Ahrens describes how the feminist principles by
which the shelter was originally established were, within two years,
subverted and the shelter developed a paid staff, a full-time admin-
istrator and other elements of hierarchical bureaucracies. The author views the former rather than the latter to be more beneficial
to the clients and gives several preventive measures that others can
use to prevent a similar occurrence with their shelters.

13   Alani, A. A.   "The Battered Husband. "   British Journal of Psy-
         chiatry 129 (July 1976): 96.
     The author, from Netherne Hospital, Coulsdon, Surrey, says
that with all the talk of battering he has heard no mention of husband
beating, but that he has run into several cases himself. The tone
of the letter indicates sympathy for the male victims.

14   "Alcohol and Domestic Violence. "   Response to Violence and
         Sexual Abuse in the Family 2 (January 1979): 4.

15   Aldrich, James R. , et al.   "Battered Wives and the Justice
         System. "   Paper presented for Dr. John Hogarth, Faculty
         of Law, University of British Columbia, Fall, 1978.

16   "The All-American Blood-Soaked Family. "   Human Behavior 5
         (February 1976): 34-5.
     General observations regarding wife abuse drawing heavily
from a talk by Murray Straus at the American Psychological Association meeting in Chicago, September 1975. Many view it to be a
husband's right to beat his wife. This is an outgrowth of the view
that the strong have the right to force their will on the weak.

17   Allen, Craig M. , and Murray A. Straus.   "Resources, Power
         and Husband-Wife Violence. "   Durham: University of New
         Hampshire, Department of Sociology, Pub. #V-12.   1975.
         Also in The Social Causes of Husband-Wife Violence.   Eds.
         Murray A. Straus and Gerald T. Hotaling.   Minneapolis:
         University of Minnesota Press, 1979, pp. 188-208.
     The authors research the relationship between the resources,
such as money, status, material, personal qualities, etc. , contributed by the husband and the wife and the amount of power either has
in the relationship. In conjunction with this, the authors determined
the amount of spousal violence that could be expected. Differences
were found between these interrelationships in middle- and working-
class couples. This article is useful for those concerned with resource theory and especially ultimate resource theory (violence).
This paper was also presented at the annual meeting of the National
Council on Family Relationships, August 2, 1975.

18   Allen, James R. , and Barbara Ann Allen.   "Violence in the
         Family. "   Family and Community Health 4 (August 1981):
         19-33.
     Overview of family violence in general, but does devote some
attention to spouse abuse. Faulty interaction between family members

is compounded by external factors. The violence is not the result
of individual personality but the system of relationships. Several
methods of interaction are suggested including transactional analysis
(TA).

19 Allwood, Rosemary, and Melanie Brown. "Women's Support
        Groups." In Identification and Treatment of Spouse Abuse;
        Health and Mental Health Agency Roles, Proceedings of
        a Conference. Eds. Abraham Lurie and Elizabeth B.
        Quitkin. New York: Editors, 1981, pp. 145-57.

20 American Bar Association. Section on Criminal Justice. Re-
        port to the House of Delegates. [Washington, D.C.]: The
        Association, 1978. 8 p.
    This resolution was adopted in February 1978 and supports
efforts to combat family violence. Shelter and counseling services
should be established, police and prosecutors must take the crime
more seriously, and data should be collected. Other recommendations along with a detailed report are included.

21 American Bar Association. Section on Criminal Justice. Victim
        Witness Assistance Project. Victim/Witness Legislation:
        Considerations for Policymakers. Washington, D.C.: The
        Association, 1981, pp. 63-71.
    Several legislative guides are provided for relief of domes-
tic violence. Protective orders are described with their purpose,
benefits, limitations, and impact on the criminal justice system
noted. Citations are made to such laws in other states with a sample given. Similar guides are provided for funding and for mandatory record-keeping legislation.

22 Anagnost, Eloise. The Angry Book. Ypsilanti, Mich.: Domes-
        tic Violence Project, 1981. 12 p.
    A coloring book used to help children in shelters express
their anger.

23 Andersen, Ingerlise. "Battered Women: The Dangerous Sex-
        Role Scenario."
    Paper presented at the IV World Congress of Sexology,
Mexico City, Mexico, 1979.

24 Andersen, Ingerlise. "Wife Battering in the Netherlands: Needs
        and Incidence." Paper presented at the International So-
        ciological Association Seminar on Sex Roles, Deviance,
        and Agents of Social Control, Dublin, Ireland, 1977.

25 Andersen, Kurt. "Private Violence." Time 122 (September 5,
        1983): 18-9.

26 Anderson, George M. "Wives, Mothers and Victims." America
        137 (August 6, 1977): 46-50.
    A good overview of the wife abuse problem incorporating
the research of Straus, J. J. Gayford, Del Martin, and others.

27 Anderson, Gordon A. Issues Relating to Domestic Violence .
    Madison: Wisconsin Legislative Council, 1977. 23 p.

28 Anderson, Gordon A. National and Wisconsin Statistics Relat-
        ing to Marriage, Divorce and Family Violence. Madison:
        Wisconsin Legislative Council, 1978. 14 p.

29 Anderson, Gordon A. ; Richard Sweet; and Stephen Lythcott.
        Information on Domestic Violence in Wisconsin: Extent
        and Services Available. (Research Bulletin 78-2). Madison:
        Wisconsin Legislative Council Staff, 1978. 75 p.
        Data were collected so the legislature could enact proper
    legislation regarding domestic violence. Questionnaires were sent
    to police and sheriffs, district attorneys, county social service agen-
    cies and others. Frequency of contact with domestic violence, how
    referred, services provided and other types of information were
    gathered. The questionnaire is appended.

30 Anderson, Ralph O. "Spouse Battering and Ohio's Domestic
        Violence Legislation. " University of Toledo Law Review
        13 (Winter 1982): 347-75.
        After a general discussion of spouse abuse, the author
    describes the process and hoped-for results of the new Ohio domes-
    tic violence laws. Good overview.

31 Ankeney, Margaret E. , ed. Family Violence: A Cycle of Abuse.
        Laramie: College of Education, University of Wyoming,
        1979. 161 p.
        This volume includes papers and some resource materials
    presented at the Wyoming Council for the Humanities, Family Vio-
    lence Conference, August 1978. All aspects of the phenomenon,
    including child abuse and spouse and elder battering, are included
    and discussed. Papers dealing with wife abuse are included in this
    bibliography as separate entries by each author.

32 Anstett, Richard E. , and Lorraine Wood. "The Patient Exhibit-
        ing Episodic Violent Behavior. " Journal of Family Prac-
        tice 16 (March 1983): 605-9.
        "Patients who present with violent behavioral eposodes or
    eccentric thought or behavioral patterns are at risk for inappropriate
    medical, as well as legal, interventions. " A diagnosis of temporal
    lobe epilepsy should be considered when the violent behavior is not
    consistent with the abuser's personality.

33 Appleton, Warren. "The Battered Woman Syndrome. " Annals
        of Emergency Medicine 9 (February 1980): 84-91.
        This study was conducted in the Emergency Department of
    Valley General Hospital of Renton, Washington. The purpose was
    to develop criteria for diagnosing battered women syndrome, to
    develop therapeutic tools, and to establish the depth of the problem.
    The findings were that this syndrome is encountered frequently in
    hospitals; it can sometimes, but not always, be identified; victims

are often not aware of assistance available to them; and therapeutic
hospital support teams should be very supportive to the victim.

34 Armstrong, Louise. The Home Front: Notes from the Family
        War Zone. New York: McGraw-Hill, 1983. 252 p.
    General discussion of various forms of family violence
including wife beating, child abuse and child molestation. Those
husbands who violate the trust of the family and abuse the other
members must be punished with jail terms. Male bias found in the
legal, judicial and helping professions works against punishing the
offender on the grounds that this would disrupt the family. Armstrong
notes that the family is already disrupted when the trust is violated.

35 Armstrong, Pamela D. Wife Battering: A Test Case for Ac-
        counts of Violence. M. A. thesis, University of Delaware,
        1983. 117 p.

36 Arndt, Nancy Yvonne. "Domestic Violence: An Investigation of
        the Psychological Aspects of the Battered Woman." Ph. D.
        dissertation, Fielding Institute, 1981. 113 p. Abstract
        in Dissertation Abstracts International 42B (February 1982):
        3405.

37 Arthur, Gary L.; P. Joe Sison; and Curtis E. McClung. "Domes-
        tic Disturbances--A Major Police Dilemma, and How One
        Major City Is Handling the Problem." Journal of Police
        Science and Administration 5, no. 4 (1977): 421.
    Arthur and Sison are associate professors of counseling
and psychological services at Georgia State University, while
McClung is Chief of Police of Columbus, Georgia. In 1974 they
set up a Family Crisis Intervention Program (based on Bard's
New York City Model) to train police officers how to better handle
family disputes. Overall the program was successful showing that
the law enforcement officer can no longer rely solely upon judo training, sophisticated weaponry, computerization and technical aids. "To
function effectively, he must be willing to develop the life skills necessary to help those victims he encounters in his day-to-day duties
and reconstruct their often shattered lives."

38 Ashley, Marta Segovia. "Shelters: Short-Term Needs." In Bat-
        tered Women: Issues of Public Policy. U. S. Commission
        on Civil Rights. Washington, D. C.: The Commission,
        1978, pp. 371-400.

39 Aviram, Yamima Rubens. "Battered Women." M. A. thesis,
        University of Illinois-Chicago Circle, 1981. 39 p.
    The author recruited eighteen battered and eighteen non-
battered women to participate in this study. Demographic intake
forms, an oral questionnaire/interview, the MMPI, Leary's Interpersonal Check List and the Gough Adjective Check List were all
used to collect information. The results, while not clearcut, indicate "that a masochistic subset of battered women exists." However,
because most of the subjects were no longer in the battering

relationship the tests measured the current mental outlook of the women. Many also had had psychiatric counseling since the incidents. More research is recommended with women still being victimized to determine the extent of the masochism.

40 BASW Working Party. "Working Party Recommendations: Battered Women." Social Work Today 9 (July 3, 1978): 12.
The British Association of Social Workers in recognition of the need to assist battered women developed this list of guidelines for identifying victims and providing aid.

41 Babcock-Williams, Carolyn. "Abused Wives: Factors Contributing to Tolerance of Abuse Among Wives Seeking Advice from Wake County Women's Aid." M.S. thesis, North Carolina State University-Raleigh, 1979. 125 p.
This paper attempts to answer two questions: Why do wives stay so long with an abusive husband? and What factors are related to the occurrence of abuse in some families? Data were collected through interviews from a sample of 57 women who contacted the Wake County Women's Aid from March to June 1979. The factors and perceptions analyzed were feelings of economic entrapment, psychological entrapment, violence experienced as a child and how all or any of these were related to the wife's willingness to seek help at the Wake County Women's Aid. No significant relationships were found. Severity of abuse, however, did seem to encourage the seeking of outside help or assistance. The questionnaire used is included.

42 Bach, George R., and Peter Wyden. "The Art of Family Fighting." In Confronting the Issues: Sex Roles, Marriage, and the Family. Ed. Kenneth C.W. Kammeyer. Boston: Allyn and Bacon, 1975, pp. 314-20.
Family fighting is common and necessary but it must be done fairly. The chief ingredients of good fighting are leveling, that is, being candid and transparent, and fighting in a spirit of goodwill and with due regard for the partner's handicaps. Physical force is unacceptable.

43 Bach, George R., and Peter Wyden. The Intimate Enemy; How to Fight Fair in Love and Marriage. New York: William Morrow and Company, 1969. 405 p.
These authors argue that many marital problems are compounded and result in unhappiness or divorce because couples have not learned to air their grievances openly and fairly. They espouse "constructive aggression," explain the philosophy behind the theory, and provide numerous examples and cases of "good" and "bad" fighting. Not directly concerned with physical abuse, this work obviously is opposed to it.

44 Bach, George R., and Peter Wyden. "Why Intimates Must Fight." In Violence in the Family. Eds. Suzanne K. Steinmetz and Murray A. Straus. New York: Dodd, Mead, 1974, pp. 98-110.

An excerpt from the book The Intimate Enemy, this article
concentrates on the need for husbands and wives to fight and argue
fairly. Numerous case examples are used. Physical fighting is
most certainly not encouraged.

45 Bacher, Adrienne E. "Battered Women: What Did I Do to Deserve
        It?" M. A. thesis, Wheaton College, 1978. 107 p.

46 Back, Susan M. , and Linda Durning. Spouse Abuse Yellow
        Pages: Transfer of Technology Directory of Spouse Abuse
        Programs. 2nd ed. Denver: Social Systems Research
        and Evaluation Division, University of Denver, 1981.

47 Back, Susan Malone; Robin Dee Post; and Genet D'Arcy. "A
        Study of Battered Women in a Psychiatric Setting." Women
        and Therapy 1 (Summer 1982): 13-26.
        The charts of 116 female patients admitted to the Colorado
Psychiatric Hospital between 1975 and 1978 were examined. The
purpose was to identify some of the characteristics of abused compared to nonabused women. Questions studied concerned the amount
of violence during childhood, education and financial status of each
group, difficulties with child rearing, incidence of alcohol or drug
abuse, suicidal behavior, and somatic disorders. One result of this
study was the conclusion that the incorporation of more routine questions regarding spouse abuse in psychiatric evaluations would improve
clinical work and research accuracy. More study of the batterer and
the dynamics of battering is needed.

48 Bader, Cheryl, and Richard Haas. Counselor Dos and Don'ts .
        Ypsilanti, Mich. : Domestic Violence Project, 1981. 12 p.
        Effective and ineffective techniques for battered-women
counselors are found in this booklet.

49 Baldwin, Roger. "Why Innovative Programs in Family Crisis
        Intervention Training Are Particularly Effective." Paper
        presented at the annual meeting of the American Society
        of Criminology, Toronto, 1975.

50 Ball, Margaret. "Issues of Violence in Family Casework." So-
        cial Casework 58 (January 1977): 3-12.
        Ball is Area Director, Family Service of Detroit and Wayne
County, Michigan. This article reports the facts collected by a committee of the district offices. Various case studies are included and
several insights are registered. Among them is the increasing aggressiveness of clients in seeking relief from abusive relationships.
More people want help and expect social agencies to provide it. Of
special interest is how many abusers come seeking help.

51 Ball, Patricia G. , and Elizabeth Wyman. "Battered Wives and
        Powerlessness: What Can Counselors Do?" Victimology:
        An International Journal 2, nos. 3-4 (1977-78): 545-52.
        The counselor can use feminist therapy. The battered wife
is a victim of learned helplessness and the best treatment is assertiveness training.

52 Bancroft, Susan, and Dianne Hamlin. Programs Providing Serv-
        ices to Battered Women . Washington, D. C. : Law Enforce-
        ment Assistance Administration, Office of Planning and
        Management, 1978. 63 p.

53 Banning, Judith. "CNJ Talks to ... Susan Lee Painter, Head
        National Clearinghouse on Family Violence. " Canadian
        Nurse 78 (June 1982): 24-5.
        Painter answers questions regarding the role of nurses and
shelters in dealing with the problem. The purpose of the new Clearinghouse, established in January 1982, will be to gather information
on the several forms of domestic violence, including wife abuse.

54 Bannon, James. Law Enforcement Problems with Intra-Family
        Violence. Detroit Police Department, 1975. (Paper pre-
        sented to the American Bar Association, August 13, 1975).
        Mimeographed, 9 p.
        As Commander of the Detroit Police Department, Bannon
finds the level of protection given to abused wives deplorable. Police departments, the judicial system, and the public at large must
learn to view spouse abuse as a public problem, not a private family
matter.

55 Bard, Morton. Family Crisis Intervention: From Concept to Im-
        plementation. Washington, D. C. : National Institute of Law
        Enforcement and Criminal Justice, 1973. 13 p. Also in
        Battered Women: A Psychosociological Study of Domestic
        Violence. Ed. Maria Roy. New York: Van Nostrand
        Reinhold, 1977, pp. 177-92.
        Bard, Professor of Psychology, City University of New
York, proposes crisis intervention, which helps to solve disputes,
rather than just make arrests. It is also safer for the officers themselves. Conflict management is indeed one of the most important
roles and duties of the police, regardless of the more romantic notion the movies, television, and novels inspire. Training is viewed
as important to the success of the program, as is genuine commitment and the rejection of the notion that to help abused wives is social work, and not the true function of the police. Methods of implementation are included. This study is directed at reforming police
departments and is therefore of interest to police and the general
public interested in police services.

56 Bard, Morton. "Family Intervention Police Teams as a Commu-
        nity Mental Health Resource. " Journal of Criminal Law,
        Criminology and Police Science 60 (June 1969): 247-50.
        This is a description of the Family Crisis Intervention Unit
as delivered at the Symposium on Innovations in Police Techniques:
Recruit Selection, Community Service and Community Relations at the
annual convention of the American Psychological Association in San
Francisco, California, September 1978.

57 Bard, Morton. The Function of the Police in Crisis Intervention
        and Conflict Management: A Training Guide . Washington,
        D. C. : Criminal Justice Associates, 1975. 359 p.

58 Bard, Morton, "Functions of the Police and the Justice System
        in Family Violence." In Violence and the Family. Ed.
        Maurice R. Green. (AAAS Selected Symposium, 47). Boul-
        der, Colo.: Westview Press, 1980, pp. 105-20.
        Bard discusses his experiment in New York City which in-
volved giving special training to police officers for domestic disturbances.   Family disturbances and spouse abuse are not the same and
the police must be trained to tell them apart.   The best approach to
providing assistance is to preserve police discretion and to reinforce
it by methods that improve their skills and competence.

59 Bard, Morton. "Role of Law Enforcement in the Helping System."
        Community Mental Health Journal 7 (1971): 151-60.   Also
        in Community Mental Health and the Criminal Justice Sys-
        tem.   Ed. John Monahan.   Elmsford, N. Y.: Pergamon,
        1976, pp. 99-109.
        A general discussion of the changing role of the police in
modern society and the need for law enforcement officials to recognize
their expanded responsibilities.   The Family Crisis Intervention Unit
is used as an example of this new role.   The program allowed for
special attention to "family disturbance" calls without interfering with
"regular" police work.   Society will benefit from bringing the police
into the helping system.

60 Bard, Morton. "The Study and Modification of Intra-Familial
        Violence." In The Control of Aggression and Violence.
        Ed. Jerome L. Singer.   New York: Academic Press, 1971,
        pp. 149-64.   Also in Violence in the Family.   Eds. Suzanne
        K. Steinmetz and Murray A. Straus.   New York: Dodd,
        Mead, 1974, pp. 127-39.
        The high level of intrafamily violence points up a glaring
need for some sort of intervention.   Since the police are often called
to render aid, it makes sense to give them special training so that
proper assistance can be given.   This article describes the special
Family Crisis Unit tested in New York City.   Battered wives, as well
as other abused family members, benefited from this experiment,
which proved successful.

61 Bard, Morton. Training Police as Specialists in Family Crisis
        Intervention.   Washington, D. C.: U. S. Government Printing
        Office, 1970.   65 p.
        Family crisis intervention is perhaps the most difficult and
dangerous police function.   This program, to train a special corps of
officers, was inaugurated to decrease that risk and to provide better
services to feuding families and help them resolve their conflicts.
Over 1,400 interventions were performed with 950 families over a
two-year period during 1967-69.   The police force incurred no injuries
in spite of handling more disputes, the community response was positive, and the professional identity of the unit officers remained intact
as they also continued to perform other police duties.   This model
was to be imitated by other police departments over the next decade.

62 Bard, Morton, and Bernard Berkowitz. "Family Disturbance as
        a Police Function." In Law Enforcement Science and Tech-

nology. Ed. S.I. Cohn. Vol. 2. Chicago: ITT Research
Institute, 1969, pp. 565-8.
In this early article, the family fight is viewed as an under-
rated and often neglected although dangerous police function. Use of
Family Crisis Intervention Specialists supported by other professionals
would go far to provide assistance to violence-prone individuals and
situations. This article was a presentation at the second National
Symposium on Law Enforcement Science and Technology.

63 Bard, Morton, and Harriet Connolly. The Police and Family
    Violence: Policy and Practice. New York: City Univer-
    sity of New York, Center for Social Research, 1978. 35 p.
    Also in Battered Women: Issues of Public Policy. U.S.
    Commission on Civil Rights. Washington, D.C.: The
    Commission, 1978, pp. 304-26; Rockville, Md.: NCJRS
    Microfiche Program, 1978.
    This report was submitted to the U.S. Commission on Civil
Rights, January 30, 1978. The police have had the most sustained,
immediate and direct exposure to disturbed families. Because of this,
the potential is high for providing much needed service and reducing
violence and injury. Wife beating and family disputes are not synony-
mous and improvements should be made in handling each. However,
any changes mandated in police management of family disputes should
be based upon objective data available through sound research.

64 Bard, Morton, and Joseph Zacker. "Assaultiveness and Alcohol
    Use in Family Disputes: Police Perceptions." Criminology
    12 (November 1974): 281-92.
    It is commonly assumed that when police are called to in-
vestigate a family dispute, an assault has taken place. It is also
usually assumed that alcohol was a causative agent in the dispute.
These assumptions are shared by both the police and by social scientists. The authors have tested the assumptions by specially trained
officers who kept records of 962 families on 1,398 occasions of disturbance. Results disprove both assumptions. In only about one-third
of the cases had an assault occurred. Alcohol was involved in from
30% to 56% of the cases, but in only 6% was there both assaultiveness
and drunkenness. This suggests that the relationship is not what
conventional wisdom would have us believe and domestic assault will
have to be viewed differently by the police and social scientists.

65 Bard, Morton, and Joseph Zacker. "How Police Handle Explo-
    sive Squabbles: New Techniques Let Police Settle Arguments
    Without Force." Psychology Today 10 (November 1976):
    71-4, 113. Also in Research into Violent Behavior: Domes-
    tic Violence. U.S. Congress. House. Committee on Sci-
    ence and Technology. Hearings. 95th Cong. 2nd Sess.
    February 14, 15, 16, 1978. Washington, D.C.: Govern-
    ment Printing Office, 1978, pp. 998-1001.
    The authors discuss the findings from a Special Family
Crisis Unit experiment where 18 police officers were given special
training and operated in West Harlem for 22 months handling all family disputes in the precinct. During that time no officers were injured
and no family disputes degenerated to homicide. A similar experiment

was then conducted in 1973 in Norwalk, Connecticut.   The program
showed that properly trained police could handle these situations better
than those using traditional methods.   Other interesting conclusions
include the fact that alcohol has no relationship to assaultiveness as
commonly believed.   Also, race was not a factor, but economic class
was.   The poorer a disputant, the more likely he would resort to
assault.

66   Bard, Morton, and Joseph Zacker.   Police and Interpersonal Con-
        flict: Third-Party Intervention Approaches. [Washington,
        D. C.]: Police Foundation, 1976.   59 p.

67   Bard, Morton, and Joseph Zacker.   "The Prevention of Family
        Violence: Dilemmas of Community Intervention. "   Journal
        of Marriage and the Family 33 (November 1971): 677-82.
        This article describes an early attempt at providing special
training of a corps of police officers for intervening in domestic crisis situations.   On the whole, the program was successful, but several
dilemmas became apparent.   For example, because no law was broken,
no arrest could be made in some cases where the officers knew a serious crime would eventually be committed.   The authors, both from
the City University of New York, note that sometimes the more innovative and successful a program is (as in this case), the more it may
conflict with society's values and ideals.   The program was conducted
in New York City.

68   Bard, Morton; Joseph Zacker; and Elliott Rutter.   Police Family
        Crisis Instruction and Conflict Management; An Action Re-
        search Analysis. New York: The Authors, 1972.   226 p.

69   Barden, Jim, and Carolyn Barden.   "The Battered Wife Syndrome. "
        Viva (May 1976): 79-81, 108-10.
        Popularized account using the research of Emily J. Goodman,
Marjory Fields, Steinmetz and Straus, and Bard and Zacker.   Case
histories are included.

70   Barman, Marcia Ringel.   "One Hospital's Very Workable Approach
        to Battering. "   RN 44 (October 1981): 26.
        A short description of the program instituted by the Brigham
and Women's Hospital in Boston, MA.

71   Barnard, George W. , et al.   "Til Death Do Us Part: A Study
        of Spouse Murder. "   American Academy of Psychiatry and
        the Law Bulletin 10, no. 4 (1982): 271-80.
        This discussion is based on the data obtained from 23 males
and 11 females who had killed their mates.   Men tended to kill because
of infidelity, rejection, or threats of separation, whereas women (70%)
killed an abusing husband.   Weapons used, presence of alcohol, and
other factors are included.   The study was conducted in Florida from
1970 to 1980.   The authors wonder if intervention or marital separation would have prevented the homicides.

72   Barnes, Paul Donald.   "Attributions by Observers in a Recreated
        Incident of Spouse Abuse. "   Ph. D. dissertation, Florida

State University, 1983. 90 p. Abstract in <u>Dissertation</u>
<u>Abstracts International</u> 44B (April 1984): 3238.

73 Barnett, Ellen R. , and Leslie Landis. <u>Handbook for Abused</u>
    <u>Women</u>. (Domestic Violence Monograph Series, no. 8).
    Rockville, Md. : National Clearing House on Domestic Vio-
    lence, 1981. 18 p.

74 Barnett, Ellen R. , et al. <u>Family Violence: Intervention Strate-</u>
    <u>gies</u>. Washington, D. C. : U. S. Department of Health and
    Human Services, 1980. 81 p.
    This manual is intended for use by professionals and para-
professionals who serve the needs of victims of family violence. The
causes of the violence, its identification, intervention strategies and
program development techniques are dealt with, for all forms of abusive activity. Child abuse, spouse abuse, sibling violence, elder
abuse are all of concern. Physical abuse as well as emotional abuse
receives attention. Emphasis here is placed on battered women.

75 Barnhill, Laurence R. "Basic Interventions for Violence in Fam-
    ilies. " <u>Hospital and Community Psychiatry</u> 31 (August
    1980): 547-50.
    The author, Coordinator of Outpatient and Emergency Serv-
ices, South Central Mental Health Center, Bloomington, Indiana, describes five stages of intervention in cases of familial violence:
crisis management of the ongoing threat of violence, an initial
assessment and contract, a more complete evaluation, brief treatment, and follow-up and longer-term treatment. The stages are
usually sequential although some regression is not unlikely. Apparently most patients drop out of the treatment after some symptom
remission and only a minority continue into the long-term treatment.
This general approach has implications for treatment of spouse abuse.

76 Barnhill, Laurence R. "Clinical Assessment of Intrafamilial Vio-
    lence. " <u>Hospital and Community Psychiatry</u> 31 (August
    1980): 543-6.
    Barnhill believes that a common problem in clinical treat-
ment of intrafamily violence is incomplete assessment resulting in
treatment intervention based on incomplete data. He identifies five
areas where analysis is necessary. They include physiological-medical
factors, individual psychological factors, interpersonal-familial factors,
cultural and family background factors and the level of life stress and
available resources. A complete evaluation of each case must be
made with appropriate action taken. Lasting change often requires
intervention at the individual psychological and interpersonal familial
levels. Cultural and family background factors are often difficult or
impossible to alter and generally require long-term work to amelio-
rate. Both spouse abuse and child abuse are discussed.

77 Barocas, Harvey A. "Crisis Intervention and Iatrogenic Reactions. "
    <u>Group Analysis</u> 6, no. 1 (1973): 36-7.
    While performing their duties during family crisis interven-
tion, policemen must avoid unintentionally causing greater violence.
Special training programs would be useful in avoiding these iatrogenic

reactions. New York, New Jersey, Massachusetts, and Ohio have
experimented with programs and found them to be successful.

78   Barocas, Harvey A.   "Iatrogenic and Prevention Intervention in
        Police-Family Crisis Situations."   International Journal of
        Social Psychiatry 20 (Spring/Summer 1974): 113-21.
        The author stresses the importance of police intervention
in domestic disputes.   Proper training is necessary, however, or the
intervention may prompt the violence it was meant to prevent.   Reference is made to New York City's Family Crisis Teams tested by
Morton Bard and found to be effective.

79   Barocas, Harvey A.   "Urban Policemen: Crisis Mediators or
        Crisis Creators."   American Journal of Orthopsychiatry 43
        (July 1973): 632-9.
        Barocas, Assistant Professor, City University of New York,
believes that police must receive special training for dealing with domestic crises or they might inadvertently create a greater danger to
themselves or the family members.   The necessary psychological
skills can be taught and this innovative training program is described.
The perspective of this article is from the police angle, that is, how
to resolve and defuse the conflict, prevent recidivism and reduce injury to everyone involved.

80   Barr, N. A. , and J. W. Carrier.   "Women's Aid Groups: The
        Economic Case for State Assistance to Battered Wives."
        Policy and Politics 6 (1978): 333-50.
        The authors investigate two questions.   Why does England,
with its welfare state orientation provide so little for battered wives,
and what resources should be provided?   The answer seems to lie in
its welfare focus.   Overall it is directed at the welfare of the children and the preservation of the family unit.   Aid to abused women
often involves disruption of the family unit and therefore seems to
work at cross purposes.   Confusion over purpose seems to explain
then why there is so little aid.   A study of efficiency of Chiswick
Women's Aid and state assistance programs seems to indicate that
the former is more efficient with fewer resources.   Since state resources are limited, funneling some of them, such as the "bed and
breakfast" programs and the children's homes, through refuge-type
operations would work better and cheaper.

81   Barry, Kathleen.   Female Sexual Slavery.   Englewood Cliffs, N. J. :
        Prentice-Hall, 1979.   274 p.
        "Female sexual slavery is present in all situations where
women or girls cannot change the immediate conditions of their existence; where regardless of how they get into these conditions they cannot get out; and where they are subject to sexual violence and exploitation."   It may be found in an Arab harem, an American pimp pad,
or a home in the suburbs.   It brings both monetary gain and personal
satisfaction to its perpetuators and is pervasive throughout patriarchal
societies.   Among its manifestations are rape, incest, prostitution,
and pornography, as well as spouse abuse.   Shelters for the abused
and decriminalization of prostitution will help.   But only with true
freedom for women as well as men; only when women are free to join

or leave institutions (such as marriage) as they choose, or change their situations, will sexual slavery end.

82 Barry, Susan. "Spousal Rape: The Uncommon Law." American Bar Association Journal 66 (September 1980): 1088-91.
    This overview of rape in marriage with discussion of historical precedents concludes that "no legal, political, or moral justifications exist to allow a man to use force to invade his wife's bodily privacy." The contractual argument and the fear that vengeful wives will accuse their husbands of rape are dismissed as having little or no merit. The current legal status of this crime in the various states and the ramifications of the Rideout case (Oregon) are detailed. Barry is a University of San Francisco law student.

83 Barshis, Victoria R. Garnier. "The Question of Marital Rape." Women's Studies International Forum 6, no. 4 (1983): 383-93.
    A general discussion, definition, and history of the marital rape exemption provides the background for the author's condemnation of its legality. It is a clear example of the protection of male privilege and must be changed. Married women have an unequivocal right to equal protection of the laws. Physical and sexual assault are unacceptable no matter when or where it occurs.

84 Bass, David, and Janet Rice. "Agency Responses to the Abused Wife." Social Casework 60 (June 1979): 338-42.
    Various authors have lamented the failure of institutions to respond to the needs of abused women. Bass and Rice, graduate students at the University of Akron (Ohio) Department of Sociology, studied the approaches of nine separate social service agencies with social workers who do family counseling. The findings indicate that most attempt to deal with abuse the same way they deal with other family problems. This results in failure to use other social service agencies in the community which could provide the victim with valuable assistance. The authors believe that integration of all agencies and persons who could help should be the goal of effective wife abuse counseling.

85 Bassett, Steve. The Battered Rich. Port Washington, N.Y.: Ashley Books, 1980. 182 p.
    The author interviewed a number of women whose husbands earned over $100,000 per year in order to determine what battered rich women shared in common with battered women of other economic classes. The interviews are reproduced in detail, but little or no interpretation or analysis of the problem is done, except perhaps that rich men also abuse their wives.

86 Bata, Evelyn J., and Sally Lemberg. "Wives in Crisis: How Students Can Help." Synergist 5 (Winter 1977): 50-3.
    Graduate students from the University of Maryland's School of Social Work were used as volunteers for the Maryland Task Force on Battered Wives, assisting with questionnaires, preparation of an informational pamphlet, gathering data, etc. Organizations and agencies needing help may wish to investigate this as a means of increasing their staff. A copy of the questionnaire is included.

87   Bates, Frank. "Domestic Violence and the Injunction in Modern
          Australian Family Law." Family Law 10 (1980): 61-3.
     The author, Reader in Law, University of Tasmania, evalu-
ates the Australian Family Law Act of 1975 with its provisions for
excluding the abuser from the matrimonial home and injunctions
against engaging in abusive behavior. The law has been helpful, but
erosion of the injunction potential is possible in its present form.
One positive effect of the law is the recognition that legal intervention
in marital dynamics is an acceptable state action.

88   Bates, Frank. "A Plea for the Battered Husband." Family Law
          11 (April 1981): 90-2.
     Bates analyzes the problem of husband abuse. Drawing
from the writings of Straus, Renvoize and others, along with the records of several court cases, the author stresses that husband abuse
is being unfairly ignored. More should be done to help these individuals.

89   Bates, Vernon. "Domestic Violence and The Law." Paper pre-
          sented at the annual meeting of the Pacific Sociological As-
          sociation, San Francisco, 1980.

90   "Battered Families: A Growing Nightmare." U.S. News and
          World Report 86 (January 15, 1979): 60-1.
     Journalistic account of battered women, children, parents
and family violence in general. Included are statistics on the amount
of family abuse that takes place in the United States.

91   "'Battered Hubby' Who Killed Wife Is Cleared." Jet 59 (1980):
          18.
     A news note about a man who killed his wife, but was not
prosecuted. She apparently battered him throughout their four-year
marriage.

92   "The Battered Husbands: Wives Aren't Always the Victim."
          Time 111 (March 20, 1978): 69. Also in Readings in Mar-
          riage and the Family 79/80. Guilford, Conn.: Annual Edi-
          tions, 1979, p. 133.
     This is a journalistic treatment of spouse abuse with empha-
sis on husband battering. The research of Steinmetz, Straus, Gelles,
Star and Pizzey provides the basis for the article.

93   "The Battered Wife." JSAC Grapevine 9 (June 1977): entire is-
          sue. Also in Appendix, Family Violence: A Workshop Man-
          ual for Clergy and Other Service Providers. Eds. Rev.
          Marie M. Fortune and Denise Hormann. Rockville, Md.:
          National Clearinghouse on Domestic Violence, 1980.
     A good general introduction to the problem of spouse abuse.
Describes the batterer and the social and legal needs of the victim.
Succinct and well done.

94   "Battered Wives ... and Coeds." Science News 124 (September
          17, 1983): 187.
     A short account of Michele Bograd's study [156] is related.

The study of violence between dating college students suggests abuse
starts early in the relationship.

95 "Battered Wives: Now They're Fighting Back." U. S. News and
        World Report 81 (September 20, 1976): 47-8.
        This popularized account of the problem of wife abuse is a
good overview aimed at a lay readership.   The types of abuser are
described, as well as the effects on the children in the family, what
can be done about the abuse and how the victims should be counseled.

96 "The Battered Woman." Emergency Medicine 11 (April 15,
        1979): 24-8.
        The role of the physician is emphasized in this article with
special attention given to shelters and the place they occupy in relieving the problem.   Doctors, particularly those in emergency room situations, should be sensitive to the possibility of abuse in suspicious
cases of trauma.   They should be familiar with the local shelters and
refer women who need assistance.

97 "The Battered Woman: Family Violence in America." Behav-
        ioral Medicine 6 (1979): 38-41.
        A general discussion of spouse abuse featuring the Women
Against Abuse Shelter in Philadelphia.   The article includes comments
from noted researchers R. J. Gelles and M. Bard, as well as local
shelter staffers, physicians and nurses.

98 "Battered Women." Children Today 11 (July/August 1982): 32.
        A discussion of two governmental reports on spouse abuse,
Under the Rule of Thumb [1620] and Federal Response to Domestic
Violence [1619].   Both are done by the U. S. Commission on Civil
Rights.

99 "Battered Women." Trial 13 (November 1977): 20, 60.
        This short general article provides comments from directors
of several shelters.   Some doubt is expressed whether counseling will
help abusive husbands.

100 Battered Women and Abused Children; Intricacies of Legal and
        Administrative Intervention.   (Issues occasional papers, no.
        4.) [Bradford, Eng.]: University of Bradford, 1979.   84 p.
        This is a collection of papers delivered at the "Violence in
the Family" Conference at the University of Bradford, March 1978.
Both spouse and child abuse are considered with emphasis on spouse
abuse.   The authors, including Jo Sutton [1566], Eileen Meredith
[1076], Richard Haselgrove [717], Errolyn Bruce [206], stress how public attitudes, social services, legal processes and procedures actually
impact on or affect abuse, rather than what should be done.   The individual articles are found under the names of the authors elsewhere
in this bibliography.

101 "Battered Women--plank 2." In The Spirit of Houston, The
        First National Woman's Conference.   Washington, D. C. :
        National Commission on the Observance of International Wom-
        an's Year, 1978, pp. 20-21.

The national plan of action approved by the conference had
26 planks.   The second plank was concerned with battered women.
Federal, state, and local action was urged to eradicate the problem.

102 "Battered Women Press Police for Equal Protection." Response
        to Violence and Sexual Abuse in the Family 2 (April 1979):
        3.

103 Battered Women: The Hidden Problem. St. Paul, Minn.: Com-
        munity Planning Organization, 1976.   58 p.
        General discussion of spouse abuse with emphasis on the
St. Paul, Minnesota area.   Numerous recommendations to relieve the
problem.

104 Bauer, Carol, and Lawrence Ritt.   " 'A Husband Is a Beating
        Animal': Frances Power Cobbe Confronts the Wife-abuse
        Problem in Victorian England." International Journal of
        Women's Studies 6 (March/April 1983): 99-118.
        The authors, both professors of history at C. W. Post Cen-
ter of Long Island University, Greenvale, New York, provide a detailed analysis of Cobbe's article in the Contemporary Review.   Placed
in its historical context, it becomes apparent that wife beating is not
a twentieth-century "discovery." Nor is Cobbe's view, that at the
heart of the wife-beating problem was the widespread notion of the
basic inferiority of women, a new revelation.

105 Bauer, Carol, and Lawrence Ritt.   "Wife Abuse, Late-Victorian
        English Feminists, and the Legacy of Frances Power Cobbe."
        International Journal of Women's Studies 6 (May/June 1983):
        195-207.
        After much lobbying and political action, the Matrimonial
Causes Act of 1878 and Summary Jurisdiction Act of 1895 were passed
and some of the worst abuses were corrected, but Victorian feminists
knew what the rest of Victorian society refused to acknowledge.   Only
when the gross disparity between men and women was recognized and
changed, and the patriarchal system ended, would real progress toward ending wife beating be made.

106 Baum, Kenneth Alan.   "Battered Women, Learned Helplessness
        and Traditional Family Ideology." Ph. D. dissertation, Unit-
        ed States International University, 1982.   117 p.   Abstract
        in Dissertation Abstracts International 43B (April 1983): 3345.

107 Baumann, Mary A.   "Expert Testimony on the Battered Wife Syn-
        drome: A Question of Admissibility in the Prosecution of
        the Battered Wife for the Killing of Her Husband." St. Lou-
        is University Law Journal 27 (April 1983): 407-35.

108 Bazemore, Gordon.   "Wife Batterers Interviewed." Criminal
        Justice Newsletter 14 (September 26, 1983): 7-8.

109 "Beating Up Hubby: Husbands Are Battered as Often as Wives."
        Human Behaviour 7 (November 1978): 60.
        A news note regarding the research by Straus, Gelles and

Steinmetz.   On their Overall Violence Index men and women are only
a half point apart, with the wives being somewhat more frequently
and severely violent.

110   Becker, Judith V. , and Gene G. Abel.   "The Physical, Psycho-
        logical and Economic Victimization of Women. "   Quarterly
        Journal of Corrections 1 (Fall 1977): 18-24.

        The authors, from the Department of Psychiatry, University
of Tennessee and the Memphis Mental Health Institute, believe that
"the victimization of women by men appears to be directly related to
our sexist society in which male supremacy is upheld at whatever
costs. " They discuss various common forms of victimization, including wife beating, which will not be eradicated from society until basic
human rights are taught to all.

111   Bedard, Virginia S.   "Wife Beating. "   Glamour 76 (August
        1978): 85-6.
        The author, an educational administrator in New York State,
describes her relationship with her abusive husband, recognizing how
she contributed to the situation.   She urges victims to recognize the
abuse early and do something before it is too late to salvage the marriage as it was in her case.

112   Bedau, Hugo Adam.   "Rough Justice: The Limits of Novel De-
        fenses. "   Hastings Center Report 8 (December 1978): 8-11.
        Several cases, including that of Francine Hughes and Rox-
anne Gay, are examined and found to stretch credibility in their patterns of defense.   The insanity plea in these cases is questionable.
Perhaps new legal lines of defense should be used when women kill
their abusive husbands.   In any case we must be willing to settle for
"rough" justice because of the imperfection of the legal system.

113   Bedrosian, Richard C.   "Using Cognitive and Systems Interven-
        tion in the Treatment of Marital Violence. "   Family Therapy
        Collections.   Vol. 3.   Clinical Approaches to Family Vio-
        lence.   Rockville, Md. :   Aspen System, 1982, pp. 117-38.

114   Behrman, Simon.   "Hostility to Kith and Kin. "   British Medical
        Journal 2 (1975): 538-9.
        The author, a consultant neurologist, London, describes a
condition found in ten male patients.   All were extremely hostile toward members of the immediate family, but no others.   In each case
this phenomenon suddenly appeared, in six cases after severe head
injuries and in one after open heart surgery.   The dynamics of Capgras' Syndrome are suspected of being similar and Behrman believes
it to be one of the many causes of conjugal conflict.

115   Bell, Garry L.   "Inter-spousal Violence: Discovery and Report-
        ing. "   In Family Violence; An International and Interdiscipli-
        nary Study.   Eds. John M. Eekelaar and Sanford N. Katz.
        Toronto: Butterworths, 1978, pp. 208-15.
        The author is assigned to youth services, Royal Canadian
Mounted Police.   He stresses that abused spouses must be aware that

they have a problem or they will not report it.   Convenient channels for reporting must be established.   Police intervention, the Mobile Family Service Society and Regina Transition House have all given valuable assistance to victims and provided documentation regarding abuse cases.

116   Bell, Joseph N.   "New Hope for the Battered Wife."   Good
        Housekeeping 183 (August 1976): 94-5, 133-4, 136, 138.
          A popularized account with cases depicting abuse.   The re-
search of J. Bannon, B. Star and others is referred to.   The "new
hope" is the shelter movement which provides temporary refuge to
victims.   Haven House in Los Angeles receives special attention.

117   Bell, Joseph N.   "Rescuing the Battered Wife."   Human Behav-
        ior 6 (June 1977): 16-23.
          This popular overview of the problem synthesizes the schol-
arly studies of others by describing the victim's circumstances with
the use of actual cases.   Why the abuser beats his wife, why she
stays and what can be done are all discussed.   The Coalition on Battered Women is coming to the rescue by forging a resource network
chain of legal aid services, hospitals, religious counselors, psychiatrists, and others to aid victims.   To round out this aid, the establishment of more shelters   like Haven House of Los Angeles is urged.

118   Bell, Norman W. , and Michael Benjamin.   "Explaining Domestic
        Murder."   Paper presented at the Conference on Violence
        in Canadian Society, 12 March 1977.

119   Bello, Teresa A.   "The Latino Patient in the Emergency Depart-
        ment."   JEN: Journal of Emergency Nursing 6 (July/August
        1980): 13-6.
          Giving assistance to Latino patients is often not the same
as for others.   Special treatment may be necessary because of cultural differences.   This is especially true with medical treatment for
abused spouses.

120   Benedek, Elissa P.   "Conjoint Marital Therapy and Spouse Abuse."
        American Journal of Family Therapy 9 (Summer 1981): 93-4.
          The question is raised regarding the decision of when to use
individual therapy and when to use conjoint therapy in cases of battering.   Suggestions are made such as these: begin with individual therapy, feel out the situation, use professional judgement, and be leery
of enraging the abuser.

121   Benich, Carol C.   "Children of Battered Women: A Descriptive
        Study of Their Behavior, Ego Functioning, and Interpersonal
        Styles."   Ph. D. dissertation, California School of Profes-
        sional Psychology, Berkeley, 1983.   120 p.   Abstract in
        Dissertation Abstracts International 44B (October 1983): 1227.

122   Benjamin, Libby, and Garry Richard Walz.   Violence in the
        Family: Child and Spouse Abuse.   Ann Arbor, Mich. :   Eric
        Counseling and Personnel Services Clearinghouse, School of
        Education, University of Michigan, 1983.   100 p.

123 Benjamin, Michael, and Susan Adler. "Wife Abuse: Implications
        for Socio-Legal Policy and Practice."   Canadian Journal of
        Family Law 3 (1980): 339-67.
        Benjamin, a doctoral candidate at the University of Toronto,
and Adler, a B. S. W. student at York University, provide an interesting and informative overview of spouse abuse, its occurrence, frequency, and various theories regarding it.   They argue that the recognition of the causes is necessary to provide a viable policy for dealing
with the abuse.   The psychopathological model, the male domination
model and the interactional model are all found inadequate.   The systems model is believed to provide a more accurate explanation for the
problem and therefore leads to better policy formation to alleviate it.

124 Berghorn, Gwen, and Anthony Siracusa.   "Beyond Isolated Treat-
        ment: A Case for Community Involvement in Family Vio-
        lence Intervention." Family Therapy Collections.   Vol. 3.
        Clinical Approaches to Family Violence.   Rockville, Md. :
        Aspen System, 1982, pp. 139-57.

125 Berk, Richard A.   "Bringing the Cops Back In: A Study of Ef-
        forts to Make the Criminal Justice System More Responsive
        to Incidents of Family Violence."   Social Science Research
        9, no. 3 (1980): 193-215.
        An analysis of the day-to-day functioning of the police and
legal systems confirms the conclusions of the feminists that there are
few incentives for the police to actively intervene in cases of domestic
violence and that minor tinkering with the system will not help much.
When the Santa Barbara Family Violence Program was established, its
goals were to increase the number of offenders subjected to the criminal judicial process, provide a counseling alternative to arrest in less
violent cases, and improve the reporting practices of the police in domestic violence cases.   Although there was much skepticism about the
value of this project when it began, it was, in the end, a success.
The reason, in part, is that the D. A. favored the program and supported it, but also because the special unit was kept separate and not
merged with the established order.

126 Berk, Richard A. , et al.   "Mutual Combat and Other Family Vi-
        olence Myths."   In The Dark Side of Families: Current
        Family Violence Research.   Eds. David Finkelhor et al.
        Beverly Hills, Ca. : Sage, 1983, pp. 197-212.
        In this study 262 domestic disturbances in Santa Barbara
County, California, were studied to determine injury to males and females involved in ongoing romantic relationships.   The authors hoped
to explore spouse abuse and determine the relative merits of the
"wife battery" and the "mutual combat" perspectives.   The results
show that alcohol does not play a direct role in the battery incidents
and that the marriage license does seem to be a hitting license for
men, but not for women.   In families where the man dominates, abuse
is more likely.   Of particular interest is the finding that mutual combat does not fairly describe the violence and although an occasional
husband is battered "it is downright pernicious to equate their experiences with those of the enormous number of women who are routinely
and severely victimized. "

127   Berk, Sarah Fenstermaker, and Donileen R. Loseke.   "Handling
         Family Violence: Situational Determinants of Police Arrest
         in Domestic Disturbances. "   Law and Society 15, no. 2
         (1980-81): 317-46.
         It is often alleged that police are too frequently not making
arrests when called to handle domestic disturbances, and thus are not
doing their job.   It is also suggested that police use this discretion
more in situations of family violences than other crimes, and they do
so because of basic sympathy with the husband.   The authors examined
262 official police calls involving domestic disturbances in Santa Barbara County in 1978.   The results suggest that it is true that there
are few arrests.   However, this class of police activity does not show
relatively fewer arrests than others.   It may be that this type of interaction may have justification for more arrests, but it also means
that courts will have to try and convict assaults more frequently than
in the past.   The problem cannot be viewed as one that can be recti-
fied only at the police contact point.

128   Berkman, Arnold S.   "The State of Michigan Versus a Battered
         Wife: A Case Study. "   Bulletin of the Menninger Clinic 44
         (November 1980): 603-16.
         In March 1977, Stephanie Howard killed her ex-husband af-
ter years of abuse.   This case study, by an associate professor of
psychiatry at Michigan State University and expert witness at the trial,
discusses the law regarding insanity, borderline syndrome, battered
wife syndrome and how the defendant's situation applies.   A better
understanding of one battered woman who kills her abuser is found here.

129   Bern, Elliot H.   "From Violent Incident to Spouse Abuse Syn-
         drome. "   Social Casework 63 (January 1982): 41-5.
         Bern, a supervisor for the Volunteer Counseling Service,
Domestic Violence Project, New York City, creates this theoretical
model by integrating various sociological and psychological views of
spouse abuse.   He shows the difference between the violent incident
and the cycle of abuse and how one progresses to the other.   Techniques for dealing with the several stages are described.

130   Bernard, Catherine Anne.   "Unmarried Battered Women: Demo-
         graphic Data, Attitudes Toward Women, and Locus of Con-
         trol. "   Ph. D. dissertation, University of Maryland, 1981.
         290 p. Abstract in Dissertation Abstracts International 43A
         (September 1982): 950.

131   Bernard, M. L. , and J. L. Bernard.   "Violent Intimacy: The
         Family as a Model for Love Relationships. "   Family Rela-
         tions: Journal of Applied Family and Child Studies 32
         (April 1983): 283-6.
         The authors, from Memphis State University, surveyed 461
college students (168 males, 293 females) to determine data regarding
incidence and frequency of physical abuse in dating relationships.   A
definite relationship exists between the type of violence engaged in and
that observed in the family of origin.   The strongest relationship is
the form the abuse takes.   Both males and females reported abusing
and being abused by their mates.

132   Berzinsky, Alyce. Battered Woman-Abused Child: The Connect-
        ed Syndrome. Dayton, Ohio: P. P. I. Publishing, 1979. 40
        p.

133   Besick, Elmer A. "Gun Control Statutes and Domestic Violence."
        Cleveland State Law Review 19 (September 1970): 556-67
        Most of Besick's article discusses the question of gun con-
trol with F. B. I. statistics showing the extent of intrafamilial murder
and murder weapons used.   Use of guns dominates.   He concludes,
"if gun control were an effective method to reduce the number of guns
available in the urban households, then it is quite possible that many
family quarrels and other arguments would not end with someone's
death."

134   Biaggi-Garcia, Rina, and Marina Corodemus. Battered Women:
        A Legal Handbook for New Jersey Women. Newark, N. J. :
        Women's Law Forum, Seton Hall University Law Center,
        [1978?]. 21 p.
        Biaggi-Garcia, Professor of Law, and Corodemus, Research
Assistant at Seton Hall, have written a guide about "where to go and
what to do if your husband or male friend beats you." The court system, laws, court actions, what can be done, what to expect, and
other legal mysteries are revealed in plain language.   Pamphlets like
this might be useful in other states.

135   Bibliographic Guide to the Files of the National Clearinghouse on
        Marital Rape. Berkeley, Ca. : Women's History Research
        Center, 1981. 33 p.

136   Biggs, John M. The Concept of Matrimonial Cruelty.   London:
        University of London, Athlone Press, 1962. 228 p.
        This book provides an overview of cruelty, which includes
willful communication of venereal disease, drunkenness, nagging, and
many other forms besides physical violence.   This is an early discussion when "cruelty" was more frequently used as grounds for divorce. This study, with a British emphasis, is notable also for its
near absence of discussion of physical abuse.   Interesting look at legal
opinions and marital cruelty.

137   Billey, Dempsey James. "Family Violence: Prosecution as a
        Constructive Response." M. A. thesis, California State Uni-
        versity, Northridge, 1982. 74 p.
        Wife abuse is a common occurrence and though other forms
of assault are covered by state statutes, until recently spouse assault
has seen little legal punishment.   The public and public agencies have
changed attitudes in recent years, many states have passed new family violence laws, and legal officers and courts are more willing to
prosecute and punish abusers.   The future will see these changes in
action.

138   Billy, B. J. "Life Patterns and Emergency Care of Battered
        Women."   JEN/Journal of Emergency Nursing 9 (September/
        October 1983): 251-3.

139 Bingham, Katherine, and Cherie Coddington. "Battered Women:
     An Emerging Social Problem." M. S. W. project, California
     State University, 1980. 133 p.

140 Binney, Val; Gina Harkell; and Judy Nixon. Leaving Violent
     Men: A Study of Refuges and Housing for Battered Women.
     [London]: Women's Aid Federation, 1981. 112 p.

141 Birnbaum, Lynn F. "Female Submissiveness, Assertiveness,
     and Aggressiveness and Situational Provocation in Relation
     to Wife Abuse." Ph. D. dissertation, Hofstra University,
     1980. 100 p. Abstract in Dissertation Abstracts Internation-
     al 41B (June 1981): 4737.

142 Birbaum, Renee. "Battered Wife--The Legal System Attempts
     to Help." University of Cincinnati Law Review 48 (1979):
     419-34.
         The author dissects the common-law view of marriage, the
inter-spousal immunity doctrine, and the inadequacies of the criminal
law and the law enforcement systems. The changing attitudes of the
court and legislatures of various states provide encouraging indications
that changes are on the way. The marital arrangement is important,
but spousal immunity should not be permitted to raise obstacles to
justice for the victim as has happened in cases of wife abuse.

143 "Black-and-Blue Marriages." Human Behavior 5 (June 1976):
     47-8.
         Popularization and restatement of the results of J. J. Gay-
ford's study of 100 battered wives in England.

144 Black, H. Campbell. "Cruelty as a Ground for Divorce." Cen-
     tral Law Journal 20 (April 10, 1885): 284-8.

145 Blair, Sandra. "Making the Legal System Work for Battered
     Women." In Battered Women. Ed. Donna M. Moore.
     Beverly Hills, Ca. : Sage, 1979, pp. 101-18.
         Blair, an attorney in private practice in San Francisco,
shows that the legal structure is merely a reflection of society-at-
large and new laws often lag behind new societal concerns. A good
discussion of using various types of laws such as civil or criminal
with the advantages and disadvantages of each. One recommendation
is the establishment of a temporary institution of advocacy for battered women, maybe along the lines of Child Protective Services. This
would allow interested parties an avenue for making appropriate facts,
information and statistics available to others.

146 Blake, Elizabeth, and Morton Bard. Three Scripts for Family
     Crisis Intervention. New York: Family Service Associa-
     tion of America, 1971. 36 p.

147 Blake, Matilda M. "Are Women Protected?" Westminster Re-
     view 137 (January 1892): 43-8.
         Opponents of women's enfranchisement argued that only un-
der male supremacy and guidance can women "develop a refinement

and gentleness otherwise unattainable." Blake points out numerous cases of abuse of women and argues that only with civil equality will moral and spiritual equality develop.

148   Blake, Matilda M.   "The Lady and the Law."   Westminster Review 137 (April 1892): 364-70.
      This argument in favor of the Parliamentary role for women includes discussion of abuses against women, such as wife beating. Enfranchisement will rectify the many hardships.

149   Blalock, Christine Lucille.   "An Examination into the History, Theoretical Causes, Treatment, and Prevention of the Problem of Battered Women: An Analytical Review of the Literature, 1972-1982." MS. thesis, Louisiana State University, 1981.   78 p.
      This paper provides a good overview of the wife abuse literature for the past decade.   Analyzed are four theories of why women stay in abusive relationships: female socialization, learned helplessness, environmental impact, and female masochism.   A comprehensive analysis of the literature dealing with these theories is presented along with an analysis of the proposals for treatment associated with each theory.

150   Blanton, Judith, "Self Study of Family Crisis Intervention in a Police Unit."   Professional Psychology 7 (February 1976): 61-7.
      The author, Project Director, Social Action Research Center, Berkeley, describes a Family Crisis Intervention Unit established in a large western city to deal with domestic disputes.   Success is achieved when the immediate problem is defused and proper referrals made.   As in other cities this experiment was viewed as successful in reducing violence, as well as family and police injury.

151   Blay-Cohen, Sue, and Dina L. Coster.   "Marital Rape in California: For Better or for Worse."   San Fernando Valley Law Review 8 (1980): 239-61.
      In this article the authors discredit such often raised arguments as the implied consent doctrine, married women's legal status, the court's reluctance to interfere with the marital relationship, concern for fabricated accusations by wives, problems of providing supporting evidence, and possibility of spousal reconciliations.   They believe that married women should be protected against sexual assault by their husbands.   They fear that the new law may not provide that protection.

152   Bloch, Donald A.   "Discussion: Violence in the Family."   In Violence and the Family.   Ed. Maurice R. Green.   (AAAS Selected Symposium, 47) Boulder, Colo.: Westview Press, 1980, pp. 32-6.
      Bloch takes issue with Straus' linear model of the causes of family violence in the article "A Sociological Perspective on the Causes of Family Violence" [1542].   A typology of violent families is necessary if one is to understand the characteristics of the people on the far end of Straus' violence continuum.   Limitations of role struc-

ture, psychological resources, poor parenting and other factors can
be considered and added to improve Straus' theory.

153 Blum, Susan E. "Battered Women." M. S. W. thesis, Smith
         College, 1977. 91 p.
     The author reviewed the literature on the subject and then
interviewed four professionals who had contacts with battered women:
a social worker, a psychologist, a psychiatrist and a police officer.
The purpose was to determine how they perceived the problem and to
what extent their opinions agreed with the literature. All viewed the
problem as multifaceted and were greatly concerned about the problem,
contrary to the tone of some of the literature.

154 Blum, Susan E. "Battered Women." Smith College Studies in
         Social Work 48, no. 1 (1977): 24-5.
     This is an abstract of Blum's thesis for her Master of So-
cial Work.

155 Bochnak, Elizabeth, ed. Woman's Self-Defense Cases: Theory
         and Practice. Charlottesville, Va.: Michie Company, 1981.
         312 p.
     This should serve as a helpful practical guide to lawyers
who defend battered women who are on trial for killing, or attempting
to kill, their husbands. Self-defense, impaired mental state, jury
selection, education of the judge, voir dire, and the value of expert
testimony are all discussed. A number of cases are used to illustrate the techniques lawyers should use.

156 Bograd, Michele. "Battered Women, Cultural Myths and Clini-
         cal Interventions: A Feminist Analysis." Women and Ther-
         apy 1 (Fall 1982): 69-77.
     Much current clinical intervention in battered women situa-
tions assumes many of the male-dominant, sexist biases of our culture. By integrating a feminist perspective into one's clinical practice many of those cultural myths can be dispelled and improper treatment will be reduced, if not eliminated. Feminist theory is not clinical theory, but it can be of assistance to the therapist by providing
insights into the problem.

157 Boland, Mary Lou. "Domestic Violence: Illinois Responds to
         the Plight of the Battered Wife--The Illinois Domestic Vio-
         lence Act." John Marshall Law Review 16 (Fall 1982):
         77-99.

158 Bolton, F. G. , Jr. "The Domestic Violence Continuum: A Press-
         ing Need for Legal Intervention." Women Lawyers Journal
         66 (Winter 1980): 11-7.
     The beauty of the law is how it reflects and responds to the
needs of society. So far, however, this is not the case with domestic
violence, which includes spouse abuse, elder abuse, and child abuse.
Violence is violence and abuse is abuse, whether done to strangers
or family. The legal profession must recognize that and become a full
partner in the prevention and rehabilitation efforts. These remarks
were delivered at the November NAWL meeting in Scottsdale, Arizona.

159   Bonaparte, Lisa A.   "Battered Women: 'One of these Days
      . . . Pow, Right in the Kisser.' "   Honors paper, Kent
      State University, 1980.   70 p.

160   Booth, Alan, and John N. Edwards.   "Crowding and Family Re-
      lations."   American Sociological Review 41 (April 1976):
      308-21.
      This study investigates the effects of human crowding on
the interfamily relationship.   Sibling relationships and parent-child
relationships are studied as well as those between spouses.   Violence
and abuse between husband and wife is not specifically dealt with, but
apparently actual crowding has little effect on the number of quarrels
they have.   The feeling either person has of being crowded does,
however.

161   Borkowski, Margaret; Mervyn Murch; and Val Walker.   Marital
      Violence: The Community Response.   London: Tavistock,
      1983.   230 p.
      This British study was conducted between 1977-1980 in
Bristol, England, commissioned by the Department of Health and Social Security.   Its purpose was to explore the attitudes of solicitors,
local social workers, health visitors and medical practitioners regarding marital violence and various policy issues.   Social characteristics
of the victims, definition of abuse, difficulties with explaining the
problem, the question of legal evidence, privacy and confidentiality
of the professional interaction, and many other related issues are
discussed.

162   Borland, Marie, ed.   Violence in the Family.   Atlantic High-
      lands, N. J. : Humanities Press, 1976.   148 p.
      The essays in this volume were presented at two confer-
ences at Manchester University in 1974 and 1975.   Emphasis was on
"physical" violence with one chapter devoted to battered women.
Medical diagnosis, legal aspects, police involvement, interagency
collaboration and other relevant factors are discussed.

163   Bosarge, Betty B.   "South Carolina Chief Calls on Congress to
      Help Police Deal with Spouse Abuse Problem."   Crime Con-
      trol Digest 17 (July 11, 1983): 1, 6-9.

164   Boskey, James B.   "Spousal Abuse in the United States: The
      Attorney's Role."   In Family Violence; An International and
      Interdisciplinary Study.   Eds. John M. Eekelaar and Sanford
      N. Katz.   Toronto: Butterworths, 1978, pp. 199-207.
      Boskey, from the Seton Hall Law School, believes the role
of the attorney in spouse abuse actions to be minimal.   He compares
and contrasts legal intervention in spouse abuse with intervention in
child abuse, pointing out that although legal intervention works in the
latter situation, it will not in the former.   Social institutions and
remedies will be more effective than legal ones.

165   Boswell, Brenda.   "The Perpetuation of Wife Assault."   Cana-
      dian Woman Studies 4 (Summer 1983): 69-71.
      Because society does not view wife assault as a crime, the

judicial system will be unlikely to punish offenders.   Without punishment, the assaults are likely to continue.   Assaulting of wives will
be perpetuated until laws are properly enforced and violators convicted.

166   Bottom, Wayne D.   "Family Violence: The Sickness of a Sys-
          tem."   Alabama Journal of Medical Science 16 (April 1979):
          124-30.
          Bottom, Assistant Professor, Department of Family Prac-
tice, University of Alabama, argues that intrafamily violence is a
sociocultural sickness which, like other illnesses, requires more than
just treatment of the patient or victim.   Injury to one segment causes
injury to the whole.   Treatment requires awareness of the full scale
dimension of the problem, recognition of the victim's numerous needs,
and the complex web of stresses and relationships from which the
needs arise.   Rather than an individual's problem, the prolonged and
deviant effects of the abuse justify reference to family violence as a
sickness of the system.

167   Bottom, Wayne, and Jeanette Lancaster.   "An Ecological Orien-
          tation Toward Human Abuse."   Family and Community
          Health 4 (August 1981): 1-10.
          Many factors contribute to family violence whether it is
child abuse, spouse abuse, or parent abuse.   They include early exposure to violence for abuser and victim, immaturity and unreasonable
expectations of others, societal and cultural support for abuse, stress
on the family through economic factors and others.   It is not just the
abuser but also the victim and nonparticipatory observers who contribute to the system of abuse which engulfs the family.   Health care
professionals must be able to detect early those characteristics which
show a family is at high risk, and then be ready to offer service.

168   Boudouris, James.   "Homicides and the Family."   Journal of
          Marriage and the Family 33 (November 1971): 667-76.
          Between 1926 and 1968, 6,389 homicides were committed
in Detroit.   About 23.6 percent involved family members and about
50 percent involved family members and close friends.   Spouse abuse
itself is not discussed, but the author says that many quarrels led
to violence and that the members in the family had had a long period
of maladjustment and discord prior to the actual homicide.   Race and
age factors are analyzed.   The author feels that properly trained
field workers or the establishment of a family problem center could
intervene in domestic problems before they become police problems.
Field workers might also be able to handle family disputes better than
the police, who tend not to view that as true police work.

169   Boulding, Elise.   "Women and Social Violence."   International
          Social Science Journal 30, no. 4 (1978): 801-15.
          Various forms of violence against women are discussed
along with wife beating.   How society (especially patriarchy) victimizes
women, how women perform when trained as warriors, and how the
future looks in terms of violence, all receive attention from Boulding,
Professor of Sociology, University of Colorado, Boulder.   In the future
there will probably be less violence as women gain greater opportunities.   In the short run however, there may be more.

170   Bowder, Bill.   "The Wives Who Ask for It."   <u>Community Care</u>
         (March 1, 1979): 18-19.
         The author discusses the two types of battered women with
the most attention devoted to the one who provokes her husband because she is "addicted" to the excitement and adrenaline that accompanies the violence.   She does not like being beaten and is not a
masochist, but she is attracted to violent men.   Gentle men are seen
as boring.   The other type of battered woman is the one who becomes
involved with the violent man by mistake.   This type needs help to
escape the violence, such as shelters, while the other type does not
really want to escape the relationship.

171   Bowen, Nancy H.   "Guidelines for Career Counseling with Abused
         Women."   <u>Vocational Guidance Quarterly</u> 31   (December
         1982): 123-7.
         Battered women who seek employment are a group which
needs special attention.   Learned helplessness and low self-esteem
will affect how they see themselves and their chances for employment.
Career counselors must keep this in mind when exposing such women
to opportunities in the working world.

172   Bowker, Lee H.   "Battered Wives, Lawyers, and District At-
         torneys: An Examination of Law in Action."   <u>Journal of</u>
         <u>Criminal Justice</u> 11, no. 5 (1983): 403-12.
         The image most often gotten of lawyers to whom battered
women have gone for help is primarily negative.   From these 146 in-
depth interviews, we get a much more positive picture, and, in fact,
the more serious the battering the more helpful the victims perceived
the lawyers to be.   Nonetheless many negative incidents were reported, meaning much needs to be done to educate the legal profession.

173   Bowker, Lee H.   "Battered Women and the Clergy: An Evalu-
         ation."   <u>Journal of Pastoral Care</u> 36, no. 4 (1982): 226-34.
         No detailed studies have been done on the effectiveness of
the clergy in counseling and providing assistance to battered women.
This study of 146 Milwaukee, Wisconsin, battered wives indicates that
overall the clergy does provide some support.   Ministers were judged
by the victims to be more effective than priests because they were
more apt to direct the women in what action they should take.   The
priests were less likely to provide direction.   Suggestions by the
author include not attempting to compete with other social services,
education, and consciousness-raising of the congregation and support
of local shelter efforts.

174   Bowker, Lee H.   <u>Beating Wife-Beating</u>.   Lexington, Mass.: D.C.
         Heath, Lexington Books, 1983.   154 p.
         In Milwaukee, Wisconsin, 136 interviews were conducted
with women who believed they had ended or severely curtailed being
beaten by their husbands.   Much information was collected making
this an important study for those who wish to learn what wives can do
to increase the possibility of ending the abuse.   It is important to
recognize that no one method seems to work in all cases.   The most
commonly successful (30 percent) was the threat of divorce.   The
threat of police or criminal legal action, and the achievement of per-

sonal growth by the wife were also important. In all of these the
most important element was that the wife made it clear that she was
serious in her pursuit of these ends. Improved training of personnel
and stable funding of shelters are needed for the victims. Batterers
Anonymous type self-help groups are necessary for the abuser.

175 Bowker, Lee H. "Marital Rape: A Distinct Syndrome?" So-
        cial Casework 64 (June 1983): 347-52.
        Bowker raises the question of whether marital rape is a
syndrome quite separate from other forms of marital violence. He
draws his conclusions from interviews with 196 battered women, of
which 33 (23 percent) experienced marital rape, and believes that
there is nothing at this point to suggest a distinct syndrome. Professionals working with battered women should be aware of the possibilities of rape and of the fact that such women may need more attention and support.

176 Bowker, Lee H. "Police Services to Battered Women, Bad or
        Not So Bad?" Criminal Justice and Behavior 9 (December
        1982): 476-94.
        Bowker interviewed 146 women who had once been abused,
but who had taken steps to end it and thus had had no incidence of
violence for at least one year. Married and cohabiting couples from
southeastern Wisconsin were included in in-depth interviews which
lasted between two and four hours. Police action in these cases was
discussed and satisfaction on the part of the abused was low. The
major reason was the unwillingness of the police to arrest the abuser
when asked to do so by the wife. The Women's Resource Network
has developed a new model of training police to handle family violence.
Interviews with these women indicate the model will help.

177 Bowker, Lee H. "A Scream in the Night: Women as Victims." In
        his Women, Crime and the Criminal Justice System. Lexing-
        ton, Mass.: D.C. Heath, Lexington Books, 1983, pp. 103-42.
        This chapter is a general discussion of violence against
women in the form of rape, murder, wife abuse and abuse of female
children and infants. The pages on wife beating discuss the difficulty
of obtaining data and detail several studies. The movement against
spouse abuse is beginning to take shape and there is no reason to believe it will be any less successful than the anti-rape movement.

178 Bowker, Lee H., ed. Women and Crime in America. New
        York: Macmillan, 1981. 433 p.
        This is a collection of essays on women as criminals and
women as victims of crime. Articles by M.D. Pagelow [1200, 1202]
and E.S. Adler [3] concerned with wife beating are annotated and included in this bibliography under the authors' names. Other studies
in Bowker's book, especially those dealing with rape, may have some
relevance to the problem of spousal violence.

179 Bowker, Lee H., and Kristen McCallum. "Women Who Have
        Beaten Wife-beating: A New Perspective on Victims as Vic-
        tors." Paper presented at the annual meeting of the Ameri-
        can Society of Criminology, San Francisco, November, 1980.

180 Boycott, Rosie. "Battered Wives Find Refuge." <u>Spare Rib</u> No.
      14 (August 1973): 18.
      A general news note about Erin Pizzey and the Chiswick
Women's Aid.

181 Boyd, V.D. "Domestic Violence: Treatment Alternatives for the
      Male Batterer." Paper presented at the meeting of the Amer-
      ican Psychological Association, Toronto, September 1978.

182 Boyd, Vicki D. , and Joan M. Morris. "Meeting Special Needs:
      Family Violence: A Look at Battered Women." <u>Nursing
      Administration Quarterly</u> 4, no. 4 (Summer 1980): 70-2.
      The Group Health Cooperative of Puget Sound has a program
for identifying battered women and providing clinical psychological or
physiological treatment.   This article describes that program and
also a program available to batterers.

183 Boylan, Ann Marie, and Nadine Taub.   <u>Adult Domestic Violence:
      Constitutional, Legislative and Equitable Issues.</u>   Parts 1
      and 2.   Washington, D.C.:   Legal Services Corporation Re-
      search Institute, 1981.   385 p. and 136 p.
      The authors believe that abused women would be well-served
by special legislation and by vigorous use of civil remedies which
currently exist in common law.   Examples of laws and court decisions
from various states are used to illustrate the point.   The authors
also support the disciplining or disqualification of judges who consis-
tently disregard the concerns of battered women.   Boylan is a member of the New Jersey Bar.   Taub is Associate Professor, Rutgers
Law School.

184 Brandon, S.   "The Violent Home: Violence in the Family."
      <u>Royal Society of Health Journal</u> 5 (1977): 201-5
      Brandon, Professor of Psychiatry, University of Leicester,
argues that although the family is changing, and although it is often
criticized, it is still important.   Proper education should be provided
to youngsters so they will be better prepared for marriage and parenthood.   With smaller families these days, children have less opportunity to learn parenting skills.   With more divorce, they have less
opportunity to learn skills for living with mates.   Some concern here
is with spouse abuse, but mostly Brandon seems to be addressing the
problem of child abuse.

185 Braverman, Mara.   "Battered Women: Special Clients with
      Special Needs."   <u>Barrister</u> 8 (Winter 1981): 10-3, 51.
      This article by Los Angeles attorney Braverman is for law-
yers who should be sensitized to the various needs of battered women.
To lawyers the most obvious need is legal assistance, but the abused
also need emotional and financial support.   Lawyers need not, and in
fact, should not, provide the latter two.   However, they should be
aware of where referrals can be made.   A list of ten phone numbers
of the ten regional offices of the National Technical Assistance Centers on Family Violence is included.

186 Braverman, Mara. Legal Rights and Remedies of Battered
         Women. Dayton, Ohio: P. P. I. Publishing, 1979. 36 p.

187 Braverman, Mara. Marital Rape. Cincinnati: Pamphlet Pub-
         lications, 1979. 26 p.

188 Breedlove, R. K. , et al. "Domestic Violence and the Police:
         Kansas City." In Domestic Violence and the Police: Studies
         in Detroit and Kansas City. Eds. G. M. Wilt et al. Wash-
         ington, D. C. : Police Foundation, 1977, pp. 22-33.

189 Breines, Wini, and Linda Gordon. "The New Scholarship on
         Family Violence." Signs 8 (Spring 1983): 490-531.
         Three areas of family violence are analyzed: child abuse,
wife beating, and incest. The authors provide a good overview of the
scholarship with attention to the sociological and the feminist approaches. Kinds of violence, who is at risk, resource theory, exchange
theory and other concerns are addressed. The scholarship of wife
abuse is seen as new and undeveloped.

190 Breiter, Toni. "Battered Women; When Violence Is Linked With
         Love." Essence 10 (June 1979): 74-5, 121, 123-4, 126,
         128-9.
         A good general article for the lay reader using the research
results of Gelles, Pizzey, Straus, Steinmetz, and others.

191 Breslin, Warren J. "Police Intervention in Domestic Confronta-
         tions." Journal of Police Science and Administration 6
         (September 1978): 293-302.
         Breslin, a Chicago police officer and Loyola University law
student, studied the problem of domestic violence and police practices
in reporting and handling incidents. Police discretion regarding arrests and the influence of court attitudes toward family-related crimes
on police practice are considered. Guidelines are proposed for police
action in these matters, as well as suggestions for when an arrest
should be made.

192 Brismar, Bo, and Kajsa Tuner. "Battered Women: A Surgical
         Problem." Acta Chirurgica Scandinavica 148, no. 2 (1982):
         103-5.
         The records for emergency injuries during 1978 and 1979
at Huddinge Hospital, Sweden, were retrospectively examined to determine how much was the result of battering. Results show that 29 percent of the women had been battered and most by husbands, cohabitees
or fiancés. Injuries to the face and head were most common and relatively few were reported to the police. The relatively high amount of
battering that shows up in these records may be because the severity
of the cases required more than 24 hours care and most battered wives
probably do not go to hospitals unless very severely injured. In any
case, physicians must be alert to battering cases and be prepared to
refer victims to proper services.

193 Brisson, Norman. "Helping Men Who Batter Women." Public
         Welfare 40 (Spring 1982): 29-34.

AMEND (Abusive Men Exploring New Directions) was founded several years ago by the Denver Commission on Community Relations. Its purpose is to help men change their abusive and violent ways by using methods similar to those of Alcoholics Anonymous.   The goals are 1) to stop the violence; 2) to get the man to accept responsibility for his violence; 3) to heighten the abuser's perception of himself; and 4) to improve his interpersonal skills.   Some comparisons are made with Boston's EMERGE program.

194   "Britain: Battered Wives."   Newsweek 82 (July 9, 1973): 39.
        A brief news account of wife abuse in Great Britain and the Chiswick Women's Aid founded by Erin Pizzey.

195   Brodribb, Somer.   "Our True North: Native Women in the
        Yukon."   This Magazine 13 (November/December 1979):
        43-4.
        A discussion of the lack of government support and sympathy for the attempts of Whitehorse women to establish a spouse abuse shelter.   "Wife abuse is truly the great unmentioned crime in the Yukon."

196   Brown, Barbara Ann, and Gina Rachele Brazzle.   "The Self-Con-
        cept and Marital Satisfaction of Women in Metroplex Shel-
        ters."   MSSW thesis, University of Texas, Arlington, 1982.
        22 p.
        The authors studied forty women from four shelters in Texas during February 1982.   Measures used were the Index of Self Esteem Scale and the Marital Satisfaction Scale.   The common belief that battered women have low self-esteem was not substantiated by this study as nearly half registered high self-esteem.   The marital satisfaction scale testing showed only 10 percent satisfied with their relationship.

197   Brown, Barbara; Barbara Carpio; and Debbie Sue Martin.   "Wife
        Abuse: An Old Family Problem, A New Health Problem."
        Canadian Nurse 78 (June 1982): 23-8.
        A good overview of the problem with attention to the person-al characteristics of the abuser, sex-role adherence, the cycle of violence and transgenerational transmission, ways of breaking the cycle and roles nurses can play.   Various myths are explored.   A Canadian perspective by Canadian practicing and teaching nurses.

198   Brown, Bruce W.   "Wife-Employment, Marital Equality and Hus-
        band-Wife Violence."   In The Social Causes of Husband-Wife
        Violence.   Eds. Murray A. Straus and Gerald T. Hotaling.
        Minneapolis: University of Minnesota Press, 1980, pp. 176-
        87.
        Much has been said about the beneficial effects of the equali-tarian marriage style, though some suggest that it may cause many problems.   This article traces the consequences of wife-employment and considers the question of whether they might increase intraspousal violence.   Violence depends upon whether or not the husband accepts the equalitarian arrangement.   His acceptance depends upon four vari-ables: 1) the degree of compulsive masculinity; 2) the degree of antici-patory socialization; 3) degree of role clarity; and 4) the degree to

which the transition facilitates goal attainment.   This is a revision
of a paper presented at the annual meeting of the National Council on
Family Relations, Salt Lake City, August 20-23, 1975.

199   Brown, Linda R. Insalaco.   "The Admissibility of Expert Testi-
         mony on the Subject of Battered Women."   Criminal Justice
         Journal 4 (Fall 1980): 161-79.
         The author, candidate for J. D. , Western State University,
San Diego (1981), in this note, argues the case for allowing expert
testimony in battered women cases where the abused wife has killed
the husband.   The Federal and California laws regarding admissibility
of expert testimony and various cases that support that right are detailed along with L. Walker's cycle theory of the battered wife syndrome.   Characteristics of the victim and the abuser and an explanation of why she stays are included.   The facts of the syndrome are
not widely known, so expert testimony is essential to the defense if a
judge or jury is to reach a proper verdict.

200   Brown, M. M. ; B. E. Aquirre; and Carol Jorgensen.   "Abusers
         of Clients of Women's Shelter: Their Socialization and Re-
         sources."   Journal of Sociology and Social Welfare 8 (Sep-
         tember 1981): 462-70.
         Female residents of the Phoenix House, a shelter for bat-
tered women in Columbus, Ohio, were interviewed for facts relating
to their abusers.   The research attempted to determine whether socialization toward violence increased its probable use.   The first hypothesis was that the abuser's occupational status, education and number of weeks worked would be inversely related to the number and
types of violence used against the spouses.   The second was that
abusers with military service or criminal records would use greater
amounts and types of violence.   The first was not proven and the second only partly.   Those with criminal records did use more violence,
but those with military service only slightly more.   Those with military service did use more violence, however, when they also had
lower education levels, less occupational status and had worked less
during the previous year.

201   Browne, A.   "Lethal Incidents in Battering Relationships Between
         Adult Intimates."   Paper presented at the Feminist Analysis
         Seminar, Union for Experimenting Colleges and Universities,
         Colorado, March 1981.

202   Browne, A. , and R. Thyfault.   "When Battered Women Kill: In-
         terviewing Techniques."   Paper presented at the annual
         meeting of the American Psychological Association, Los
         Angeles, August 1981.

203   Browne, Irving.   "Wife-Beating and Imprisonment."   American
         Law Review 25 (1891): 557-68.
         In this article of some historical interest (1891), Browne dis-
cusses the notion that an English husband had the right to chastise his
wife.   He concludes that there never was such a right, except in self-
defense.   In America he has no such right and never did except in
Mississippi and North Carolina.   In England the husband did not have

the right to imprison his wife for misconduct and in America the husband has never had that right for any reason.

204 Browne, Stephen F.   " 'In Sickness and in Health ... ': Analysis of a Battered Women Population." Denver, Colo. : Denver Anticrime Council, 1980. 56 p.
  This study was done through use of a questionnaire developed by Lenore Walker. The instrument became part of the normal admitting procedures at Safehouse, a Denver, Colorado shelter. Data were collected and analyzed regarding attitudes toward and incidence of abuse. Overall, the survey shows a population who are committed to their marriages and even their abusive spouses, but who prefer to live without the beatings. The wives seem to view a service such as Safehouse as a way to preserve the relationship. A copy of the questionnaire is included.

205 Brownmiller, Susan. Against Our Will: Men, Women, and Rape. New York: Simon and Schuster, 1975. 472 p.
  In her discussion of rape the author says, "It is nothing more or less than a conscious process of intimidation by which all men keep all women in a state of fear." Some attention is paid to marital rape. Excellent overview of sexual violence directed at women.

206 Bruce, Errolyn. "Attitudes of Social Workers and Police in the Select Committee Reports on Violence to Women and Children." In Battered Women and Abused Children. (Issues occasional papers, no. 4.) [Bradford, Eng.]: University of Bradford, 1979, pp. 50-61.
  The attitudes of British police and social workers are similar as they relate to children. Both feel the abused child deserves complete protection of the law and society. When dealing with battered women they again agree, but practice indicates they are less apt to be as sympathetic as they are toward children. Privacy of home and the family take on stronger meanings when battered women are concerned. There is also more commitment to prevention of child abuse than wife abuse.

207 Bruner, Idamay Marjory Bunting. "Wife Abuse: The Effects on Young Children." Ph.D. dissertation, Fuller Theological Seminary, 1983. 119 p.
  In this study 20 nonabused children from homes with physical wife-abuse were compared with 20 from nonabusive homes. Using Travis story pictures, the Bene-Anthony Family Relations Test, and projective drawing, the effects of the abusive family situation on the children were analyzed. Results show that the violence does have an effect on children and there is no age that the children can "safely" witness (that is, not suffer from) the conflict. Children as young as four years can become emotionally distressed by this exposure. Lawyers may wish to note here that while paternal custody may have some merits in some cases, it has none if he was an abusive husband.

208 "Bruno v. Codd: A Summary." Response to Violence in the Family 3 (February 1980): 6.

209 Bryan, Marilyn, and Eugene N. Smith. A Resource Manual for
        Battered Spouses. New York: Harper and Row, [1978]. 39 p.

210 Bulcroft, Richard A. , and Murray A. Straus. Validity of Hus-
        band, Wife, and Child Reports of Conjugal Violence and
        Power. Mimeographed. (Family Violence Research Pro-
        gram, V-14). Durham: University of New Hampshire,
        1975. 18 p.
     Because of the high visibility of violence, there is more
agreement about the incidence data provided by husbands, wives, and
children than there is regarding power imbalance. On the other hand,
there is also a tendency for husbands to underreport their own violence when compared to observer reports and for the observers to
underreport the violence of the wives. Child reports of conjugal violence should therefore be viewed as useful, but as suspiciously as
self reports by the wife and husband.

211 Burns, Ligerie Peterson. "Criminal Law-Evidence-Expert Testi-
        mony Relating to Subject Matter of Battered Women Admissi-
        ble on Issue of Self-Defense." Seton Hall Law Review 11
        (1980): 255-64.
     This is a discussion of Ibn-Tamas v. United States, the
first time that expert testimony regarding a "battered woman" was ad-
missible on the grounds that it would not invade the province of the
jury and that its probative value was not outweighed by its prejudicial
impact. The court did have some problem establishing that Lenore
Walker was an "expert," however. A step forward in the court's
recognition that battered wives who kill their husbands must be seen
from a different perspective.

212 Burns, Sarah. "On Being an Abused Wife ... and Living in
        Fear." Mademoiselle 85 (December 1979): 56, 58.
     The author tells her story of life with an abusive husband
and her decision to divorce him. If she had to do it over, she would
not have waited so long to leave.

213 Busch, Ken, ed. Woman Abuse. Boston: EMERGE, n. d. 24 p.

214 Business and Professional Women's Foundation. "Battered Wom-
        en." Info Digest. Washington, D. C. : Author, 1978. 11 p.
     A general fact sheet useful for informing interested individu-
als and groups regarding the myths and facts of spouse abuse. A
short bibliography of some of the better items is included.

215 Buzawa, Eva S. "Police Officer Response to Domestic Violence
        Legislation in Michigan." Journal of Police Science and
        Administration 10 (December 1982): 415-24.
     Traditional attitudes of the police toward domestic violence
show why it is not given high priority. Police see themselves as
crime fighters, are not rewarded for social service functions, and do
not feel equipped to handle such situations. Rewards for proper handling of these cases and effective training programs are recommended
as major improvements. Revision of a paper presented at the annual
meeting of the American Society of Criminology, 1980.

216 Buzawa, Eva S. , and Carl G. Buzawa. "Legislative Responses
          to the Problem of Domestic Violence in Michigan. " Wayne
          Law Review 25 (March 1979): 859-81.
          The authors first provide a general discussion of the prob-
lem of domestic violence with emphasis on spouse abuse, then a description of the new Michigan laws. Officers will be able to make
warrantless arrests at the scene, and courts will be able to provide
for counseling alternatives to jail sentences, etc. More legislation
is suggested. The authors consider the Michigan laws a start, but
only a start.

217 Byles, J. A. "Family Violence in Hamilton. " Canada's Mental
          Health 28 (March 1980): 4-6.
          Byles studied the data on 605 family dispute calls received
during a six-month period in 1974-1975 by the Hamilton-Wentworth
Regional Police. The results indicate a sufficient level of violence
to justify a concerted program of action. Late evening and weekends
had the most incidents and alcohol was a contributor in many cases.
Many more questions were raised for future study.

218 Byles, John A. "Family Violence in Hamilton--Revisited. "
          Canada's Mental Health 30 (December 1982): 10-1.
          This is a second study to correct biases in the first article
[217]. Previously only police reports were used, but this study includes information from shelters, the United Family Court, and other
sources. During the time period between surveys, spouse abuse did
not appear to be on the increase. Services are available to the victims, but they are fragmented and inadequate. More funding is needed;
however, society cannot wait for better times before taking action.

219 Byles, J. A. "Family Violence. Some Facts and Gaps: A Sta-
          tistical Overview. " In Domestic Violence: Issues and Dy-
          namics. Ed. Vincent D'Oyley. Toronto: Ontario Institute
          for Studies in Education, 1978, pp. 53-68.
          Data regarding domestic disputes were taken from the calls
of the Hamilton police for a six-month period in 1974-75. The police
responded to more calls in summer than winter, the weekend rather
than weekdays, and evening to early morning rather than other hours
of the day. Data on marital status, age of offender, method of assault, presence of alcohol, etc. were also reported.

220 Byles, John A. "Violence, Alcohol Problems and Other Prob-
          lems in Disintegrating Families. " Journal of Studies on
          Alcohol 39 (March 1978): 551-3.
          Byles, Professor, Department of Psychiatry, McMaster
University Medical Center, studied 139 individuals (130 women) who
appeared in Hamilton Ontario Family Court from May-July 1974. The
strong association between violence and alcohol is confirmed. Indebt-
edness and incompatibility, however, seem to be independent of both.
Although violence occurs without the presence of alcohol, it is twice
as likely to happen when alcohol use is a problem.

221 Byrd, Doris E. "Intersexual Assault: A Review of Empirical

Findings." Paper presented at the annual meeting of the
Eastern Sociological Society, New York, March, 1979.

222 C., H. D. "Constitutional Law--State Misdemeanor Statute Which
          Provides That a Male over the Age of Eighteen Who As-
          saults a Female May Be Given a Longer Prison Sentence
          Than May a Female or a Male Not over Eighteen Who Com-
          mits an Identical Assault upon Either a Male or Female,
          Does Not Deny Equal Protection, State v. Gurganus." Jour-
          nal of Family Law 18, no. 1 (1979): 202-208.
     The defendant appealed a sentence for assaulting his wife
that was based on his sex. He claimed that if he were female he
would have received less than his eighteen months' imprisonment.
The North Carolina Court of Appeals agreed, but argued that since
the average adult male is taller, heavier and possesses greater body
strength than the average adult female, he also presents a greater
threat and therefore the fourteenth amendment was not violated.

223 California Commission on Crime Control and Violence Preven-
          tion. An Ounce of Prevention: Toward an Understanding
          of the Causes of Violence, Preliminary Report to the People
          of California. Sacramento, Cal.: The Commission, 1981.
          114 p.
     Various root causes of domestic violence are studied, in-
cluding biological factors, the birth experience, violence in the media,
education and the role of schools, diet, drugs, individual biochemistry,
and economic and social factors. A less violent society is possible,
but a commitment of resources will be required.

224 California Department of Justice. Handbook on Domestic Vio-
          lence. (Information Pamphlet no. 11.) [Sacramento]: Au-
          thor, 1979. 61 p.
     This handbook is designed to be a useful reference for law
enforcement officials, as well as for victims and for people in government and private shelters who assist victims of domestic violence.
Special attention is given to California laws and service agencies.

225 Calvert, Robert. "Criminal and Civil Liability in Husband-Wife
          Assaults." In Violence in the Family. Eds. Suzanne K.
          Steinmetz and Murray A. Straus. New York: Dodd, Mead,
          1974, pp. 88-91.
     The author observes that although a husband may have been
legally able to physically chastise his wife in the past, this is no
longer the case. This change has been brought about through gradual
increases in the socioeconomic level and education of the population
rather than by legislation.

226 Campbell, Don. "Battered Wives: Will the New Act Really Help?"
          Police Review 85 (May 6, 1977): 585.
     The author, policeman turned lawyer, discusses the Domestic
Violence and Matrimonial Proceedings Act of 1976, but does not believe
it will accomplish much.

227 Campbell, Jacquelyn. "Misogyny and Homicide of Women."
      Advances in Nursing Science 3 (Jan. 1981): 67-85.
            Campbell, Instructor, Community Health Department, Wayne
      State University, argues that misogyny is an important but often miss-
      ing element from theories of violence.   Misogyny derives from patri-
      archy, the basic family structure in American society.   Misogyny,
      patriarchy, machismo, gynocide, witch burning, suttee, footbinding,
      female circumcision, rape and wife abuse are all placed in context.
      All are ways males have asserted their dominance throughout history.
      In this study of Dayton, Ohio, murders of women, along with similar
      studies in Kansas City and Detroit, the males in many cases were
      found to be defining the female as an object of personal property and
      acting on that basis.   The article is directed at nurses who are urged
      to work to end the hold partriarchy has on society.

228 Campbell, Margaret. "Battered Wives." In Domestic Violence:
      Issues and Dynamics.   Ed. Vincent D'Oyley.   Toronto: On-
      tario Institute for Studies in Education, 1978, pp. 141-52.
            A general overview of wife abuse using numerous examples
      and the research of Pizzey, Gingold, Dutton, and others.   A unified
      Family Court System, specialized police Family Crisis Units, and
      social service assistance for victims, abusers and the children are
      all suggested as means to provide relief.

229 "Canadian Programs for Men Who Batter." Response to Family
      Violence and Sexual Assault 5 (September/October 1982): 5-6.

230 "Canadians Join Forces to Improve the Justice System's Response
      to Abused Women." Response to Violence in the Family
      and Sexual Assault 6 (July/August 1983): 5-6, 12.

231 Cantoni, Lucile. "Clinical Issues in Domestic Violence." So-
      cial Casework 62 (January 1981): 3-12.
            Domestic violence in general is discussed on the premise that
      the dynamic is similar whether the victim is a child, sibling, parent, or
      spouse. Common characteristics of such families include role reversal
      or role confusion, inappropriate sexual expression, lack of trust, fear
      of dependence or independence, expectations of perfection and others.
      To end the violence the family members must be ready to change and ac-
      cept new relationship patterns. It is the responsibility of the social
      worker to help. The parent-surrogate relationship is the principal
      treatment tool for helping violence-prone families.

232 Carlson, Bonnie E. "Battered Women and Their Assailants."
      Social Work 22 (November 1977): 455-60.
            Carlson, Adjunct Lecturer, School of Social Work, Univer-
      sity of Michigan, Ann Arbor, provides information on a sampling of
      101 battered women studied in 1976.   Marital status, education levels,
      race, age, number of children, etc., are data analyzed.   The rela-
      tionship of alcohol to this problem, why separation or divorce may
      not help, and the helpfulness of the police are also discussed.   Im-
      proving a family's financial situation might help alleviate the problem,
      but wife beating will not really go away until men accept the fact that
      physical force and violence are not answers to stress and frustration.

233 Carpenter, Stanley Roland. "Spousal Rape." American Bar
      Association Journal 66 (December 1980): 1494-5.
        This letter to the editor states that a spousal rape law, as
suggested in Susan Barry's "Spousal Rape: The Uncommon Law" ABA
Journal (September 1980), "is totally lacking in merit." Divorce is
always available to the victim.

234 Carr, Brian F. , and Joseph Mathews III. Woman Abuse Bibli-
      ography. (Public Administration Series: Bibliography,
      P-351) Monticello, Ill. : Vance Bibliographies, 1979. 16 p.
        A brief bibliography of fewer than 200 citations, about one-
tenth of which are annotated. The authors are from the School of
Social Work, University of Missouri. Better lists are available.

235 Carr, John J. "Treating Family Abuse Using a Police Crisis
      Team Approach." In The Abusive Partner: An Analysis
      of Domestic Battering. Ed. Maria Roy. New York: Van
      Nostrand Reinhold, 1982, pp. 216-29.

236 Carroll, Joseph C. "A Cultural-Consistency Theory of Family
      Violence in Mexican-American and Jewish-Ethnic Groups."
      In The Social Causes of Husband-Wife Violence. Eds.
      Murray A. Straus and Gerald T. Hotaling. Minneapolis:
      University of Minnesota Press, 1980, pp. 68-81.
        In an attempt to determine the effects of subcultural charac-
teristics on family violence, Carroll, Assistant Professor of Sociology at Colby-Sawyer College in New London, N. H. , compares Jewish families with Mexican-American families. The results indicate
that the strong patriarchal, male dominant approach of the Mexican-
Americans, with lack of intimacy and encouragement, and the emphasis on coercion, especially in the father-son relationship, promotes
violent interactions. The violence is used on the children and the wife.
In Jewish families more interaction is allowed, if not encouraged, and
disagreements are handled verbally and intellectually, not with violence.
Sons in each case pattern their adult behavior on their fathers' modes
of handling disputes.

237 Carroll, Joseph C. "The Intergenerational Transmission of Fam-
      ily Violence: The Long-Term Effects of Aggressive Be-
      havior." Aggressive Behavior 3 (Fall 1977): 289-99. Also
      in Advances in Family Psychiatry 2 (1980): 171-81.
        Carroll studies the contention that family violence is passed
from one generation to the next. Spouse abuse is not directly linked
here, but some relevance is apparent. Using a group of 14 clients
and a control group of 82, the author finds there is some relationship,
especially in families low in warmth and high in stress. The violence
characteristic is also more likely to be transmitted in same-sex patterns. That is, sons will be more violent if their fathers were,
whereas this transmission is not so obvious in daughters of violent
fathers.

238 Carter, Jack P. 'The Batterer: An Empirical Assessment of
      the Generational Transfer Hypothesis and the Severity of

Abuse. " M. A. thesis, University of Texas, Arlington,
1983.   108 p.

The author studied 542 battered women to learn what factors
influence the severity of abuse.   Results show external factors such
as youth (under 30 years old), low income, high school education or
less, blue collar occupation or unemployed status characterized the
most severe batterers.   Internal factors, including having witnessed
abuse between parents as children, also show a high relationship thus
supporting the thesis that family violence is transferred from one generation to the next.

239 CASA: New Directions: A Program Model for Battered Women.
        Citizens Assisting and Sheltering the Abused, U. S. Depart-
        ment of Labor and the Women's Bureau.   Washington, D. C. :
        Government Printing Office, 1981.   32 p.

This experimental program was designed through experience
in Hagerstown, Maryland.   Begun in 1977, the success of the program
required a more structured approach.   The organization of the program, staffing, funding, use of CETA help, a description of the actual
program, evaluation, and future plans are included.   A manual for
those wishing to set up a shelter for abused women who do not want
to return to the abuser.

240 Cate, Rodney M. , et al.   "Premarital Abuse: A Social Psycho-
        logical Perspective. " Journal of Family Issues 3 (March
        1982): 79-90.

While there is much study of marital violence, there is
relatively little research on violence between dating couples.   Factors
studied were how early abuse began, how the violence was interpreted
by the partners, whether violence was reciprocal, and why the abuse
occurred.   The subjects were 355 college students (153 male and 202
female) ages 18-31.

241 Cavanagh, Teri.   "Battered Women: Avenues for Community
        Response. " M. S. W. Essay, San Diego State University,
        1978.   131 p.

242 Cazenave, Noel A. , and Murray A. Straus.   "Race, Class, Net-
        work Embeddedness and Family Violence: A Search for
        Potent Support Systems. " Journal of Comparative Family
        Studies 10 (1979): 280-99.

Family violence in general, with some attention to child,
parent and spouse abuse, is considered here.   The relationship of
race, class, income, neighborhood, and network embeddedness factors
are sought with some success.   The author finds that "overall, the
black respondents in this study appear to be more embedded in family-
kin networks than their white counterparts, and these networks appear
to be more operative in reducing family violence as compared to whites
at similar socioeconomic levels.   This is especially true for the reduction of spousal violence. "

243 "The CETA Amendments and Battered Women. " Response to
        Violence and Sexual Abuse in the Family 2 (January 1979):
        1-2.

244 Celarier, Michelle. "I Kept Thinking Maybe I Could Help Him."
       In These Times (January 10-16, 1979): 3, 8.
       Interview with Greta Rideout regarding her marital rape
legal case.

245 Center for Women Policy Studies. A Comprehensive Bibliogra-
       phy: Part I--Domestic Violence; Part II--Crisis Interven-
       tion. Washington, D. C. : Author, 1977. 20 p.
       One of the early bibliographies that included spouse abuse,
this was quite comprehensive for the time. It has no annotations and
is now dated.

246 Center for Women Policy Studies. Films and Videotapes on
       Spouse Abuse. Washington, D. C. : Center for Women
       Policy Studies, 1980. Also in Abuse of Women: Legisla-
       tion, Reporting, and Prevention. Ed. Joseph J. Costa.
       Lexington, Mass. : Lexington Books, D. C. Heath, 1983,
       pp. 323-36.
       An annotated filmography with ordering and rental informa-
tion for about 130 films, TV programs, and videotapes.

247 Center for Women Policy Studies. Programs Providing Services
       to Battered Women. 4th ed. (Domestic Violence, Informa-
       tion Series, no. 2, April, 1981.) Rockville, Md. : National
       Clearinghouse on Domestic Violence, 1981. 247 p.
       This directory of services available to battered women is
arranged alphabetically by state, then by city. Information for each
entry includes mailing addresses, phone numbers, funding source,
contact persons, and services provided.

248 Chan, Kwok Bun. Husband-Wife Violence in Toronto. Ph. D.
       dissertation, York University, 1978. 350 p. Abstract in
       Dissertation Abstracts International 39A (May 1979): 6995-6.

249 Chan, Kwok B. "Intrafamilial Violence: Myth-making vs.
       Theory-building." Paper presented at the Canadian Soci-
       ology and Anthropology Meeting, University of New Bruns-
       wick, Fredericton, Canada, June 1977.

250 Chapman, Jane Roberts. "The Economics of Women's Victim-
       ization." In The Victimization of Women. Eds. Jane Rob-
       erts Chapman and Margaret Gates. (Sage Yearbooks in
       Women's Policy Studies, 3.) Beverly Hills, Cal. : Sage,
       1978, pp. 251-68.
       This discussion does not attempt to put a dollar value on
suffering. It does, however, point out two ways women suffer economically from the various forms of abuse and victimization they endure. First they must pay for the physical damage itself. This is
done in medical bills, time lost at work, and a myriad of other ways.
Secondly, if they leave the battering situation they will no doubt suffer
a reduction in their standard of living. Overall society supports this
system whereby only the victims (women) do the most, if not the total,
suffering.

251 Chapman, Jane Roberts, and Margaret Gates, eds. The Victim-
      ization of Women. (Sage Yearbooks in Women's Policy
      Studies, 3.) Beverly Hills, Cal.: Sage, 1978. 282 p.
      This volume has a fine selection of articles related to vic-
timization of women, including essays on spouse abuse, rape, sexual harassment, prostitution and the general effects of this victimization on women and on society at large. Spouse abuse articles by
Jane R. Chapman [250], Del Martin [1028], and Lenore E. Walker
[1670] are annotated elsewhere in this bibliography.

252 Chappell, Duncan. "Rape in Marriage: The South Australian
      Experience." In Violence in the Family: A Collection of
      Conference Papers. Ed. Jocelynne Scutt. Canberra: Aus-
      tralian Institute of Criminology, 1980, pp. 137-44.

253 "Characteristics of Battered Women: Two Approaches." Re-
      sponse to Violence and Sexual Abuse in the Family 2 (No-
      vember/December 1978): 2.
      Irene Frieze and Lenore Walker both received large grants
to study wife abuse, but each will use a different research methodology.

254 Charney, Israel. "From Marital Love and Hate." In Confront-
      ing the Issues: Sex Roles, Marriage, and the Family. Ed.
      Kenneth C. W. Kammeyer. Boston: Allyn and Bacon, 1975,
      pp. 303-13.
      Several myths of the "happy family" are discussed. The
family relationship is filled with tension and anger which must be
released. Physical violence is never acceptable. Aggression is natural, but fighting must be fair discussions which release constructive
forces.

255 Charney, Israel W. "Marital Love and Hate." In Violence in
      the Family. Eds. Suzanne K. Steinmetz and Murray A.
      Straus. New York: Dodd, Mead, 1974, pp. 52-8.
      Charney believes aggressiveness and conflict in marriage
are natural and should not be avoided. Fighting is necessary, but
physical violence cannot be tolerated. In fact, he believes, managed
conflict will prevent violence.

256 Chattanooga Metropolitan Council for Community Services. Study
      Committee. Spouse Abuse. Chattanooga: The Council,
      1980. 17 p.

257 Chavez, Beatrice. "Domestic Violence in Three Cultures." M. A.
      thesis, New Mexico Highlands University, Las Vegas, 1981.
      48 p.

258 Chegwidden, Paula; Lawrence F. Felt; and Anne Miller. "Bat-
      tered Women: Myths, Realities and New Directions for
      Future Research." Atlantis 6 (Spring 1981): 186-93.
      This article is a revision of a paper presented to the At-
lantic Association of Anthropologists and Sociologists, March 16-18,

1979, Mount Saint Vincent University, Halifax, Nova Scotia. It is a general overview of the problem based on American and Canadian research. Myths about the batterer and the victim, social class, alcohol, masochism, and the sanctity of marriage are discussed.

259 Chernok, Norma B. "The Battered Woman: A Domestic Matter of Public Concern." Professional Medical Assistant 13 (March/April 1980): 13-6.
          A general discussion based on monographs by D. Martin, T. Davidson, Steinmetz and Straus, Langly and Levy, and others. Medical assistants can play an important role by recognizing abused women and providing intelligent and sympathetic support and encouragement.

260 Chester, Robert, and Jane Streather. "Cruelty in English Divorce: Some Empirical Findings." Journal of Marriage and the Family 34 (November 1972): 706-12.
          The authors, from the Department of Social Administration, University of Hull, review the concept of "cruelty" as grounds for divorce. In the popular mind this appears to mean physical violence and is the single most frequently claimed reason. The authors suggest that even though cruelty need not include actual violence in the eyes of the courts, it may be used at the suggestion of the lawyer to insure a successful ending of the marriage. The implication, therefore, is that there may not be as much actual physical abuse as divorce court records suggest.

261 Child Welfare Resource Information Exchange. Wife Abuse: The Role of the Social Worker. n. p. : Author, 1980. 13 p.

262 Chimbos, Peter D. Marital Violence: A Study of Interpersonal Homicide. San Francisco, Cal. : R and E Research Associates, Inc. , 1978. 109 p.
          This is one of the few studies of inter-spouse homicide. Although the author does not claim that the 34 cases studied here are representative, they do have some general relevance to the crime. Among the findings is that the homicides do not suddenly occur in an otherwise blissful marriage, but rather the marriages are filled with violence and battering. Important study.

263 Citizens Committee for Victim Assistance. A Service Guide for Professionals Who Assist Victims of Rape, Child Abuse and Domestic Violence. Chicago: Author, 1978. 15 p.
          This is a service guide for workers in public and private Illinois service organizations who come into contact with victims of rape, child abuse, and wife abuse. It had been prepared to familiarize workers with laws that directly relate to victims of these crimes and to provide a listing of specialized and general service organizations that serve these clients. Could serve as a good model for other states.

264 Claerhout, Susan; John Elder; and Carolyn Janes. "Problem-Solving Skills of Rural Battered Women." American Journal

of Community Psychology 10 (October 1982): 605-12.
This study of 64 women in rural West Virginia indicates
that battered women were far less likely to have effective response
mechanisms to the situation and were more apt to use avoidance or
dependent responses than were nonbattered clients. It appears then
that the treatment strategy should include training in problem solving
skills. Earlier intervention will improve the battered woman's situation.

265 Clancy, Thomas K. "Equal Protection Considerations of the
     Spousal Sexual Assault Exclusion." New England Law Re-
     view 16, no. 1 (1981): 1-30.
     The author, an instructor at Vermont Law School, takes
issue with the Vermont marital rape exclusion. The theories which
support the immunity--including irrevocable consent, marital privacy,
difficulty of proof, and concern with reconcilability of the couple--all
promote the relationship at the expense of fundamental human rights.
This is inconsistent with the primacy given the individual by the con-
stitution. The marital rape immunity must be eliminated.

266 "Class Action to Protect Battered Wives." Response to Intra-
     family Violence and Sexual Assault 1 (February 1977): 6.

267 "Cleaver Tells Why He's Wifebeater--and More." Jet 58 (June
     12, 1980): 41.

268 Climie, R. C. "The Paradox of Family Violence." Canadian
     Medical Association Journal 129 (August 1, 1983): 221.

269 "Closing Chiswick's Open Door" Economist 266 (January 28,
     1978): 25.
     A recent legal battle between Erin Pizzey's Chiswick Wom-
en's Aid and the Hounslow Borough Council is discussed. General information regarding the shelter's activities is included. Complaints
of overcrowding have been made.

270 Clout. Ann ... et al. Manchester: Commonword, [1981?].
     68 p.

271 Coates, Carolie J. , and Deborah J. Leong. Conflict and Com-
     munication for Women and Men in Battering Relationships.
     Denver, Colo. : Denver Anti-Crime Council, 1980. 87 p.

272 Cobbe, Frances Power. "Wife Torture in England." Contempo-
     rary Review 32 (April 1878): 55-87.
     The article was written in support of a bill the author pro-
poses: "An act for the protection of wives whose husbands have been
convicted of assaults upon them." Numerous examples of wife battering are given showing that the problem is not a new one. An interesting depiction of family violence in Victorian England.

273 Coddington, F. J. O. "Rape of a Wife." Justice of the Peace
     and Local Government Review 96 (March 26, 1932): 199-201.

The intent of the Hale doctrine was not to allow spousal immunity in all cases of marital rape. When there has been a non-cohabitation order or a deed of separation there can be no "obligation of marital submission."

274   Cohen, Susan. "Employment Training for Battered Women." Response to Violence in the Family 3 (February 1980): 1-2.

275   Cohen, Susan. "Funding Family Violence Programs: Sources and Potential Sources for Federal Monies." Prosecutor 15 (November/December 1979): 128-32. Also, Washington, D.C.: Center for Women Policy Studies, 1979. 19 p.
        Government agencies are a rich source of funding for domestic violence projects and have not been tapped to full potential. The author, a staff member from the Center for Women Policy Studies, provides information on various agencies and programs. Though now dated it is of interest because it shows the range of possible sources for those willing to pursue the matter.

276   Cohn, Ellen, and David B. Sugarman. "Marital Abuse: Abusing the One You Love." Victimology: An International Journal 5, nos. 2-4 (1980): 203-12.
        This study examined how male and female observers attributed responsibility to victims and offenders for sexual and physical abuse of women. Both male and female observers believed the male offender to be more responsible for the abuse than the female victim. Interestingly, offenders were held more responsible for physical abuse than sexual abuse, probably because physical abuse was seen as more spontaneous and therefore the victim was not a willing partner.

277   Coleman, D.H., and Murray A. Straus. "Alcohol Abuse and Family Violence." Paper presented at the annual meeting of the American Sociological Association, February 1979.

278   Coleman, Karen Howes. "Conjugal Violence: What 33 Men Report." Journal of Marital and Family Therapy 6 (April 1980): 207-13.
        The author, researcher and family therapist, Marriage and Family Clinic, Texas Research Institute of Mental Sciences, interviewed 33 men who had abused their wives. Each man also completed a short questionnaire regarding sociodemographic characteristics, his nuclear family and family of origin as well as the BEM Sex-Role Inventory. Most men believed that both partners were responsible for the violence and the majority blamed the wife's verbal aggressiveness for provoking the physical fights. Explanation for the majority of fights fall into three groups: 1) chronic dissatisfaction with the wife; 2) retaliation for verbal aggressiveness; and 3) jealousy of past or present male friendships. Data regarding sociodemographic factors and strategies for treatment are included. This study is especially important since previously most information about abusers had been gathered from the victims.

279   Coleman, Karen H.; Maxine L. Weinman; and Bartholomew P.

Hsi. "Factors Affecting Conjugal Violence." <u>Journal of</u>
<u>Psychology</u> 105 (July 1980): 197-202.
This study includes 30 couples involved in marital violence
seeking psychiatric assistance for the conflict. The purpose was to
determine the variables which might be the most prominent predictors
of marital violence. Sociodemographic questionnaires and the BEM
Sex-Role Inventory (BSRI) were completed by husbands and wives.
The results indicate that a background of family violence, frequent
alcohol use, low education level, and frequent marital arguments
among abusing husbands increase probability of violence. This also
indicates that the variables of the abuser, as opposed to the victim,
are the most important for predicting marital violence.

280   Collins, Lisa. "The Wife-Beaters." <u>Sepia</u> 28 (February 1979):
      52-4, 63.
      General overview. The magazine is directed at a Black
readership, but the article is of interest to all. Popular presentation
for a lay audience.

281   Colorado Advisory Committee to the United States Commission
      on Civil Rights. <u>The Silent Victims: Denver's Battered</u>
      <u>Women.</u> Washington, D.C.: U.S. Commission on Civil
      Rights, 1977. 22 p.
      The committee reports that spouse abuse is more widespread
that commonly thought, and affects all ethnic and economic groups.
The purpose of the committee was to determine the extent of the problem and available assistance. Eighty persons including social workers,
law enforcement personnel, attorneys and 19 battered women were
interviewed. Findings include the fact that Denver has no city or
county services specifically for battered women. Recommendations
include a hotline, shelter funding, better police service for battered
women, and the establishment of crisis intervention teams. A good
local study.

282   Colorado Association for Aid to Battered Women. <u>A Monograph</u>
      <u>on Services to Battered Women.</u> Washington, D.C.: U.S.
      Department of Health and Human Services, 1980. 146 p.

283   Combo, Mary Ellen. "Wife Beating: Law and Society Confront
      the Castle Door." <u>Gonzaga Law Review</u> 15 (1979): 171-202.
      Combo provides a general overview of the problem and ex-
plains current legal remedies in the State of Washington. She is especially interested in the new Domestic Violence Act and the new
Shelter Act. Included in the provisions is the recognition that the
legal, police, and medical professions need education and increased
awareness regarding the problem. Such civil remedies as divorce, protective orders and tort action are discussed along with criminal provisions, including assault and battery, rape, spouse abuse statutes
and Washington's new laws. These new laws could solve the problem,
but, she says, it will depend upon how rigorously they are enforced.

289   Connecticut Advisory Committee to the U.S. Commission on Civil
      Rights. <u>Battered Women in Hartford, Connecticut.</u> Washing-

ton, D. C. :   U. S. Commission on Civil Rights, 1979.   28 p.
The committee reviewed the problems faced by abused women in Hartford and examined especially the policies and practices of the police, the criminal justice system, social service agencies, hospitals, welfare agencies, spouse abuse shelters, etc.   Thirty-six witnesses testified and Hartford police files were reviewed.   The findings were that despite growing awareness of the problem, the assistance battered women need is not forthcoming.   Police and social service agencies are lacking in the requisite training and funds for services are insufficient.

285   Conroy, Kathryn.   "Long-Term Treatment Issues with Battered
        Women. "   In The Many Faces of Family Violence.   Ed.
        Jerry P. Flanzer.   Springfield, Ill. :   Charles C. Thomas,
        1982, pp. 24-33.
        Among the more important problems facing the counselor
of battered women is the victim's ambivalence.   Women are socialized in that vein and overcoming it is often very difficult.   Other attitudes to be overcome are the notion that they are somehow at fault, or that the wife is responsible for holding the marriage together.   Economic factors, "love", and concern for the welfare of the children are also important considerations for the therapist to keep in mind.

286   Conroy, Kathryn, and Barbara Gordon.   "The Impact of Abuse
        on the Family. "   In Identification and Treatment of Spouse
        Abuse; Health and Mental Health Agency Roles, Proceedings
        of a Conference.   Eds. Abraham Lurie and Elizabeth B.
        Quitkin.   New York: Editors, 1981, pp. 101-15.

287   Coon, Liston F.   "Felony Assaults in Family Court. "   Criminal
        Law Bulletin 1 (May 1965): 11-4.
        The New York Family Court Act went into effect in September 1962, and within weeks a controversy arose over whether its jurisdiction included felonious assault of a wife by the husband.   The author believes that criminal court is the appropriate place to handle marital assault since family court lacks adequate penal sanctions.

288   Coonan, Helen.   "Rape Law Reform: Proposals for Reforming
        the Substantive Law. "   In Rape Law Reform.   Ed. Jocelynne
        A. Scutt.   Canberra: Australian Institute of Criminology,
        1980, pp. 37-47.
        Various aspects of the Australian rape laws need reform including the rape immunity clause for husbands.   Overall there can be no meaningful social progress until there is a fundamental change in the way men and women treat each other.   Sexism, of which rape is but an extreme example, must go.

289   Cooper, Barbara.   Wife Beating: Counselor Training Manual #2.
        Ann Arbor, Mich. :   NOW Domestic Violence and Spouse Assault Fund, 1976.   35 p.

290   Cooper, Margo.   "Duties and Enforcement Mechanisms for the

Rights of Battered Women." Suffolk University Law Review
16 (Winter 1982): 937-82.

291   Coote, Anna.   "Hellbent on Destroying the Act." New Statesman
         95 (June 16, 1978): 814.
         A criticism of the way judges and others are not enforcing
the Domestic Violence Act 1977 in England.

292   Coote, Anna, and Tess Gill.   Battered Women and the New Law.
         Rev. and extended ed.   London: Inter-Action Inprint and
         National Council for Civil Liberties, 1979.   40 p.

293   Corea, Gena.   "Northern Ireland: The Violence Isn't All in the
         Street."   Ms 8 (July 1979): 94, 97-9.
         Description of family violence in Northern Ireland with em-
phasis on spouse abuse and incest.   Masculinity roles of Irish men
and partriarchy are seen as the causes.

294   Corenblum, B.   "Reactions to Alcohol-related Marital Violence:
         Effects of One's Own Abuse Experience and Alcohol Prob-
         lems on Causal Attributions."   Journal of Studies on Alcohol
         44 (July 1983): 665-74.
         Several studies show that more blame will be attributed to
a batterer who has been drinking than one who has not.   In a study
of the opinions of 85 recovering alcoholics attending A. A. , it appears
that long-term members are less likely than short term members to
attribute responsibility for the abuse to the one who had been drinking.
They are also more likely to attribute the abuse to other factors.
Alcoholic victims too are more likely to blame other victims.   Para-
doxically this probably stems from a recovering alcoholic's perceptions
of a "just" world.   "One way to preserve justice is to see others as
personally responsible for their own fate. "

295   Cormier, Bruno M.   "Psychodynamics of Homicide Committed
         in a Marital Relationship. "   Corrective Psychiatry and Jour-
         nal of Social Therapy 8, no. 4 (1962): 187-94.
         Cormier, Department of Psychiatry, McGill University, in-
vestigates eight cases of men who killed their wives.   Unlike most
studies, which interview husbands shortly after the murder or during
the trial, this one concerns itself with the attitudes of the murderers
two to eight years after the event.   The intent is to determine if they
would kill again, or if something was learned from the experience.
The latter appears to be true.   The murderers eventually make a
truer assessment of their marital relationship and see where they
could have done things differently.   "Years after the murder, we see
men who have changed greatly and for the better. "   During the marriage the most important characteristic is the inability of the husband
to make the final separation from a troubled marriage.   This paper
was originally presented at the Third World Congress of Psychiatry,
Montreal, 1961.

296   "Corporal Punishment for Wife Beating. "   Central Law Journal
         2 (February 26, 1875): 134.

A short discussion suggesting that abolition of corporal punishment in England may have been a mistake, at least when it comes to wife beaters.

297   Costa, Joseph J.   Abuse of Women: Legislation, Reporting and Prevention.   Lexington, Mass.: Lexington Books, D.C. Heath, 1983.   674 p.
This compilation contains an original article by Stephen Couch [301], and several reprinted studies by R.J. Gelles [602], L. G. Lerman [937], and the Center for Women Policy Studies [246]. While much of this material is not new, including a long bibliography, it is a convenient resource for those wanting directory information on services for battered wives and abusive husbands.   Extreme caution must be exercised when using the bibliography since it is filled with typos and other errors.

298   Costantino, Cathy.   "Battered Women"   Social Work 24 (July 1979): 359.
The author of this letter to the editor suggests several alternatives to the proposals advanced by Claudette McShane in "Community Services for Battered Women" [1067].

299   Costantino, Cathy.   "Intervention with Battered Women: The Lawyer-Social Worker Team."   Social Work 26 (November 1981): 456-60.

300   Costello, Carol Norma.   "Wife Battering: Attributions of Blame and Responsibility."   Ph.D. dissertation, Adelphi University, 1983.   164 p.   Abstract in Dissertation Abstracts International 44B (September 1983): 953.

301   Couch, Stephen R.   "Research on Wife Abuse: A Scan of the Literature."   In Abuse of Women: Legislation, Reporting and Prevention.   Ed. Joseph J. Costa.   Lexington, Mass.: Lexington Books, D.C. Heath, 1983, pp. 1-11.
A good scholarly review of the literature dealing with the extent of abuse, characteristics of abuser and victim, research perspectives, an evaluation of them, and suggestions for further research. Deterrence of abuse will only come with greater equality between the sexes and less violence and stress in society in general.

302   Court, Joan.   "Violence in the Home."   Social Work Today 9, no. 27 (1978): 1.
Court provides general comments regarding family violence, especially child and spouse abuse.   Shelters are useful for interrupting the abuse and enabling the individuals to see their condition in a different light.   Forms of socially approved violence must be reevaluated.   Children need more family life education and social workers need different training to deal with the problems of sexual frustration which often lie behind marital violence.

303   Cox, W.J.E.   "Law Reform and Rape Under the Tasmanian Criminal Code."   In Rape Law Reform.   Ed. Jocelynne A.

Scutt.   Canberra: Australian Institute of Criminology,
1980, pp. 49-65.
Some attention is devoted to marital rape.

304   Crawford, Mabel Sharman.   "Maltreatment of Wives." West-
        minster Review 139 (March 1893): 292-303.
      The failure of the courts and magistrates to enforce the
wife beating sections of the Matrimonial Causes Act of 1878 is de-
plored.   Numerous cases of cruelty are cited.

305   Creach, Donald L.   "Partially Determined Imperfect Self-de-
        fense: The Battered Wife Kills and Tells Why." Stanford
        Law Review 34 (February 1982): 615-38.
      Creach discusses the problem of the battered wife who kills
her abusive husband and claims self-defense when there are other options to homicide.   He points out how traditional self-defense pleas
do not work well here and suggests that courts assimilate the concept
of partial determination into it.   Reasonable force, imminent danger,
reasonable belief, retreat and other factors of the law are noted.   The
problem juries face is choosing between two extremes, the intention-
alist or the determinist positions.   The case of battered wives falls
somewhere between the two and justice is not served by forcing a jury
to choose one over the other.   These cases would be seen as imperfect self-defense.

306   Crimes Against Women: Proceedings of the International Tri-
        bunal.   Compiled and edited by Diana E. H. Russell and
        Nicole Van De Ven.   Millbrae, Cal.:   Les Femmes, 1976.
        298 p.
      The 1st Tribunal was held in Brussels in March 1967 and
was attended by over 2,000 women from 40 countries.   Many of the
proceedings consist of testimony regarding a wide assortment of cruelty and abuse of women.   A small part is devoted to testimony of
battered women and a resolution that governments recognize the extent
of the problem and provide refuges, financial aid, and legal protection for these women.

307   Crist, Karen.   "Battered Women in Rural Communities." Women
        and Environments 5 (Summer 1982): 17-9.   Also in Response
        to Violence in the Family 4 (November/December 1980): 1-2.
      The author describes the special problems faced by battered
women who live in rural areas of the United States.   Certain characteristics of rural life make it extremely difficult for rural battered
women to seek help and find alternatives to living with violence.   Social services are in short supply even if rural women were inclined
to seek them out.   Rural service providers have begun to overcome
their isolation from each other by forming coalitions and networks to
exchange information and technologies for solving problems.   Two examples of this are the Rural Domestic Violence Conference and National Coalition Against Domestic Violence Rural Task Force.

308   Crist, Karen.   "Federal Response to Battered Women Inadequate."
        Response to Family Violence and Sexual Assault 5 (January/

February 1982): 3.
A discussion of two government studies, Under the Rule of
Thumb and Federal Response to Battered Women.

309   Crist, Karen. "Guidelines for Obtaining Foundation Funds."
       Response to Violence in the Family 3 (July 1980): 3.

310   Crist, Karen, and Lois A. West. "Federal Initiatives to End
       Family Violence Blocked." Response to Violence in the
       Family 4 (March/April 1981): 3, 6.

311   Cristall, Linda May. "A Comparison of Androgyny and Self-
       Actualization in Battered Women." Ph. D. dissertation,
       United States International University, 1978. 128 p. Ab-
       stract in Dissertation Abstracts International 39B (April
       1979): 5039.

312   Croft, Elizabeth Benz. FACIT: Family Conflict Intervention
       Team Experiment, Experimental Action Program. Roch-
       ester, N. Y.: University of Rochester, 1974. 33 p.

313   Cross, Meredith Brinegar. "The Expert as Educator: A Pro-
       posed Approach to the Use of Battered Woman Syndrome
       Expert Testimony." Vanderbilt Law Review 35 (April 1982):
       741-68.
       Since the use of expert testimony is not universally accepted
in cases where the battered wife has killed the abuser, the author suggests that courts can use the information provided by experts to educate the jury. The Ibn-Tamas case allowed expert testimony, but in
Ohio (State v. Thomas), Wyoming (Buhrle v. State), and Georgia
(Smith v. Smith), testimony by battered wife experts was not allowed.
Even if the testimony is not allowed to show the wife's perception of
imminent harm, it could be used to inform the court of the facts regarding her psychological condition.

314   Crowley, Charles, et al. Physically Abused Women and Their
       Families: The Need for Community Services. Program De-
       velopment Guide. Trenton: New Jersey Department of Hu-
       man Services, 1978. 96 p.
       The purpose of this report is to summarize what is known
regarding the problems of abused wives and their children and to
identify programs that would meet their needs. The scope of the problem is described, followed by current program development activity
and recommendations for program development. A good basic overview.

315   Cunningham, Laura. "Love and Rage: The Threat of Male Vio-
       lence." Vogue 172 (July 1982): 60, 62.
       Cunningham discussed how "nice" men become violent.
Sometimes they are provoked, but it is their own personality which
is at fault. Most of the article discusses violence in the context of
the movie with Albert Finney and Diane Keaton, Shoot the Moon.

316 Curran, William J. "Women's Rights in the Courts: Some
        Gains and Losses." American Journal of Public Health 70
        (February 1980): 178-9.
        Some attention is devoted to the Ibn-Tamas v. U. S. case
wherein an abused wife killed her husband. Testimony by a psychologist regarding battered-women syndrome is not allowed by the judge.
This is one of the losses.

317 Dahl, Tove Stang. "Domestic Violence: Crimes Against Women."
        In Crime and Crime Control in Scandinavia. Ed. Norman
        Bishop. Scandinavian Research Council for Criminology,
        1980, pp. 24-8.
        The 1976 Brussels Tribunal on Crimes Against Women
prompted an interest which resulted in the first shelter in Norway.
Prior to that there was little willingness by the public to recognize
wife abuse. Most of the abuse was concealed in the police logs under
"domestic violence." Since 1976 the problem has received more publicity, legal concerns are being aired, and more shelters have been
established.

318 Dalto, Carol Ann. "Battered Women: Factors Influencing
        Whether or Not Former Shelter Residents Return to the
        Abusive Situation." Ph. D. dissertation, University of Mas-
        sachusetts, 1983. 208 p. Abstract in Dissertation Ab-
        stracts International 44B (October 1983): 1277.

319 Dalton, Debra A., and James E. Kantner. "Aggression in Bat-
        tered and Non-battered Women as Reflected in the Hand
        Test." Psychological Reports 53 (December 1983): 703-9.
        Dalton, Rehabilitation Group of Santa Barbara, and Kantner,
University of North Carolina, administered the Hand Test to 52 women
(26 battered and 26 nonbattered) to determine each participant's potential anger, aggression and acting out. It appears that this test is
useful in assessing the emotional states of abused women. The test
is easy to administer and nonthreatening. Results show the battered
women to be more aggressive and less able to interact appropriately
with their environment than the nonvictim.

320 Daly, Liam. "Family Violence: A Psychiatric Perspective."
        Irish Medical Association Journal 68 (October 11, 1975):
        450-3.
        Family violence is viewed as a community mental health
problem. Services should be provided by a specialized team, including a psychiatrist, social worker, psychologist, community nurse and
occasionally representatives of other relevant agencies such as clergy,
police, and the courts. Therapy should focus on the options to violence.

321 Daniel, A. E., and P. W. Harris. "Female Homicide Offenders
        Referred for Pretrial Psychiatric Examination: A Descrip-
        tive Study." American Academy of Psychiatry and the Law

Bulletin 10, no. 4 (1982): 261-9.
Twenty-two women murderers were referred to the authors
for pre-trial psychiatric examinations.   A high proportion were victims of spouse abuse.   If domestic violence is recognized by helping
professionals earlier, some killings could be prevented.   Law enforc-
ment officials must be prepared to intervene in family disputes, since
90 percent of family homicides are precipitated by domestic disturbances.

322   Daniels, Mark.   "Wife Abuse and Public Policy: A Conceptual
         Model."   Free Inquiry in Creative Sociology 9 (November
         1981): 190-4, 197.
         In order to provide relief to victims of spouse abuse, poli-
cymakers should construct a model of the problem.   The model would
consist of the various elements of the problem, such as the characteristics of the abuser and the victim, the policies and services available
from community agencies, and the results of those services, both
positive and negative.   This visual depiction would make the problem
and possible solutions more visible and planning easier.

323   Daniels, Robin.   "Battered Women--The Role of Women's Aid
         Refuges."   Social Work Today 9, no. 12 (1977): 10-3.
         The need for battered-women shelters and the growth of the
National Women's Aid Federation in Britain shows the glaring need
for a reevaluation of the popular attitudes and view of family life.
Shelters are seen as necessary, but only providing temporary relief.
They are not a final solution to the problem.   The role shelters play
and the emotional needs of the wives and their children are clearly
detailed.   The shelter movement is always in need of financial aid
and public support.

324   Dank, Barry M.   "Six Homosexual Siblings."   Archives of Sexu-
         al Behavior 1, no. 3 (1971): 193-204.
         In a family of ten children, six were found to be predomi-
nantly homosexual.   Since all the siblings had been exposed to the
same family dynamics, Dank stresses the need to consider family relations as contributing to homosexuality.   The father's behavior toward
the children and the mother was characterized as hostile, violent, and
alcoholic.   One son's description of the father shows him to be a
chronic batterer.   The emphasis of this article is on the causes of
homosexuality, not spouse abuse, but the possible relationship demands
some consideration.

325   Davidson, Terry.   Conjugal Crime: Understanding and Changing
         the Wife Beating Pattern.   New York: Hawthorn Books,
         1978.   274 p.
         This is a highly readable overview of the problem of wife
abuse by one who had witnessed her father, a minister, beat her
mother.   Detailed explanations of why the abuser does it, why the
victim takes it, the effects on the children and what can be done.
Shelters should be provided, as well as legislation, and more support
by the community, churches and social service agencies.   Interestingly,
she suggests that the abuser be placed in a shelter, thereby allowing

the victim to remain in the family home.   Included is a list of over
50 shelters for battered wives in the United States.

326   Davidson, Terry.   "Wifebeating: A Recurring Phenomenon
            Throughout History."   In Battered Women: A Psychosocio-
            logical Study of Domestic Violence.   Ed. Maria Roy.   New
            York: Van Nostrand Reinhold, 1977, pp. 2-23.
            Interesting overview of wife abuse in history with some at-
tention to biblical and pre-biblical times.   The author believes that
even with such strong tradition the public can be educated to view
such abuse as wrong.   Christian understanding and above all Christian
Church advocacy of the changes will help.   Religion aided in justifying
abuse, but now can reverse that attitude.

327   Davidson, Terry.   "Wife Beating: It Happens in the Best of
            Families: In the Eyes of Acquaintances He May be a Nice
            Guy."   Family Circle (November 15, 1977): 62, 68, 70, 72.
            A general discussion of the problem, describing the person-
ality characteristics of the abuser and the abused.   The article includes a list of hot lines in various cities for those who want help.

328   Davies, D. L.   "Alcoholism."   Midwife Health Visitor and Com-
            munity Nurse 20 (April 1983): 124-6.

329   Davis, Liane V. , and Bonnie E. Carlson.   "Attitudes of Service
            Providers Toward Domestic Violence."   Social Work Re-
            search and Abstracts 17 (Winter 1981): 34-9.
            The authors, both assistant professors at the School of So-
cial Welfare, State University of New York, Albany, surveyed by
questionnaire the attitudes of five hundred social workers, police officers, family court judges, and health service providers regarding family violence.   The results indicate a strong tendency to blame the victim or to at least put some responsibility for the violence on the
abused.   Service providers tend to concentrate on those factors that
are least subject to change such as personality characteristics.   The
less educated the respondents, the less sympathetic they were toward
the victims.   The outcome is that the victims often do not receive the
aid that is needed or even available, because they are led to believe
that there is little that can be done.

330   Day, L. Edward.   Report on Technical Assistance Project: Do-
            mestic Violence Survey.   Chicago: Statistical Analysis Cen-
            ter, Illinois Law Enforcement Commission, 1978.   6 p.
            A questionnaire was sent to 780 local police departments
and 99 sheriff's departments to learn how domestic violence calls were
handled.   The overall response rate was 25.5 percent with the conclusion that the emphasis placed on these cases by the law enforcement
agencies was equal to that of other crimes.   On the other hand, only
a small number had written policies for dealing with the calls.   Among
the findings are the facts that arrests are not common and there is a
lack of records kept pertaining to domestic violence.   A copy of the
survey instrument was included.

331 "Decisions on Sentencing: Offences Against the Person." Crim-
        inal Law Quarterly 17, no. 4 (1975): 343-4.
        A short discussion of a case (R. v. Chaissen) in which a
husband was arrested and convicted for abusing his wife. The author
objects to the use of imprisonment periods longer than what treatment
would normally be. This is especially objectionable when no treatment had initially been proposed or contemplated.

332 Delacoste, Frederique, and Felice Newman, eds. Fight Back!
        Feminist Resistance to Male Violence. Minneapolis: Cleis
        Press, 1981. 398 p.
        This volume contains many short articles and essays address-
ing the problem of male violence directed at women. Several about
spouse abuse are listed and annotated in this bibliography by author.
The opinions contain a feminist, lesbian perspective.

333 Delaware Commission for Women. Facing Crisis: A Guidebook
        for Delaware Families. Ed. Barbara Herr. Wilmington,
        Del.: Author, 1982. 62 p.
        Most of this booklet is an essay, "Understanding Family
Violence," written by Suzanne K. Steinmetz, which discusses all forms
of family abuse. Causes and examples of abuse are discussed along
with some steps to take which might stop the abuse. Other sections
include information on social and legal services available. More
states should make materials such as this available to their citizens.

334 Dellapa, Fred M. "Domestic Violence: Alternative Processes to
        Resolve Interpersonal Family Conflicts." Conciliation Courts
        Review 17 (June 1979): 15-20.
        The way criminal justice currently operates is punitive, not
preventative and as such does not fully meet the needs of battered wives
who seek the latter not the former. One alternative might be the Citizen
Dispute Settlement Center as developed by a Dade County program, funded
by a LEAA Grant. This program, which was tested in 1975, proved successful; though not touted as a cure-all, it does offer an alternative to the
criminal courts.

335 Dellapa, Fred. "Mediation and the Community Dispute Center." In
        Battered Women: A Psychosociological Study of Domestic Vio-
        lence. Ed. Maria Roy. New York: Van Nostrand Reinhold,
        1977, pp. 239-49.
        The author, Director of the American Bar Association's Spe-
cial Committee on Resolution of Minor Disputes, proposed the establishment of a community dispute settlement center, like the experiment conducted in Miami in 1975. Problems are handled more quickly and at less
expense than if handled by regular court procedures. With a 94.9 percent
successful resolution rate and a recidivist rate of 4.1 percent, this method appears to be one that might merit serious consideration in cases of
wife abuse. The traditional courtroom may not be the only place to dis-
pense justice.

336 Delorto, Diane O., and Alyce D. Laviolette. "Spouse Abuse." Occu-
        pational Health Nursing 28 (August 1980): 17-9.

This paper was presented at the tenth annual Tri-Association Educational Seminar, Long Beach, California, February 23, 1980, by the authors, two volunteers for the Long Beach YWCA Women Shelter. It is a good general overview of the problem.

337 Del Tosto, Doris. "The Battered Spouse Syndrome as a Defense to a Homicide Charge Under the Pennsylvania Crimes Code." Villanova Law Review 26 (November 1980): 105-34.
Three hypothetical cases of spouse abuse resulting in the killing of the attacker are used by the author as illustrations of how the Pennsylvania law would accommodate a homicide defense based on Battered Spouse Syndrome. The author argues that the legal system with its general unresponsiveness to domestic violence contributes to the feeling abused women have, that their only recourse is to strike back at the attacker. Use of Battered Spouse Syndrome could reduce the charges and if the circumstance were right, self-defense could be claimed. That would be preferable to an argument of impaired mental state.

338 Dewsbury, Anton R. "Battered Wives: Family Violence Seen in General Practice." Royal Society of Health Journal 95 (December 1975): 290-4.
A pilot study of marital violence in England using fifteen cases. The cause of violence is perceived to be from personality difficulties of the husbands, often aggravated by physical causes, especially alcohol. The author believes the treatment of family violence will be largely a matter of counseling and coping.

339 DiAnna, Carol. "The House of Ruth: A Healing Perspective; An Interview with Three Battered Women." Women: A Journal of Liberation 7, no. 3 (1981): 46-50.
Three women staying at the Baltimore shelter, the House of Ruth, tell their stories. Of special interest is the value of the shelter experience as seen by these victims.

340 Dibble, Ursula, and Murray A. Straus. "Some Social Structure Determinants of Inconsistency Between Attitudes and Behavior: The Case of Family Violence." Journal of Marriage and the Family 42 (February 1980): 71-80.
The authors surveyed 2,143 American couples in an attempt to determine if there was a relationship between one's attitude toward violence and their actual use of violence toward children and spouses. The relationships between these and economic status were also considered. The results indicate what consistency there is depends more on other factors than one's actual belief about violence. This study disputes the notions of some that occurrence of violence is an outgrowth of an individual's beliefs or personality traits. An important study.

341 DiCarlo, Melinda S. "The Marital Rape Exemption in Pennsylvania: 'With This Ring ...'" Dickinson Law Review 86 (Fall 1981): 79-114.
DiCarlo reviews the question of marital rape and especially the legal situation in Pennsylvania. Protection there for married women forced to have sex by their husbands is afforded only if she is living in a

residence separate from him, or if in the same residence only if there is a written separation agreement or court order. Basically the view that a husband cannot be prosecuted for raping his wife remains intact in most of the United States. The seriousness of spousal rape is not diminished because it occurs in the context of marital or cohabital relationship. To allow it to go unpunished is a threat to the moral principles that underlie society and the criminal law.

342 Diebel, Linda. "Curbing the Wife-Beaters." MacLeans 96 (January 17, 1983): 40-1.
      This news account relates efforts in Canada during 1982 to provide relief to abused wives. Several case histories are given, legislative action (or inaction) and Calgary's new police department policy of arresting batterers with the officers laying charges are described.

343 Dierking, Anne V. "How to Lose a Court Case." Social Action and the Law 11, no. 6 (1978): 58-60.
      A divorce case which included abuse of the wife was lost because of the lack of apparent male involvement in the case. Women lawyers must learn to play the game. Being right is often not enough.

344 Dierking, Anne V. "What Should the Police Do in Spouse Abuse Incidences?" Social Action and the Law 4, no. 6 (1978): 61-3.
      The author compares the approach of Bard and Connolly with that of Marjory Fields. She argues that the philosophy of each is too exclusive for such a wide range of human behavior. Resolution is more likely if domestic disturbances are reclassified as family arguments (nonviolent) and family assaults, and then treated appropriately.

345 Dierking, Anne V.; Daniel Katz; and Katherine W. Ellison. "Domestic Violence: Attitudes and Implications." Social Action and the Law 4, no. 6 (1978): 51-7.
      The authors surveyed 221 registered voters in New York and New Jersey, a cross section eligible for jury duty, to determine if the popular attitude "a man's home is his castle" includes wife beating. If found to be true, then women seeking relief in criminal court may have difficulty with juries. The results indicate that usual methods of jury selection may not be as valuable in cases of wife beating. Overall the general public seems to believe family issues and problems are private, not legal issues.

346 Dion, Mark. "On Men in the Battered Women's Movement." Response to Violence in the Family 4 (July/August 1981): 2.

347 Disney, Dorothy Cameron. "I Was a Battered Wife." Ladies Home Journal 96 (April 1979): 18, 20, 44.
      This is a case study from the magazine's series "Can This Marriage Be Saved?" The wife tells her side of the story and the husband tells his. Finally the counselor discusses the situation and in this case appears optimistic. No particular relationship between this case and the research that has been conducted on the problem has been drawn.

348 Divver, Elizabeth Johnson; Judith Ann Dunlap; and Kathryn Atkins Morgan.

"Community Services to Battered Wives in Spartanburg County: An Explanatory Study and Model." M. S. W. thesis, University of South Carolina, 1978. 323 p.

349 Do You Feel Like Beating Up on Someone? Boston: Emerge, 1980. 4 p.
This leaflet utilizes a question and answer approach for frustrated males who take their stress out on their wives. Various bits of advice are provided.

350 Dobash, R. Emerson. "The Negotiation of Daily Life and the 'Provocation' of Violence: A Patriarchal Concept in Support of the Wife Beater." Paper presented at the 9th World Congress of Sociology, Uppsala, Sweden, August 1978.

351 Dobash, R. Emerson, and Russell P. Dobash. "The Antecedents and Nature of Violent Episodes." Paper presented at the annual meeting of the American Sociological Association, San Francisco, August 1982.

352 Dobash, R. Emerson, and Russell P. Dobash. "Explanations of Wife Beating That Blame the Victim." In Conflict in the Family: A Continuing Education Course. Milton Keynes, England: Open University, 1980.

353 Dobash, R. Emerson, and Russell Dobash. "If You Prick Me Do I Not Bleed?" Community Care no. 262 (May 3, 1979): 26-8.
The authors respond to the article by Bill Bowder [170] in an earlier issue of the same journal which suggests that some battered women are thrill seekers whose thrills get out of hand. The Dobashes argue that the existence of such a group of women is not proven and Bowder's unsubstantiated suggestions may encourage counselors and police to not take the needs of battered women seriously.

354 Dobash, R. Emerson, and Russell P. Dobash. "The Importance of Historical and Contemporary Contexts in Understanding Marital Violence." Paper presented at the annual meeting of the American Sociological Association, New York, August 1976. 13 p.

355 Dobash, R. Emerson, and Russell P. Dobash. "Love, Honour and Obey: Institutional Ideologies and the Struggle for Battered Women." Contemporary Crises 1 (1977): 403-15.
The authors argue that changing the words in the marriage vows "to love, honour and obey" does little to effect any real changes. The reason is that patriarchy is the basis of marriage and all institutions in society see it to their advantage to preserve the notion of male domination. Much attention is directed at changing the wife's behavior or providing counseling and/or shelter. Nothing of importance can be done so long as the patriarchy remains. This essay was originally delivered at the annual meeting of the Society for the Study of Social Problems, New York, August 1976.

356 Dobash, R. Emerson, and Russell P. Dobash. "Patterns of Violence

in Scotland. " In International Perspectives on Family Violence.
Eds. Richard J. Gelles and Claire Pedrick Cornell. Lexington,
Mass. : Lexington Books, D. C. Heath, 1983, pp. 147-57.
    This is an abridged version of the authors' "Wives: The 'Ap-
propriate' Victims of Marital Violence" [364].

357 Dobash, R. Emerson, and Russell P. Dobash. "Social Science and
    Social Action: The Case of Wife-beating. " Journal of Family
    Issues 2 (December 1981): 439-70.
    The authors investigate the relationship between social science
and social action as it pertains to wife abuse and its accompanying issues
and problems. When spouse abuse became a public issue in the early
seventies many psychiatrists responded to the media's desire for information. Their message was that abuse was the result of an individual's
own psychological problem. Social scientists who know better (that it is
a sociocultural problem) must come forward to educate the public. Researchers should attempt to incorporate research findings into positive
social action. Association of social scientists with community action
groups does not necessarily taint the research and no blanket judgment of that nature should be permitted to go unchallenged.

358 Dobash, R. Emerson, and Russell P. Dobash. Violence Against
    Wives: A Case Against the Patriarchy. New York: Free
    Press, 1979. 339 p.
    A scholarly overview of the problem. This study sees the
maintenance of patriarchy as the primary reason for wife abuse. Historically (the last several centuries at least) women have been excluded
from the positions and professions with power. The reason was to prevent them from changing the patriarchal social order. Social, legal, economic, religious, and political traditions are all reviewed. One of the
more important books on wife abuse.

359 Dobash, R. Emerson, and Russell P. Dobash. "The Violent Event. "
    In The Changing Experience of Women. Eds. Elizabeth White-
    legg et al. Oxford: Martin Robinson, 1982, pp. 190-206.
    This chapter consists of excerpts from their book, Violence
Against Wives, and concentrates on the violent event itself. Observations
regarding the sources of the conflict, the verbal exchange and efforts to
avoid the conflict, response of the wife once the violence began, the nature
of the injuries and the aftermath are detailed.

360 Dobash, R. Emerson, and Russell P. Dobash. "Wifebeating: Past
    and Present. " Paper presented to the first meeting of the
    Anglo-French Exchange on Violence Against Women, London,
    November 1975.

361 Dobash, R. Emerson, and Russell P. Dobash. "Wife-Beating: Pa-
    triarchy and Violence Against Wives. " In Conflict in the Fami-
    ly: A Continuing Education Course. Open University Course
    Team. Milton Keynes, England: Open University, 1980.

362 Dobash, R. Emerson, and Russell P. Dobash. "Wife-Beating--Still
    a Common Form of Violence. " Social Work Today 9 (November
    15, 1977): 14-7.

The authors, using police and court records from Glasgow and Edinburgh in 1974 and through interviews with battered women, find abuse to be the second highest violent offense that police must handle. Personal male attitudes and those of society in general support the notion that a husband may chastise his wife, with violence if necessary. Shelters are useful for immediate relief, but societal changes are necessary for the long run. The results of this research are published in detail in their book, Violence Against Wives: A Case Against Patriarchy.

363 Dobash, R. Emerson, and Russell P. Dobash. "With Friends Like These Who Needs Enemies--Institutional Supports for the Patriarchy and Violence Against Women." Paper presented at the Ninth World Congress of Sociology, Uppsala, Sweden, August 1978. 43 p.

364 Dobash, R. Emerson, and Russell P. Dobash. "Wives: The 'Appropriate' Victims of Marital Violence." Victimology: An International Journal 2, nos. 3-4 (1977-1978): 426-42.
The authors discuss the legal, religious and cultural legacies that support patriarchy. They had examined the police records of Glasgow and Edinburgh and had interviewed numerous battered women. The results of their research show that violence is used by the husband to chastise the wife for real or perceived transgressions of his authority, and to reaffirm or maintain a hierarchical and moral order within the family. Thus the desire to preserve patriarchy causes wife abuse, not personality defects in the abuser or his victim.

365 Dobash, R. Emerson; Catherine Cavanagh; and Monica Wilson. "Violence Against Wives: The Legislation of the 1960's and the Policies of Indifference." Paper presented at the meeting of the National Deviancy Conference, Sheffield, England, April 1977.

366 Dobash, R. Emerson; Russell P. Dobash; and C. Cavanagh. "Contact Between Battered Women and Service and Medical Agencies." Paper presented to DHSS Conference on Violence in the Family--Recent Research on Services for Battered Women and Their Children. University of Kent at Canterbury, September 1981.

367 Dobash, R. Emerson; Russell P. Dobash; and C. Cavanagh. "The Professions Construct the Problems of Women: Medical and Social Work Responses to Battered Wives." Paper presented at the 31st annual meeting of the Society for the Study of Social Problems, San Francisco, August 1982.

368 Dobash, R. Emerson; Russell P. Dobash; Cathy Cavanagh; and Monica Wilson. "Victimology Interview, Wife Beating: The Victims Speak." Victimology: An International Journal 2 (1978): 608-22.
Extensive interviews with three victims of spouse abuse comprise this article. The purpose is to show the technique utilized in their study of abused women in Scotland as well as to illustrate the structure

and dynamics of a violent family episode. The interviews were selected
from the 109 that were part of the research for the authors' study, Violence Against Wives: The Case Against the Patriarchy.

369 Dobash, Russell P. , and R. Emerson Dobash. "Battered Women:
        The Importance of Existing Perspectives. " Paper presented
        to the British Sociological Association Study Group on Sexual
        Divisions in Society, London, November 1975.

370 Dobash, Russell P. , and R. Emerson Dobash. "Community Re-
        sponse to Violence Against Wives: Charivari, Abstract Justice
        and Patriarchy. " Social Problems 28 (June 1981): 563-81.
        The authors review societal response to spouse abuse and find
that in past centuries the community helped the abused in very severe
cases. Never, however, was the right to chastise the wife, nor any serious objection to patriarchy, allowed. Modern women's movements are
posing threats to patriarchy with their insistence upon a more egalitarian
relationship in the family. The authors sympathize with that movement.

371 Dobash, Russell P. , and R. Emerson Dobash. "The Context-Specific
        Approach; Do We Need New Methods for Studying Wife Abuse? "
        in The Dark Side of Families: Current Family Violence Re-
        search. Eds. David Finkelhor et al. Beverly Hills, Cal. :
        Sage, 1983, pp. 261-76.
        The authors explain their research methodology which they call
the context-specific approach. Other sociological research strategies
are reviewed, but logical-positivism especially is taken to task. The
authors' approach "leads the researcher to attempt to develop thorough
explanations of social phenomena through a substantively informed theoretical discourse in which concepts, propositions, and assertions are
rooted in specific delimited empirical contexts. Thus theoretical discourse and empirical analysis and evidence cannot be isolated and separated from one another but must be interrelated. "

372 Dobash, Russell P. , and R. Emerson Dobash. "Violence Between
        Men and Women Within the Family Setting. " Paper presented
        at the VIII World Congress of Sociology, Toronto, August 1974.

373 "Documenting a Problem: Are There Battered Women? " Response
        to Intrafamily Violence and Sexual Assault 1 (October 1976): 2.
        The extent of wife abuse is difficult to document because of the
lack of statistics. A few that are available are reproduced here.

374 Doherty, Diane. "Salvation Army Study of Battered Women Clients. "
        Response to Violence in the Family 4 (March/April 1981): 5.

375 "Dollars and Sense: Transition Houses Seek Stable Funding. " Re-
        sponse to Family Violence and Sexual Assault 5 (May/June
        1981): 5-6.
        A discussion of the funding needs of Canadian shelters for bat-
tered women.

376 Domestic Violence: A Directory of Services for Victims of Domestic

Violence in New York State. 3rd ed. [Albany]: New York State
Department of Social Services, 1983. 78 p.

377 Domestic Violence, Final Report. Washington, D. C. : Department
of Health and Human Services, 1981. 3v.

378 Domestic Violence: The Hidden Crime. Eds. Julie A. Hatchard and
Gloria Krys Klose. Ypsilanti, Mich. : Assault Crisis Center,
1977. 19 p. Also in Domestic Violence, 1978. U. S. Congress.
Senate. Committee on Human Resources, Subcommittee on
Child and Human Development. Hearings. 95th Cong. 2nd
Sess. on Domestic Violence and Legislation with Respect to
Domestic Violence, March 4 and 8, 1978. Washington, D. C. :
Government Printing Office, 1978, pp. 421-40.
This pamphlet discusses the causes of wife abuse and what can
be done to change the situation. The services of the assault crisis center
are listed. A typical guide given to women faced with this problem.

379 Doran, Julie B. "Conflict and Violence in Intimate Relationships:
Focus on Marital Rape." Paper presented at the annual meeting of the American Sociological Association, New York, 1980.

380 Doucette, Serge R. , Jr. "Navy and Marine Corps Members and
Families: An Advocacy Position." U. S. Navy Medicine 71
(May 1980): 27-30.
The military has gradually become more of a family man's
occupation than a single man's. How the military family perceives the
military services is important to retention and reenlistment of its personnel. If various forms of domestic violence are believed by the family to
be caused by military life, the chance of losing personnel increases. The
goal of the Family Advocacy Program is to respond to domestic violence,
including wife abuse, and initiate educational and other measures to prevent it.

381 Doucette, Serge R. , Jr. , and Robert D. McCullah. "Domestic Violence: The Alcohol Relationship." U. S. Navy Medicine 71
(March 1980): 4-8.
The literature of alcohol abuse and the literature of family
violence are each studied to determine similarities between them. It
appears that personal characteristics of both family member abusers
and alcohol abusers are similar and there is often alcohol involvement
in cases of abuse. The domestic violence literature reports that children
of abusers often themselves become abusers and the same happens with
children of alcohol abusers. To stop this cycle abusers must be identified
and treatment begun. The sooner done the better for future victims.

382 Downey, Joanne, and Jane Howell. Wife Battering: A Review and
Preliminary Enquiry into Local Incidence, Needs and Resources.
Vancouver, B. C. : United Way of Greater Vancouver, 1976.
93 p.
This study is meant to determine the frequency of abuse in the
Vancouver area and the service needs of the victims. A long literature
review is followed by an analysis of the relationship between alcohol use

and abuse. The needs of victims and available resources are described
in later sections. Results show that abuse is more common than widely
believed; society tends to see it as a social problem, not a crime; the
connection with alcohol is inconclusive; and present social services are
inadequate to deal with the problem. A good example of the type of research communities must do before any program of assistance can hope
to succeed. A useful annotated bibliography concludes the study.

383 D'Oyley, Vincent, ed. Domestic Violence: Issues and Dynamics.
         Toronto: The Ontario Institute for Studies in Education, 1978.
         268 p.
    The majority of the articles in this collection were papers read
at the seminar on Domestic Violence Between Mates: Couples in Conflict,
held at OISE, Toronto, March 11-12, 1977. The major concerns of the
papers are child and spouse abuse with emphasis on the latter. The most
important papers have been annotated elsewhere in this bibliography by
author. D'Oyley is Associate Dean, Faculty of Education, University of
British Columbia.

384 Drake, Virginia Koch. "Battered Women: A Health Care Problem
         in Disguise." Image 14 (June 1982): 40-7.
    A limited clinical study by doctoral student Drake to initiate a
nursing profile of battered women coming into contact with the health care
system. Uses Walker's Cycle Theory of Violence as a backdrop for her
study. She provides more clinical data, but no new insights. A good description of the Cycle Theory, this article is of value to the reader for
that reason alone. No intervention plans were developed.

385 Dreas, Gale N.; Dorothy Ignatov; and Thomas P. Brennan. "The
         Male Batterer: A Model Treatment Program for the Courts."
         Federal Probation 46 (December 1982): 50-5.
    Since batterers do not often seek treatment voluntarily, it may
be necessary for the courts to adopt a mandatory program of treatment
in order to protect other members of the family. The program's focus,
philosophy, goals, content and structure are all described. In the past
the integrity of the family system has been emphasized over the safety
and civil rights of the individual members.

386 "Drinking Alcohol Linked with Assault on Spouse by Study." Juven-
         ile Justice Digest 4 (December 3, 1976): 4.
    This is a short news note regarding John Flynn's study [519]
of spouse abuse in Kalamazoo County, Michigan.

387 Driscoll, James M.; Robert G. Meyer; and Charles F. Schanie.
         "Training Police in Family Crisis Intervention." In Commu-
         nity Mental Health and the Criminal Justice System. Ed. John
         Monahan. Elmsford, N.Y.: Pergamon Press, 1976, pp. 111-
         30.
    Using Bard's New York Family Crisis Intervention Unit as a
model, a similar although adapted version was attempted in Louisville.
This project is described and compared with the New York experiment.
Both were found to be useful, but needing some fine tuning. In sum, the
experiments show that with training police officers can produce more

satisfactory and effective family crisis intervention. Reprinted from
Journal of Applied Behavioral Science 9, no. 1 (1973): 62-82.

388 Drucker, Dennis. "The Common Law Does Not Support a Marital
      Exception for Forcible Rape." Women's Rights Law Reporter
      5 (Winter/Spring 1979): 181-200.
      The marital exception for rape is analyzed and found to be
lacking any support in common law. The basis for this article is the New
Jersey case State v. Smith in which it was held that a husband as a sole
actor could not be charged with rape for a forcible sexual attack upon his
wife in a state without an explicit statutory spousal exception. He states
that such an exception has no place in a society which recognizes women
as having equal rights with men and are not the mere property of their
husbands.

389 Duncan, Darlene. "Cognitive Perceptions of Battered Women."
      Ph. D. dissertation, University of Southern California, 1981.
      Abstract in Dissertation Abstracts International 43B (July
      1982): 245.

390 Duncan, Darlene. Handbook for Battered, Abused Women. Holly-
      wood, Cal.: CAN-DU Publications, 1977. 34 p.

391 Dunkle, Margaret. Cracking the Corporations: Finding Corporate
      Funding for Family Violence Programs. Washington, D. C.:
      Center for Women Policy Studies, 1981. 26 p.
      Corporations have money they would be willing to contribute
to family violence programs. This source of funding, though not easy to
crack, has thus far been inadequately tapped. It also provides some advantages over the traditional funding foundations. Dunkle's pamphlet provides tips on how best to mesh your needs with those organizations which
are most likely to sponsor projects.

392 Dunkle, Margaret. "Finding Corporate Funding for Family Violence
      Programs." Response to Violence in the Family 4 (November/
      December 1981): 5-6.
      This article is excerpted from the author's Cracking the Corpo-
rations [391].

393 Dunn, Mike, and Erin Pizzey. "Violence Between the Sexes." Jour-
      nal of Psychosomatic Research 23 (1979): 369.
      In this short article the authors argue that short-term shelters
are not the answer to the battered-wife problem. Indeed a more proper
term would be "violence-prone families" rather than battered wives.
Many individuals are raised in an atmosphere of fear and rage which
causes noradrenaline to flow, creating a noradrenaline high. When deprived of this high, in shelters or new relationships, many will tend to
recreate the "thrill" which may often result in family violence. Because
of the recurrence of the violence, many helping agencies quickly weary
of providing assistance. More research is needed to deal with this element of the problem.

394 Dunwoody, Ellen. "Battered Women Receive Help at Kentucky Army
      Post." Response to Violence in the Family 3 (July 1980): 1-2.

395 Dunwoody, Ellen. "Battering in Indochinese Refugee Families. "
      Response to Family Violence and Sexual Assault 5 (September/
      October 1982): 1-2, 12.

396 Dunwoody, Ellen. "Beating Wife-Beating: Strategies to End Abuse. "
      Response to Violence in the Family and Sexual Assault 5 (Janu-
      ary/February 1982): 4-5.
      A discussion of the Wisconsin study by Lee Bowker [174].

397 Dunwoody, Ellen. "Canada Holds Hearings on Family Violence. "
      Response to Violence in the Family and Sexual Assault 5
      (March/April 1982): 8-9.

398 Dunwoody, Ellen. "The Clergy: New Partners in the Response to
      Family Violence. " Response to Violence in the Family and
      Sexual Assault 6 (July/August 1983): 1-2.

399 Dunwoody, Ellen. "Counseling Men Who Batter: A CWPS Work-
      shop. " Response to Family Violence and Sexual Assault 5
      (January/February 1982): 9-10.

400 Dunwoody, Ellen. "Courts' Response to Battered Women Evaluated. "
      Response to Family Violence and Sexual Assault 5 (March/April
      1982): 4, 10.

401 Dunwoody, Ellen. "Family Violence: The Canadian Response. " Re-
      sponse to Family Violence and Sexual Assault 5 (January/Feb-
      ruary 1982): 1-2, 10.

402 Dunwoody, Ellen. "First National Conference on Violence in Mili-
      tary Families. " Response to Violence in the Family 4 (March/
      April 1981): 1-2, 5.

403 Dunwoody, Ellen. "House Passes Federal Domestic Violence Legis-
      lation. " Response to Violence in the Family 3 (January 1980):
      1.

404 Dunwoody, Ellen. "How to Develop a Military Spouse Abuse Pro-
      gram. " Response to Violence in the Family 4 (May/June 1981):
      12-3.

405 Dunwoody, Ellen. "A Literature Review on Domestic Violence Pro-
      gramming. " Response to Violence in the Family and Sexual
      Assault 6 (January/February 1983): 1-4, 10, 12-4.

406 Dunwoody, Ellen. "The National Coalition Against Domestic Vio-
      lence: A Grassroots Movement. " Response to Violence in the
      Family 4 (March/April 1981): 4.

407 Dunwoody, Ellen. "Premarital Violence: Battering on College Cam-
      puses. " Response to Violence in the Family 4 (July/August
      1981): 1.

408 Dunwoody, Ellen. "Senate to Determine Destiny of Domestic Vio-
        lence Legislation. " Response to Violence in the Family 4
        (October 1980): 1.

409 Durbin, Karen. "The Intelligent Woman's Guide to Sex. " Mademoi-
        selle 82 (December 1976): 60, 66.
     General discussion of spouse abuse with Del Martin's Battered
Wives [1026] as the focus.

410 Durbin, Karen. "Wife-Beating. " Ladies Home Journal 91 (June
        1974): 62, 64, 66-7, 72.
     General discussion of the problem using cases and examples
directed at a popular readership. Early action is advised in the form of
marriage counseling or psychiatric help to avoid divorce. In the end,
however, divorce may be the only solution.

411 Dutton, Don; Beverly Fehr; and Hope McEwen. "Severe Wife Bat-
        tering as Deindividuated Violence. " Victimology: An Interna-
        tional Journal 7, nos. 1-4 (1982): 13-23.

412 Dutton, Don, and Susan Lee Painter. "Traumatic Bonding: The
        Development of Emotional Attachments in Battered Women and
        Other Relationships of Intermittent Abuse. " Victimology: An
        International Journal 6, nos. 1-4 (1981): 139-55.
     Professionals who work with battered women are struck by the
strength of the emotional ties between the couple. Several reasons why
she stays or returns are reviewed, but traumatic bonding is seen as a
partial explanation. The experiences and belief systems are not unlike
those which cult members and hostages sometimes acquire. Intermittent
violence combined with periods of warm and friendly contact seem to
strengthen rather than weaken the relationship.

413 Dutton, Donald G. "Training Police Officers to Intervene in Domes-
        tic Violence. " In Violent Behavior: Social Learning Approaches
        to Prediction Management and Treatment. Ed. Richard B.
        Stuart. New York: Brunner/Mazel, 1981, pp. 173-202.
     The author discusses the reasons why police officers do not
treat "domestic disputes" as seriously as they should, and proceeds to
describe a step-by-step approach for the proper training of officers for
these duties. A follow-up seven months after the training showed no de-
terioration of that training over time. This experiment was done with the
Vancouver Police Department.

414 Dutton, Donald, and Bruce Levens. "Domestic Crisis Intervention:
        Attitude Survey of Trained and Untrained Police Officers. "
        Canadian Police College Journal 1 (Autumn 1977): 75-92.
     One hundred and eighty police recruits (140 from the Vancouver
Police Department) were given six weeks' specialized training in family
crisis intervention. The purpose was to shape their attitudes towards
such activity in a positive manner. The attitudes of experienced officers
with no special training were compared to the attitudes of three classes
of trainees. The effects of the training and the attitudes of the officers
toward it were detailed. Results indicated the trained officers were more

apt to attempt negotiation of the problem for long-term results, perceived their training valuable, and believed they provided real assistance. This differed from the attitudes of untrained officers.

415 Dvoskin, Joel Alan. "Battered Women: An Epidemiological Study of Spousal Violence." Ph. D. dissertation, University of Arizona, 1981. 64 p. Also Dissertation Abstracts International 42B (December 1981): 2525.
   Ten trained interviewers gathered data from 175 married women in Tucson, Arizona. The purpose was to determine the relationship of abuse to various stressors. The results indicate a multicausal theory of spouse abuse is justified. Money and the husband's drinking were most frequently the issues, but number and age of children still at home were also significant. Abuse is not likely to be reduced until the environmental stresses are reduced and/or satisfactory means of dealing with the stress are developed.

416 Dvoskin, Joel. "Legal Alternatives for Battered Women Who Kill Their Abusers." American Academy of Psychiatry and the Law Bulletin 6, no. 3 (1978): 335-54.
   The author, Ph. D. candidate in clinical psychology, University of Arizona, reviews the history of wife abuse and its legality. He analyzes the legal defenses of women who kill their abusers and concludes that insanity and temporary insanity, duress, and some aspects of crime prevention cannot be used as defenses. Self-defense can, however, so long as the jury can be convinced that the action is undertaken to prevent future injury, not to avenge past battering.

417 Dworkin, Andrea. "The Bruise That Doesn't Heal." Mother Jones 3 (July 1978): 31-6.
   An insightful look at abuse through the eyes of one who lived in a violent marriage. The wife's anger at her fate, the isolation she feels from family and friends, and how the abuse conflicts with her view of what love, marriage, and the family should be are all described compassionately.

418 Dwyer, Vincent T. "Interspousal Violence: A Response." Paper presented at the Second International Conference on Family Law, Montreal, June 13-17, 1977.

419 Eber, Loraine Patricia. "The Battered Wife's Dilemma: To Kill or to Be Killed." Hastings Law Journal 21 (March 1981): 895-931.
   Eber recounts the historical and sociological background to spouse abuse and the general reluctance of the legal system to get involved in domestic matters. Why abuse occurs, why the wife stays, the inadequacies of the criminal remedies, shelters, and other factors and problems receive consideration. The self-defense plea would be a reasonable defense in many cases of spouse abuse, but all the surrounding circumstances, especially the wife's perception of her conditions and danger, must be considered.

420 Eberle, Patricia A. "Alcohol Abusers and Non-users: A Discrimi-
       nant Analysis of Differences Between Two Subgroups of Batter-
       ers." Journal of Health and Social Behavior 23 (September
       1982): 260-71.
    Research indicates that abuse victims have low frequencies of
alcohol use and that the abuser uses alcohol more than the victim. Interviews were conducted with 390 battered women, most of whom came from
the Denver area. There is indication that victims who use alcohol are
more apt to be battered by men who use alcohol and they are likely to be
older than nonalcohol users. At the same time it appears that only a
small percentage of interpersonal assaults involve excessive alcohol use.

421 Edmiston, Susan. "If You Loved Me, You Wouldn't Hurt Me." Red-
       book 153 (May 1979): 99-100, 102, 104-5.
    A popular overview of the problem with many examples told
by victims. The research of R. J. Gelles, N. Shainess, W. Goode, L.
Walker and others provides the theoretical basis. Fear of dependence,
insecurity, and need to control the wife's behavior are what cause many
men to use violence on their spouses. Those who can repair their marriages and live without violence are in the minority.

422 Edmiston, Susan. "The Wife Beaters." Woman's Day (March 1976):
       61, 110-1.
    A good general overview of the problem using the research of
Gelles, Straus, Goode and others. Why wife abuse occurs and what can
be done about it are the major thrusts of the article.

423 Edwards, Betty. "Sojourner Trouble." Amazon 11 (February/March
       1983): 8-9.
    Sojourner Truth House, one of Milwaukee, Wisconsin's bat-
tered women shelters, is undergoing organizational structure changes.
This situation is not unlike that of other shelters that have been begun with strong feminist influence but had to face economic realities.
This news article explains some of the changes. A useful article
for those interested in the politicizing of shelters.

424 Edwards, Rob. "Battered Women Rejected." New Statesman
       106 (August 5, 1983): 5.
    News note on lack of shelters in Scotland where shelters
turned away two-thirds (1,659) of the women seeking refuge. The
increased number of those seeking aid is blamed on unemployment,
but women's groups say the incidence has not increased. Public awareness is causing more women to seek help.

425 Eekelaar, John M. , and Sanford N. Katz, eds. Family Violence;
       An International and Interdisciplinary Study. Toronto, But-
       terworths, 1978. 572 p.
    A collection of articles concerned with various aspects of
family violence, including wife abuse, child abuse, incest, etc. Some
of the material has been published elsewhere. Contributors include
Maidment [1007], Straus [1548], Parnas [1226], Freeman [544], and
others. Essays by the editors tie the articles/chapters together. The
articles on wife abuse are annotated elsewhere in this bibliography.

426   Egger, Sandra J. , and James Crancher. "Wife Battering: Anal-
         ysis of the Victim's Point of View." Australian Family
         Physician 11 (November 1982): 830-2.
      This general overview is for the information and education
of Australian physicians.   Data include the age and sex of the victims,
the causes of violence, why victims stay and the sources of help.   The
survey of sheltered women shows doctors are not perceived as helpful in most cases.   Effective intervention is not impossible and physicians can contribute to its success.

427   Egley, Lance C.   A Shelter Based Group Counseling Plan for
         Men Who Batter.   Madison, Wis. :   Men's Place, 1981.
         155 p.

428   Eisenberg, Alan D. "Changes in the Law Affecting Battered
         Women.   Past, Present and Future." American Journal of
         Trial Advocacy 3 (1979): 45-62.
      This is an overview of the legal alternatives and problems
facing battered women.   The inadequacy of the legal system, the police, the criminal complaint, injunctive relief and breaches of contract
are detailed.   When women kill their abusers several legal defenses
are available, such as self-defense, the flight rule, and defense of
others (e. g. , the children).   Society is finally beginning to recognize
this as a problem and that some corrective action is required.   Police must take stronger action against the abuser and courts must be
willing to recognize the need for more liberal rules of evidence.

429   Eisenberg, Alan D. "Overview of Legal Remedies for Battered
         Women, Part I. " Trial 15 (August 1979): 28-31.
      An attorney in private practice, the author discusses the
legal remedies available to battered women with the strengths and
weaknesses of each.   The value of police protection, restraining orders, orders of protection and peace bonds are evaluated.   Good review.

430   Eisenberg, Alan D. , and David A. Dillon.   "Medico-Legal As-
         pects of Representing the Battered Women." Oklahoma
         City University Law Review 5 (Fall 1980): 645-57.
      A lawyer and physician co-authored this article, which pro-
poses that the two professions can and should work together to eradicate spouse abuse.   The medico-legal investigation of each case must
be conducted with future litigation in mind.   Documentation and accurate records are necessary.   When a traumatized woman comes to
a doctor he must query her regarding the possibility of abuse.   Lawyers must be prepared to argue the Wanrow-Patri equalizer principle,
which says that when an abused wife arms herself and the husband
does not, she is not using excessive force but only making her position equitable.

431   Eisenberg, Alan D. , and Earl J. Seymour.   "Defending Battered
         Women: A Model Voire [sic] Dire." Trial 16 (December
         1980): 30-3, 61.
      This article details a strategy for selecting a jury in cases

of homicide involving spouse abuse. The theory of androgyny, what
constitutes a fair fight and a grounding in case law which would impact on trials of this type would aid the defense lawyer. A long list
of questions to ask prospective jurors is included. These questions
would facilitate uncovering biases and attitudes detrimental to a favorable verdict. A practical guide for defense lawyers.

432   Eisenberg, Alan D. , and Earl J. Seymour, "Overview of Legal
          Remedies for Battered Women, Part II." Trial 15 (Octo-
          ber 1979): 42-5, 60, 69.
      The authors in this part discuss damages and restitution to
the victim, which are found to be woefully inadequate. Women and
use of violence must be viewed differently by society. This change
can be made only by education and socialization.

433   Eisenberg, Alan D. , and Earl J. Seymour. "The Self-defense
          Plea and Battered Women." Trial 14 (July 1978): 34-6,
          41-2, 68.
      Attorney Eisenberg is president of the Wisconsin Criminal
Defense Bar and defended Jennifer Patri, an abused wife who killed
her husband. He discusses the problem of spouse abuse with the Patri
case as a backdrop and favors the use of self-defense in cases where
the victim strikes back against the abuser. Two prosecution arguments are dealt with: 1) the flight rule and 2) immediate bodily
harm. He believes it hypocritical to allow one form of violence, but
then punish victims for using violence to protect themselves. Seymour is a law clerk in the Eisenberg law firm.

434   Eisenberg, Sue E. , and Patricia L. Micklow. "The Assaulted
          Wife: 'Catch 22' Revisited." Women's Rights Law Reporter
          3 (Spring/Summer 1977): 138-61.
      The authors approach the problem from a legal perspective.
They believe most attempts at resolving the issue have revolved
around use of the mediation-conciliation approach, which deprecates
the severity of the complaints. The only way any real progress can
be made is to view domestic violence as the serious crime it is,
rather than a social problem.

435   Elbow, Margaret. "Children of Violent Marriages: The For-
          gotten Victims." Social Casework 63 (October 1982): 465-
          71.
      The effects of a violent marriage on the children have not
been adequately dealt with other than the notion that seeing and living
in abusive families teaches children that violence is a legitimate
means of dealing with conflict. This author discusses the effects on
the child's personality, explaining that the intensity and characteristics
of such marriages overshadow the developmental needs of the children. Suggestions for social worker intervention and counseling of these
children and parents are included.

436   Elbow, Margaret, ed.   Patterns in Family Violence. New York:
          Family Service Association of America, 1980.   144 p.

437 Elbow, Margaret. "Theoretical Considerations of Violent Mar-
         riages." Social Casework 58 (November 1977): 515-26.
         Ms. Elbow is Executive Director, Family Service Associ-
ation, Lubbock Texas. Her opinions are based upon her observations
with no attempts made to submit them to a statistical analysis. She
provides an analysis of the common personality characteristics of
abusers and a discussion of four common abuser syndromes, including the controller, the defender, the approval seeker, and the incorpo-
rator. Some implications of these characteristics and techniques of
intervention are given.

438 Elliot, Elizabeth, and Wendy Susco. "Legal Briefs." Working
         Woman 4 (May 1979): 10.
         These authors deal with the question of marital rape.

439 Elliott, Frank A. "Biological Contributions to Family Violence."
         Family Therapy Collections. Vol. 3. Clinical Approaches
         to Family Violence. Rockville, Md.: Aspen Systems, 1982,
         pp. 35-58.

440 Elliott, Frank A. "The Neurology of Explosive Rape: The Dys-
         control Syndrome." In Battered Women: A Psychosocio-
         logical Study of Domestic Violence. Ed. Maria Roy. New
         York: Van Nostrand Reinhold, 1977, pp. 98-109.
         This article is reprinted from The Practitioner (July 1976).
The term "dyscontrol syndrome" is sometimes used for symptoms
arising from poor impulse control. Sometimes this is a personality
disorder, but other times it is caused by neurological and metabolic
disease. In the case of spouse abuse and explosive rape, this latter
possibility should be investigated. It may not be just a question of
socialization which makes violence an "acceptable" method of conflict
resolution.

441 Ellis, Rhian. "The Legal Wrongs of Battered Women." In Es-
         says in Law and Society. Eds. Zenon Bankowski and Geoff
         Mungham. Boston: Routledge and Kegan Paul, 1980, pp.
         143-56.
         The law and legal systems support the patriarchal order.
That helps explain why wife abuse has historically been given little
attention by the British courts. Times are changing, however. The
Domestic Violence Act 1976 now provides the victim with some much
needed weapons. The problem now is the lack of law enforcement by
those who persist in supporting the male-dominated order. The roots
of the problem are to be found in society at large, not just in the
particular abusing family.

442 Ellis, Rhian M. "The Problem of the Legal Regulation of Vio-
         lence in the Family (Battered Wives)." Ph.D. dissertation,
         University College, Cardiff, 1976.

443 Emener, William G., Jr.; William E. Stilwell; and Barbara J.
         Witten. "Delivering Human Services for Abused Clients:
         A Systems and Individual Approach." Family and Commu-
         nity Health 4 (August 1981): 71-83.

The organization of a Human Abuse Service Team (HAST) composed of counseling psychologists, clergymen, social workers and other helping professionals can provide meaningful assistance to the abused and the abusers. There is much stress that must be dealt with, however. The clients need the HAST to help them with stress management, but because of the difficulty of working with abuse clients, the HAST must beware of the stress they themselves are under. If both are not handled properly, success is not possible. Guidelines for both are detailed.

444 Emerge: A Men's Counseling Service on Domestic Violence. Rockville, Md. : National Clearing House on Domestic Violence, 1981. 96 p.

445 Emergency Procedures in Matrimonial Cases. (College of Law Lectures). [Guildford]: College of Law, [1978?]. 74 p. Supplements, 1978. [Guildford]: College of Law, [1978]. 14 p.

446 Emerson, Charles D. "Family Violence: A Study of the Los Angeles County Sheriff's Department." Police Chief 46 (June 1979): 48-50.
The Los Angeles County-wide Task Force on Domestic Violence was set up in 1978 to assess the extent of the problem and make recommendations for public action. The survey lasted two months, involved 19 sheriff stations, and collected much useful information. The data helped establish the need for professional referral services and shelters. They also helped to identify specific training needs, to correct myths, etc. Very useful study.

447 English, Peter. "The Husband Who Rapes His Wife." New Law Journal 126 (December 9, 1976): 1223-5.
English, Lecturer in Law at Exeter University, England, takes issue with the 1975 DPP v. Morgan decision in which a man was convicted only of helping others rape his wife. The author believes the old rule that a husband could not commit rape on his wife should be changed. Then Morgan and others who engage in such activity could be convicted. The fear that wives will seek revenge on husbands with false charges is not justified.

448 Englund, Steven. Man Slaughter. Garden City, N. Y. : Doubleday, 1983. 419 p.
This is a detailed description of the background and trial of Jennifer Patri of Waupaca, Wisconsin, who killed her husband after years of alleged abuse. Billed by some as a classic case of spouse abuse, Englund shows this to be an oversimplification. Many interviews with friends, relatives, and local citizens, as well as observations at the trial, indicate the abuse was mutual, and rarely physical. A readable account, this should be read as a balance to some of the articles written by Alan Eisenberg, who acted as Mrs. Patri's defense attorney.

449 Epstein, Judy. "Police Intervention in Family Violence." In

Domestic Violence: Issues and Dynamics. Ed. Vincent
D'Oyley. Toronto: Ontario Institute for Studies in Education, 1978, pp. 69-83.
A general discussion of how police handle spouse abuse.
Police are poorly trained to handle such conflict, tend to empathize
with the husband and give inconsistent and/or conflicting signals to
the wife regarding her rights and the advisability of her pressing
charges. Some success has been seen with training programs, but
more needs to be done.

450   Errington, Gene. "Family Violence--Is It a Woman's Problem?"
      Paper presented at the Symposium on Family Violence, Van-
      couver, British Columbia, March 1977.

451   Everett, Henry C. "Battered Husbands." American Journal of
      Psychiatry 137 (May 1980): 635.
      This physician, in a letter to the editor, claims to have
treated battered husbands in his practice, but hears little about it and
much about battered wives. He believes chivalry and humiliation to
be the reasons for underreporting by husbands of these assaults.

452   The Existing Research into Battered Women. [Leeds]: National
      Women's Aid Federation, [1976?]. 20 p.

453   The Experiences of Women with Services for Abused Spouses in
      New York City. New York: Victim Services Agency, 1982.
      138 p.

454   Fagan, Jeffrey A.; Douglas K. Stewart; and Karen V. Hansen.
      "Violent Men or Violent Husbands?: Background Factors
      and Situational Correlates." In The Dark Side of Families:
      Current Family Violence Research. Eds. David Finkelhor
      et al. Beverly Hills, Cal.: Sage, 1983, pp. 49-67.
      The information for this study was obtained from 270 victims
in face-to-face interviews from March 1980 to February 1981. The
results indicate that witnessing spousal violence as a child or being
physically abused as a child was a strong and consistent predictor of
both severity and frequency of violence. Age and education were also
strong predictors. Younger men were inclined to severe and widespread violence. Education was an indicator for severity of injury,
but not involvement in extra domestic violence. Another finding was
that actual violence was a predictor of subsequent violence. To end
this violence one must look at the problem of violence in the home.
Exposure here increased the probability that it would be used later in
life. Programs for batterers to unlearn violence may be the answer.

455   Fain, Constance Frisby. "Conjugal Violence: Legal and Psycho-
      sociological Remedies." Syracuse Law Review 32 (Spring
      1981): 497-579.
      Fain is Assistant Professor of Law at Thurgood Marshall
Law School. Her lengthy article presents an overview of conjugal

violence, especially assault and marital rape, with emphasis on such proposed and existing criminal and civil remedies as the new Pennsylvania law and proposed federal legislation. Psychological and sociological factors, historical background, law enforcement responses, and recommendations for enhancing existing remedies as well as a good overview of extra-legal assistance are included.

456 Family Violence: A Comprehensive Approach to the Community Problem. Project Director, Penny Davis. University: Law Center, University of Alabama, 1980. 95 p.
This is a collection of papers presented at the Alabama Conference on Family Violence, University of Alabama, January 29, 1980. Experts from academia and professional practice reviewed Alabama's practices and procedures regarding spouse abuse, child abuse and abuse of the elderly. The experts were drawn from medicine, psychology, social work, the clergy and many other fields. The recommendations include more and better services to the abused, increased public awareness of the problem, and more shelters.

457 "Family Violence: A Perspective on the Abuse of Women and Children." Urban Reader 5, no. 4 (1977): 9-12.
This is an interview with Pat Ross, coordinator of the United Way Task Force on Family Violence in Vancouver, B.C. Frequency of abuse, what the victim can and should do, what help police and physicians provide along with other general observations regarding the problem are discussed. Most of the comments are directed at spouse abuse with a few at child abuse.

458 "Family Violence Study Purports Physical Force Is Commonplace." Crime Control Digest 10 (March 1, 1976): 3-4.
A short comment on the paper by Gelles, Straus, and Steinmetz presented at the 142nd annual meeting of the American Association for the Advancement of Science.

459 Farragher, T. "The Police and Marital Violence." Paper presented at the DHSS seminar on Violence in the Family-- Recent Research on Services for Battered Women and Their Children. University of Kent at Canterbury, September, 1981.

460 Farrar, Mimsie Minor. "Spouse Abuse." Imprint 28 (February 1981): 17, 64-5.
General discussion of spouse abuse including the common myths surrounding it and what action should be taken by nurses who come into contact with it.

461 Farrington, K. "Family Violence and Household Density: Does the Crowded Home Breed Aggression?" Paper presented at the annual meeting of the Society for the Study of Social Problems, Chicago, August 1977.

462 Farrington, Keith M. "Stress and Family Violence." In The Social Causes of Husband-Wife Violence. Eds. Murray A.

. Straus and Gerald T. Hotaling. Minneapolis: University
of Minnesota Press, 1980, pp. 94-114.

Much of the violence occurring in the family setting can be
attributed to stress operating within the family environment. Not only
does the family by its nature produce stress, it is poorly equipped to
handle it. This being the case, the current family structure must
change if child abuse and spouse abuse are to be reduced. Portions
of this article were in "Toward A General Theory of Stress and Family Violence," a paper presented at the annual meeting of the National
Council on Family Relations, 1975.

463   Fassberg, Evelyn, et al. Crimes of Violence Against Women:
         Rape, Battered Women. Hackensack, N. J. : Bergen County
         Advisory Commission on the Status of Women, 1977. 161 p.

464   Faulk, M. "Men Who Assault Their Wives." Medicine, Science,
         and the Law 14 (July 1974): 180-3. Also in Battered Wom-
         en: A Psychosociological Study of Domestic Violence. Ed.
         Maria Roy. New York: Van Nostrand, 1977, pp. 119-26.

A British survey of 23 men in custody for seriously assaulting their wives. The author attempts to determine the nature of the
psychiatric disturbance which caused the assault. Comparison with
abusers of the Battered Baby Syndrome produced no comparable psychological similarities.

465 Faulk, M. "Sexual Factors in Marital Violence." (With commen-
         tary by Richard J. Gelles and John R. Lion) Medical As-
         pects of Human Sexuality 11 (October 1977): 30-43.

Faulk concentrates on the sexual factors and provocations
which cause or become a part of spousal violence. They include sexual jealousy, desire for sex after abuse, use of sex as punishment,
marital rape, etc. The management of abuse by medical professions
takes two forms. The physician may have to provide emergency medical service and be prepared to provide advice about community social
services. Gelles points out the bleakness of the situation and how few
shelters and services are available (in 1976). Lion suggests that many
wives provoke their husbands, and others do not know any other way
of marital interaction.

466   "Federal Legislation Introduced on Domestic Violence." Re-
         sponse to Intrafamily Violence and Sexual Assault 1 (April
         1978): 1.

An overview of two bills, S2759 and H. R. 12299 [1621 and
1626], being discussed by Congress.

467   "Federal Legislation Introduced to Aid Victims of Domestic Vio-
         lence." Response to Intrafamily Violence and Sexual Assault
         1 (October 1977): 1.

A discussion of Congressional bills HR8948, HR7927, and
S1728, which would provide assistance for battered women.

468   Feldman, Linda, and Murray Bloom. "Conciliation Court: Cri-
         sis Intervention and Research Project on Domestic Violence."

Conciliation Courts Review 17 (June 1979): 1-14.

Feldman, psychologist in San Diego, and Bloom, Director
of Counseling Services, Conciliation Court Superior Court, San Diego,
discuss the communication problem of abusing partners, showing how
its breakdown is usually the cause or precipitating factor in violent
episodes.   Counseling couples in communication techniques proved in-
valuable in many cases.   The need for hotlines, shelters, public education, etc. is stressed for dealing with persistent cases of violence.
A new (1978) procedure for obtaining counseling was instituted for the
San Diego jurisdiction.   The central issue must be the prevention of
domestic violence.   A copy of a petition for a restraining order is
appended.   Of special interest is the large amount of violent activity
by the wife in these cases.

469   Feldman, Susan Ellen.   "Battered Women: Psychological Corre-
        lates of the Victimization Process."   Ph. D. dissertation,
        Ohio State University, 1983.   341 p.   Abstract in Disser-
        tation Abstracts International 44B (October 1983): 1221.

470   Felthous, Alan R.   "Crisis Intervention in Interpartner Abuse."
        American Academy of Psychiatry and the Law Bulletin 11,
        no. 3 (1983): 249-60.

Felthous discusses interpartner abuse wherein both aggress
against each other.   This is called the "Saturday Night Brawl" by
S. K. Steinmetz, and Felthous objects to that term.   How it differs
from the unilateral spouse abuse, its effects on the children, intervention techniques, fear of separation, homicide threats, and other
elements are investigated.   Professionals are strongly advised to determine early in the case whether the violence is unilateral.   Treatment for the two types is quite different.

471   Ferraro, Kathleen.   "Battered Women and the Shelter Movement."
        Ph. D. dissertation, Arizona State University, 1981.   390 p.
        Abstract in Dissertation Abstracts International 42A (August
        1981): 879.

472   Ferraro, Kathleen J.   "Definitional Problems in Wife Battering."
        Paper presented at the annual meeting of the Pacific Socio-
        logical Association, Anaheim, 1979.

473   Ferraro, Kathleen J.   "Hard Love: Letting Go of an Abusive
        Husband."   Frontiers 4 (Summer 1979): 16-8.

"Hard love" is a term used to describe the intense caring
which allows women to let go of their husbands' problems.   It grew
out of the Al-Anon philosophy toward alcoholics and in this article is
applied to wife batterers.   It promotes the idea that refusal to take
abuse is in the best interest of the abuser and recognizes the fact that
nothing the wife does to modify her own behavior will stop the abuse.
The wife must leave the husband and refuse to return unless the battering ends.   She must be prepared to leave permanently if need be.
While not appropriate to all battering situations, it has been effective
in some cases.

474   Ferraro, Kathleen J.   "Physical and Emotional Battering: As-
          pects of Managing Hurt."   California Sociologist 2 (Summer
          1979): 134-49.
      The main idea in this article is that there can be no sepa-
ration of physical abuse from emotional abuse.   The latter problem
is as difficult to deal with, if not more so, as physical violence.   The
difficulty is illustrated by a discussion of the personality conflict and
power struggle among the leadership and staff of a women's shelter.
In this case there was no physical abuse, but the author notes that
responsibility for pain is no less serious because there are no broken
bones.   More research must be done on the relationship between the
two.

475   Ferraro, Kathleen J.   "Physical vs. Emotional Battering: A
          Study of Responsibility."   Paper presented at the annual
          meeting of the Pacific Sociological Association, Anaheim,
          1979.

476   Ferraro, Kathleen J.   "Processing Battered Women."   Journal
          of Family Issues 2 (December 1981): 415-38.
      The author, from the University of Arizona, studied the ac-
tivities of a shelter for battered women over a two-year period as a
participant/observer.   The influence of the staff organization, funding
agency, board of directors, and other factors are discussed.   Although
all clients are seen as having problems and needing help, some are
seen by the counselors as good clients.   Those not accepting the shelter rules were viewed as troublemakers and therefore bad.   Development of self-sufficiency was seen as the primary goal.   This was seen
in economic terms, an approach which ignores "loneliness."   Even
women who had been helped financially, who had jobs and were not
economically dependent upon their abusers, sometimes returned to the
violent home.   Ferraro sees the need for emotional support as the
reason.   Shelters do not sufficiently provide this.

477   Ferraro, Kathleen J.   "Rationalizing Violence: How Battered
          Women Stay."   Victimology: An International Journal 8, nos.
          3-4 (1983): 203-12.
      In this article Ferraro describes the techniques used by bat-
tered women to rationalize their staying with abusive men.   Six specific techniques are appealing to the salvation ethic, denial of injury,
denial of victimization, denial of the victimizer, denial of options,
and appealing to higher loyalties.   Economic reasons are often men-
tioned in the literature, and in fact do play a part, but the rationales
listed here are probably more important.   The same rationales are
used to justify why people remain in other unpleasant situations.

478   Ferraro, Kathleen J., and John M. Johnson.   "How Women Ex-
          perience Battering: The Process of Victimization."   Social
          Problems 30 (February 1983): 325-39.
      Over a hundred battered women were interviewed to gain in-
sights regarding the feelings they experience about themselves, the
abuser, and the incidents.   Six denials are listed as mechanisms by
which victims avoid dealing with the problem.   Six catalysts for changing their lives are also given.   The whole process requires the

realization of "victimization" by the abused.   Until the wife actually sees herself as a victim no change usually occurs.

479 Fessenden, Christy Lee. "Perceiver Bias in the Evaluations Made of a Battered Woman." M. A. thesis, California State University, Fullerton, 1980. Abstract in Masters Abstracts 18 (December 1980): 323.

480 Field, Martha H. , and Henry F. Field. "Marital Violence and the Criminal Process: Neither Justice nor Peace." Social Service Review 47 (June 1973): 221-40.
The prevalence of marital violence and the inability of the legal system to effectively deal with it are all reviewed. Problems are encountered by the police, the prosecutors, the courts, and others. Several alternatives to criminal law are suggested, including easier and less expensive divorce, use of Bard's model for training family crisis units, use of family courts, and counseling services. If any real relief of this problem of marital violence is to be attained it must be separated from other forms of criminal behavior in the legal process.   One of the early scholarly approaches.

481 Fields, Marjory D. "The Battered Wife: How the Lawyer and Psychologist Can Work Together." Family Advocate 2 (Fall 1979): 20-2, 39.
Effective help to resolve the problems experienced by the battered wife requires cooperation and coordination between the psychologist and the lawyer. The lawyer can use the psychologist's insights relative to abuse and the particular client and the psychologist can help reassure the client regarding the lawyer and the legal problems encountered. Much mutual assistance can be performed for the benefit of the abused client.

482 Fields, Marjory. "Does This Vow Include Wife Beating?" Human Rights 7 (Summer 1978): 40-5.
Fields, an attorney with Brooklyn Legal Services, argues that the legal system does little to provide relief to battered wives. The attitudes of the police as well as the prosecuting attorneys must be changed and their male bias discouraged.   The federal government is in the best position to make these changes.

483 Fields, Marjory. "Legal Remedies: Part of the Care for Battered Women." In Identification and Treatment of Spouse Abuse; Health and Mental Health Agency Roles, Proceedings of a Conference. Eds. Abraham Lurie and Elizabeth B. Quitkin. New York: Editors, 1981, pp. 49-59.

484 Fields, Marjory. "Representing Battered Wives, or What to Do Until the Police Arrive." Family Law Reporter (Monograph no. 25) 3 (April 5, 1977): 4025-9.
This article is a guide for giving legal assistance to battered women. Discusses useful strategies and tactics, but argues that in the last analysis, real reforms are necessary. These include shelters and attitudinal changes in the police and courts.   The Family Law Bar is in a good position to push for that reform.

485 Fields, Marjory D. "Wife-Beating: Facts and Figures." Vic-
     timology: An International Journal 2, nos. 3-4 (1977-78):
     643-7.
        The lack of data and statistics regarding abuse is noted.
     This author then discusses a few items that have been published by
     other researchers, such as R. Parnas, G. Levinger, and R. J. Gelles.
     Of special interest are those regarding child support, alimony, and
     social costs of abuse in general. Economic dependency contributes
     to the frequency of abuse of wives.

486 Fields, Marjory D. Wife Beating: Government Intervention Pol-
     icies and Practices. Rockville, Md. : NCJRS Microfiche
     Program, 1978. 96 p. Also in Domestic Violence, U. S.
     Congress. House. Committee on Education and Labor, Sub-
     committee on Select Education. 95th Cong. 2nd Sess.
     Hearings on H. R. 7927 and H. R. 8948, March 16 and 17,
     1978. Washington, D. C. : Government Printing Office, 1978,
     pp. 132-228; Battered Women: Issues of Public Policy.
     Washington, D. C. : U. S. Commission on Civil Rights, 1978,
     pp. 228-87.

487 Fields, Marjory D. "Wife Beating: The Hidden Offense." New
     York Law Journal 175 (April 28, 1976): 1, 4.
        A good overview of the problems of wife abuse with statis-
     tics from New York, Chicago, England, and elsewhere. Includes in-
     formation on the institutional responses to abuse and their inadequacies.
     Among other things New York City needs shelters like those of other
     cities.

488 Fields, Marjory D. , and Elyse Lehman. "Guide for Beaten Wom-
     en: How to Get Help If Your Husband or Boyfriend Beats
     You. " In Sheltering Battered Women. Albert R. Roberts.
     (Springer Series, Focus on Women, v. 3.) New York:
     Springer, 1981, pp. 111-22.
        This is a revised version of a pamphlet (A Handbook for
     Beaten Women. New York: Brooklyn Legal Services Corp. B, 1977)
     originally developed for New York women. Step-by-step instructions
     and advice are given on how best to deal with an abusive situation and
     how to involve the police and courts. Advice on obtaining and retain-
     ing a lawyer is especially useful for the uninitiated.

489 Fields, Marjory D. , and Elyse Lehman. A Handbook for Beaten
     Women; How to Get Help If Your Husband or Boyfriend Beats
     You. New York: Brooklyn Legal Services, Corporation B. ,
     1977. 29 p. Also in Research into Violent Behavior: Domes-
     tic Violence. U. S. Congress. House. Committee on Sci-
     ence and Technology. Hearings. 95th Cong. 2nd Sess.
     February 14, 15, 16, 1978. Washington, D. C. : Government
     Printing Office, 1978, pp. 591-622.
        A newer edition is called "Guide for Beaten Women: How
     to Get Help if Your Husband or Boyfriend Beats You" [488].

490 Fields, Marjory D. , and Rioghan M. Kirchner. "Battered Wom-
     en Are Still in Need: A Reply to Steinmetz. " Victimology:

An International Journal 3, nos. 1-2 (1978): 216-22. Also
in U. S. Congress. House. Committee on Education and
Labor, Subcommittee on Select Education. 95th Cong. 2nd
Sess. Hearings on H. R. 7927 and H. R. 8948, March 16
and 17, 1978. Washington, D. C. : Government Printing
Office, 1978, pp. 241-55.
    This is a challenge to the article by S. K. Steinmetz "The
Battered Husband Syndrome" in Victimology: An International Journal
2 (1977-78): 499-509 [1502]. The authors claim that not only are the
data on husband abuse misinterpreted, but their publication does a
great disservice to needy battered wives.

491 Fields, Marjory D. , and Rioghan M. Kirchner. Summary of
     English and Scottish Shelters. [Brooklyn, N. Y. : Brooklyn
     Legal Services, 1976]. 30 p.

492 Finesmith, Barbara K. "Police Response to Battered Women:
     A Critique and Proposals for Reform" Seton Hall Law Re-
     view 14 (Winter 1983): 74-109.
     Historically police response to domestic violence has been
highly discretionary and arrests have not been common. In fact, this
lack of response is not what society expects and is not how police respond to other crimes. Legislatures should enact strong legislation,
since where this has been done police have made more arrests and
more prosecutions have occurred. Full enforcement of these laws
would serve the victim and reduce the psychological effects of learned
helplessness. Lawyers, the courts, and prosecutors must be educated,
shelters supported, counseling and other services provided. The author is Instructor of Law, Chicago-Kent College of Law.

493 Finkelhor, David. "Common Features of Family Abuse." Paper
     presented at the National Conference for Family Violence
     Researchers, Durham, New Hampshire, July 1981.

494 Finkelhor, David, ed. The Dark Side of Families: Current
     Family Violence Research. Beverly Hills, Cal. : Sage,
     1981. 384 p.
     This is a diverse collection of articles based on papers pre-
sented at the tenth annual National Conference for Family Violence Researchers, Durham, N. H. , 1981. Noted scholars including sociologists, psychologists, psychiatrists, social work researchers and others
all contributed original articles. Each of the articles is listed in this
bibliography under the author. Familiar names include Kalmuss [846],
Stark and Flitcraft [1494], Straus [1535], Dobash and Dobash [371],
Yllo [1773], Gelles [605], and Walker [1663], to list only a few.

495 Finkelhor, David, and Kersti Yllo. "Forced Sex in Marriage:
     A Preliminary Research Report." Crime and Delinquency
     28 (July 1982): 459-78.
     Part of a larger research project, this study contains the
results of the analysis of twenty interviews of women who had had
forced sex with husbands or live-in lovers. To date it is an ignored
topic and in many states not even illegal. The purpose of this report

is to show that this type of research is possible and should be given
attention in political, legal, academic and clinical arenas. Several
case histories are given.

496   Finkelhor, David, and Kersti Yllo. "Rape in Marriage: A
        Sociological View." In The Dark Side of Families: Cur-
        rent Family Violence Research. Eds. David Finkelhor et
        al. Beverly Hills, Cal.: Sage, 1983, pp. 119-30.
        Concerned with lack of sociological studies of marital rape,
these authors interviewed in-depth 50 women whose husbands had
forced them to have sex. The results show three types of cases:
1) battering rapes, wherein rape is just one more aspect of a violent,
abusive relationship; 2) nonbattering rapes, wherein the marriages
may have conflict, but not conflicts over sex; 3) obsessive rapes,
which may or may not involve battering, but did involve sexual obses-
sion with the husbands' interested in pornography and wanting the
wives to imitate it. In most cases of marital rape the wife did not
put up a fight as it was thought wiser not to. Trauma of rape by a
loved one is as great or even greater than rape by a stranger. The
incidence of marital rape is not rare.

497   Finlay, H. A. "The Battered Mistress and the Violent Paramour."
        Australian Law Journal 52 (November 1978): 613-25.
        An analysis of the Domestic Violence and Matrimonial Pro-
ceedings Act 1976 (U.K.) which says the husband, even if the house
is in his name, can be barred from the home, and three court cases
involving unmarried couples. Australian lawyer Finlay agrees with the
courts that this violates one's property rights. Interesting legal discussion of property rights vs. assault.

498   Finley, Britt. "Nursing Process with the Battered Woman."
        Nurse Practitioner 6 (July/August 1981): 11-3, 29.
        An informative discussion for health care professionals.
More treatment is needed by the abused than for just the physical injury. Intervention by the nurse in the battered-wife syndrome should
be grounded in sound theory and psychosocial skills.

499   Fiora-Gormally, Nancy. "Battered Wives Who Kill: Double
        Standard Out of Court, Single Standard In?" Law and Human
        Behavior 2, no. 2 (1978): 133-65.
        The author, College of Law, University of Arizona, provides
a lengthy and readable discussion and analysis of the social and legal
environment of the battered woman. Everything seems to be constructed
to work against the woman who kills her abuser--the society she is
raised in, and the legal system which shows the bias of a male orientation. Her conclusion is that until there is a set of social and behavioral norms that are similar for males and females, it is unfair
to apply the same standards to defendants of different sexes in the
courtroom.

500   Fisher, Susan. "Family Law Issues of the 1980's: Battered
        Women." District Lawyer 5 (September/October 1980): 48-
        52, 75.

Fisher, Assistant Attorney for the Family Abuse Project of Catholic University, describes in detail the legal and civil remedies available to battered women under the D. C. Intrafamily Offense Act of 1970. Victims are directed to the Citizens Complaint Center, where they are advised as to the proper way of proceeding with their charges. Civil protection orders and temporary protection orders are available for relief and the effectiveness of each is dealt with by Fisher.

501   Fitch, Frances J. , and Andre Papantonio. "Men Who Batter: Some Pertinent Characteristics. " Journal of Nervous and Mental Disease 17 (March 1983): 190-2.
Fitch (Department of Psychiatry, University of Maryland and House of Ruth) and Papantonio (House of Ruth) interviewed 188 battering clients at the shelter's batterers program. Several characteristics of the group are noted. Seventy-one percent saw abuse between their parents, 49 percent were themselves abused as childre, 59 percent abused alcohol, 18 percent abused drugs, and 22 percent were unemployed. This study lends support to others which suggest the transgenerational transfer of abuse, and that alcohol abuse is related to domestic violence.

502   Flaherty, Kathleen M. The Domestic Violence Order of Protection: Civil Court Practice. Springfield: Illinois Coalition Against Domestic Violence, [1983]. 36 p.

503   Flammang, C. J. Police Crisis Intervention. [Urbana, Ill.]: Police Training Institute, 1972. 92 p.

504   Flanzer, Jerry P. "Alcohol and Family Violence: Double Trouble. " In The Abusive Partner: An Analysis of Domestic Battering. Ed. Maria Roy. New York: Van Nostrand Reinhold, 1982, pp. 136-42.

505   Flanzer, Jerry P. ed. The Many Faces of Family Violence. Springfield, Ill. : Charles C. Thomas, 1982. 132 p.
This is a collection of articles by several contributors dealing with family violence. Several concern themselves with the effects of alcohol on family relations and violence and two are devoted specifically to wife abuse. These articles, by Barbara Star [1487] and Kathryn Conroy [285], are annotated elsewhere in this bibliography. The editor maintains no member of the family is immune to possible violence by the others. More public awareness is necessary if family violence is to end. The articles were selected from the presentations made at the annual symposia, Mid-America Institute on Violence in Families, from 1978 to 1980 in Hot Springs, Arkansas.

506   Flax, Morton L. "Couples Therapy in Battering Relationships. " Paper presented at Colorado Women's College Conference on Battered Women, Denver, March 31, 1977.

507   Flax, M. L. ; L. E. Walker; and K. J. Schreiber   "The Battered Woman Syndrome. " Symposium presented at the annual meeting of the American Psychological Association, Washington, D. C. , September 3, 1976.

508   Fleming, Jennifer. "Family Violence: A Look at the Criminal
        Justice System." In Domestic Violence. U. S. Congress.
        House. Committee on Education and Labor, Subcommittee
        on Select Education. 95th Cong. 2nd Sess. Hearings on
        H. R. 7927 and H. R. 8948, March 16 and 17, 1978. Wash-
        ington, D. C. : Government Printing Office, 1978, pp. 116-26.

509   Fleming, Jennifer Baker. "Stopping Wife Abuse: A Feminist
        Approach." In Identification and Treatment of Spouse Abuse,
        Health and Mental Health Agency Roles, Proceedings of a
        Conference. Eds. Abraham Lurie and Elizabeth B. Quitkin.
        New York: Editors, 1981, pp. 41-8.

510   Fleming, Jennifer Baker. Stopping Wife Abuse: A Guide to the
        Emotional, Psychological, and Legal Implications for the
        Abused Woman and Those Helping Her. Garden City, N. Y. :
        Anchor Press, Doubleday, 1979. 532 p.
        The purpose of this book is to provide guidance to individu-
als interested in providing services for battered women. Attention is
also devoted to advice for battered women, legislative changes needed,
working with the legal system, guidelines for establishing shelters and
support services and many other problems the abused encounter. A
good practical guide which also provides an overview of the research
on the topic.

511   Fleming, Jennifer Baker, and Carolyn Kott Washburne. "Vio-
        lence Within Marriage." In their For Better, For Worse:
        A Feminist Handbook on Marriage and Other Options. New
        York: Charles Scribners Sons, 1977, pp. 314-27.
        A general overview of the problem with attention to the po-
lice and legal response to abuse, how married women are entrapped
emotionally and financially, and options available to the victim.

512   Fleming, Thomas S. "Violent Domestic Assault." M. A. thesis,
        University of Toronto, 1975. 133 p.

513   Flint, Susan, and Margaret Hunt. Wife Battering: A Packet of
        Articles Examining the Problem and Exploring Responses
        to It. Cambridge, Mass. : American Friends Service Com-
        mittee, [1977]. 47 p.

514   Flitcraft, Anne. "Battered Women: A Case for Preventive Med-
        icine." Presented at the annual meeting of the American
        Public Health Association, Miami Beach, Florida, October
        1976.

515   Flitcraft, Anne. Battered Women: An Emergency Room Epide-
        miology with a Description of a Clinical Syndrome and Cri-
        tique of Present Therapeutics. M. D. thesis, Yale Univer-
        sity, 1977. 45 p.

516   Flynn, Deborah. "Domestic Relations--The Protection from
        Abuse Act." Temple Law Quarterly 51 (1978): 116-26.

The Pennsylvania act is viewed as a vanguard measure in dealing with the problem of wife abuse. While not adequate as the ultimate solution, it does provide adequate temporary and emergency relief. This article traces prior methods of dealing with both child and spouse abuse, the efficacy of those methods and the potential impact of the new law.

517 Flynn, Janice B. , and Janice Craddoch Whitcomb. "Unresolved Grief in Battered Women." JEN: Journal of Emergency Nursing 7 (November/December 1981): 250-4.
Battered women are in a state of unresolved and chronic grief which engulfs them until they change their situation. The stages of grief as described by Kubler-Ross are correlated to grief symptoms of battered women. The authors believe the victims are caught in the first four stages with the fifth stage, acceptance of the situation, never being reached. They may seem to be resigned to their fate, but they have not really achieved acceptance. The role of the emergency nurse is described. Specific nursing interventions can facilitate normal grieving in the battered woman.

518 Flynn, John P. "Recent Findings Related to Wife Abuse." Social Casework 58 (January 1977): 13-20.
This is a summary of Spouse Assault: Its Dimensions and Characteristics in Kalamazoo County, Michigan, 1975 [519]. The purpose was to establish the extent and characteristics of the problem and offer solutions. Silence about abuse and victim blaming are common and agencies which are supposed to report incidence often do not. Besides general attitude, lack of community resources hindered resolution. The findings are not unique. Other communities would find themselves in a similar situation.

519 Flynn, John. Spouse Assault: Its Dimensions and Characteristics in Kalamazoo County, Michigan. Patrick Anderson et al. (Field Studies in Research and Practice, no. 3.) Kalamazoo, Mich. : School of Social Work, Western Michigan University, 1975. 93 p.

520 Fojtik, Kathy. "Ann Arbor Overview." Do It Now 9 (June 1976): 4-5.

521 Fojtik, Kathleen M. The Bucks Start Here: How to Fund Social Service Projects; A Practical Guide to Grant Funds and Fund Raising. Ann Arbor, Mich. : Domestic Violence Project, 1978. 142 p.

522 Fojtik, Kathleen M. "The NOW Domestic Violence Project." Victimology: An International Journal 2, nos. 3-4 (1977-78): 653-7.
The background and inspiration for the Ann Arbor project and the several studies and publications that resulted are discussed. Also included are statistics regarding victims served by the project and their assailants.

523   Fojtik, Kathleen M.   Wife Beating--How to Develop a Wife As-
        sault Task Force and Project.   3rd ed.   Ann Arbor, Mich. :
        NOW Domestic Violence Project, 1976.   41 p.
        Prompted by a presentation by Micklow and Eisenberg, "The
Assaulted Wife: 'Catch 22' Revisited," the Ann Arbor-Washtenaw
County NOW Chapter organized their wife-abuse task force.   Their
experiences in that community provided the background information
for this guide.   Numerous newspaper articles are included describing
abuse and giving examples, along with police and court watching procedures.   Useful guide for those wishing to take action at the local
community level.

524   Foland, Carolyn Ann.   "Battered Women: An Exploratory Study
        of the Phenomenon of Wife Abuse and Institutional Response
        to Its Victims. "   M. S. N.   thesis, Yale University, 1978.
        84 p.

525   Follingstad, Diane R.   "A Reconceptualization of Issues in the
        Treatment of Abused Women: A Case Study. "   Psychother-
        apy: Theory, Research and Practice 17 (Fall 1980): 294-
        303.
        The author is a member of the Department of Psychology,
University of South Carolina, Columbia.   Rather than encouraging the
victim to change her environment (leave the abuser), the first thing
should be the changing of faulty conceptions (learned helplessness) the
wife has acquired after years of mistreatment.   Once her attitudes and
behavior are modified, the change of environment may be considered.
In this case, not only did the method work, but the abuser changed
his behavior without even attending therapy.   MMPI Personality Scales
and Mood Scales showed a definite change in the subject as a result
of her attempted environment change.   This study is important in that
it indicates that extreme passivity and helplessness came as a result
of her situation, not the reverse.

526   Fonseka, S.   "A Study of Wife-Beating in the Camberwell Area. "
        British Journal of Clinical Practice 28 (December 1974):
        400-2.
        This was a study of assault cases which came to King's
College Hospital in London, during 1971, 1972, and 1973.   An analysis
of injuries to assault victims in general and to battered wives showed
a disposition to more facial injuries for the latter, whereas both had
injuries over much of the body.   Attempts to see if wife beating
showed more distinct radiological patterns of injury did not produce
positive results.

527   "Food Stamps for Residents of Shelters for Battered Women and
        Children. "   Clearing House Review 15 (June 1981): 144.
        The Food Stamp Act of 1977 with the 1980 amendments would
allow women living in shelters, under some circumstances, to qualify
for food stamps.   In some cases it might require the shelters to change
some of their eating arrangements.   This should be investigated for
the benefit of the residents.

528 Footlick, Jerrold K. , and Elaine Sciolino. "Wives Who Batter
         Back." Newsweek 91 (January 30, 1970): 54.
     General discussion of abused wives who murdered their hus-
bands. Authors express some concern for the apparent lessening of
sentences when the defendant has a history of being abused. A trend
that "smacks uncomfortably of frontier justice."

529 "For Battered Women and Kids, 'Room in the Inn'--A Trailer."
         National Catholic Reporter 20 (December 30, 1983): 3.

530 For Shelter and Beyond: An Educational Manual for Working
         With Women Who Are Battered. Boston: Massachusetts
         Coalition of Battered Women Service Groups, 1981. 75 p.
     Composed of about thirty short essays by many authors, this
collection is meant to fill a gap in the literature for the training of
new staff of battered women's programs. Though not covering all
aspects of such work, the authors do draw on their own experiences
and offer them up as a starting point for other training manuals. A
general introduction, working with victims and their children, welfare
and legal advocacy, racial and cultural concerns, mental health, and
alcohol are all dealt with here.

531 Ford, D. A. "Wife Battery and Criminal Justice: A Study of
         Victim Decision-Making." Paper presented at the annual
         meeting of the American Sociological Association, New York,
         1978.

532 Ford, David A. "Wife Beating and Criminal Justice: A Study
         of Victim Decision-Making." Family Relations 32 (October
         1983): 463-75.
     Ford, Assistant Professor of Sociology, Indiana University,
Indianapolis, studied the relationship between 235 battered women and
the legal system in Marion County, Indiana. Information gathered
from the police, the prosecutor's office, court records, and other legal sources indicates that the outcome is as much a result of the victim's needs as her interaction with the legal system's representative.
Chance has as much to do with the outcome as do other factors.

533 Forney, D. G. "Abuse of Spouses." American Medical Associa-
         tion Journal 240 (December 1, 1978): 2539.
     Issue is taken with statements in Petro's article [1251] in
this journal regarding beaten women deserving the abuse.

534 Forte, A. D. M. "Marital Rape: A Cautionary Note." Law
         Quarterly Review 99 (October 1983): 513-4.
     The case of H. M. A. v. Duffy is reviewed, along with the
question of separation and marital rape as it applies in Scottish law.
While the decision of the couple to separate may be important, it
overlooks the question of the withdrawal of consent regardless of the
couple's separation plans.

535 Fortune, Rev. Marie M. , and Denise Hormann. Family Violence:
         A Workshop Manual for Clergy and Other Service Providers.

(Domestic Violence: Monographic Series, no. 6, April 1981.) Rockville, Md.: National Clearinghouse on Domestic Violence, 1980. 100 p.

A how-to-do-it booklet explaining how to conduct a workshop for providing assistance to victims of family violence. Background planning, educational formats, sample presentations, sample questionnaires and evaluation forms, and several reprinted articles are included. Spouse abuse, as well as child abuse and incest, receives attention. Excellent guide for developing a workshop. This was originally published as Family Violence: A Workshop Manual for Rural Communities.

536 Foss, Joyce E. "The Paradoxical Nature of Family Relationships and Family Conflict." In The Social Causes of Husband-Wife Violence. Eds. Murray A. Straus and Gerald T. Hotaling. Minneapolis: University of Minnesota Press, 1980, pp. 115-35.

Foss, Assistant Professor of Sociology, Sangamon State University, Springfield, Illinois, concludes that in intimate groups like the family, structural constraints work against effective conflict resolution. High emotional investment, total personality involvement, and difficulty of leaving the relationship militate against using conflict resolution techniques. Avoidance is often used to escape conflict, but in an intimate relationship it is likely to lead to more conflict. This theory helps to explain conflict resolution problems between spouses as well as between other family members.

537 "Founder of English Shelter Visits USA." Response to Intrafamily Violence and Sexual Assault 1 (April/June 1977): 2.

A short overview of Pizzey's work with the Chiswick Women's Aid.

538 Fradin, Judith Bloom. "The Battered Women: Can Anything Be Done?" Illinois Issues 6 (February 1980): 9-11.

This article is a general discussion of the problem with emphasis on legal remedies Illinois could adopt.

539 Francke, Linda Bird. "Battered Women." Newsweek 87 (February 2, 1976): 47-8.

General article and brief overview with some indication of the scope of the problem.

540 Frank, Phyllis B., and Beverly D. Houghton. Confronting the Batterer: A Guide to Creating the Spouse Abuse Educational Workshop. Ed. Judi Fisher. New York: Volunteer Counseling Service, 1982. 76 p.

The old method was to teach women not to antagonize the husband or to help them leave the relationship. The new method described in this book is directed at the batterer, not the victim. This six-week course is viewed as the first step in rehabilitating the offender. The various features of the program, training volunteers, therapy and counseling methods are all detailed.

541 Frederick, Robert E. Domestic Violence: A Guide for Police
       Response. Harrisburg: Pennsylvania Coalition Against Do-
       mestic Violence, 1979. 58 p.

542 Freeman, Michael D. A. " 'But If You Can't Rape Your Wife,
       Who[m] Can You Rape?': The Marital Rape Exemption Re-
       examined." Family Law Quarterly 15 (Spring 1981): 1-29.
    Freeman draws a connection between marital rape and
spouse abuse and then provides an overview of the legal history of
the marital rape immunity. The major arguments in favor of the immunity are retold. American laws and those of other countries are
discussed with the conclusion that most countries exempt the husband.
Freeman believes this should be changed since it is one more symptom of the disadvantageous position of women in a patriarchal society.

543 Freeman, M. D. A. "Legal Systems, Patriarchal Ideologies and
       Domestic Violence: A Case Study of The English Legal
       System." In Research in Law, Deviance and Social Control.
       V. 4. Eds. Steven Spitzer and Rita J. Simon. Greenwich,
       Conn. : JAI Press, 1982, pp. 131-61.
    Many concerned with domestic violence believe legal reform
to be the answer. Part of their belief rests on the notion that the
purpose of government is to provide protection and justice. In fact,
he says, it has historically only provided a surface illusion of justice.
The legal system reflects the society it supports. English society is
patriarchal and the law reflects that condition. As contemporary social and economic values are reevaluated so will the legal system
change. It is patriarchy that must be challenged if violence against
women is to end.

544 Freeman, Michael D. "The Phenomenon of Marital Violence
       and the Legal and Social Response in England." In Family
       Violence; An International and Interdisciplinary Study. Eds.
       John M. Eekelaar and Sanford N. Katz. Toronto: Butter-
       worths, 1978, pp. 73-109.
    This article also appears in modified form as "Le Vice
Anglais" Family Law Quarterly 11 (1977): 199-251. A member of the
Faculty of Laws, University College of London, Freeman has produced
an excellent overview of the social and legal aspects of the problem.
The answer to spouse abuse is a complete redefinition of the status
of women and the elimination of violence as an acceptable method of
resolving conflict.

545 Freeman, M. D. A. "Rape by a Husband?" New Law Journal
       129 (April 5, 1979): 332-3.
    The spousal rape immunity in England is explained along
with the recommendation that the law be changed. The arguments
against repealing the immunity are reviewed and rejected. The law
is not as clearcut as it appears at first. For example, the husband
can be charged with rape if a judicial separation or a noncohabitation
order has been issued. If force or violence was used, the husband
can be charged with assault. Several other legal alternatives are also
given. The 1976 Delaware law is suggested as a possible model for
England's rape laws.

546   Freeman, Michael D. A.   "Le Vice Anglais?: Wife-battering in
         English and American Law."   Family Law Quarterly 11 (Fall
         1977): 199-251.   Also in Fathers, Husbands and Lovers;
         Legal Rights and Responsibilities.   Eds. Sanford N. Katz
         and Monroe L. Inker.   n. p. : American Bar Association,
         1979, pp. 183-235.
              An excellent overview of the legal problems associated with
spouse abuse.   Studies by American and British scholars as well as
court cases from those two countries are discussed and analyzed.
Legal aids and solutions--including injunctions, divorce, magistrate
courts, criminal action, and torts--are proposed.   In the last analysis
the author feels that nothing can be done without a complete redefinition of the status of women.   So long as preservation of the existing
family unit and belief in the inferiority of women are overriding considerations, force will be used to control women.   If force is thought
by society as acceptable, then violence will occur.

547   Freeman, Michael D. A.   "Violence Against Women: Does the
         Legal System Provide Solutions or Itself Constitute the Prob-
         lem?"   British Journal of Law and Society 7 (Winter 1980):
         215-41.   Also in Canadian Journal of Family Law 3 (1980):
         377-401.
              The author argues that it is the ideology of patriarchy that
encourages the acceptance of wife beating in our societal and legal systems, not simply that husbands have too much stress, or that men
are just more violent than women.   Until this patriarchal ideology is
eliminated, women will not be safe.   The legal system is part of the
problem because it is based on the patriarchal assumptions.   This
paper was delivered at the annual meeting of the Law and Society Association, Madison, Wisconsin, June 5-8, 1980.

548   Freeman, Michael David Alan.   Violence in the Home.   Farn-
         borough, England: Saxon House, 1979.   257 p.
              Written by a lawyer and from a legal perspective, this vol-
ume is concerned with family violence, especially child and spouse
abuse.   Some attention is also devoted to elder abuse, sibling violence
and husband beating.   A heavily footnoted scholarly study with an English emphasis, this is one of the first good monographs.

549   Freeman, M. D. A.   "Violence in the Home: The New Law."
         New Law Journal 127 (February 17, 1977): 159-60.
              The British Domestic Violence and Matrimonial Proceedings
Act of 1976 is analyzed and its faults and failings are detailed.   The
author, Lecturer in Law at University College in London, believes the
act will solve few problems and may instead create new ones.

550   Freeman, M. D. A.   "What Do We Know of the Causes of Wife
         Battering?"   Family Law 7, no. 7 (1977): 196-201.
              This article provides a good review of the literature up to
1977, including the myths surrounding wife abuse and various theories
regarding its cause.

551   Freilicher, Elizabeth.   "Pilot Program Takes Hard Line on

Violence." New Directions for Women 9 (January/ February
1980): 3, 17.
This news item discusses a pilot program in Santa Barbara,
California funded by Law Enforcement Assistance Administration
(LEAA) in 1979.   The Santa Barbara Shelter and Family Violence
Unit are also described.

552   Friedman, Kathleen O'Ferrall.   Battered: A Survival Manual
        for Battered Women.   Baltimore: Maryland Commission
        for Women, [1976].   14 p.
A short practical guide for women seeking relief from a
violent marriage.   This pamphlet includes general information on
spouse abuse, how to deal with uncooperative police, where to seek
legal advice, and other counsel.

553   Friedman, Kathleen O'Ferrall.   "Image of Battered Women."
        American Journal of Public Health 67 (August 1977): 722-3.
This is an editorial response to the Parker and Schumacher
article [1218], which also appeared in this issue.   She argues that
the health professions have much influence and should be using some
of it to help eliminate the crime of spouse abuse.

554   Frieze, Irene H.   "Causes and Consequences of Marital Rape."
        Paper presented at the annual meeting of the American Psy-
        chological Association, Montreal, September 1980.

555   Frieze, Irene.   "Consequences of Rape in Marriage."   Paper
        presented at the National Conference for Family Violence
        Researchers in Durham, New Hampshire, July 1981.

556   Frieze, Irene Hanson.   "Investigating the Causes and Conse-
        quences of Marital Rape."   Signs: Journal of Women in
        Culture and Society 8 (Spring 1983): 532-53.
For this study the author interviewed 137 women who had
reported physical assaults by their husbands to determine the extent
of the violence and the occurrence of marital rape.   The results were
analyzed in conjunction with a group of women who were battered, but
not raped, and a group that experienced neither rape nor battering.
A number of observations were made.   Marital rape, for example,
was rare in nonviolent marriages.   Raped women believed its occurrence was a result of the husband's personality, not their own fault.
The most violent men were the most likely to rape their wives.   Also,
the majority of the raped women felt anger or some other form of
negative emotion toward the husband.   Overall marital happiness and
the general pattern of sexual relations were more negative for the
raped women.   Very important study.

557   Frieze, Irene Hanson.   "Perceptions of Battered Wives."   In
        New Approaches to Social Problems.   Eds. Irene Hanson
        Frieze, Daniel Bar-Tal and John S. Carroll.   San Francisco,
        Cal.:   Jossey-Bass, 1979, pp. 79-108.
Attribution theory is used to make predictions about the future of a battering relationship.   What the woman does often depends

upon to whom the wife attributes blame for the abuse. Is it her own
fault, or her husband's? Are there social, cultural, economic, personality, or other factors involved? Are these seen as temporary or
permanent conditions? Does she have any control over them? Insightful analysis.

558   Frieze, Irene H.   "Power and Influence in Violent and Non-violent
       Marriages." Paper presented at the annual meeting of the
       Eastern Psychological Association, Philadelphia, 1979.

559   Frieze, Irene Hanson. "Self Perceptions of the Battered Women."
       Paper presented at the annual meeting of the Association for
       Women in Psychology, Pittsburgh, 1978.

560   Frieze, Irene Hanson, and C. Washburn. "Battered Women's
       Response to Battering." Paper presented at the annual meet-
       ing of the Association for Women in Psychology, Houston,
       1979.

561   Frieze, Irene H.; Marylynn McCreanor; and Kathy Shome. "Male
       Views of the Violent Marriage." Paper presented at the
       annual meeting of the Association for Women in Psychology,
       Santa Monica, California, 1980.

562   Fromson, Terry L.   "The Case for Legal Remedies for Abused
       Women." New York University Review of Law and Social
       Change 6 (Spring 1977): 135-74.
       A good description of the problem and what the legal com-
munity must do. The first section describes the characteristics of
spouse abuse which make legal remedies necessary. The next part
shows the inadequacy of the present responses to abused women by
police, prosecutors, and the courts. The final sections analyze strategies to reform the law. The legal system cannot solve the whole
problem, but it can do more to protect the victims, deter the perpetrators, and reduce the incidence of wife beating.

563   Fromson, Terry. "The Prosecutor's Responsibilities in Spouse
       Abuse Cases." In Prosecutor's Responsibility in Spouse
       Abuse Cases. Washington, D.C.: LEAA: U.S. Department
       of Justice, 1980. 24 p. Also in The Victim Advocate.
       Chicago: National District Attorneys Association, 1978.
       24 p.
       Although the role of the prosecutor is limited, there are
things the prosecutor should know. The appropriateness of criminal
prosecution, which cases to prosecute and the probability of conviction,
what the victim can and should have to aid the case, overcoming proof
and evidentiary problems, alternatives for prosecution, etc. all receive
ample attention. The overall view is that spouse abuse is a crime
and should be taken as seriously as other crimes by prosecuting attorneys.

564   Frost, Lynn, et al. Household Violence Study. Hartford: Con-
       necticut Task Force on Abused Women, 1977. 2v.

565 Frye, Ellen. "Abused Women: Two Freed, Three Murdered, Wife-Killer Walked." Off Our Backs 8 (November 1978): 2.
Five cases of abuse and homicide show the bias of the press and courts in this news note.

566 Fuszara, M.; J. Kurczewski; J. Tropea; and N. Wityak. "Battery, Women and the State." Paper presented at the annual meeting of the American Sociological Association, New York, 1980.

567 Gabbard, Glen O., and Jan Larson. "Masochism: Myths or Human Need." American Journal of Psychiatry 138 (April 1981): 533-4.
This letter to the editor challenges the dismissal of masochism in Elaine Hilberman's article [741] in the same journal (November 1980, pp. 1336-47) and suggests that her feminist leanings fog her objectivity. They further suggest that just because female masochism has been overemphasized does not mean it is a myth. Hilberman, in turn, provides a short defense.

568 Gabor, Agota. "I Am Joe's Punching Bag!" Homemaker's Magazine 11 (May 1976): 137-48.
A good popularized article for a Canadian readership, this discussion is peppered with real-life recountings. The research of Don Dutton and the experiences of Interval House and Transition House provide the reading with a solid base.

569 Galant, Lawrence L. "The Relationship Between Intrafamily Violence and Self-concept." Ph.D. dissertation, University of North Carolina, Greensboro, 1977. 153 p. Abstract in Dissertation Abstracts International 38B (October 1977): 1950.

570 Galaway, Burt, and Joe Hudson, eds. Perspectives on Crime Victims. St. Louis, Mo.: C.V. Mosby, 1981. 443 p.
This is a collection of articles relating to the victims of crime with some emphasis on the role played in one's own victimization. Authors Del Martin [1027], Suzanne Steinmetz [1502], and Oberg and Pence [1160] have articles directly concerned with the problem. These essays are annotated elsewhere in this bibliography. Several other essays may be useful.

571 Galvin, June R. "Ohio's New Civil Remedies for Victims of Domestic Violence." Ohio Northern University Law Review 8, no. 2 (1981): 248-64.

572 Ganley, Anne. "Counseling Programs for Men Who Batter: Elements of Effective Programs." Response to Violence in the Family 4 (November/December 1981): 3-4.
This article is excerpted from the author's Court-mandated Counseling for Men Who Batter [573].

573   Ganley, Anne L.   Court-mandated Counseling for Men Who Bat-
          ter: A Three-Day Workshop for Mental Health Profession-
          als.   Participant's Manual.   Washington, D.C.:   Center for
          Women Policy Studies, 1981.   122 p.
      Designed as a participant's manual for workshops to train
mental health professionals to deal with batterers, this guide has several assumptions.   Spouse abuse is a crime; it is learned behavior;
it is not a mental illness; batterers must have treatment, probably
court-mandated since they will avoid voluntary programs; and the purpose of counseling is to get the abuser to stop.   A good program
aimed at the cause of the problem, not the result.

574   Ganley, Anne L., and Lance Harris.   "Domestic Violence: Is-
          sues in Designing and Implementing Programs for Male Bat-
          terers."   Paper presented at the annual meeting of the
          American Psychological Association, Toronto, September,
          1978.   Also in Appendix, Family Violence: A Workshop
          Manual for Clergy and Other Service Providers.   Eds. Rev.
          Marie M. Fortune and Denise Hormann.   Rockville, Md.:
          National Clearinghouse on Domestic Violence, 1980.
      The emphasis here is on the abuser.   The authors believe
too much attention is paid to the victim, whose primary need is only
safety.   If the abusing situation is to change, it is the abuser who must
behave differently.   The characteristics of batterers are explored,
along with suggestions for modifying their actions.   Somewhat surpris-
ingly, the abuser is viewed by the authors as being too dependent
emotionally on the victim.   This they feel is what makes him want to
control her completely.   The authors are therapists at the Domestic
Assault Program of American Lake Veterans Hospitals in Tacoma,
Washington.

575   Ganley, Anne, and N. Nickles.   "Counseling Men Who Batter
          Their Mates."   Presented at a workshop sponsored by the
          Center for Women Policy Studies, Coral Gables, Florida,
          February 1981.

576   Gaquin, Deirdre A.   "Spouse Abuse: Data from the National
          Crime Survey."   Victimology: An International Journal 2,
          nos. 3-4 (1977-1978): 632-43.
      This article presents findings about the victims of spouse
abuse in the U.S. who were identified in the national crime survey.
It includes data from over a million interviews conducted during 1973,
1974, and 1975, such as details about the victims, their households,
their neighborhoods, and the victimizations that they experienced.
Sample households were interviewed every six months until seven interviews were completed for each.

577   Garfinkle, Max.   "Couple Education to Prevent Family Violence."
          American Journal of Orthopsychiatry 44 (March 1974): 221.
      This is a digest of a paper presented at the 51st annual
meeting of the American Orthopsychiatric Association, San Francisco,
April 8-12, 1974.   The author, from the University of Montreal, recommends that couples be educated during the formative period of their

relationship regarding their basic compatability and personal needs.
This will allow them to make more reasoned choices about marital
partners and thereby increase the probability of a violence-free future.

578   Garnet, Shelley E. "How to Set up a Counseling Program for
       Self-referred Batterers: The AWAIC model. " In The Abu-
       sive Partner: An Analysis of Domestic Battering. Ed.
       Maria Roy. New York: Van Nostrand Reinhold, 1982,
       pp. 267-76.

579   Garnet, Shelley, and Irwin L. Lubell. "From Inmate to Ex-
       offender: A Prevention Program for Abusive Partners in
       Transition. " In The Abusive Partner: An Analysis of Do-
       mestic Battering. Ed. Maria Roy. New York: Van Nos-
       trand Reinhold, 1982, pp. 126-35.

580   Garnet, Shelley, and Phyllis Frank. "Working with the Abuser. "
       In Identification and Treatment of Spouse Abuse; Health and
       Mental Health Agency Roles, Proceedings of a Conference.
       Eds. Abraham Lurie and Elizabeth B. Quitkin. New York:
       Editors, 1981, pp. 83-99.

581   Gates, Margaret. "The Battered Woman: Criminal and Civil
       Remedies. " Paper presented at the annual meeting of the
       American Psychiatric Association, Toronto, May 1977.

582   Gates, Margaret. "Victims of Rape and Wife Abuse. " In Wom-
       en in the Courts. Eds. Winifred L. Hepperle and Laura
       Crites. Williamsburg, Va. : National Center for State
       Courts, 1978, pp. 176-201.
       A founder and co-director of the Center for Women Policy
Studies, Gates compares the court/legal attitudes toward rape and
spouse abuse. In both cases it is victimization of women by men and
in both cases the courts seem unwilling to treat the offenses as seriously as they should be treated. Male offenders are given more benefit of the law than they would be in cases where women were not involved. Reform is imperative.

583   Gault, Cinda. "Discussion Forum: Wife Battery. " Canadian
       Newsletter of Research on Women 7 (March 1978): 8-9.
       A short general review of the myths surrounding spouse
abuse, such as economic hard times cause abuse, women like the
abuse, it's a lower-class problem, it's caused by alcoholism, etc.
The cause, she says, is social, and abuse has always occurred because women are viewed in the same light as children. Use of force
and violence is seen as legitimate for both.

584   Gault, Cinda. "Role of the Police in Domestic Violence: A
       Discussion with Deputy-Chief James Bannon. " Canadian Po-
       lice College Journal 4, no. 3 (1980): 184-8.
       In an interview Bannon, Deputy-Chief of the Detroit police,
states that police are not therapists and he prefers increasing the arrest powers and practices of the patrolman in matters of domestic

violence. He takes issue with Morton Bard's approach suggesting that
his "successful" programs are not convincingly proven.

585   Gayford, J.J. "The Aetiology of Repeated Serious Physical As-
           saults by Husbands on Wives (Wife Battering)." Medicine,
           Science and the Law 19, no. 1 (1979): 19-24.
      This article is derived from the author's study of 100 bat-
tered wives and the information presented here is similar to his other
articles. Nearly half of the wives had lost at least one parent by age
15 and a small group had a history of social and sexual disturbance.
There was also an association between childhood unhappiness and adult
attempted suicide. The author believes the wives' role as provocateur
is important, but underreported by them. No solutions were offered.
This is a presentation of causes and factors contributing to abuse.

586   Gayford, J.J. "Battered Wives." British Journal of Hospital
           Medicine 22 (November 1979): 496, 498, 500-3; Also in
           International Perspectives on Family Violence. Eds. Rich-
           ard J. Gelles and Claire Pedrick Cornell. Lexington,
           Mass. : Lexington Books, D. C. Heath, 1983, pp. 123-37.
      Gayford presents definitions of various terms associated
with spouse abuse, explanations of factors contributing to the frequency and severity of the beatings, and the types and locations of injury.
He believes that to really understand how and why it occurs it must be
seen in terms of the couple's frustration tolerance. The problem of
violence begins when a man with low frustration is paired with a highly
provocative woman. Alcohol is very important, because it removes
inhibitions and allows violence to erupt.

587   Gayford, J.J. "Battered Wives." Medicine, Science and the Law
           15, no. 4 (1975): 237-45.
      General overview of spouse abuse using some details from
a study of 100 battered wives in England. Types of injuries, need for
shelters and prevention of violence, and the cycle of violence are discussed.

588   Gayford, John. "Battered Wives I: Facts and Figures." Nurs-
           ing Mirror 143 (July 15, 1976): 62-5.
      This illustrated article is taken from a film prepared by
CameraTalks Production in London. Types of injuries, characteristics of the assaulters and the victims, effect on the children and other
facts are discussed. The report is continued in another article [1268]
by Pizzey and Gayford in this same journal.

589   Gayford, J.J. "Battered Wives One Hundred Years Ago." The
           Practitioner 219 (July 1977): 122-8.
      Gayford provides a historical account of wife beating in Eng-
land during the latter half of the nineteenth century. A good analysis
of Cobbe's article is given with some reference to Charles Dickens and
J. S. Mill. Shelters are a valuable service, but need better funding.
Encouraging advances have been made in dealing with wife abuse, but
more needs to be done.

590   Gayford, J.J.   "Battered Wives: Research on Battered Wives."
         Royal Society of Health Journal 95 (December 1975): 288-9.
      Reports results on research conducted with victims at the
Chiswick Women's Aid Hostel.   The influences of family background,
alcohol, jealousy, etc. on the incidence of abuse and the need for
safe shelter are discussed.   Not only the abused, but also the abuser
needs treatment and help.

591   Gayford, John J.   "The Plight of the Battered Wife."   Interna-
         tional Journal of Environmental Studies 10, no. 4 (1977):
         283-6.
      This article is the substance of a lecture given at the Na-
tional Conference on Crime and Violence at the Royal Society of Medicine, London, March 16, 1976.   Gayford describes the results of his
survey of 100 battered women.   Characteristics of the victim, such
as age, nationality, length of relationship, and psychological symptoms,
are listed.   He believes his findings are not at variance with those
of other researchers.   He believes that society can no longer tolerate
wife abuse.

592   Gayford, J.J.   "Wife Battering: A Preliminary Survey of 100
         Cases."   British Medical Journal 1 (January 25, 1975):
         194-7.
      The author interviewed 100 women, mostly from the Chis-
wick Women's Aid Hostel.   Much useful information comes to light in
this article concerning injuries, medical history, social and economic
factors, types and frequency of aid sought, characteristics of the
abuser as well as the abused and involvement of alcohol in the problem.   Among the conclusions Gayford reaches is that repeated violence
often occurs because the women had no place to go.   Shelters are
necessary.

593   Gaylin, Jody.   "Battered Wives Find It Hard to Get Help."   Psy-
         chology Today 11 (June 1977): 36, 88.
      This is a restatement of the findings of R.J. Gelles' article
in Journal of Marriage and the Family [602].

594   Gee, Pauline S.   "Ensuring Police Protection for Battered Wom-
         en: The Scott v. Hart Suit."   Signs: Journal of Women in
         Culture and Society 8 (Spring 1983): 554-67.
      This article describes in detail the Scott v. Hart case, which
challenged the procedures of the Oakland Police Department in response
to wife assault calls.   The question of due process, the First Amendment right to petition the government for redress of grievances, and
equal protection are seen as possible arguments; this case depended
upon the last.   Whether successful or not, this type of case is useful
in providing leverage for voluntary changes in policy by government
agencies.

595   Gehr, Marilyn.   Women as Victims of Violence: Battered
         Wives/Rape; A Selected Annotated Bibliography.   Albany:
         State University of New York, State Education Department,
         State Library Legislative Service, 1978.   23 p.

Includes seven pages on wife abuse. Very select bibliography with short annotations. Limited value and now dated.

596   Geis, Gilbert. "Rape-in-Marriage: Law and Law Reform in
            England, the United States, and Sweden. Adelaide Law Re-
            view 6 (June 1978): 284-303.
            Surveys the legal history of rape in marriage laws and legal
opinions, discussing the current climate and possibilities for reform
in England, the United States, and South Australia. Fears that wives
would frivolously charge husbands with rape are not borne out by the
Swedish experience. The author strongly supports the idea that sexual choice is the prerogative of the woman and her consent is necessary, even for her husband.

597   Gelb, Lenore. Plain Talk About Wife Abuse. Rockville, Md. :
            U. S. Department of Health and Human Services, [1983?].
            3 p.
            This public information flier provides general information
about wife abuse, including a definition, how the victim feels about
the situation, why abuse occurs, why the wife stays with the abuser,
what she can do, and the patterns of abuse.

598   Geller, Janet. "Conjoint Therapy: Staff Training and Treatment
            of the Abuser and the Abused." In The Abusive Partner:
            An Analysis of Domestic Battering. Ed. Maria Roy. New
            York: Van Nostrand Reinhold, 1982, pp. 198-215.

599   Geller, Janet A. "Reaching the Battering Husband." Social Work
            with Groups 1 (Spring 1978): 27-37.
            Since many battered wives do not want to leave their mar-
riages, and would not if the battering stopped, a program of therapy
for the husband was instituted. A ten-week voluntary program is discussed. An interesting hypothesis advanced by Geller is that since
batterers seem to be identical to non-batterers except for the violence
which is directed exclusively at the family, it may be a lack of tolerance for close contact and intimacy that causes the husband to lash
out. This idea merits more research.

600   Geller, Janet A. , and James C. Walsh. "A Treatment Model
            for the Abused Spouse." Victimology: An International
            Journal 2, nos. 3-4 (1977-78): 627-32.
            The Victims Information Bureau of Suffolk, Inc. (VIBS) of
Long Island, N. Y. , which directs its attention toward victims of spouse
abuse, rape and sexual assault, claims to have found an effective
method of therapy. They assume abuse is not victim precipitated and
discussions with the abused show that most do not want to end their
marriages. Those whose husbands will come in for counseling will
receive therapy as couples; when husbands will not come in the wives
are treated in group therapy. Clients in couple therapy or group therapy all have had positive results.

601   Geller, Janet, and Louise Garin. "Working with Couples." In
            Identification and Treatment of Spouse Abuse; Health and

Mental Health Agency Roles, Proceedings of a Conference.
Eds. Abraham Lurie and Elizabeth B. Quitkin. New York:
Editors, 1981, pp. 71-81.

602 Gelles, Richard J. "Abused Wives: Why Do They Stay." Journal of Marriage and the Family 38 (November 1976): 659-68.
Also in Abuse of Women: Legislation, Reporting and Prevention. Joseph J. Costa. Lexington, Mass. Lexington
Books, D. C. Heath, 1983, pp. 13-28; Marriage and Family
in a Changing Society. Ed. James M. Henslin. New York:
Free Press, 1980, pp. 373-88.
Gelles interviewed 80 New Hampshire women for this study
and concludes that there are several major reasons for abused women
staying with their husbands. The less severe and the less frequent
the abuse, the less likely the victim will seek outside help. Another
factor is how frequently she was struck by her parents. She is also
less likely to leave if she has few occupational or educational options.
Lack of legal and police support influences her reluctance to leave
also. All of these factors are discussed in detail.

603 Gelles, Richard J. "Applying Research on Family Violence to
Clinical Practice." Journal of Marriage and the Family 44
(February 1982): 9-20.
Discusses the problems encountered while applying the findings of ten years of research to actual cases during a year of diagnostic and therapeutic work with abused wives and children. Certain
aspects transfer more readily than others. A research background
helped enchance and sharpen the diagnostic focus.

604 Gelles, Richard J. "Domestic Criminal Violence." In Criminal
Violence. Eds. Marvin E. Wolfgang and Neil Alan Weiner.
Beverly Hills, Cal. : Sage, 1982, pp. 201-35.

605 Gelles, Richard J. "An Exchange/Social Control Theory." In
The Dark Side of Families: Current Family Violence Research. Eds. David Finkelhor et al. Beverly Hills, Cal. :
Sage, 1983, pp. 151-65.
Gelles reviews and summarizes the popular theories of family violence and the dilemmas of each. He personally favors exchange
theory. Simply put, the exchange theory says that human interaction
is guided by the pursuit of reward and the avoidance of punishment
and cost. For the batterer the rewards of using violence outweigh the
costs. The solution then is to make the costs greater than the rewards. Husband counseling, reducing the isolation of the family, and
democratizing the family decision-making will also help change the
situation.

606 Gelles, Richard J. Family Violence. (Sage Library of Social
Research, v. 84.) Beverly Hills, Cal. : Sage Publications,
1979. 219 p.
Gelles discussed many aspects of family violence, including
spouse abuse. To eliminate the violence, which is in large measure
caused by the way families and society are organized, several steps

are advanced. The norms and values that glorify and legitimize violence must be eliminated. Stress on individuals and families must be reduced and coping skills increased. Sexism in society must be ended and the cycle of transgenerational transfer of violence in the family must be broken. The laws and courts must reflect this changed attitude. In short, no meaningful change will occur unless we change the fundamental way we organize our lives, families and society.

607   Gelles, Richard J. "Methods for Studying Sensitive Family
        Topics." American Journal of Orthopsychiatry 48 (July
        1978): 408-24. Also in Research into Violent Behavior:
        Domestic Violence. U. S. Congress. House. Committee
        on Science and Technology. Hearings. 95th Cong. 2nd
        Sess. February 14, 15, 16, 1978. Washington, D. C. :
        Government Printing Office, 1978, pp. 668-710.
        General discussion of the problems faced by researchers
who wish to research family violence. Besides the limitations of research methods and techniques (most rely on the use of interviews and questionnaires), society frowns on the invasion of family privacy. If family violence is to be dealt with effectively, however, more must be done to understand family dynamics.

608   Gelles, Richard J. "The Myth of Battered Husbands and New
        Facts About Family Violence." Ms 8 (October 1979): 65-6,
        71-3.
        In the process of researching family violence for the book
Behind Closed Doors [1551], Straus, Steinmetz, and Gelles found a surprising amount of husband abuse. The media quickly picked up on this and sensationalized it without relating all the facts. In this article Gelles tries to do just that. Stressing that one needs to be careful with the data, it appears that as many women use violence on men as men do on women. However, the outcomes of each of those acts of violence are quite different with the wives suffering far worse injury then the men. It also seems that even though men did not report the abuse to the police, they were not reluctant to discuss it with the researcher.

609   Gelles, Richard J. "No Place to Go: The Social Dynamics of
        Marital Violence." In Battered Women: A Psychosociologi-
        cal Study of Domestic Violence. Ed. Maria Roy. New
        York: Van Nostrand Reinhold, 1977, pp. 46-63.
        This essay is synthesized from two chapters (3 and 5) of
the author's The Violent Home [615], (Sage, 1974). Its primary concern is where and when the violence takes place. Most takes place in the home, especially the kitchen, but also in the living room and bedroom. Most happens in the evening between 8:00 and 11:30, that is, from after dinner to bedtime. Morning violence is either on weekends or a spillover from the previous night. Verbal violence seems more likely to stimulate physical violence than do more civil approaches to family problem-solving Overall, it appears that the victim is beaten in a place, at a time of the day, and day of the week that gives her no place to go. Shelters are a necessity.

610   Gelles, Richard J.   "The Other Side of the Family: Conjugal
         Violence." Ph.D. dissertation, University of New Hamp-
         shire, 1973.   294 p.   Abstract in Dissertation Abstracts
         International 34A (March 1974): 6141.

611   Gelles, Richard J.   "Power, Sex, and Violence: The Case of
         Marital Rape." The Family Coordinator 26 (October 1977):
         339-47.   Also in Marriage and Family in a Changing Society.
         Ed. James M. Henslin.   New York: Free Press, 1980,
         pp. 389-402.
     Gelles discusses the question of married women being forced
to have sexual relations with their husbands through violence or intimidation.   Most women apparently do not view it as rape or even a violent act.   He argues that although there is no legal recognition of
marital rape (when this was written) social scientists can no longer
respond to the problem with the "head-in-the-sand" approach.   An
analysis of the phenomenon of marital rape suggests that sex and violence are means which husbands can use to dominate and intimidate
their wives without fear of outside intervention.   This is a revised
version of the paper presented at the annual meeting of the Western
Social Science Association, April 30, 1976.

612   Gelles, Richard J.   "Research Findings and Implications from
         a National Study on Domestic Violence."   In Domestic Vio-
         lence: Issues and Dynamics.   Ed. Vincent D'Oyley.   To-
         ronto: Ontario Institute for Studies in Education, 1978, pp.
         25-43.
     A general discussion of family violence with some attention
to spouse abuse.   Some of the results of the study with Murray A.
Straus and Suzanne K. Steinmetz for the book Behind Closed Doors:
Violence in the American Family [1551], are found here.   There are
many variables, including the social-psychological makeup of individuals and the structure of society itself, which encourage resolution of
problems with violence.

613   Gelles, Richard J.   "Violence and Pregnancy: A Note on the
         Extent of the Problem." Family Coordinator 24 (January
         1975): 81-6.
     The author investigated cases of wife abuse during pregnancy
and found a disturbingly high frequency of it.   Reasons for its occurrence were these: 1)   sexual frustration of the husband; 2)   the stress
of the transition to parenthood and its role changes; 3)   biochemical
changes in the wife, causing her to be more critical of the husband's
activities; 4)   hoping for miscarriage from prenatal abuse; and 5)   de-
fenselessness of the wife.   Planned parenthood and pre-birth counseling would help relieve anxiety and eliminate unwanted children.

614   Gelles, Richard J.   "Violence in the Family: A Review of Re-
         search in the Seventies." Journal of Marriage and the Fam-
         ily 42 (November 1980): 873-85.
     A useful literature review of family violence, especially
child and spouse abuse.   During the 1960's, researchers tended to
view domestic violence as rare and confined to the poor or mentally

disturbed. In the seventies, it was realized that the violence was by
far more widespread than previously thought and the reasons more than
economic or psychological. The major theories and discoveries are
discussed with suggestions for future research. This review will provide the reader with an excellent overview of the scholarship about
the topic during the last decade.

615 Gelles, Richard J. The Violent Home: A Study of Physical
        Aggression Between Husbands and Wives. (Sage Library of
        Social Research, vol. 13.) Beverly Hills, Cal. : Sage
        1972. 230 p.
        This ground-breaking empirical study makes several impor-
tant points regarding intraconjugal violence. It basically rejects the
idea that wife beating is the result of individual pathology, claiming
that most abusers are "normal." He does claim, however, that violence is learned behavior and that learning occurs during childhood.
It is the structure of society that must be changed if family violence
is to end. An important early study.

616 Gelles, Richard J. , and Claire Pedrick Cornell, eds. Interna-
        tional Perspectives on Family Violence. Lexington, Mass. :
        Lexington Books, D. C. Heath, 1983. 171 p.
        This volume pursues the notion that intrafamily violence is
widespread and if it is to be understood researchers must consider
macrosocial factors. To do this a historical, cross-cultural perspective is essential. This compilation of articles by several authors
does just that. A number of them are concerned with spouse abuse
and a few have been published elsewhere. Authors include M. Straus
[1540], J. J. Gayford [586], D. Levinson [960], T. M. Mushanga [1128],
and the Dobashes [356]. Their contributions are all annotated in this
bibliography under their respective names.

617 Gelles, Richard J. , and Murray A. Straus. "Determinants of
        Violence in the Family: Toward a Theoretical Integration. "
        In Contemporary Theories About the Family. Eds. Wesley
        R. Burr et al. Vol. I. New York: Free Press, 1979,
        pp. 549-81.
        These authors argue that physical violence between family
members is a normal part of family life in most societies and especially American society. "Normal" is used in the context of statistical frequency and approval by the culture and the one who commits
the violence. They believe that conflict in the family is inevitable,
but violence is not. The various aspects of family violence and the
importance of each are considered. Fifteen theories of interpersonal
violence are analyzed and applied to the family setting. A causal
flowchart of 13 of the theories is included. While the study has self-
admitted limitations, it is a valuable attempt at formulating a theory
to explain the determinants of family violence.

618 Gelles, Richard J. , and Murray A. Straus. "Toward an Inte-
        grated Theory of Family Violence. " Paper presented at the
        Conference of the National Council on Family Relations,
        1974.

619 Gelles, Richard J. , and Murray A. Straus. "Violence in the
         American Family." Journal of Social Issues 35, no. 2
         (1979): 15-39. Also in Relationships: The Marriage and
         Family Reader. Jeffrey P. Rosenfeld. Glenview, Ill. :
         Scott, Foresman, 1981, pp. 422-44.
         The question of family violence is reviewed with data gathered
from a national survey measuring the extent of child abuse, wife abuse,
husband abuse, and violence between siblings. The organization of the
family and cultural norms are seen as being the root cause. Family
intimacy provides love but also conflict. However, since other groups
provide both, why does the family often include violence when other
groups do not? The answer seems to reside in the privacy granted
to family activity and society's implicit legitimization of violence within family confines.

620 Gemmill, Francine B. "A Family Approach to the Battered
         Woman." Journal of Psychosocial Nursing and Mental Health
         Service 20 (September 1982): 22-4, 37-9.
         It is easy for psychiatric nurses to become too involved with
abuse victims or to adopt the other extreme and ignore their plight.
This article provides general information regarding abuse and suggests
that the Bowen Family Systems Theory can be used to help women
assess their situation and make changes in their lives. Since battered-
wife syndrome can be viewed as a symptom of a dysfunctional family,
treatment is best done with the whole family. If that is not possible,
the victim must view therapy as a means of becoming emotionally
reactive, which means the victim must be interested in changing herself, not other members of the family. The author is a psychiatric
clinical nurse specialist, Children's Hospital National Medical Center,
Washington, D. C.

621 Gentry, Charles E. , and Virginia Bass Eaddy. "Treatment of
         Children in Spouse Abusive Family." Victimology: An
         International Journal 5, nos. 2-4 (1980): 240-50. Also in
         Domestic Violence. U. S. Congress. House Committee on
         Education and Labor, Subcommittee on Select Education.
         Hearing, 98th Cong. , 1st Sess. , 23 June 1983. Washington,
         D. C. : Government Printing Office, 1983, pp. 63-73.
         Based on the belief that violence is learned behavior and
children who live in violent families learn that violence can be viewed
as appropriate behavior. The treatment of children in Spouse Abusive
Families Program in Knox County, Tennessee, is aimed at breaking
that cycle. Intervention is not punitive, but instead therapeutic and
educational.

622 Gentzler, Rie. The Abused. Harrisburg: Pennsylvania Coali-
         tion Against Domestic Violence, 1980. 88 p.

623 Gentzler, Rie. The Abused-advocacy Programs for Abused Wom-
         en. Harrisburg: Pennsylvania Coalition Against Domestic
         Violence, 1977. 75 p.
         Basically a guide for those providing assistance to the abused.
The information is drawn from Pennsylvania, but much is applicable

elsewhere. Budgets, proposal writing, setting up a hot line, selecting
staff, etc. are all discussed. Useful how-to-do-it guide.

624   Gentzler, Rie.   Advocacy Programs for Abused Victims: Shelter,
      Hot Line, Counseling, Accompaniment.   Lancaster: Penn-
      sylvania Coalition Against Domestic Violence, 1977.   98 p.

625   Geracimos, Ann.   "How I Stopped Beating My Wife."   Ms 5
      (August 1976): 53.   Also in Domestic Violence, 1978.   U. S.
      Congress.   Senate.   Committee on Human Resources, Sub-
      committee on Child and Human Development.   Hearings.
      95th Cong.   2nd Sess. on Domestic Violence and Legislation
      With Respect to Domestic Violence, March 4 and 8, 1978.
      Washington, D. C. :   Government Printing Office, 1978, p.
      653.
      An interview with a self-confessed wife-beater, this short
article gives some insight into the problem.   Better communication
between the couple and willingness to leave the relationship are seen
as ways to handle the situation.

626   Gesino, Jack Paul; Holly Hamlett Smith; and Walter A. Keckich.
      "The Battered Woman Grows Old."   Clinical Gerontologist
      1 (Fall 1982): 59-67.
      The authors, psychiatric social workers, Institute of Living,
investigate the conditions of two elderly women who had been physically abused by their husbands throughout their married lives.   Their
rationales for not leaving parallel those of their younger counterparts.
When their husbands died or became ill, the marital power relationship
was changed, causing depression in these wives since they were not
equipped to take control of their own lives.

627   Gibbens, T. C. N.   "Violence in the Family."   Medico-Legal Jour-
      nal 43, no. 3 (1975): 76-88.
      A general overview of family violence with information on
both the battered-child and the battered-wife syndromes.

628   Gilboa, Netta.   "When the Whip Comes Down: 300 Abusive Im-
      ages of Women in the Media."   Paper presented to the Illi-
      nois Sociological Association, 1983.

629   Giles-Sims, Jean Grindell.   "Stability and Change in Patterns of
      Wife-beating: A Systems Theory Approach."   Ph. D. disser-
      tation, University of New Hampshire, 1979.   373 p.   Ab-
      stract in Dissertation Abstracts International 41A (December
      1980): 2781.

630   Giles-Sims, Jean.   Wife Battering: A Systems Theory Approach.
      New York: Guilford Press, 1983, 193 p.
      The author studied 31 women who had been abused to deter-
mine how their patterns of interacting with their husbands affected the
outbreak of violence.   The "general systems theory" approach is the
theoretical framework used.   The first interview took place at a shelter, and the second, four to six months later, was designed to determine if changes in the interaction system had occurred and if the

changes were effective.   Of the 24 women in the follow-up study over
half had returned to their abusing husbands and most of these had
failed to reconstitute their marriages on a new and nonviolent basis.

631   Gill, Tess, and Anna Coote.   Battered Women: How to Use the
        Law.   London: Cobden Trust, 1975.   25 p.
      A guide explaining to British women the rights they have
if their husbands or male friends are abusing them.   Some of this
changed with the Domestic Violence and Proceedings Act of 1976.

632   Gillman, Irene S.   "An Object-relations Approach to the Phenom-
        enon and Treatment of Battered Women."   Psychiatry 43
        (November 1980): 346-58.
      Gillman, of Hofstra University, attempts in this article to
put spouse abuse in the context of the object-relations approach as
proposed by Keinberg in his Object Relations Theory and Clinical Psychoanalysis, 1976.   This approach is learned by the patient in the
pre-oedipal stage and is the key to her relationship with her parents,
later with her husband, and finally also with her therapist.   It helps
to explain why the wife can live with an abusing husband for years
and even say she still loves him.   The author rejects the traditional
Freudian interpretation and places abuse in the context of contemporary psychiatric theory.

633   Gilmore, Anne.   "Psychiatrists Look at Violence."   Canadian
        Medical Association Journal 129 (November 15, 1983):
        1135-8.
      The theme of the 1981 Canadian Psychiatric Association held
in Ottawa was "Violence, Society and Psychiatry."   Gilmore, a free-
lance writer, recounts several of the speakers' opinions.   The discussions of family violence included some information about, and concern with, wife abuse.

634   Gingold, Judith.   "One of These Days--Pow Right in the Kisser."
        Ms 5 (August 1976): 51-2, 54, 94.   Also in Domestic Vio-
        lence, 1978.   U.S. Congress.   Senate.   Committee on Hu-
        man Resources, Subcommittee on Child and Human Develop-
        ment.   Hearings.   95th Cong.   2nd Sess. on Domestic Vio-
        lence and Legislation with Respect to Domestic Violence,
        March 4 and 8, 1978.   Washington, D.C.:   Government
        Printing Office, 1978, pp. 651-5; Domestic Violence.   U.S.
        Congress.   House.   Committee on Education and Labor,
        Subcommittee on Select Education.   95th Cong.   2nd Sess.
        Hearings on H.R. 7927 and H.R. 8948, March 16 and 17,
        1978.   Washington, D.C.:   Government Printing Office, 1978,
        pp. 372-6.
      A good general review of the problem written for a popular
audience using a variety of noted authorities on the topic.

635   Glasgow, Jan M.   "The Marital Rape Exemptions: Legal Sanc-
        tion of Spouse Abuse."   Journal of Family Law 18, no. 3
        (1980): 565-86.
      A general discussion of the marital rape exemption, its his-
torical origins and current attempts to change it.   Legal reasoning

for revision, American case law, state statutes and reform legislation, and the advantages and disadvantages of various remedies are
discussed.   Reform is necessary and there is no reason to assume
that such reform would put an intolerable burden on the judicial system or on marriage itself.   Besides, women have a right to restrict
their sexual activity as they choose and legal reform would recognize
that right.

636   Goffman, Jerry M.   Batterers Anonymous: Mutual Support
              Counseling for Women-Batterers.   Redlands, Cal. : Coali-
              tion for the Prevention of Abuse of Women and Children,
              1980.   18 p.
        This pamphlet is designed to briefly describe the problem
and to provide guidelines for establishing Batterers Anonymous Chapters elsewhere.   Usually attention is focused on sheltering the abused,
but programs such as this may be useful in easing the problem at its
source.

637   Goffman, Jerry M.   Mutual Support Counseling for Women-
              batterers.   Redlands, Cal. : Coalition for the Prevention
              of Abuse of Women and Children, 1980.   31 p.

638   Goldberg, Herb.   "The Dynamics of Rage Between the Sexes in
              a Bonded Relationship. " Family Therapy Collections.   Vol.
              3.   Clinical Approaches to Family Violence.   Rockville,
              Md. : Aspen Systems, 1982, pp. 59-67.

639   Goldberg, Wendy, and Anne L. Carey.   "Domestic Violence Vic-
              tims in the Emergency Setting. "   Topics in Emergency
              Medicine 3 (January 1982): 65-76.
        Goldberg, a clinical specialist in psychiatric nursing at
Henry Ford Hospital, Detroit, and Carey, Director of Social Work,
William Beaumont Hospital, Troy, Michigan, stress the need and
value of health professionals making contact with abuse victims when
they seek emergency medical attention.   The problem is generally
described and a model form is provided for gaining information regarding the abuse.   The purpose is to provide the hospital with data for
treatment and to encourage in the victim a willingness to discuss her
situation and seek relief.

640   Golde, Madeleine.   "Federal Programs Provide Housing Assist-
              ance for Battered Women. "   Journal of Housing 37 (August/
              September 1980): 443-7.
        Projects for providing housing and shelter for battered wom-
en are eligible for funding with community development block grants.
Local officials and women's organizations must be willing to aggres-
sively apply for these funds.   The need abused women have for shelters, transition housing, etc. is discussed.

641   Goldstein, Diane.   "Spouse Abuse. " In Prevention and Control
              of Aggression.   New York: Pergamon Press, 1983, pp.
              37-65.

This essay is a review of the research regarding spouse abuse with an examination of current and recommended control and prevention programs. A historical overview with the theories which explain the abuse and describe the actors is presented. She also proposes her own theory of "vulnerability" which may be helpful in early identification and treatment of couples who are at high risk for violence.

642 Goode, William J. "Force and Violence in the Family." Journal of Marriage and the Family 33 (November 1971): 624-36. Also in Violence in the Family. Eds. Suzanne K. Steinmetz and Murray A. Straus. New York: Dodd, Mead, 1974, pp. 25-44; Crime and Justice, 1971-1972; An AMS Anthology. New York: AMS Press, 1974.
Goode discusses general theories of family violence. The theory he puts forth in this article can be called a social control or a resources theory of family violence. He argues that violence can be used to achieve desired ends. It tends to be used when other resources (such as money, respect, love, shared goals) are lacking, or found to be insufficient.

643 Goode, William J. "Violence Among Intimates." In Crimes of Violence; A Staff Report to the National Commission on the Causes and Prevention of Violence. Eds. Donald J. Mulvihill and Melvin M. Tumin, with Lynn A. Curtis. Vol. 13, Appendix 19. Washington, D.C.: Government Printing Office, 1969, pp. 941-77. Also in his Explorations in Social Theory. New York: Oxford University Press, 1973, pp. 145-97.
An interesting study of violence and rape between spouses and friends. Social conditions and conditioning are major contributors to the problem. Better police training, gun control, changes in childrearing practices and changes in society, especially in class and racial discrimination, will all help to alleviate the situation.

644 Goodman, Elizabeth. America's Battered Women. Cincinnati, Ohio: Pamphlet Publications, 1978. 54 p.
A general pamphlet popularizing the studies of a number of scholars and researchers for a lay readership. A history of the problems, a look at the abuser and the victim, the role of the police, the courts and the community are all included. Establishment of shelters is seen as the "only feasible solution existing at this time."

645 Goodman, Elizabeth. America's Battered Women: A Look into the 80's. Dayton, Ohio: P.P.I. Publishing, 1982. 47 p.

646 Goodman, Emily Jane. "Legal Solutions: Equal Protection Under the Law." In Battered Women: A Psychosociological Study of Domestic Violence. Ed. Maria Roy. New York: Van Nostrand Reinhold, 1977. pp. 139-44.
A general discussion of the irony that women receive little protection from the law if their husbands are the assaulters. Since

laws are sexist and supportive of male supremacy, statutory modifi-
cations are unlikely to solve the problem.   Only radical social and
legal changes in the current attitude toward women will make any real
difference.

647   Goodstein, Richard K., and Ann W. Page.   "Battered Wife Syn-
          drome: Overview of Dynamics and Treatment." American
          Journal of Psychiatry 138 (August 1981): 1036-44.
          This is an overview of the studies done regarding spouse
abuse.   No new information is added but the authors do hope to shed
light on this psychosocial subject for clinicians and health care professionals.   Aspects of the syndrome including characteristics of the
wives and the abusers, influence of alcohol and family backgrounds,
coping responses of victims, and other factors are discussed and
highlighted.

648   Gordeuk, Anita Rose.   "Characteristics of Abused Wives in the
          Salt Lake City Area."   M. S. thesis, University of Utah,
          1979.   98 p.
          The purpose of this study was to determine which character-
istics of abused wives identified in the literature were unique to a
group of abused women as opposed to a nonabused group.   Thirty abused
and 60 nonabused women from Salt Lake City were studied by questionnaire.   The results show the abused had more shared household
conjugal relationships, greater age differences between the spouses,
more discord during pregnancy, more dependency of the wife on the
husband, more unemployment, lower self-esteem, and more experience
with abuse in the home of origin than nonabused women.   Nurses will
encounter this problem and must be prepared to offer assistance and
refer the victim to appropriate agencies.   Recommendations for local
services are included.

649   Gordon, James S.   "The Runaway Center as Community Mental
          Health Center." American Journal of Psychiatry 135
          (August 1978): 932-5.
          The value of the services provided by the community health
center for runaway youth is detailed.   It is suggested that it would
serve as an effective model for battered-women shelters.

650   Gordon, Marie.   "Battered Wives: The Gagged Victims."
          Branching Out 6, no. 2 (1979): 26-9.
          This article surveys the Canadian legal situation as it re-
lates to spouse abuse.   Comparison is made with the English Domestic and Matrimonial Proceedings Act.   Deficiencies of Canadian Law
are examined.

651   Goudy, Frank William.   "Wife Abuse: A Legal Bibliography."
          Behavioral and Social Sciences Librarian 2 (Summer 1982):
          1-11.
          About eighteen selected articles regarding spouse abuse and
marital rape are annotated.   A list of additional citations is appended.
Useful beginning source for the researcher or the general public.

652   Grab, Frederick. "Spousal Rape." American Bar Association
            Journal 66 (December 1980): 1494.
            This letter to the editor denies the need for heavier penal-
ties for spousal rape than for nonspousal rape.

653   Graff, Thomas Theodore. "Personality Characteristics of Bat-
            tered Women." Ph. D. dissertation, Brigham Young Univer-
            sity, 1979. 53 p. Abstract in Dissertation Abstracts Inter-
            national 40B (February 1980): 3395.

654   Grambs, Marya, and Pam Miller. Dollars and Sense: A Com-
            munity Fund-raising Manual for Shelters and Other Non-
            profit Organizations. San Francisco: Western States Shel-
            ter Network, 1982. 155 p.

655   Grant, Bernadette Clarke. " '... Till Death Us Do Part': A
            Social Psychological Analysis of Women Who Kill Their
            Spouses." Ph. D. dissertation, Mississippi State University,
            1983. 162 p. Abstract in Dissertation Abstracts Interna-
            tional 44A (September 1983): 871.

656   Grau, Janice L. "Restraining Order Legislation for Battered
            Women: A Reassessment." University of San Francisco
            Law Review 16 (Summer 1982): 703-41.
            This author discusses the value and limitations of restrain-
ing orders, sometimes also referred to as protection orders.   As a
civil resolution to the problem of spouse abuse, she believes they
have become a popular alternative to criminal sanctions.   Her article
is divided in three parts.   The first is an overview of current restraining order legislation while the second part discusses the problems inherent in such legislation, such as the difficulty of implementation and ultimate effectiveness.   Part three suggests improvements
in such legislation and improved methods of dealing with wife abuse.

657   Gravdal, Beverly Wigen. "A Study of Locus of Control and Sex-
            role Typology in Two Groups of Battered Women." Ph. D.
            dissertation, Washington State University, 1982. 127 p.
            Abstract in Dissertation Abstracts International 43B.
            (August 1982): 556.

658   Gray, D. J. Pereira. "Law and the General Practitioner. Legal
            Aspects of Violence in the Family." British Medical Jour-
            nal 282 (June 20, 1981): 2021-2.
            A short description of the British law as it relates to vio-
lence between adults, and between children and adults and its implications for physicians.

659   Grayson, Joann, and Gary Smith. "Marital Violence and Help
            Seeking Patterns in a Micropolitan Community." Victim-
            ology: An International Journal 6, nos. 1-4 (1981): 188-97.
            This study of the questionnaire responses of 327 women
(158 abused, 169 not abused) from a rural area of Southeastern U. S.
collects demographic data and patterns of help seeking.   Results show

similarities to Gelles' research, that those suffering occasional or
frequent abuse were less likely than moderately abused to seek help.
Of special note is how many never have sought help and probably are
not aware of how much and what services are available to them.

660   Great Britain. Department of Health and Social Security; Depart-
         ment of the Environment; Home Office; Scottish Office and
         Welsh Office. Observations on the Report from the Select
         Committee on Violence in Marriage.   London: HMSO, 1976.
         (Command paper 6690.)   37 p.
      After reviewing the recommendation of the select committee,
these government agencies made further recommendations and observations for another such committee to consider.   Serious governmental
attention is recommended.

661   Great Britain. Parliament. House of Commons. "Report to the
         Secretary of State for the Home Department on the State of
         the Law Relating to Brutal Assaults." Vol. 61 (C1138)
         London: HMSO, 1875. 173 p.

662   Great Britain. Parliament. House of Commons. Select Com-
         mittee on Violence in the Family. Battered Wives. "First
         Report ... Together with Appendices. Session 1975-76."
         Vol. 45. Sessional Paper 473. London. HMSO 1976.   36 p.
      This is a collection of letters, memorandums, and other
materials from special interest groups and local government bodies,
such as the Scottish Women's Aid, Police Federation, Chiswick Wom-
en's Aid, National Women's Aid Federation, the London Boroughs of
Hounslow, Richmond on Thames, and The Lord Chancellors Office.
These items were published without comment by the select committee.

663   Great Britain. Parliament. House of Commons. Select Com-
         mittee on Violence in the Family. Battered Wives. "Second
         Report ... Together with the Proceedings of the Committee
         and Appendices. Session 1976-77." Sessional Paper 431.
         Vol. 46. London: HMSO, 1977. 26 p.
      This report is a publication of the responses of the govern-
ment, the Scottish Women's Aid, and the National Women's Aid Federation to the Report of the Select Committee on Violence in Marriage
(HC Sessional paper 553, 1974-75).   Discontent is evident because of
the feeling that the government is not fully committed to ending the
problem.

664   Great Britain. Parliament. House of Commons. Select Com-
         mittee on Violence in Marriage. "First Special Report ...
         Session 1974-75." Vol. 35. Sessional Paper 229. HMSO,
         1975. 3 p.
      A call for memoranda from members of Parliament and in-
terested persons and organizations regarding spousal violence to be
considered by the committee.

665   Great Britain. Parliament. House of Commons. Select Com-
         mittee on Violence in Marriage. "First Special Report ...

Session 1975-76." Sessional Paper 260. Vol. 45. London:
HMSO, 1976. 3 p.
This report tells what will be done in future committee
meetings.

666 Great Britain. Parliament. House of Commons. Select Committee on Violence in Marriage. "Report ... Together with
the Proceedings of the Committee, Session 1974-75." Vol.
2. Report Minutes of Evidence and Appendices. London:
HMSO, 1975. 536 p. Session Paper 553-II Vol. 35.
This report contains a general overview of the problem in
Great Britain and a listing of recommendations for dealing with spouse
abuse. This is followed by the minutes of 15 days of testimony by
many witnesses including Pizzey, Gayford, Gill and Coote, to name
only a few. Also included are letters, written statements and memos
from public and private social agencies, and government offices and
officials.

667 Great Britain. Parliament. House of Commons. Select Committee on Violence in Marriage. "Second Special Report ...
Session 1975-76." Vol. 45. London: HMSO, 1976. 3 p.
Recommends a new committee to deal with battered women
since violence toward children took most of the current committee's
time.

668 Greater Egypt Regional Planning and Development Commission.
Inquiry into Family Violence in Southern Illinois. Carbon-
dale, Ill.: The Commission, 1979. 56 p.

669 Green, Maurice R., ed. Violence and the Family. (AAAS
Selected Symposium, 47.) Boulder, Colo.: Westview Press,
1982. 134 p.
The articles in this volume are drawn from the annual meeting of the American Association for the Advancement of Science in
Houston, Texas, January 3-8, 1979. Articles by M. Straus, [1542],
J. P. Spiegel [1475], and M. Bard [58], with discussion by others are
included. Each is included elsewhere in this bibliography under the
author. Cultural and social aspects of family violence are analyzed
with little direct concern with spouse abuse. Useful for theories of
general family violence.

670 Greenblat, Cathy Stein. "A Hit Is a Hit Is a Hit ... or Is It?:
Approval and Tolerance of the Use of Physical Force by
Spouses." In The Dark Side of Families: Current Family
Violence Research. Eds. David Finkelhor et al. Beverly
Hills, Cal.: Sage, 1983, pp. 235-60.
Greenblat, Professor of Sociology, Rutgers University, in
a study of the attitudes of 97 New Jersey residents regarding permis-
sibility of striking one's spouse, found little evidence of general approval. Less than a quarter of the sample believed it to be appropriate behavior. When it was approved, it was in cases of self-defense
or the other person's transgressions, particularly sexual infidelity.

Also found was a tolerance for violence.   While not acceptable to themselves, they could see how others might be driven to it.

671   Greenland, Cyril.   "Health Topic: Violence and the Family."
        Canadian Journal of Public Health 71 (January/February
        1980): 19-24.
        This paper was originally presented at the Ontario Public
Health Association, 29th annual conference, November 1978.   A general discussion of family violence including child abuse; some attention
is paid to spouse abuse.   Includes information from research with
Canadian families.

672   Greenland, Cyril.   "Sex Law Reform in an International Perspec-
        tive: England and Wales and Canada." American Academy
        of Psychiatry and the Law 11, no. 4 (1983): 309-30.
        This article includes minor comments regarding the spousal
immunity for marital rape.

673   Greenstone, James L. , and Sharon Leviton.   Hotline: Crisis
        Inventory Directory.   New York: Facts on File, 1981.
        310 p.

674   Gregory, Margaret.   "Battered Wives." In Violence in the Fam-
        ily.   Ed. Marie Borland.   Atlantic Highlands, N. J. : Human-
        ities Press, 1976, pp. 107-28.
        This essay is a good general description of the problem in
England.   Among her recommendations for relief of the problem is a
financial allotment to one-parent families.   This would give some economic independence so return to an abusing husband would not be necessary.   Creation of a family court to deal with disintegrating marriages
and the making available of medical and social services would be high
on the priority list.   More research must be encouraged since it is
difficult to solve the problem if its dimensions are not exactly known.

675   Griffin, Moira K.   "In 44 States, It's Legal to Rape Your Wife."
        Student Lawyer 9 (September 1980): 21-3, 57-61.
        An overview of the question of marital rape in the U. S.   The
literature supporting the exemption for husbands is reviewed and authors B. Schlachet, D. Finkelhor, A. N. Groth, and D. Drucker, among
others, are quoted.   The status of the law in each state is given.

676   Griffin, Moira K.   "Rape: A Family Affair." Student Lawyer
        9 (September 1980): 22-3.
        An overview of the Rideout case in Oregon.   The court case,
for marital rape, and the aftermath are discussed.

677   Griffith, Marie Gardner.   "Some Characteristics of Battered Wom-
        en at Womenshelter in Long Beach." M. S. thesis, Califor-
        nia State University, Long Beach, 1980.   52 p.   Abstract
        in Masters Abstracts 19 (June 1981): 195.

678   Griffiths, Aled.   "The Legacy and Present Administration of
        English Law.   Some Problems for Battered Women in Con-
        text. " Cambrian Law Review 11 (1980): 29-39.

The results of interviews with 17 battered women in Wales
in January 1979.   Police must take a more active role either in prosecution or providing other aid.   Safety of the victim is also paramount.

679   Griffiths, Aled.   "Some Battered Women in Wales: An Interac-
         tionist View of Their Legal Problems."   Family Law 11
         (February 1981): 25-9.
         Seventeen battered women were interviewed to determine
their knowledge of their rights and their satisfaction with the aid they
had received from legal, social, and medical agencies.   Most believed
their husbands had the right to beat them.   This was reinforced by
the lack of assistance and the attitudes displayed by the police.   Assistance by solicitors, the courts, and physicians was better, but
still inadequate.   The paramount consideration must be the personal
safety of the victim.   Therefore the helping professions should be
aware of the shelters and services available so victims can be referred.   Courts and police must also take injunctions more seriously.

680   Grim, Nancy, E.   "Domestic Relations: Legal Responses to
         Wife Beating: Theory and Practice in Ohio."   Akron Law
         Review 16 (Spring 1983): 705-45.
         The Ohio Domestic Violence Act of 1979 is studied, especial-
ly its practice and interpretations in the realm of spouse abuse.   The
civil protection order and the temporary restraining order are compared with observations regarding available relief.   Civil and criminal
provisions are detailed.   Although Ohio's Domestic Violence Act is
the most comprehensive recent law, and while it does provide more
relief than previous laws, there are several improvements that would
enhance its effectiveness.   This is especially true of the civil domestic
violence protection orders.   Lawyers must become more familiar with
the law and prosecutors must see spouse abuse as a crime against
the state and should promote victim cooperation with its prosecution.

681   Grohmann, Stephen W.   Dane County Advocates for Battered
         Women Emergency Shelter Facility: Monitor Report.
         Madison: Wisocnsin Council on Criminal Justice, 1979.
         5 p.

682   Gropper, Arlene, and Janet Currie.   A Study of Battered Women.
         [Vancouver?]:   Authors, 1976.   100 p.
         This study of women who stayed at Ishtar Transition House,
Vancouver, British Columbia, was meant to investigate the needs of
battered women and whether the community was meeting them.   If so,
to what degree and if not, why?   Medical, police, legal and other
forms of assistance were evaluated.   Results indicate that those who
leave the abusive situation permanently have more self-esteem than
those who do not.   Individual motivation is therefore requisite for success.   Shelters can help by providing personal support, counseling,
and a source of income.   Community services are also important.

683   Grosfeld, Sharon.   "Rape Within Marriage: A Sociological and
         Historical Analysis."   Paper presented at the Society for the
         Psychological Study of Social Issues Meetings, August 1980.

684   Groth, A. Nicholas, with H. Jean Birnbaum. Men Who Rape:
        The Psychology of the Offender. New York: Plenum Press,
        1979. 227 p.
        This work contains a short chapter on marital rape. Sev-
eral case examples are given along with motivations, such as sex
being equated to power, virility, debasement, and love and affection.
The author believes that marital rape may be the most prevalent form
of sexual assault, but because of societal attitudes and legal codes it
goes undetected.

685   Groth, A. Nicholas, and Thomas S. Gary. "Marital Rape."
        Medical Aspects of Human Sexuality 15, no. 3 (March 1981):
        122-32.
        A general overview with emphasis on the rapist, his person-
ality, and motivation. The act is not an aggressive expression of sexuality, but rather a sexual expression of aggression.

686   Gullattee, Alyce L. "Spousal Abuse." National Medical Associ-
        ation Journal 71 (April 1979): 335-40.
        Three sociopolitical concerns are viewed as significant to
behaviorists: 1) the disintegration of the institution of the family and
what it means for the future; 2) increasing nihilism in the white Judeo-
Christian world population; and 3) researching the preconceived theories of violence and the need to develop national sanctions to deter
violent behavior. These are analyzed in the context of spouse abuse.
The author is Professor of Psychiatry at Howard University.

687   Gully, Kevin J., et al. "Research Note: Sibling Contribution
        to Violent Behavior." Journal of Marriage and the Family
        43 (May 1981): 333-7.
        A questionnaire was completed by 216 undergraduate students
regarding the degree of violence they witnessed in their families.
They also reported on the amount of violence they themselves had inflicted on family members. Findings indicate that recollections of
family violence were consistent with their own violent behavior, thus
confirming that observing violence does teach others to do it. Another
observation of interest is that the family also provides a training ground
since children were able to practice violence, not just observe it.
Violence observed was between parents, between siblings, and between
parent and children. The authors are all from the Department of
Psychology, Washington State University, Pullman.

688   Haas, Richard. How Do You Answer That One? Ypsilanti,
        Mich.: Domestic Violence Project, 1981. 14 p.
        A booklet for counselors dealing with family violence.

689   Haffner, Sarah. "Victimology Interview: A Refuge for Battered
        Women, a Conversation with Erin Pizzey." Victimology:
        An International Journal 4, no. 1 (1979): 100-12.
        Pizzey discusses the beginnings of the Chiswick Women's
Aid and the policies and philosophy by which it operates. Her attitudes

regarding the problem of abuse in society, how much can be done to provide relief, and how she perceives the abuser, the victim, and their children are all discussed frankly. She concludes that the government is not
willing to look closely at the problem because it will require much money
and change in current methods of assistance if it is seen how widespread
the problem really is.

690 Haffner, Sarah. "Wife Abuse in West Germany." Victimology: An
			International Journal 2, nos. 3-4 (1977-78): 472-6.
		This article gives a view of wife abuse in West Germany and
reports the establishment of the first shelter in Berlin. Abuse seems to
be frequent in Germany with an accompanying disinclination to discuss
it. Public attitudes range from helpless sympathy to shoulder-shrugging
complacency to outright cynicism. Numerous observations regarding
wife abuse are made.

691 Haines, Janine. "Women, the Law and Provocation." Australasian
			Nurses Journal 10 (August 1981): 1, 3.
		Haines, Senator from South Australia, in response to a 1981
trial of a woman convicted of murder rather than manslaughter after 27
years of violence and abuse, argues that the rules of provocation should
be changed. Because of the difference in the socialization of men and
women, it is unjust and unfair to judge women by the current male standards of provocation. Included is a resolution passed by a public meeting
of 550 citizens at North Adelaide, urging changes in the law in such cases,
and improved services for battered women.

692 Haka-Ikse, K. "Domestic Violence." In Domestic Violence: Issues
			and Dynamics. Ed. Vincent D'Oyley. Toronto: Ontario Insti-
			tute for Studies in Education, 1978, pp. 183-8.
		Why do family members commit violence against each other?
There may be medical-psychiatric reasons, such as psychosis, schizo-
phrenia, or personality disorders like hostility or passive-dependence
or rigid-compulsive personality. Disturbed family roles, neurotic traits,
outside stress, cultural influences and numerous others may also be
reasons.

693 Hake, Lois M. Diary of a Battered Housewife. Independence, Ky.:
			Feminist Publications, 1976. 38 p.
		This "diary" tells the story of a woman's childhood, courtship
and thirty-year marriage, characterized by heavy drinking and violence,
but also many good times. Battered wives may find this pamphlet useful
for comparison with their own experiences.

694 Hake, Lois M. What You Can Do If You Are a "Battered" Woman.
			Cincinnati, Ohio: Pamphlet Publications, 1977. 31 p.
		This useful pamphlet gives advice to battered women seeking
legal and other answers to what they should or should not do. It especially addresses situations where the wife is in real physical danger
and is considering leaving her abuser. A list (now dated) of shelters
is included.

695 Hall, Ruth; Selma James; and Judit Kertesz. The Rapist Who

Pays the Rent; Evidence Submitted by Women Against Rape, Britain, to the Criminal Law Revision Committee. Bristol, England: Falling Wall Press, 1981. 64 p.

In 1980 the Home Secretary issued a "Working Paper On Sexual Offenses" asking for comment and criticism. This is a response regarding the problem of marital rape, which is not considered illegal. The authors argue the case for declaring marital rape illegal, whether it is coerced by physical, emotional, financial or other power means. Numerous legal and social myths are challenged. Spouse abuse, incest, and rape are all dealt with.

696   Hall-Apicella, Virginia. "Correlates of Attitudes Toward Battered Women Among Selected Mental Health Practitioners." Ph.D. dissertation, University of Pennsylvania, 1983. 188 p. Abstract in Dissertation Abstracts International 44A (September 1983): 708.

697   Haller, Susan Kay. "Wife Abuse: The Exploitation of Women by Society." M.S. thesis, George Williams College, 1977. 48 p.

698   Hamilton, Claire Jo, and James J. Collins, Jr. "The Role of Alcohol in Wife Beating and Child Abuse: A Review of the Literature." In Drinking and Crime: Perspectives on the Relationships Between Alcohol Consumption and Criminal Behavior. Ed. James J. Collins, Jr. New York: Guilford Press, 1981, pp. 253-87.

A good analysis of the theories of family violence is done with emphasis on the influence of alcohol in family violence. In sum, it appears that the relationship is not well understood. Alcohol seems to be involved in spouse abuse more than child abuse. Wife abusers and child abusers are more likely than the general public to be alcohol abusers. However, there is no proof that alcohol causes family violence. It is often present, but its role is uncertain. More serious and objective research is necessary.

699   Hamlin, Diane. "The Nature and Extent of Spouse Abuse." In Prosecutor's Responsibility in Spouse Abuse Cases. Washington, D.C.: LEAA, U.S. Department of Justice, 1980. 14 p. Also in The Victim Advocate. Chicago: National District Attorneys Association, 1978. 14 p.

This essay is a general discussion of the problem and answers questions regarding the nature of spouse assault, the extent of the problem, who are the victims and who are the batterers, why victims stay with the abuser, the role of alcohol and what intervention methods are effective.

700   Hamlin, Diane. "Violence Among Relatives and Friends: A National Crime Survey." Response to Violence in the Family 3 (July 1980): 5.

The author highlights the National Crime Survey's Intimate Victims: A Study of Violence Among Friends and Relatives and compares it with Mark Schulman's A Survey of Spousal Violence Against Women in Kentucky.

701 Hamlin, Diane E.; Dorothy B. Hurwitz; and Gisela Spieker.
    "Perspectives: Family Violence." Alcohol Health and Re-
    search World 4 (Fall 1979): 17-22.
    Hamlin, Director of the Clearinghouse on Battered Spouses,
Center for Women Policy Studies; Hurwitz, former director of the
National Conference on Social Welfare; and Spieker, Graduate School
of Social Work, University of Arkansas, Little Rock, all respond to
questions regarding the relationship between alcoholism and family
violence. They believe more cooperation between the various helping
agencies is necessary.

702 Hammond, Nancy. Domestic Assault: A Report on Family Vio-
    lence in Michigan. Lansing: Michigan Women's Commis-
    sion, 1977. 141 p.
    In 1976 the Michigan Women's Commission received a re-
port from the Task Force on Public Information called "Hearings on
the Physically Abused Woman." Domestic Assault is the response to
that initial interest. Numerous cases of abuse are described along
with lack of formal aid to the abused. Recommendations include improved police and legal action in domestic cases. Spouse abuse should
be treated more like other cases of assault. A good introduction to
the problem with graphic case histories.

703 Hamos, Julie E. Illinois Domestic Violence Act: A State's At-
    torney's Manual. Springfield: Illinois Coalition Against
    Domestic Violence, [1983]. 19 p.

704 Hamos, Julie E. State Domestic Violence Laws and How to Pass
    Them; A Manual for Lobbyists. (Domestic Violence, Mono-
    graph Series, no. 2, June 1980.) Rockville, Md. : National
    Clearinghouse on Domestic Violence, 1980. 170 p.
    "This manual focuses on one response to the issue of do-
mestic violence: the substance and process of state legislation. The
manual is designed to serve as a 'how-to' primer on domestic violence
legislation and the lobbying process." Emphasis is placed on four
types of legislation: 1) legislation intended to create public awareness
of the issues; 2) legislation intended to alter institutional response to
the issue; 3) legislation intended to fund services for domestic violence
victims; and 4) legislation intended to eliminate or prevent domestic
violence. The lobbying process is described with suggestions on how
to use it to advantage. Numerous examples of current state legislation are appended.

705 Hancock, Mary. Battered Women: An Analysis of Women and
    Domestic Violence and the Development of Women's Refuges.
    Wellington, New Zealand: The Committee on Women, 1979.
    33 p.
    Originally an honors paper for the B. Ed in women's studies
at Massey University, this begins with an excellent overview of the research literature regarding wife abuse. Of interest, too, is the overview of the emergence and development of refuges and shelters in
western society, including the U. S. , Canada, France, Australia, Switzerland, and elsewhere. The final part of the study is the analysis

of the five refuges in New Zealand. Of concern are the aims and objectives of the shelters, how they are organized and operated, finances, and general problems faced by each.

706   Handal, Kathleen, and Toni Ruffolo. "Crisis Intervention in the
       Emergency Room." In Identification and Treatment of Spouse
       Abuse; Health and Mental Health Agency Roles, Proceedings
       of a Conference. Eds. Abraham Lurie and Elizabeth B.
       Quitkin. New York: Editors, 1981, pp. 117-31.

707   A Handbook for Domestic Violence Victims. Springfield: Illinois
       Coalition Against Domestic Violence, [1983]. 32 p.

708   Hands Up. Domestic and Personal Violence. [Washington, D. C. :
       General Federation of Women's Clubs], n. d. 22 p.   Also
       in Domestic Violence: Prevention and Services.   U. S. Con-
       gress.   House.   Committee on Education and Labor.   Hear-
       ings.   96 Cong.   1st Sess.   July 10 and 11, 1979, Washing-
       ton, D. C. :   Government Printing Office, 1979, pp. 509-29.
       This booklet provides general information on several facets
of domestic violence. The section on spouse abuse attempts to explain why it happens, the role of law enforcement agencies, the purpose of shelters, and information regarding special programs.

709   Hanks, Susan E. , and C. Peter Rosenbaum. "Battered Women:
       A Study of Women Who Live with Violent Alcohol-abusing
       Men." American Journal of Orthopsychiatry 47 (April 1977):
       291-306.
       Twenty-two women living with violence-prone, alcohol-abusing
husbands were studied to determine how they became involved with such men, why they remained and how they contributed to the violence. The authors find that these women choose mates similar to the fathers they had, or wanted to have. They believe that the violence cannot be explained away simply with psychological theories of sadomasochistic behavior or social theories of male dominance and female submission. The women did not cause the men to be violent, but their pattern of interaction did cause the violence to ignite. To stop the abuse the woman must leave the husband or change her behavior during angry interchanges.

710   Hanmer, Jalna. "Community Action. Women's Aid and the
       Women's Liberation Movement." In Women in the Commu-
       nity. Ed. Marjorie Mayo. London: Routledge and Kegan
       Paul, 1977, pp. 91-108.

711   Hanmer, Jalna. "Violence and the Social Control of Women."
       In Power and the State. Eds. Gary Littlejohn et al. New
       York: St. Martin's Press, 1978, pp. 217-38.
       Hanmer argues that the threat of force in Western industri-
alized society is recognized as a major component of social control of women by men. It is the basis for the extraction of all benefits that men make of women, including economic, sexual and prestige gains. In a woman's life fear of violence from men is subtle and pervasive.

Of special importance is the notion that force, or its threat, is never
a secondary mode of influence; rather, it is the ultimate sanction but-
tressing other forms of control.   Wife abuse is only one such manifestation of those forms.   Based on a paper presented at the annual
meeting of the British Sociological Association, Sheffield, 1977.

712   Harrison, Paul.   "Refuges for Wives."   New Society 34 (No-
        vember 13, 1975): 361-4.
        The Chiswick refuge administered by Erin Pizzey is the only
one which maintains an open-door policy.   This policy has put her at
odds with the other shelters and public officials.   A good description
of Chiswick and its problems.

713   Hartik, Lorraine M.   Identification of Personality Characteristics
        and Self-concept Factors of Battered Wives.   Palo Alto,
        Cal. :   R and E Research Associates, Inc. , 1982.   83 p.
        Research for this book began with the assumption that bat-
tered women and nonbattered women would exhibit different personality
characteristics.   The Tennessee Self-Concept Scale and the Sixteen
Personality Factor Questionnaire were given to 60 women (30 battered,
30 nonbattered) from San Bernardino County, California.   The results
indicate that battered women tend to have lower self-esteem and more
self-conflict, and they were found to be "significantly more generally
maladjusted" than nonbattered women.   This research tends to confirm
the more informal observations made by others.

714   Hartik, Lorraine Mae.   "Identification of Personality Character-
        istics and Self-concept Factors of Battered Wives."   Ph. D.
        dissertation, United States International University, 1978.
        91 p.   Abstract in Dissertation Abstracts International 40B
        (August 1979): 893.

715   Harvey, Campbell J.   "Marital Violence and the Divorce Court:
        Seen But Not Heard."   Paper presented at the annual meet-
        ing of the American Society of Criminology, Washington,
        D. C. , 1981 and at the National Conference for Family Vio-
        lence Researchers, University of New Hampshire, July 1981.

716   Harvis, Barbara.   "The Progress of State Domestic Violence
        Legislation."   Family Law Reporter (Monograph no. 5) 4
        (July 25, 1978): 4027-31.   Also in Battered Women: Issues
        of Public Policy.   U. S. Commission on Civil Rights.   Wash-
        ington, D. C. :   The Commission, 1978, pp. 628-35.
        Prepared by the Center for Women Policy Studies, this chart
indicates the growing state legislative concern with spousal abuse.
Now dated, this chart does show how quickly many states reacted once
the issue of wife abuse was recognized as a problem.

717   Haselgrove, Richard.   "Homelessness Legislation and Experiences
        in Bradford."   In Battered Women and Abused Children.
        (Issues occasional papers, no. 4.)   [Bradford, Eng.]   Uni-
        versity of Bradford, 1979, pp. 42-9.
        The Housing Act of 1977 was an attempt to provide certain

classes of British citizens with a home and battered women are included in this group.   Actual experience in Bradford indicates that
there are problems preventing quick provision of the housing.   For
example, a woman who petitions for housing because her husband has
threatened violence cannot receive it until the need and reasons have
been verified by other authorities.

718   Hauser, William J.   Differences in Relative Resources, Familial
             Power and Spouse Abuse.   Palo Alto, Cal. : R and E Re-
             search Associates, Inc. , 1982.   104 p.
       The author's purpose was to determine the degree to which
the relative difference in resources between spouses affects their per-
ceptións of family power and, in turn, their utilization of abusive behavior as a viable resource.   This study, originally a doctoral dissertation for the Department of Sociology, University of Akron, points up
discrepancies between perceived power and resources and the use of
violence.   Useful study with few solid conclusions.   Need for more
research in resource theory recommended.

719   Hauser, William Joseph.   "Differences in Relative Resources,
             Familial Power and Spouse Abuse. "   Ph. D. dissertation,
             University of Akron, 1979.   145 p.   Abstract in Dissertation
             Abstracts International 40A (July 1979): 486.

720   Havemann, Paul L.   "Professional Education and the Violent
             Family. "   In Family Violence; An International and Inter-
             disciplinary Study.   Eds. John M. Eekelaar and Sanford N.
             Katz.   Toronto: Butterworths, 1978, pp. 231-8.
       Discusses professional training in law, social work, medi-
cine, etc.   Determined that cooperation between the schools and departments was minimal as it related to family violence in the United
Kingdom.   Not specifically concerned with spouse abuse, but relevant.

721   Haviland, Mary.   "Starting a Safe Home Network for Battered
             Women. "   In Fight Back!   Feminist Resistance to Male Vio-
             lence.   Eds. Frederique Delacoste and Felice Newman.
             Minneapolis: Cleis Press, 1981, pp. 120-2.
       Haviland urges establishment of community-based safe home
programs like the Park Slope Safe Homes Project.   The rationale and
advantages of this type of sheltering are provided.

722   Heale, William.   An Apologie for Women.   Oxford: J. Barnes,
             1609.   In Classics of English Legal History in the Modern
             Era.   New York: Garland, 1978.

723   " 'He's Got to Show Her Who's Boss': The National Women's
             Aid Federation Challenges a Man's Right to Batter. "   Spare
             Rib no. 69 (1978): 15-8.
       This article provides a detailed look at the philosophy of the
National Women's Aid Federation, an English feminist, socialist organization, as it pertains to spouse abuse.   Capitalist society abuses all
women, and spouse abuse is only one such manifestation.   The differences between the NWAF philosophy and that of the Chiswick Women's

Aid (Pizzey) is noted on occasion. Useful for understanding the British shelter movement.

724 Heintzelman, Carol Ann. "Differential Utilization of Selected Community Resources by Abused Women." DSW dissertation, Catholic University of America, 1980. 157 p. Abstract in Dissertation Abstracts International 41A (August 1980): 806-7.

725 "Help for Wife Abusers." Response to Violence and Sexual Abuse in the Family 2 (October 1978): 1-2.

726 "Helping Battered Women." Children Today 10 (January/February 1981): 30.

727 Hemmons, Willa M. "The Need for Domestic Violence Laws with Adequate Legal and Social Support Services." Journal of Divorce 4 (Spring 1981): 49-61.
New and stronger legislation should be enacted to protect victims of spouse abuse. Total success will not be achieved, however, until the economic, political, medical, educational, religious, and other community resources are mobilized in an all-out effort. Not much can be done if the problem goes undetected, so all service agencies that interact with such victims should be aware of the possibility that any client could be abused and proper referrals made if interviews prove the suspicion true. It is especially important that comprehensive programs are developed that minister to all aspects of the problem.

728 Hendricks, Jim. "Transactional Analysis and the Police: Family Disputes." Journal of Police Science and Administration 5, no. 4 (1977): 416-20.
The author, Assistant Professor of Corrections and Law Enforcement, School of Technical Careers, Southern Illinois University, discusses the importance of communication when handling family disturbances. He believes transactional analysis (TA) to be a useful way of improving interpersonal communications.

729 Hendricks-Matthews, Marybeth. "The Battered Woman: Is She Ready for Help?" Social Casework 63 (March 1982): 131-7.
The literature often refers to women who have left their husbands many times and did not take the advice of counselors or utilize all the services available to them. This author, doctoral candidate in counseling psychology, Kent State University, believes it imperative that counselors learn to tell when a battered wife is psychologically ready to take action to end the abuse, or leave the situation permanently. The counselor must be aware of the victim's locus of control, who the victim believes causes the conflict, and what stage of learned helplessness the victim is experiencing. Only when these are perceived accurately can the counselor know what help to offer.

730 Hendrix, Melva Jo. "Home Is Where the Hell Is." Family and Community Health 4 (August 1981): 53-9.

A general overview of the problem and the lack of responsiveness of the helping professions. Health professionals must be aware of the extent of the problem and be sensitive to such women when they seek assistance. They should also be aware of the various community services available and help prepare the women for using them.

731   Hendrix, Melva Jo; Gretchen E. LaGodna; and Cynthia A. Bohen. "The Battered Wife." American Journal of Nursing 78 (April 1978): 650-3.
      General article on abuse directed at educating nurses to the problem. The nature of the problem, theories about wife battering, and how to recognize an abuse victim are all discussed.

732   Hennon, Charles B. "Interpersonal Violence and Its Management by Cohabiting Couples." Paper presented at the Western Social Science Meetings, Tempe, Arizona, 1976.

733   Heppner, Mary J. "Counseling the Battered Wife: Myths, Facts, and Decisions." Personnel and Guidance Journal 56 (May 1978): 522-5.
      This article is directed at professional counselors with an aim at dispelling the myths that surround the problem of battered women. Group sessions, assertiveness training, and changes in attitudes and assistance by the various helping professions are seen as the beginning of resolution.

734   Herman, E. R. , and C. B. Pittman. "Interspousal Abuse: Identification and Intervention." Paper presented at the Conference on the Family: Perspectives for Intervention, Mt. Vernon Center for Community Mental Health, April 20, 1978.

735   Herrmann, Kenneth J. , Jr. "Getting Action from Social Agencies." Trooper 3 (July/August 1978): 55-7.
      The community is better served if the police and social workers can combine their efforts. Tips for doing so are provided.

736   Hewson, Martha. "Outlawing Marital Rape." McCall's 109 (October 1981): 48-9.
      The arguments for ending the exemption of husbands from prosecution are presented to a lay readership. The opinions of David Finkelhor and Joanne Schulman are used to support the major thesis.

737   Hien, Loke Kwok, and K. Alves. "Social Problems Encountered in the Rehabilitation of Physically-abused Women: Two Case Reports." Medical Journal of Malaysia 38 (September 1983): 232-6.

738   Higgins, J. G. "Social Services for Abused Wives." Social Casework 59 (May 1978): 266-71.
      The author's purpose was to review all the kinds of social services for battered wives that are presently offered in the United

States and Canada. His general belief is that while there is a wide variety of services available and more in the offing, additional assistance will be needed. Crisis lines, shelters, hospital emergency rooms, financial and legal aid, and counseling are all discussed.

739   "Highlights of the Domestic Violence Bill." Response to Violence in the Family 4 (October 1980): 2.

740   Hikida, Robin Rei. "Counselors' Responses to and Knowledge of Marital Violence." Ph.D. dissertation, Ohio State University, 1982. 126 p. Abstract in Dissertation Abstracts International 43B (April 1983): 3347.

741   Hilberman, Elaine. "Overview: The Wife-beater's Wife Reconsidered." American Journal of Psychiatry 137 (November 1980): 1336-47.
A detailed review of the victim of wife abuse and the literature which describes her. The psychological effects of the abuse are discussed along with treatment possibilities. One of the better descriptions of the wife.

742   Hilberman, Elaine, and Kit Munson. "Sixty Battered Women." Victimology: An International Journal 2, nos. 3-4 (1977-1978): 460-70.
Hilberman and Munson have written an excellent article describing the perceived characteristics of the wife beater and especially the victim. A list of symptoms and circumstances was compiled to aid the clinical staff of health clinics and hospitals in identifying victims of spouse abuse. Of the sixty cases referred for psychiatric help by the medical staff of a rural health clinic, 56 did not admit to being beaten until directly asked. The importance of frank questioning is stressed when abuse is suspected. The article especially focuses on the psychological impact of marital violence on the women.

743   Hilf, Michael Gary. "Marital Privacy and Spousal Rape." New England Law Review 16, no. 1 (1980): 31-44.
Hilf takes issue with the recent trend of states to allow prosecution of husbands for spousal rape. He argues that married persons have lesser expectations of personal autonomy and therefore spousal rape is less harmful to the victim than nonspousal rape. "While a married persons' interest in bodily integrity is not inconsiderable, a balance must be struck between the individual's interest in private autonomy and the public policy favoring spousal immunity." To allow prosecution for marital rape exposes marital privacy to public scrutiny, thereby jeopardizing chances for reconciliation. Most importantly it violates the constitutional right to marital privacy.

744   Hinchey, Frances S., and James R. Gavelek. "Empathic Responding in Children of Battered Mothers." Child Abuse and Neglect 6, no. 4 (1982): 395-401.
A study to determine the effects of observing parental violence was conducted with 32 pre-school children ages 4 to 5. Half had observed such violence while half had not. Those who came from

violent homes were less empathic and less able to recognize the emotional state of others. It suggests that this may contribute to the
tendency for children witnessing abuse to be abusers or victims later
themselves. The ability to develop intimate relationships may have
been inhibited. More study is recommended.

745   Hindman, Margaret H. "Family Violence." Alcohol Health and
        Reserach World 4 (Fall 1979): 2-11.
        This overview of the problem stresses child and spouse
abuse and its connection with alcoholism. Most research shows that
alcohol is often associated with abuse, but while some victims believe
alcohol use causes the abuse, few researchers do. Counselors treating alcoholics and their family must probe to determine if physical
abuse too is occurring and not wait for the clients to mention it. In
these situations the whole family must be treated.

746   Hirsch, Miriam F. Women and Violence. New York: Van Nos-
        trand Reinhold, 1981. 385 p.
        Discusses the many forms of violence directed at women.
One chapter "To Love, Cherish and Batter" deals with wife beating.
She hopes that since wife abuse is no longer a taboo topic, remedies
may be forthcoming.

747   Hofeller, Kathleen H. Battered Women, Shattered Lives. Palo
        Alto, Cal. : R and E Research Associates, 1983. 120 p.
        This is a highly readable account of spouse abuse based on
three detailed case histories of women from distinctly different backgrounds. A historical overview of wife beating, the social factors
which contribute to its occurrence, descriptions of the battered women
and the abuser, the interactive pattern of violent couples, and advice
about what to do if you are abused will be found here. Tips for those
hoping to make changes in society at large or provide assistance at
the community level are also given.

748   Hofeller, Kathleen H. Social, Psychological, and Situational Fac-
        tors in Wife Abuse. Palo Alto, Cal. : R and E Research
        Associates, Inc. 1982. 171 p.
        This study reviews the history of wife abuse and the atti-
tudes of church and society from the Greeks to the present. One hundred women, half battered and half with nonviolent marriages, were
interviewed and completed questionnaries to measure the social, psychological and environmental factors which might contribute to an
abusive relationship. Much interesting and useful information was
found. There seems to be no particular type of man likely to be an
abuser, but lower-class men with a need to dominate were more common. Violence by men is of two types. One is to attain a certain
goal, whereas other men use abuse to win total domination. The best
predicters of violence are violence in the background of both husband
and wife, inequality of status between the two and heavy alcohol use
by the men. Community response to the problem is definitely inadequate.

749   Hofeller, Kathleen Hartsough. "Social, Psychological and Situ-
        ational Factors in Wife Abuse." Ph. D. dissertation,

Claremont Graduate School, 1980.   216 p.   Abstract in
Dissertation Abstracts International 41B (July 1980): 408.

750   Hoffman, Lois Jean.   "A Study of Battered Women Who Resided
        at 'The Family Place': A Shelter in Dallas, Texas."   M. A.
        thesis, Sam Houston State University, 1980.   116 p.
        The purpose of this paper is to determine the service needed
by the battered women of Dallas, Texas, to be best assisted in the
transition to a nonabusive relationship.   The results of 100 questionnaires from women at "The Family Place" show that although shelters are helpful, most victims need continued aid after they leave
them.   Aids to insure an end of the violence are required if the victim returns home.   If she sets up a different household, economic,
psychological and other supports are necessary.   A total delivery system is required and not currently available in Dallas.

751   Hoffman, Maxine.   "Christianity, Battered Wives and Hope."
        Pentecostal Evangel no. 3466 (October 12, 1980): 4-6.
        Christian groups must provide services for abused wives
since feminists often do not provide Christian advice.   Divorce is
never the answer, but separation might be in very rare cases.

752   Hollis, Florence.   Women in Marital Conflict.   New York: Fam-
        ily Association of America, 1949.   236 p.
        A casework study of women seeking counseling regarding
unhappy marriages.   Concentration is on such problems as interfering
relatives, parental ties, difference in cultural background, and economic factors.   Spouse abuse receives fleeting attention in a chapter
entitled "The Need to Suffer."   Here the interpretation is the standard
female masochism explanation.

753   Holmes, Sally Ann.   "A Holistic Approach to the Treatment of
        Violent Families."   Social Casework 62 (December 1981):
        594-600.
        The author believes violence is taught in the home.   This
causes problems when family violence extends into the community as
in the case of abused children growing up and committing violence on
others.   Family abuse has traditionally been hidden because family
affairs were private and viewed as of no concern to the community.
If the community at large is to be protected, the necessary supports
must be provided to mitigate the creation of violent individuals.
Holmes, District Supervisor, Family Trouble Clinic, Detroit, Michigan, proposes that the police and social workers must work together
to provide the necessary supports that families and individuals need
to prevent violent outbursts.   A holistic approach recognizes violence
as a waste product of an inefficient society.

754   "Home Violence--Is There an Answer?"   BASW News 6 (October
        2, 1975): 409-13.
        In October 1974 the Professional Development and Practice
Committee of the British Association of Social Workers began a one-
year project to examine child and spouse abuse.   The discussion docu-
ment is the result.   Many questions are raised to provoke discussion
of the problem and possible remedies available.

755 Hopayian, K. , et al. "Battered Women Presenting in General
        Practice." Journal of the Royal College of General Practi-
        tioners 33 (August 1983): 506-7.

756 Horgan, Patrick T. "Legal Protection for the Victim of Marital
        Violence." The Irish Jurist 13 (Winter 1978): 233-53.
        Horgan, Lecturer in Law, University College, Cork, com-
pares the domestic violence legislation passed by English and Irish
legislatures in 1976. The law before and after this new enactment
is discussed. Both countries have taken an important step forward,
but the English version is thought to be much better and more effective.

757 Hornung, Carlton A. ; B. Claire McCullough; and Taichi Sugimoto.
        "Status Relationships in Marriage: Risk Factors in Spouse
        Abuse." Journal of Marriage and the Family 43 (August
        1981): 675-92.
        The authors Hornung and Sugimoto from the School of Medi-
cine and McCullough from the Computer Services Division, University
of South Carolina, first presented this paper at the annual meeting of
the American Sociological Association, August 1980, in New York.
Three levels of abuse were analyzed: psychological abuse, physical
aggression, and life-threatening violence. The differences in occupational and educational status and differences between the husband's
and wife's achievement were studied in conjunction with how this affected the marital relationship. The study produced several insights:
psychological abuse is more common than generally recognized, working women are more likely to be abused than housewives, and couples
are at a higher risk of psychological abuse when the woman has more
postgraduate education than the man. Regarding life-threatening force,
couples with a post-college-trained man and a woman with less education are at higher risk. A valuable study which is must reading for
serious scholars of spouse abuse.

758 "Hospital-based Family Services Help S. I. D. S. Families, Bat-
        tered Wives." Hospitals 53 (April 1, 1979): 32.
        Informative, albeit short, discussion of the Park Slope Safe
Homes Project in Brooklyn.

759 "Hospital Staff Learns to Identify Battered Women." Response
        to Violence and Sexual Abuse in the Family 2 (July 1979):
        2, 7.

760 Hotaling, Gerald T. "Attribution Processes in Husband-wife
        Violence." In The Social Causes of Husband-Wife Violence.
        Eds. Murray A. Straus and Gerald T. Hotaling. Minneapo-
        lis: University of Minnesota Press, 1980, pp. 136-54.
        Hotaling believes that "intent" is imputed rather than ob-
served. Therefore an action is intentionally aggressive or violent only
when the imputation is made. He concentrates on the proceses by
which minor issues between spouses escalate into violence. The transformation is seen as being facilitated by organizational or structural
features of the marriage bond. Much attention is dedicated to

attribution theory and mutual expectations. A revised version of this
paper was presented at the annual meeting of the National Council on
Family Relations, August 19-20, 1975.

761 Hotaling, Gerald T.   "Facilitating Violence: Why Intimates At-
         tribute Aggression. " Paper presented at the annual meeting
         of the National Council on Family Relations, August 19-20,
         1975. 27 p. Also Washington, D. C. : National Criminal
         Justice Reference Service, 1976. 1 microfiche.

762 Hotaling, Gerald T. , and Murray A. Straus. "Culture, Social
         Organization, and Irony in the Study of Family Violence. "
         In their The Social Causes of Husband-Wife Violence.   Min-
         neapolis: University of Minnesota Press, 1980, pp. 3-22.
         This is the introductory essay for the book and discusses
the ironies that spring from marriage where increased violence may
result from increased intimacy.   1)   Cultural norms which make family violence legitimate help to maintain the family system, but they
also perpetuate violence in that relationship.   2)   Those social organizational features which encourage intimacy also encourage a high
degree of intraspousal violence.   3)   The change from a patriarchal
sexist to a more equalitarian relationship may also lead to more violence.   Attempts to reduce the cause of violence may increase it
instead.

763 Houghton, Beverly D. "Domestic Violence Training: Treatment
         of Adult Victims of Family Violence. " New York State
         Nurses Association Journal 12 (December 1981): 25-33.
         This article is directed at emergency room nurses who may
come in contact with battered women.   Guidance is given in assisting
the nurse to recognize the abused and suggestions are presented for
ways to make the victim aware of shelters and other services available.

764 Houghton, Beverly. "Review of Research on Women Abuse. "
         Paper presented at the annual meeting of the American So-
         ciety of Criminology, Philadelphia, November 1979.

765 Houts, Marshall. They Asked for Death. New York: Cowles,
         1970. 241 p.
         The author, using case histories, suggests that in many
murders the victims played an important role in their own demise.
One chapter, "Risks of the Chronic Wife Beater," is relevant to the
problem of a wife killing an abusive husband.   He says that in a great
many cases the murderers are rather reasonable people, whereas the
victims were the discordant individuals.

766 "How to Avoid Zoning Problems. " Response to Violence in the
         Family 3 (November 1979): 2.
         Local laws and ordinances may sometimes present a problem
to those establishing shelters.   Practical advice is provided: hire an
attorney with zoning experience; locate near other facilities that clients
will need, such as hospitals, day care centers, etc. ; and work closely
with city officials.

767 How to Get Your Own Injunction Under the Domestic Violence Act
     1976. 2nd ed. Manchester: Manchester Law Centre; Lon-
     don: National Women's Aid Federation, 1978. 38 p.

768 "How to Help the Battered Female Patient." Practical Psychol-
     ogy for Physicians (January 1977): 11-4.
     This general article is directed at physicians who are vis-
ited by beaten wives seeking medical aid. Tips on how to approach
the victim and offer information regarding shelters and other resources
are provided along with addresses and phone numbers. By making
proper referrals the cycle of violence may be broken and a life saved.

769 "How Women Raised an Issue That Mass Media Was Ignoring:
     Women Battering." Media Report to Women 6 (May 1978):
     9.
     This is essentially a series of excerpts from the foreword
from the American edition of Pizzey's Scream Quietly or the Neighbors Will Hear and an afterword by Mildred Daley Pagelow. The
American press is attacked for ignoring the problem until they could
no longer do so.

770 Howard, Janet. "Battered and Raped: The Physical/Sexual
     Abuse of Women." In Fight Back! Feminist Resistance to
     Male Violence. Eds. Frederique Delacoste and Felice New-
     man. Minneapolis: Cleis Press, 1981, pp. 71-84.

771 Howard, Melissa. My Neighbor Is a Battered Woman. Albuquer-
     que: New Mexico Commission on the Status of Women, 1981.
     39 p.

772 Howard, Pamela F. Wife Beating: A Selected, Annotated Bibli-
     ography. San Diego, Cal. : Current Bibliography Series,
     1978. 57 p.
     This selected annotated bibliography includes monographs,
journal articles, newspaper articles, films and a list of agencies providing service to abused women.

773 Howard, R. M. "Rape of a Wife." Justice of the Peace and
     Local Government Review 118 (February 13, 1954): 99-100.
     Howard, Barrister-at-Law, discusses marital rape in the
context of a recent case, R. v. Miller, and finds that there is little
legal remedy for the wife. What little there is consists of a possible
charge of "cruelty" in divorce cases or assault, if there was bodily
injury. Otherwise the Hale doctrine, while not justifiable, remains
the recognized principle.

774 Howe, Mary E. "An Analysis of the Factors in Determining
     Police Response in Wife Abuse Cases." M. A. thesis, Uni-
     versity of Iowa, 1982.

775 Hudson, Walter W. , and Sally Rau McIntosh. "The Assessment
     of Spouse Abuse: Two Quantifiable Dimensions." Journal
     of Marriage and the Family 43 (November 1981): 873-85, 888.

Hudson, School of Social Work, Florida State University, and McIntosh, Department of Psychology, University of Hawaii, have constructed a new short-form scale called the Index of Spouse Abuse. It is to be used by clinicians to measure progress in treatment. Both physical and nonphysical abuse can be measured in the test which takes only five minutes to administer. Although it has a few shortcomings, the attempts to test it resulted in the opinion that the ISA was a highly reliable and valid measure of the degree or magnitude of the abuse women receive. The scales can be used with women and men victims, but the tests were conducted only with women. A copy of the test is included.

776   Huggins, Martha D., and Murray A. Straus. "Violence and the Social Structure as Reflected in Children's Books from 1850-1970." In The Social Causes of Husband-Wife Violence. Eds. Murray A. Straus and Gerald T. Hotaling. Minneapolis: University of Minnesota Press, 1980, pp. 51-67.
This survey of children's books shows that much violence is depicted but relatively little between members of the same family. As with television, children's books show an idealized view of the family. Violence usually occurs between strangers. The books also teach the lesson that violence is acceptable, if not advisable, for achieving some valued end, such as justice.

777   Hughes, Honore M. "Advocacy for Children of Domestic Violence: Helping the Battered Woman with Non-sexist Childrearing." Victimology: An International Journal 6, nos. 1-4 (1981): 262-71.
Hughes, Assistant Professor of Psychology, University of Arkansas, studied children at the Fayetteville Shelter and found that a major portion of the time spent in advocacy involved helping with parenting. It is believed that nonsexist childrearing is important and must be addressed at two levels, the parent-child and the societal. The results of the experience suggest that even short-term exposure to these ideas provide the residents with new ways of dealing with violence.

778   Hughes, Honore M. "Brief Interventions with Children in a Battered Women's Shelter: A Model Preventative Program." Family Relations: Journal of Applied Family and Child Studies 31 (October 1982): 495-502.
This intervention model requires four separate points of approach: the children themselves, their mothers, their schools, and the staff at the shelter. The results, though difficult to evaluate, show children to be quite resilient and this program helps them quickly get on with the business of living.

779   Hughes, Honore M., and Susan J. Barad. "Changes in the Psychological Functioning of Children in a Battered Women's Shelter: A Pilot Study." Victimology: An International Journal 7, nos. 1-4, (1982): 60-8.
The authors studied 12 children who stayed at a shelter for battered women twelve days or longer. It was thought that if a violent

home life caused the children to have social functioning problems, re-
moval from that atmosphere would help. After three weeks, the anxiety level of the children was reduced substantially, but self-esteem
and behavioral problems had not improved.

780   Hughes, Honore M. , and Susan J. Barad. "Psychological Func-
          tioning of Children in a Battered Women's Shelter: A Pre-
          liminary Investigation." American Journal of Orthopsychiatry
          53 (July 1983): 525-31.
          "This study of the psychological functioning of 65 child resi-
dents of a battered women's shelter provided data on differences between children exposed to domestic violence and normative groups,
differences between boys and girls whose mothers have been physically
abused, and differences in the way child behavior was perceived by
mothers and staff." Results indicate school-age boys are more aggressive than girls; the preschool children have lower self-esteem than
peers, while others were closer to their normative peers; and mothers
viewed their children more negatively than did the staff.

781   Hughes, Honore, et al. A Training Manual for Children's Serv-
          ices in Battered Women's Shelters. Fayetteville, Ark. :
          Project for Victims of Family Violence, 1982. 160 p.

782   Hulett, Linda Louis. "Learned Helplessness in Battered Women."
          M. A. thesis, Southern Methodist University, 1979. 57 p.
          Three groups of women (20 battered, 10 nonbattered) from
the Fort Worth, Texas, area were studied. Of the battered group,
ten were separated from their abusers and ten were still living with
them. The purpose of the study was to determine how learned helplessness affected each group. Results indicate women who stayed
were more external in locus of control, which may have contributed
to their being ineffective in controlling their lives. These women
also tended to be more depressed and anxious than the others. Shelter workers then must pay attention to the learned helplessness of the
victims and help them overcome it. The appendix includes the survey
instruments used.

782a Hunt, Morton. "Legal Rape." Family Circle (January 9, 1979):
          14, 37-8, 125.
          A general discussion of marital rape for a popular reader-
ship. Rape by a spouse is as traumatic as rape by a stranger, but
goes unrecognized as a crime. At most it is seen by society as
brutish, not criminal.

783   Husain, A. ; D. E. Anasseril; and P. W. Harris. "A Study of
          Young-age and Mid-life Homicidal Women Admitted to a
          Psychiatric Hospital for Pre-trial Evaluation." Canadian
          Journal of Psychiatry 28 (March 1983): 109-13.

784   "Husband Cannot Be Guilty of Raping His Wife." Dickinson
          Law Review 82 (Spring 1978): 608-16.
          In this article the case of Smith v. Smith is reviewed. The
New Jersey court questioned the common-law principle that a husband

could not be found guilty of raping his wife. The court did uphold the
state rape statute which would not allow for such prosecution, but it
did strongly oppose that principle. The various rationales for defense
of the statute were discussed but without the sympathy of the author.
The legislature is put on notice by the courts to change the law.

785 "Husband Convicted of Raping Wife." Response to Violence in
     the Family 3 (November 1977): 4.
     A short discussion of the Chretien case in Massachusetts.

786-7 "Husband Sues Shelter That Aided Wife." Response to Violence
       in the Family 3 (October 1979): 4.

788 "I Was a Battered Wife." Good Housekeeping 188 (May 1979):
     34, 37-8, 40, 42.
     An anonymous personal account by a woman who endured
abuse for several years before finally leaving. She now has few if
any regrets about her decision although recognizing the road ahead is
not easy.

789 Iazzo, Anthony Nicolas. "The Attitudes Toward Men Scale."
     Ph. D. dissertation, California School of Professional Psy-
     chology, Fresno, 1982. 111 p. Abstract in Dissertation
     Abstracts International 43B (September 1982): 853.

790 Iazzo, Anthony N. "The Construction and Validation of Attitudes
     Toward Men Scale." Psychological Record 33 (Summer
     1983): 371-8.
     The Attitudes Toward Men Scale (AMS) was developed and
tested using rape victims, lesbians, feminists, and battered women.
The results show all groups, including battered women have a more
negative attitude toward men than the general population of adult wom-
en. The cause, however, is their experiences, not their own characteristics or psychopathology.

791 Illinois Coalition Against Domestic Violence. Five Year Report:
     1978-1983. Springfield, Ill.: The Coalition, [1983]. 12 p.

792 Illinois Domestic Violence Act: Finally--Relief for Victims of the
     Hidden Crime. [Springfield: Illinois Coalition Against Do-
     mestic Violence, 1983]. 5 p.

793 Illinois Domestic Violence Act: Public Act 82-621 as Amended
     by Public Acts 82-888 and 83-0101. Springfield: Illinois
     Coalition Against Domestic Violence, [1983]. 16 p.

794 "Incidents of Battered Wives Said Under-reported." Psychiatric
     News 13, no. 10 (1978): 25-9, 31.
     This news article synthesizes the ideas of Elissa P. Benedek,
M. D., and especially Martin Symonds, M. D. The latter's speech was
called "Psychodynamics of Violence Prone Marriages" and was delivered
at the annual meeting of the Association for the Advancement of Psychoanalysis. Provocative overview. These results were also published
in the American Journal of Psychoanalysis later in 1978.

795 Inglis, M. "Wife Assaulting--A Social Ill Rediscovered." Paper
     presented at the Conference on Women and Health, Welling-
     ton, New Zealand, 1977.

796 Inter-action Advisory Service. Battered Women and the Law.
     Rev. ed. (Service Handbook, 3.) London: Author, 1975.
     31 p.

797 International Association of Chiefs of Police. Training Key #245
     [Wife Beating]. In Battered Women: A Psychosociological
     Study of Domestic Violence. Ed. Maria Roy. New York:
     Van Nostrand Reinhold, 1977, pp. 144-53.
     This information guide is prepared for police officers who
must deal with and respond to domestic disturbance calls. It stresses
that abuse is to be treated as a crime and that the victim needs assistance. The husband often needs more than a talking to and a walk
around the block. A discussion guide is included.

798 International Association of Chiefs of Police. Training Key #246
     [Investigation of Wife Beating]. In Battered Women: A Psy-
     chosociological Study of Domestic Violence. Ed. Maria Roy.
     New York: Van Nostrand, 1977, pp. 153-64. Also in Shel-
     tering Battered Women. Ed. Albert R. Roberts. New
     York: Springer, 1981, pp. 123-32.
     The complaint is often made that the police routinely refuse
to give meaningful assistance to battered women. The advice given
to police by the International Association is "...one fact should always
remain clear and should be the basis for police action. The wife has
been physically assaulted and must be treated as a victim of a crime.
The husband is a violent lawbreaker who should not be shielded from
legal action." The Training Key then proceeds to explain step-by-step
the officer's duties and responsibilities. Basic guide for police officers who may confront domestic violence.

799 " 'It Can't Happen Here'--But It Does." Graduate Woman 75
     (May-June, 1981): 31.
     A news item regarding the establishment of Villa de Fidelis
as an abuse shelter in Prescott, Arizona. A survey of need prior to
its establishment showed over 600 cases of reported abuse in six
months. Some details regarding its purpose and operation are included.

800 "An Interview with Sara Smith--One Woman's Experience with
     the Cycle of Violence." In Women and Crime in America.
     Ed. Lee H. Bowker. New York: Macmillan, 1981, pp.
     320-8.
     Sara Smith (a fictitious name) killed her abusing husband and
was subsequently sent to a state mental institution. She tells how she
was abused as a child and later as a wife. Her husband had also suffered abuse as a child. Her case has ramifications for social agencies
dealing with abused women and children. The interview took place in
February, 1979.

801 " 'It's Outrageous': Old Myths Plague Battered Wives." LEAA

Newsletter 6 (October 1977): 1, 19.
A newsy account of abuse and funding programs available
from the Law Enforcement Assistance Administration.

802 Iyer, Patricia W. "The Battered Wife." Nursing 80 10 (July
     1980): 53, 55.
     Provides a general discussion of spouse abuse and why wom-
en stay with the abuser. The author then gives the nursing readership advice on how to identify victims of abuse and how to treat them.

803 Jackson, Stevi, and Peter Rushton. "Victims and Villains: Im-
     ages of Women in Accounts of Family Violence." Women's
     Studies International Forum 5, no. 1 (1982): 17-28.
     The authors contend that the real cause of abuse and family
violence lies in the power structure of the family itself. Gayford,
Gelles, Goode and others all fall victim to an inability to see that.
Instead they blame individuals and their upbringing. Either abusers
are abnormal or inadequate as individuals or have been raised in abnormal families. Too many social scientists also want to attribute
the problem to women or class and avoid any serious examination of
the power structure in the family where the problem really begins.

804 Jackson, Susan. "In Search of Equal Protection for Battered
     Wives." Paper presented to the Conference of Mayors on
     Victimology, 1975.

805 Jacobs, Phillip E. , and Pearl Levine. "Alcoholism and Spouse
     Abuse." In Identification and Treatment of Spouse Abuse;
     Health and Mental Health Agency Roles, Proceedings of a
     Conference. Eds. Abraham Lurie and Elizabeth B. Quitkin.
     New York: Editors, 1981, pp. 159-77.

806 Jacobson, Beverly. "Battered Women." Collegiate Women's
     Career Magazine 7 (Winter 1979/80): 23-4, 26-8.
     The author, a free-lance writer, has written a good general
overview of the problem of spouse abuse using the research of Del
Martin, Murray Straus, Erin Pizzey, and others, along with the
Brooklyn Legal Services files of Marjory Fields. The historical and
social background of the problem, characteristics of abuser and victim, efforts to end the violence, legal concerns and practices, police
interaction, role of the Family Court of New York and other elements
of the problem are discussed. In the last analysis nothing significant
will happen to provide relief until the criminal justice system lives up
to its moral and legal obligations to women.

807 Jacobson, Beverly. "Battered Women: The Fight to End Wife
     Beating." Civil Rights Digest 9 (Summer 1977): 2-11.
     General discussion of spouse abuse and the need for legal
reform to deal with the question.

808 Jacobson, Rebecca Hanson. "Changing Causal Attributions and

Person Perceptions in a Case of Wife Abuse." Ph. D. dissertation, University of Georgia, 1982. 180 p. Abstract in Dissertation Abstracts International 43B (May 1983): 3734.

809 Jacques, Karen N. "Perceptions and Coping Behaviors of Anglo-American and Mexican Immigrant Battered Women: A Comparative Study." Ph. D. dissertation, United States International University, 1981. 488 p. Abstract in Dissertation Abstracts International 42B (June 1982): 4933.

810 Jaffe, Natalie. Assaults on Women: Rape and Wife-beating. Public Affairs Pamphlet, no. 579. New York: Public Affairs Committee, Inc., 1980. 29 p.
A good overview of the problems of rape and wife abuse. Each is dealt with separately although some comparisons are made. Abuse victims and abusers are described, along with what seems to cause it and what can be done to help remedy the problem. For a popular readership.

811 Jaffe, Peter, and Judy Thompson. "The Family Consultant Service with the London (Ontario) Police Force." In Family Violence; An International and Interdisciplinary Study. Eds. John M. Eekelaar and Sanford N. Katz. Toronto: Butterworths, 1978, pp. 216-23.
The Family Consultant Service was set up to provide assistance to the police in cases of family crisis. The consultants are available evenings and weekends when most other social agencies are not available. These consultants are called in by police when making calls for domestic disputes. The service assists with many problems, but spouse abuse is the single most frequent. Novel and interesting service.

812 Jaffe, Peter; Judy Thompson; and Jim Rae. "The Responsibility of the Police in Domestic Violence." In Domestic Violence: Issues and Dynamics. Ed. Vincent D'Oyley. Toronto: Ontario Institute for Studies in Education, 1978, pp. 85-90.
The attitudes of the police officer working with domestic disputes are reviewed and the concept of the Family Consultant Service is promoted. This service provides for five individuals from several mental health disciplines to be available at all times to the police for immediate consultation in crisis situations. This service would be more widespread except for lack of financial support and resistance of some police and community leaders to this method of dealing with the problem.

813 James, Ed. "Treatment Approach with Abused Spouses in a Military Setting." Paper presented at the Biennial Army Social Work Symposium, San Antonio, Texas, March 1980.

814 Jansen, Mary A., and Judith Meyers-Abell. "Assertive Training for Battered Women: A Pilot Program." Social Work 26 (March 1981): 164-5.
The authors, both Associate Professors of Psychology,

Jansen at Purdue University and Meyers-Abell at the University of Dayton, describe a pilot program of basic communication skills and assertiveness training in a support group environment. The fifteen participants had all been abused by husbands or boyfriends and all had extremely low self-esteem. The authors stress a special program on the grounds that "assertiveness training for battered women that does not address the problems of women who have never felt worthwhile and secure in their own behavior is worthless at best and harmful at worst."

815 Jayewardene, C. H. S. "The Nature of Homicide: Canada 1961-1970." In Crime in Canadian Society. Eds. Robert A. Silverman and James J. Teevan, Jr. Toronto: Butterworths, 1975, pp. 279-310.
         Detailed charts and analysis of homicide during the decade of the 1960's. There is much information on the family relationship of the killer and the victim, but none relative to spouse abuse precipitating the incident.

816 Jeffery, Linda, and Jan Pahl. "Battered Women and the Police." Paper presented at the annual conference of the British Sociological Association, April, 1979.

817 Jeffords, Charles R. , and R. Thomas Dull. "Demographic Variations in Attitudes Towards Marital Rape Immunity." Journal of Marriage and the Family 44 (August 1982): 755-62.
         The authors, Jeffords of Wichita State University and Dull of Memphis State University, surveyed 1,300 Texans by mail regarding the marital rape exemption. Two basic issues were examined, the public attitude toward that immunity and the impact of demographic variation on the issue. Only 35 percent felt a wife should be allowed to accuse her husband of rape. They tended to be single younger white females. Since Texas is a conservative state it may be that this question might receive a more positive response in some other states.

818 Jens, K. S. , and L. Museo. "Group Therapy with Battered Women." Paper presented at the meeting of the Colorado Mental Health Conference, Vail, Colorado, September 1977.

819 Jensen, Rita Henley. "Battered Women and the Law." Victimology: An International Journal 2, nos. 3-4 (1977-78): 585-90.
         Discusses the plight of abused wives when they seek help and protection from the criminal justice system. Several examples of abuse and case histories are given. Discusses the New York law.

820 Jenson, M. Katherine. "State v. Thomas: The Final Blow to Battered Women?" Ohio State Law Journal 43 (Spring 1982): 491-511.
         This is a discussion of the Ohio Supreme Court case State v. Thomas, which ruled that the trial judge had not made a reversible error by excluding expert testimony regarding battered-wife syndrome. Thomas had been convicted of murder in 1978 after killing her abusive

common-law husband. The Supreme Court using the Ohio test for
relevancy and the Ohio Rules of Evidence felt the expert testimony
should not be included. This ruling only serves to confuse the issue
since the court actually went beyond the question at hand. Judges
who disagree with this decision should feel free to allow such expert
testimony in the future.

821   Jeter, Verona Middleton. "Sheltering the Battered Women." In
        Identification and Treatment of Spouse Abuse: Health and
        Mental Health Agency Roles, Proceedings of a Conference.
        Eds. Abraham Lurie and Elizabeth B. Quitkin. New York:
        Editors, 1981, pp. 61-7.

822   Jobling, Megan. "Battered Wives: A Survey." Social Service
        Quarterly 47 (April/June 1974): 142-4, 146.
        During 1972-3 the Citizens Advisory Bureau in England re-
ceived nearly two million requests for advice and information regarding abuse. The extent of the problem, the men and women involved,
effects on the children, and the availability of assistance are all
briefly reviewed.

823   Johnson, Bernice, and Jennifer Baker-Fleming. "Working with
        the Individual." In Identification and Treatment of Spouse
        Abuse; Health and Mental Health Agency Roles, Proceedings
        of a Conference. Eds. Abraham Lurie and Elizabeth B.
        Quitkin. New York: Editors, 1981, pp. 133-44.

824   Johnson, Billy, and Marilyn Trimble. "Battered Women: Some
        Relevant Variables." Free Inquiry in Creative Sociology 8
        (November 1980): 150-4.
        After a general overview of the problem, the authors reveal
the results of a six-month study at the YWCA Women's Resource Center in Oklahoma City. Data were collected from calls for help from
86 women. Results indicate the role of alcohol was overwhelming, 85
percent of the women were unemployed, 88 percent were mothers and
33 percent had no access to transportation. Many wanted only counseling and a third wanted legal advice. Both the abuser and the victim
are seen as having low self-esteem and being locked in a battering
relationship which reaffirms their "loser" positions in society.

825   Johnson, Carolyn; John Ferry; and Marjorie Kravitz. Spouse
        Abuse: A Selected Bibliography. Rockville, Md. : U.S.
        Department of Justice, Law Enforcement Assistance Admin-
        istration, National Institute of Law Enforcement and Criminal
        Justice, 1978. 61 p.
        A good selected bibliography with long and detailed annotations.
The purpose is to provide interested individuals with information on
the nature of the problem and role of law enforcement in intervention.
One of the better early attempts to draw relevant literature together.

826   Johnson, John M. "New Research in Family Violence." Journal
        of Family Issues 2 (December 1981): 387-90.
        Much new research is being done on family violence and

this author introduces three articles concerned with spouse abuse that
add to that knowledge. The articles by Mildred Pagelow [1196],
Kathleen Ferrero [476], and R. Emerson Dobash and Russell P. Dobash [357] are listed elsewhere in this bibliography under the authors'
names.

827 Johnson, John M. "Program Enterprise and Official Cooperation
     in the Battered Women's Shelter Movement." American Be-
     havioral Scientist 24 (July-August 1981): 827-42.
     Johnson, from Arizona State University, argues the impor-
tance and influence of welfare state corruption, social control enterprise and professional enterprise on the rapid acceptance of the shelter as a service for battered women. He also points out how any
feminist ideological influence is quickly eliminated by those who supply
the funding. Official government funding is necessary in most cases
because the shelters are so expensive to open and operate.

828 Johnson, Margie N. , and Yvonne Boren. "Sexual Knowledge and
     Spouse Abuse: A Cultural Phenomenon." Issues in Mental
     Nursing 4, no. 3 (1982): 217-31.
     Johnson, Associate Professor, Psychiatric-Mental Health
Nursing, College of Nursing, Texas Woman's University, Denton, and
Boren, Consultant Psychiatric Mental Health Nurse, hypothesize that
there may be a relationship between the sexual knowledge of a couple
and the occurrence of spouse abuse. Fifty-nine women were tested
with the Sex Knowledge and Attitude Test (SKAT) and the Method of
Conflict Resolution Questionnaire (MCRQ). Support for the hypothesis
was not found.

829 Johnson, Sally. "Abused Wives Strike Back." Majority Report
     4 (May 3, 1975): 9.

830 Johnson, Sally. "What About Battered Women?" Majority Re-
     port 4 (February 8, 1975): 1, 4.

831 Johnson, Vivien. "Children and Family Violence: Refuges."
     In Violence in the Family: A Collection of Conference
     Papers. Ed. Jocelynne A. Scutt. Canberra: Australian
     Institute of Criminology, 1980, pp. 195-203.

832 Johnston, Pamela. "Attack from the Right." In Fight Back!
     Feminist Resistance to Male Violence. Eds. Frederique
     Delacoste and Felice Newman. Minneapolis: Cleis Press,
     1981, pp. 85-92.
     Ms. Johnston was coordinator of a battered women's shelter
in Lawrence, Kansas, from August 1979 to May 1980. This article
details the struggle between the shelter leadership and a conservative
community group, the Pro-Family Forum.

833 Jones, Ann. "When Battered Women Fight Back." Barrister
     9 (Fall 1982): 13-5, 48-51.
     Jones, in a very readable manner, describes the legal prob-
lems facing women who kill their abusive mates. The male bias of

the police, courts, prosecutors and, indeed, the whole legal system
is clearly portrayed. The underlying assumptions regarding sex roles,
rights and privileges need to undergo serious rethinking by male pre-
servers of law and order. Ironically, focusing solely on the battered
woman syndrome may result in worse treatment by the courts.

834   Jones, Ann. Women Who Kill. New York: Holt, Rinehart, and
          Winston, 1980. 408 p.
          Jones has produced here an intriguing study of women who
have killed and the reasons why. Chapter 6 "Totaling Women" studies
women who have killed their abusing husbands. She includes discussions of the cases of Roxanne Gay, Francine Hughes, Jennifer Patri,
Kathy Thomas, and others. She is very critical of press coverage
which gave much space to women who received light or no prison sentences and ignored those who received heavy sentences. Contrary to
the belief of some that these women tend to be feminists or "libbers,"
Jones contends that they are more likely to be desperate and disillu-
sioned proponents of Marabel Morgan's The Total Woman.

835   Jones, Carolyn Okell, and Geraldine Peacock. "The Family."
          In Conflict in the Family: A Continuing Education Course
          (Block 2, Units 3-4) Open University. Milton Keynes:
          Open University Press, 1980. 63 p.

836   Jones, Val. "Abused Women's Shelter Opens." Off Our Backs
          8 (December 1978): 4.
          A description of the efforts that were required to establish
"My Sisters Place," a Washington, D. C. , shelter.

837   Jones, Valle. "Federal Legislation Concerning Spouse Abuse."
          Victimology: An International Journal 2, nos. 3-4 (1977-78):
          623-7.
          An explanation of the Boggs-Steers and Mikulski Bills intro-
duced in 1977. Both are appropriations bills which would provide
funds for research, direct services, clearinghouse activities, and coordination among federal agencies. Their shortcomings are also described.

838   Jones, Valle. "The Washington D. C. Conference on Battered
          Women." Victimology: An International Journal 1, no. 4
          (1976): 581-5.
          A conference on battered women was held in Washington,
D. C. , in November 1974 and was attended by about 200 people. Jones
details the events of the conference. Lisa Leghorn was the keynote
speaker, debunking alcohol and economic pressure as causes of wife
abuse. Instead it is the powerlessness of women and the disdain men
have for women that makes wife beating an occupational hazard of
housewives. The various panel discussions served an educational
function for attendees.

839   Jorgenson, Anne D'Arcy. The Psyche Squad (Therapist on
          Housecall for Domestic Violence). Dayton, Ohio: P. P. I.
          Publishing, n. d.

840   Jorgenson, Anne D'Arcy. The Wifebeaters Guide to Rage Writ-
         ing Therapy. Dayton, Ohio: P. P. I. Publishing, 1980.
         52 p.

841   "Jury Selection in Battered Women's Trials." Response to Vio-
         lence and Sexual Abuse in the Family 2 (January 1979): 5.
         Tips are provided to lawyers interested in selecting the best
and most empathetic jurors.

842   Kaas, Carolyn Wilkes. "The Admissibility of Expert Testimony
         on Battered Woman Syndrome in Support of a Claim of Self-
         defense." Connecticut Law Review 15 (Fall 1982): 121-39.
         Kaas considers the question of expert testimony regarding
Battered Woman Syndrome as it applies to Connecticut self-defense
law. Four roles that expert testimony can play and specific applications are described. The author concludes that such testimony is
relevant to a woman's claim of self-defense and that the syndrome is
beyond the understanding of the average juror. It should therefore
be allowed in Connecticut.

843   Kabakov, Marsha, and Carol Levenson. Summary of Research
         on Wife Abuse Programs and Guidelines. Boston: Massa-
         chusetts Department of Public Welfare, 1978. 14 p.
         This is a request and justification for priority funding by the
Massachusetts Department of Public Welfare for wife abuse programs
in the state. Emergency shelters should be given top priority.

844   Kahn, Marvin W. , et al. "Wife Beating and Cultural Context:
         Prevalence in an Aboriginal and Islander Community in
         Northern Australia." American Journal of Community Psy-
         chology 8 (December 1980): 727-31.
         While spouse beating may not be acceptable to the middle
class of western society, it does not follow that other cultures view
it similarly. An investigation of aboriginals in Australia indicates
wife beating to be a social norm--neither unusual, nor abnormal, and
in fact an accepted part of the living pattern. To attempt to provide
service and interfere with that pattern may disrupt the established
culture. Attempts to change must come from within the culture itself,
not from the outside.

845   Kalmuss, Debra S. "The Attribution of Responsibility in a Wife-
         abuse Context." Victimology: An International Journal 4,
         no. 2 (1979): 284-91.
         Kalmuss' study explores the attitude of the general public
toward wife abuse. Using several variations on the same vignette,
responses to over 330 questionnaires from males and females over
eighteen years old from the Detroit SMA were analyzed. Over 25
percent attributed at least partial responsibility to the wife/victim.
Women seemed to do so at a rate similar to men. The author believes that the psychological and economic dependence of the wife on
the marital relationship explains why women stay with abusers. Attri-
butional patterns must be considered when abuse programs are developed.

846 Kalmuss, Debra S. , and Murray A. Straus. "Feminist, Political and Economic Determinants of Wife Abuse Services. "
In The Dark Side of Families: Current Family Violence Research. Eds. David Finkelhor, et al. Beverly Hills, Cal. :
Sage Publications, 1981, pp. 363-76.
   More affluent states, as well as those with more liberal political traditions might be expected to provide more spouse abuse services. This study indicates, however, that the level of feminist organization in a state is the strongest determinant of the amount of service
to abuse victims. Grass-roots program development will probably be
a more effective strategy than traditional lobbying efforts.

847 Kalmuss, Debra, and Murray Straus. "Ideological and Social
Organizational Factors Associated with State and Local Response to Domestic Violence. " Paper presented at the annual
meeting of the Academy of Criminal Justice Sciences, Philadelphia, March 1981.

848 Kalmuss, Debra S. , and Murray A. Straus. "Wife's Marital
Dependency and Wife Abuse. " Journal of Marriage and the
Family 44 (May 1982): 277-86.
   The authors investigate the relationship between dependency,
both actual and perceived, of wives on their husbands and the amount
and severity of spouse abuse. Results indicate that women who are
subjectively dependent will tolerate much minor abuse, but this is also
true of most women. However, severe abuse will only be tolerated
by those who really are economically dependent upon their husbands.
The dependence does not cause the violence, but it does increase the
likelihood of its being tolerated. In short, the study indicates that it
is economics not psychological dependency which keeps women in severely abusive marriages.

849 Kamisher, Michele. "Battered Women. " The Women's Yellow
Pages: Original Sourcebook for Women. Eds. Carol Edry
and Rosalyn Gerstein. New England Edition. Boston: The
Public Works, 1978, pp. 114-8.
   A good overview of the question using the research of J. J.
Gayford, M. Straus, R. J. Gelles, J. E. O'Brien, G. Levinger, and
many others. Is violence normal? why are women beaten? why do
victims stay? why does he do it? and other questions are considered.
The solution is seen in an equalitarian society, but shelters are needed
in the meantime.

850 Kane, Maureen. Male Violence Against Women. Dayton, Ohio:
P. P. I. Publishing, 1981. 50 p.

851 Kappel, Sybille, and Erika Leuteritz. "Wife Battering in the
Federal Republic of Germany. " Victimology: An Interna-
tional Journal 5, nos. 2-4 (1980): 225-39.
   This article outlines the development of the German Women's
Aid Movement and the role shelters play.

852 Karl, Marilee. "Refuges in Europe. " Victimology: An International Journal 2, nos. 3-4 (1977-78): 257-66.

Descriptions of the shelter movement in Great Britain, Holland, France, Norway, and Switzerland along with addresses and recommendations regarding resources are provided. The general climate for providing shelter in each country is described. In most it is less than positive.

853   Kashimer, Michele. "Where to Get Help." MS 5 (August 1976): 97-8.
This is a listing by state of shelters and organizations which will assist battered women.

854   Katzman, Elaine. "Interview with a Battered Wife." Do It Now 9 (June 1976): 7.

855   Kaunitz, Paul E. "Sadomasochistic Marriages." Medical Aspects of Human Sexuality 11 (February 1977): 66-9, 74, 80.
Kaunitz, Clinical Professor of Psychiatry, Yale University School of Medicine details four cases of spouse abuse and labels them sadomasochistic marriages. Dealing with them requires patience, skill, luck, and temerity. One should avoid taking sides. The problem in dealing with these marriages is the masochist's need to blame all the problems on the other and the sadist's disdainful disclaiming of any role in the problem. Both partners contribute to the continuance of the beatings.

856   Kaye, J. W. "Outrages on Women." North British Review 26 (May 1856): 233-56.
This mid-nineteenth-century English article paints an interesting portrait of wife beating at that time. A number of solutions are proposed including a bill to punish wife beating with flogging. In the last analysis the author suggests that women should be trained for employment to make themselves independent. When this is done wife abuse will disappear.

857   Kelly, Janis. "On Powerlessness." Off Our Backs 10 (October 1980): 14.
The August 8, 1980, conference in Washington, D.C. "Poverty, Police Brutality, and Woman Abuse" is briefly described.

858   Kemp, Martin; Betty Knightly; and Michael Norton. Battered Women and the Law. Rev. ed. London: Inter-action Inprint, 1975. 31 p.

859   Kemp, Mary Ellen. Domestic Violence Handbook. [Raleigh]: Domestic Violence Project, North Carolina Council on the Status of Women, 1981. 14 p.

860   Kenny, D. , and J. Q. Thompson. Refuges for Battered Women in London--Provision and Need. London: Greater London Council, 1978. 35 p.
Since the first English refuge was established in 1972 by Erin Pizzey, many more have been opened. This report describes the current need and shows how it is being met. The relationships between

refuge administrations and local authorities are detailed, along with
the effects of local housing policies on the operation of the shelters.

861 "Kentucky Survey Documents Incidence of Spouse Abuse." Re-
       sponse to Violence in the Family 3 (December 1979): 3.
     A recounting of the study A Survey of Spousal Violence
Against Women in Kentucky by Mark A. Schulman.

862 Kerr, Mary Ann. "The Social Networks of Twenty Battered
       Women." M. A. thesis, University of Kansas, 1982. 124 p.
     The notion that social isolation is often a condition associ-
ated with spouse abuse is widely accepted, but not often studied or
proved. This author investigated social networks of 20 women from
two shelters in two Southern towns to determine their depth and
breadth. The results indicate that half of the sample were isolated
through deliberate attempts by the husband and that the majority of
the victims were dissatisfied with their network interaction. The networks turned out to be small and dominated by relatives. The kinsmen
were often not of much assistance for the problems dealing with abuse.
The help provided by the shelters was needed for that part of the victim's life.

863 Kessler, Gail. "Some People Are Just Born Caring." Quest 3
       (June 1979): 9-10.
     The focus of this article is the Hackensack, N. J. , shelter
for battered women, "Shelter Our Sisters" (SOS), founded by Sandy
Ramos. This shelter was in the founder's own home for several years
until she was finally able to obtain state funding in 1978.

864 Ketterman, Thomas, and Marjorie Kravitz. Police Crisis Inter-
       vention; A Selected Bibliography. Washington, D. C. : Na-
       tional Institute of Law Enforcement and Criminal Justice,
       U. S. Department of Justice, 1978. 40 p.
     This bibliography lists 63 items related to police intervention
in family violence situations. Monographs, journal articles, films,
pamphlets, etc. are included. The abstracts are well done, and the
materials are available from the National Criminal Justice Reference
Service. Although becoming dated, it still has value to researchers.

865 Khan, Anwar N. "Better Law for Battered Wives." Solicitors
       Journal 122, nos. 24, 25 (1978): 391-2, 409-12.
     This two-part article discusses new changes in battered
wives' legal situation in Australia. Police were given more arrest
powers in these cases. Still needed is the extension of protection to
unmarried couples.

866 Khan, Anwar, and Jeanette Hacket. "The Law and the Battered
       Wife." Legal Service Bulletin 3 (1978): 5-7.
     A general discussion of spouse abuse with special attention
to the legal situation in Australia. The Family Act (1975) did give
some relief, but not enough. Police should have more powers in domestic disputes and the law should apply to cohabiting couples.

867   Kiebert, Irene, and Susan Schechter, eds.   Park Slope Safe
        Homes Project; Technical Assistance Manual.   How to Set
        Up a Community-based Program for Battered Women and
        Their Families. [New York]: The Project, 1980.   153 p.
        This is a practical guide on how to set up a shelter in your
community based on the experiences of Park Slope Safe Homes Project
in Brooklyn, begun in 1976.   Especially useful are the many forms
which others can quickly revise to meet their own needs, or use as
they are.   Cooperation with other public and private agencies and services is stressed.   Comprehensive and well-planned guide.   A videotape
is also available.

868   Kieviet, Thomas G. "The Battered Wife Syndrome: A Potential
        Defense to a Homicide Charge." Pepperdine Law Review 6
        (Fall 1978): 213-29.
        Kieviet discusses the legal remedies available to battered
women.   He finds them to be inadequate.   For battered women who
have suffered the "last straw" and kill the abuser, a number of ideas
are suggested for consideration by the defense.

869   Kilgore, Nancy. Every Eighteen Seconds; A Personal Journey
        into Domestic Violence. 2nd ed. Eugene, Oregon: L. I. F. T.
        Press, 1983.   87 p.
        Personal account of the feelings, despair, and anguish of
being a battered wife.   Written in the form of letters to her son.

870   "A Killing Excuse; Expanding the Limits of Self-defense." Time
        110 (November 28, 1978): 108.
        News article and general discussion of wives killing their
husbands after years of abuse.   Emphasis here is on the Patri case
in Waupaca, Wisconsin.

871   Kimball, Don. "Marital Violence Syndrome: Psychosocial Ap-
        proach." Smith College Studies in Social Work 48 (November
        1977): 31.
        This abstract of a master's paper from Smith states that the
purpose of the project was to review the literature and isolate major
factors that contribute to the phenomenon.   More research is necessary
if effective intervention is to be achieved.

872   King, Linda Silverman. "Elements and Standards for Shelters
        and Family Violence/Social Service Programs." Response
        to Violence in the Family and Sexual Assault 6 (March/April
        1983): 9-12.

873   King, Linda Silverman. "Family Service Association Responds
        to Domestic Violence." Response to Violence in the Family
        3 (March 1980): 1.
        Most of the nation's 250 Family Service Associations now
offer assistance to family abuse victims.   The programs in Wayne
County (Michigan), Pawtucket (R. I.), Milwaukee (Wisconsin), Charlotte
(N. C.), and Lubbock (Texas) are singled out for attention.

874   King, Linda Silverman. "Responding to Spouse Abuse: The Men-
         tal Health Profession." Response to Violence in the Family
         4 (May/June 1981): 9.

875   King, Linda Silverman. "Training Social Workers to Serve Bat-
         tered Women." Response to Violence in the Family 3 (Janu-
         ary 1980): 2.

876   King, Linda Silverman, and Karen Crist. "ODV Advocacy Proj-
         ects to Increase Use of Community Services." Response to
         Violence in the Family 4 (November/December 1980): 1-2.

877   King, Linda Silverman, and Robert Gotwald. "More Federal Aid
         for Battered Women." Response to Violence in the Family
         4 (October 1980): 2.

878   Kirchner, Rioghan M. Relationships Between Early Pregnancy,
         Early Marriage, Education and Wife Beating. Brooklyn Legal
         Services, 1978. 11 p. Also in Domestic Violence. U. S.
         Congress. House. Committee on Education and Labor, Sub-
         committee on Select Education. 95th Cong. 2nd Sess. Hear-
         ings on H. R. 7927 and H. R. 8948, March 16 and 17, 1978.
         Washington, D. C.: Government Printing Office, 1978, pp.
         256-66.
              During the period from May 1976 to May 1977, 600 women
      applied to the Family Law Unit of the Brooklyn Legal Services for help
      in obtaining a divorce, separation, or annulment. Of these 59.5 per-
      cent had been beaten by their husband. The hypothesis that there was
      a relationship between being beaten and early pregnancy was affirmed;
      white women were beaten more than other ethnic groups; beaten women
      tended to have married earlier; and more education of the women in-
      creased the odds of her being beaten.

879   Kirchner, Rioghan M. The Social Worker, the Battered Woman,
         and the Criminal Justice System. Brooklyn, New York:
         Brooklyn Legal Services, 1979. 18 p.

880   Kirkland, Karl. "Assessment and Treatment of Family Violence."
         Journal of Family Practice 14 (April 1982): 713-8.
              Because family physicians are probably the second most
      likely (police are first) professionals to have contacts with abuse vic-
      tims, they have a great potential for helping put an end to it and rec-
      ommending treatment. This can be done by physicians analyzing their
      own attitudes regarding the problem, being aware of the characteristics
      of abusive relationships, being aware of local resources and methods
      of dealing with the problem, and routinely assessing the anger control
      skills of their patients. In the long run, performing this service is
      the best approach for protecting the rights of individuals and strength-
      ening the family.

881   Klatt, Michael R. "Rape in Marriage: The Law in Texas and
         the Need for Reform." Baylor Law Review 32 (Winter 1980):
         109-21.

In 1979 amendments were proposed to the Texas Penal Code which would remove the spousal immunity from rape. The amendment failed and the author reviews the arguments against the proposed law. Klatt believes that at the very least, women who are separated from their husbands should be protected. This law should be reconsidered.

882   Kleckner, James H. "Wife Beaters and Beaten Wives: Co-
      conspirators in Crimes of Violence." Psychology 15
      (February 1978): 54-6.
         Dr. Kleckner, a clinical psychologist and marriage counselor,
believes that women who allow themselves to be beaten more than once
are co-conspirators in the act. He believes the repeatedly abused wife
is one who sends messages to her husband that his physical violence is
a legitimate and tolerable activity. He also claims never to have
seen a chronically abused wife who truly objected to being abused.
Only when they take serious action will it stop.

883   Klein, Dorie. "Can This Marriage Be Saved?--Battery and
      Sheltering." Crime and Social Justice 12 (Winter 1979):
      19-33.
         This is a good overview of the problem and a survey of
studies of wife abuse. The victim blaming theory is analyzed, as well
as that of conflict management. The use of shelters is supported,
but some feminist separatist concepts are rejected. One of the better
surveys.

884   Klein, Dorie. "The Dark Side of Marriage: Battered Wives and
      the Domination of Women." In Judge Lawyer Victim Thief;
      Women, Gender Roles, and Criminal Justice. Eds. Nicole
      Hahn Rafter and Elizabeth Anne Stanko. Boston: North-
      eastern University Press, 1982, pp. 83-107.
         In this chapter, the author analyzes battering "as the extreme
end of a continuum of institutionalized asymmetry in marriage." It is
seen as an aspect of the overall structure of patriarchy which in turn
is a result of capitalist modes of production and reproduction. The
feminist shelter movement and the subsequent takeover by nonfeminist
interests encouraged by "state" concern and funding are described.
The end of battering is of importance not only to the immediate victims,
but all men and women.

885   Klein, Dorie. "Violence Against Women: Some Considerations
      Regarding Its Causes and Its Elimination." Crime and De-
      linquency 27 (January 1981): 64-80.
         Klein reviews various facets of violence directed against
women, including rape, spouse abuse, marital rape, incest, child
molestations and pornography. Violence of this type is caused by a
concerted effort of males to dominate females. Systematic gender
domination must be eliminated and more democratic orientations to
society must emerge. The feminist movement will help in this effort.

886   Klingbeil, K. "A Treatment Program for Male Batterers."
      Paper presented at the annual meeting of the American Psy-
      chological Association, Toronto, September 1977.

887   Knoble, J. , and Irene Frieze. "General Beliefs About Violence
      Towards Women. "   Paper presented at the annual meeting
      of the Association for Women in Psychology, Dallas, 1979.

888   Knox, Robert.   Report on Battered Women and Children Confer-
      ence.   Albuquerque: New Mexico Commission on the Status
      of Women, 1977.   10 p.   Also in Domestic Violence, 1978.
      U. S. Congress.   Senate.   Committee on Human Resources,
      Subcommittee on Child and Human Development Hearings.
      95th Cong.   2nd Sess.   On Domestic Violence and Legisla-
      tion with Respect to Domestic Violence, March 4 and 8,
      1978.   Washington, D. C. :   Government Printing Office,
      1978, pp. 697-707.
      A conference was held at Shiprock, N. M. , on May 5 and 6,
      1977, to identify services and procedures for addressing problems re-
      lated to domestic violence, to identify the national and local needs of
      victims, to identify gaps in services, and to coordinate existing re-
      sources.   Both child and wife abuse are investigated.   Results indicate
      much local interest and support.

889   Korlath, Maureen J.   "Alcoholism in Battered Women: A Report
      of Advocacy Services to Clients in a Detoxification Facility. "
      Victimology: An International Journal 4, no. 2 (1979): 292-8.
      The Hennepin County Minnesota Alcoholism Receiving Center
      established a program for alcoholic battered wives in 1977.   Thirty-
      three women were interviewed and the results indicate that more re-
      search should be done.   Emphasis should be on practical, not esoteric
      theoretical, results.   A unified attack should be made by family vio-
      lence workers and chemical-dependecy professionals, service structures
      should be flexible and receptive to client needs, and the abuser him-
      self must be confronted and encouraged to obtain help.   Of importance,
      too, is the strengthening of legal advocacy for chemical dependent
      battered women.

890   Korman, James W.   "To Love, Honor and Do Violence. "   Fami-
      ly Advocate 2 (1979): 2-5, 38.
      This article provides advice to lawyers with clients suing
      for financial compensation for damages in spouse battering and spouse
      homicide cases.   Of special interest is how to deal with interspousal
      immunity claims by the defendant.   A useful collection of advice by a
      practicing lawyer from Arlington, Virginia, whose recent case sub-
      stantially eroded interspousal immunity.

891   Koslof, Karen E.   "The Battered Women: A Developmental Per-
      spective. "   M. S. W. thesis, Smith College, 1983.   107 p.
      Nine battered women were compared with nine nonbattered
      women to determine whether abuse in the childhood of the victim or
      the abuser has any relationship to acceptance of marital violence in
      later life.   The T. E. D. (Task of Emotional Development) test was
      used to generate the data.   Results indicate that all participants were
      subjected to verbal and physical abuse as children.   In the battered
      group the major difference was that even though women were more

abused as children than the nonbattered group, they also chose husbands who had been more abused by parents than husbands in the nonbattered group. Contrary to other research, having witnessed their parents being abused did not have an effect. The survey instrument is appended.

892 Koval, James E.; James J. Ponzetti, Jr.; and Rodney M. Cate.
       "Programmatic Intervention for Men Involved in Conjugal
       Violence." Family Therapy 9, no. 2 (1982): 147-54.
          If marital violence is to be ended, attention must be paid
    to both partners, not just the victim. Abusers have special characteristics and thus can be treated as a unique population. Abusers
    must first acknowledge their abusiveness. The various factors such
    as stress, role expectations, and cultural norms can be addressed by
    the treatment.

893 Kratcoski, Peter C., and Lucille Dunn Kratcoski. "Explaining
       Family Violence." USA Today 108 (January 1980): 30-2.
          A general discussion of domestic violence including child
    and spouse abuse. The causes are essentially sociological with learned
    responses to frustrations. The cycle of violence, that is, children
    learning violence in the home, must be broken. Social agencies can
    and must help.

894 Kremen, Eleanor. "The 'Discovery' of Battered Wives: Consideration for the Development of Social Service Network."
       Paper presented at the annual meeting of the American Sociological Association, New York, August 1976.

895 Krisst, Ilze. Spouse Abuse. (Issue paper no. 15). Hartford:
       Office of Legislative Research, Connecticut General Assembly,
       1978. 16 p.

896 Kuhl, Anna F. "Community Responses to Battered Women."
       Victimology: An International Journal 7, nos. 1-4 (1982):
       49-59.

897 Kuhle, S. J. "Domestic Violence in Rural America: Problems
       and Possible Solutions." Paper presented at the First World
       Congress of Victimology, Washington, D. C., August 20-24,
       1980.

898 Kuhn, Mary Ann. "Domestic Battleground: The Violent Family
       Image." Criminal Justice Digest 3 (November 1975): 6-9.
          This general discussion by a reporter for the Washington
    Star is especially concerned with intrafamily murder, although some
    attention is devoted to husband-wife murder. Most of the information
    found here is taken from Donald T. Lunde's Murder and Madness and
    Murray A. Straus' Violence in the Family.

899 Kultgen, Rebecca A. "Battered Women Syndrome: Admissibility
       of Expert Testimony for the Defense." Missouri Law Review
       47 (Fall 1982): 835-48.

In this legal note, the author discusses the Georgia case,
Smith v. State, in which the court overruled the trial court for im-
properly excluding expert testimony regarding battered-woman syndrome.
The pros and cons are detailed and in the end the author concludes
that such testimony should not be allowed, because L. Walker herself,
one of the leading subscribers to the syndrome, says that this theory
is unproven. Expert testimony is too influential with juries. To allow
unproven theories into the courtroom would not serve justice.

900   Kumagai, Fumie. "Social Class, Power and Husband-Wife Vio-
        lence in Japan." Journal of Comparative Family Studies.
        10 (Spring 1979): 91-105.
        Kumagai's earlier study reported that the level of conjugal
violence in Japan was significantly lower than in the U.S. To test
whether that held true in all social classes, Straus' Family Conflict
Resolution Study questionnaires were distributed to 635 Jananese high
school seniors to determine the power and violence of their parents.
The findings indicate that there is no significant difference between
classes. The Japanese woman holds dominant power in the family.
This results from the nature of Japanese society and culture, not
one's social class or background. Family structure in Japan is best
explained by the resource theory.

901   Kumagai, Fumie, and Gearoid O'Donoghue. "Conjugal Power
        and Conjugal Violence in Japan and the U.S.A." Journal of
        Comparative Family Studies 9 (Summer 1978): 211-21.
        Japanese and American couples were studied to determine
if a relationship existed in the sharing of conjugal power and family
violence. Family Conflict Resolution Study questionnaires were given
to high school students to complete in the belief that their observations
would be more accurate than the spouses'. Results show both societies
have considerable violence. The egalitarian nature of American families brings the wife's use of violence to near equality with the husband.
Traditional Japanese values and supremacy of the wife in the home, as
well as more use of reasoning, accounts for less use of violence by
Japanese women. A high relationship between verbal and physical aggression exists in both societies.

902   Kurland, Albert A.; Jacob Morganstern; and Carolyn Sheets. "A
        Comparative Study of Wife Murderers Admitted to a State
        Psychiatric Hospital. Journal of Social Therapy 1 (1955):
        7-15.
        The records of 12 men who had murdered or attempted to
murder their wives were analyzed. The personality characteristics
of the men are detailed as well as those of the wives who survived.
No distinct reference is made to battering behavior, but the description
of the sadomasochistic interaction which the authors say characterizes
the relationship makes wife beating likely.

903   Kutun, Barry. "Legislative Needs and Solutions." In Battered
        Women; A Psychosociological Study of Domestic Violence.
        Ed. Maria Roy. New York: Van Nostrand Reinhold, 1977,
        pp. 277-87.

As state representative in the Florida House of Representatives, Kutun found in 1975 that no state agency was keeping any statistics on wife abuse.   Therefore it was impossible to tell the exact extent of it in that state.   Several laws were proposed, among them one that would make reporting of abuse mandatory.   Another would set up shelters and other forms of assistance to abuse victims.   Copies of the bills are included and commented upon.

904   Labell, Linda S.   "Wife Abuse: A Sociological Study of Battered
        Women and Their Mates."   Victimology: An International
        Journal 4, no. 2 (1979): 258-67.
        The author is a counselor at Hubbard House of Jacksonville,
Florida, where this study was conducted.   From November 1976 to
October 1978, 512 physically abused women were questioned regarding
history of the violence, demographic data, information about the spouse,
etc.   These data were then compared with that discovered by Richard
Gelles, Terry Davidson, Maria Roy, La Casa de las Madres, and
others.   Various methods of reducing the amount of wife beating are
suggested.   These include counseling, stress management, and assertiveness training.

905   La Casa de las Madres.   "Legal Rights of Battered Women."   In
        Battered Women.   Ed. Donna M. Moore.   Beverly Hills, Cal. :
        Sage, 1979.   Appendix A, pp. 145-89.
        This handbook is designed for the battered woman who needs
practical and legal advice, including how to get the police and judicial
system to pay attention and practical information regarding divorce.
While directly relevant for Californians, the information can be useful
to others, also.   Other states might like to copy this example and use
it as a prototype.

906   Lacey, Bobbi.   Domestic Violence Services in Rural Communities:
        Direct Services and Funding.   Lincoln: Nebraska Task Force
        on Domestic Violence, n. d.

907   Lacey, Bobbi.   Domestic Violence Services in Rural Communities:
        First Steps of Organization.   Lincoln: Nebraska Task Force
        on Domestic Violence, n. d.

908   Lafata, Lorraine.   The Effective Coordination of Volunteers.
        (Domestic Violence, Monograph Series, no. 1, May 1980.)
        Rockville, Md. : National Clearinghouse on Domestic Violence,
        1980.   133 p.   Also Rockville, Md. : National Criminal Justice Reference Service, 1980.   2 microfiche sheets.
        The author is a volunteer coordinator with the Domestic Violence Project.   The manual is designed to facilitate the recruiting,
screening, training, and supervising of a volunteer staff in abuse shelters.   Interviewing techniques, training methods, orientation procedures
are all detailed.   The appendixes include many sample forms that other
organizations and services which utilize volunteers might find useful.

909 Lancaster, Jan, and Ajax Quinly. "Vancouver's Munroe House:
         A Second-stage Transition House." Canadian Woman Studies
         4 (Summer 1983): 56-7.
     The purpose of Munroe House is to provide battered women
with interim housing between their stay at the Vancouver Transition
House, a shelter for abused wives, and more permanent accommoda-
tions. This secondary housing provides the women with the extra time
some need to plan their future. Munroe House was established in
September 1979.

910 Laner, Mary Riege, and Jeanine Thompson. "Abuse and Aggres-
         sion in Courting Couples." Deviant Behavior 3 (April/June
         1982): 229-44.
     The authors, from Arizona State University, originally pre-
sented this revised paper at a Western Social Science Association meeting, San Diego, California, April 1981. Their results indicate that
much more research is necessary, but essentially that involved relationships have more violence than those that are less involved. Individuals who had been exposed to violence at home were more inclined
to use it themselves. On the other hand, an inverse relationship between socioeconomic status and violence did not exist.

911 Langley, Roger, and Richard C. Levy. "The Shocking Truth
         About Wife Beating." Cosmopolitan 189 (August 1980): 212-5,
         220-1.
     This is an excerpt from their book Wife Beating: The Silent
Crisis. A general overview of the problem.

912 Langley, Roger, and Richard Levy. "Wife Abuse: Why Will a
         Woman Stay and Take It?" New Woman 7 (July/August 1977):
         89-98.
     A general discussion of the problem with case studies. This
is an excerpt from the authors' book Wife Beating: The Silent Crisis.

913 Langley, Roger, and Richard C. Levy. "Wife Abuse and the
         Police Response." FBI Law Enforcement Bulletin 47 (May
         1978): 4-9.
     A general article aimed at policemen, urging them to view
spouse abuse as a criminal matter, not just a civil one. Concern for
"paperwork" does the abused a disservice. The "paper chase" and
"clogged courts" are not the officer's problem. His duty is to provide safety.

914 Langley, Roger, and Richard C. Levy. Wife Beating: The Si-
         lent Crisis. New York: E. P. Dutton, 1977. 242 p.
     General discussion of the problem using the research of
numerous scholars and a variety of case studies. A historical look
at the problem, why the victim stays with the abuser, husband abuse
and remedial options available to the abused and society are all discussed at length. Good overview by investigative journalists.

915 LaPrairie, Carol Pitcher. "A Socio-legal Perspective of Domes-
         tic Violence." In Domestic Violence: Issues and Dynamics.

Ed. Vincent D'Oyley.   Toronto: Ontario Institute for Studies in Education, 1978, pp. 119-38.
What is often considered criminal behavior between strangers or friends is sometimes seen quite differently by society when it occurs between intimates.   This is because of the lack of willingness of government to interfere in family matters.   Freedom from assault must be seen as a basic right and must not be tied to the victim's willingness to seek counseling or treatment.

916   LaRossa, Ralph.   "'And We Haven't Had Any Problems Since':
        Conjugal Violence and the Politics of Marriage."   In The
        Social Causes of Husband-Wife Violence.   Eds.   Murray A.
        Straus and Gerald T. Hotaling.   Minneapolis: University of
        Minnesota Press, 1980, pp. 157-75.
        This interview with "Joe and Jennifer" is an excerpt from the author's Conflict and Power in Marriage: Expecting the First Child, Beverly Hills, Cal. : Sage, 1977, pp. 69-82.   The interview portrays a couple, both strong and independent who will not be "dominated" by the other.   An incident of spousal violence had occurred earlier in the marriage which both partners viewed as normal consequence of a conflict between them.   Conflict is seen by the author as the prevailing mode of marital interaction.   Marital politics is based on ideology (the way marriage is supposed to be) and exchange (power goes to whoever brings home the most in rewards such as money, status, etc.)   This particular couple had basic disagreements over both.

917   Laskin, David M.   "Looking Out for the Battered Woman."   Jour-
        nal of Oral Surgery 39 (June 1981): 405.
        This editorial urges doctors to be familiar with the problem of battered women and aware of the various resources available for the victims.   Doctors have an obligation to the patient's overall welfare and can meet those responsibilities by being alert to suspicious injuries and by making proper referrals.

918   Lasok, D.   "Domestic Violence and Rights of Property."   New
        Law Journal 128 (February 9, 1978): 124-5; (June 1, 1978):
        124-5.
        Several cases involving barring the batterer from the home as approved by the Domestic Violence and Matrimonial Proceedings Act, 1976, and how this might be a violation of property rights is the focus of this two-part article.   The question which arises is whether he is temporarily removed or whether the ownership of the property is transferred to the victim and children on a more permanent basis.

919   Laszlo, Anna T. , and Thomas McKean.   "Court Diversion: An
        Alternative for Spousal Abuse Cases."   In Battered Women:
        Issues of Public Policy.   U. S. Commission on Civil Rights.
        Washington, D. C. :   The Commission, 1978, pp. 327-57.
        Also Rockville, Md. : NCJRS Microfiche program, 1978.

920   Lauter, David.   "Assault on Shelter Data Heats Up: Files on
        Rape, Abuse."   National Law Journal 5 (February 28, 1983):
        5.

921   LaViolette, Alyce D. "An Attitudinal Study of the Male Batterer."
      M. S. thesis, California State University, Long Beach, 1980.
      46 p.
      LaViolette is interested in the relationship between the atti-
tudes men hold toward women and spousal violence. Two groups (15
nonbattering and 16 battering) of men were given a battery of tests
to determine how batterers and nonbatterers differed. The study
shows a connection between alcohol or drug abuse and violence. Non-
batterers tend to have better family relations with their parents during
childhood and they also tend to be more androgynous than the battering group.

922   "The Law in Relation to Women." Westminster Review 128
      (September 1887): 698-710.
      This article discusses suffrage, adultery, cruelty, divorce
and wife beating. While women are physically and intellectually inferior to men, they are morally superior so their influence in government is desirable.

923   "LEAA Releases Draft Guidelines for Family Violence Funding."
      Response to Intrafamily Violence and Sexual Assault 1
      (December 1977): 1-2.

924   League of Women Voters of Minneapolis. Family Violence: A
      Focus on Handguns. Minneapolis: The League, [1983].
      26 p.

925   League of Women Voters of Minneapolis. Family Violence: How
      the Systems Respond. Minneapolis: The League, [1978].
      42 p.

926   Leavy, Walter. "Battered Women, Why So Many Suffer Abuse
      for So Long." Ebony 36 (February 1981): 94-6, 98, 100.
      A general article discussing spouse abuse. Although directed
to a Black readership, no attempt is made to suggest it occurs more
or less frequently in Black families. No Black-White comparisons are
made.

927   Leevers, Maureen. Violence in Marriage. London: Shelter
      Housing Aid Centre, [1978]. 38 p.

928   Leghorn, Lisa. "Social Responses to Battered Women." Speech
      given at the Wisconsin Conference on Battered Women, 2
      October 1976. Pittsburgh, Pa.: Know, Inc., 1979. 16 p.

929   Lennon, Madonna, and Sara Blanchard. Attitudes and Percep-
      tions of Family Violence Professionals: Survey Results.
      St. Paul, Minn.: Crime Control Planning Board, 1980.
      61 p.
      Questionnaires were designed to measure the attitudes of
professionals working in family violence, including police officers,
county health nurses, social workers, judges, county attorneys, doctors, family therapists, and probation agents. Two thousand four

hundred and seventy-six questionnaires were returned with data regarding child abuse, incest, and spouse abuse. Results show lack of written procedures, inadequate training, negative attitudes from legal and police professionals, and lack of communication and coordination of efforts. Changes in these would improve the needed services.

930   Lenzner, Anne R.   "Selected Psychological and Social Aspects of Battered Women: A Grounded Theory Approach." Ph. D. dissertation, Arizona State University, 1981. 169 p. Abstract in Dissertation Abstracts International 42A (August 1981): 551.

931   Lepley, E. Joan Edwards.   "Pastoral Counseling: Battered Women." American Protestant Hospital Association Bulletin 42, no. 2 (1978): 32-5.
Directed at ministers who may be confronted with abused wives, this essay explains why the wife stays and why she may not fight back. The author interviewed eleven ministers in the Greater Portland area, giving a hypothetical case of abuse and asking what advice and counsel he would give. Responses indicate that real help would be in short supply.

932   Lerman, Lisa G.   "Civil Protection Orders: Obtaining Access to Court." Response to Violence in the Family 3 (April 1980): 1-2.
At least twenty-seven states provide civil protection orders for battered women. This article explains their use and value.

933   Lerman, Lisa.   "Criminal Prosecution of Wife Beaters." Response to Violence in the Family 4 (January/February 1981): 1-4.

934   Lerman, Lisa.   "Court Decisions on Wife Abuse Laws: Recent Developments." Response to Family Violence and Sexual Assault 5 (May/June 1982): 3-4, 21-2.

935   Lerman, Lisa G.   "Elements and Standards for Criminal Justice Programs on Domestic Violence." Response to Family Violence and Sexual Assault 5 (November/December 1982): 9-14.

936   Lerman, Lisa G.   "Expansion of Police Arrest Power: A Key to Effective Intervention." Response to Violence in the Family 3 (June 1980): 1-2.
Why the police must be encouraged to arrest the abuser, the constitutional limits of the Fourth Amendment regarding warrantless arrests, new state arrest laws, and other concerns are addressed. Police must be made aware of their expanded powers of arrest if the victims of family violence are to be helped.

937   Lerman, Lisa.   Legal Help for Battered Women. Washington, D. C.: Center for Women Policy Studies, 1981. 13 p. Also in Abuse of Women: Legislation, Reporting, and Prevention. Ed. Joseph J. Costa. Lexington, Mass.: Lexington Books, D. C. Heath, 1983, pp. 29-38.

This is a short guide to legal terminology and remedies for
those who find the difference between civil and criminal action, the
purpose of a protection order, peace bonds, torts, arrests, plea bar-
gaining, trials, and many other legal matters elusive.

938   Lerman, Lisa G. Prosecution of Spouse Abuse: Innovations in
        Criminal Justice Response. Washington, D.C.: Center for
        Women Policy Studies, 1981. 227 p.
        Written for prosecutors, this book describes the legal ex-
perience of those who have solved some of the problems that face lawyers involved with wife abuse cases. Practical options are given
with changes suggested in the policies for screening cases, charging
and dismissal of charges, protection of victims, rehabilitation of batterers, and more.

939   Lerman, Lisa G. "A Self-assessment Guide for Domestic Vio-
        lence Programs: Criminal Justice and Social Service Agen-
        cies." Response to Violence in the Family and Sexual As-
        sault 6 (January/February 1983): 15-8.

940   Lerman, Lisa G. "Senate Hearing on Domestic Violence Bill."
        Response to Violence in the Family 3 (March 1980): 3.
        An overview of the February 6, 1980, hearing of the Senate
Subcommittee on Child and Human Development for the Domestic Violence Prevention and Services Act, S. 1843.

941   Lerman, Lisa G.; Franci Livingston; and Vicky Jackson. "State
        Legislation on Domestic Violence." Response to Violence
        in the Family and Sexual Assault 6 (September/October 1983):
        1-28.

942   Lerman, Lisa G.; Leslie Landis; and Sharon Goldzweig. "State
        Legislation on Domestic Violence." Response to Violence in
        the Family 4 (September/October 1981): 1-18.

943   Lerman, Lisa G.; Leslie Landis; and Sharon Goldzweig. "State
        Legislation on Domestic Violence." Response to Violence in
        the Family 4 (September/October 1981): 1-18. Also in
        Abuse of Women: Legislation, Reporting and Prevention.
        Ed. Joseph J. Costa. Lexington, Mass.: Lexington Books,
        D. C. Heath and Company, 1983, pp. 39-74.
        State laws regarding domestic violence are changing rapidly.
An extensive and detailed chart in this article shows the status of the
law in each state of the U. S. as of 1981. Also included is a section
on the relevant laws, such as protection orders, police intervention,
etc. for each state. A quick and easy guide.

944   Lerman, Lisa G.; Mary Bottum; and Susan Wiviott. "State Leg-
        islation on Domestic Abuse." Response to Violence in the
        Family 3 (August/September 1980): 1-16.
        A detailed commentary and chart of the current status of
the actual law and pending legislation in each state of the U. S.

945 Lerman, Lisa, and Sharon Goldzweig. "Protection of Battered
         Women: A Survey of State Legislation." Women's Rights
         Law Reporter 6 (Summer 1980): 271-84.
     This article includes an extensive chart indicating which
states have what provisions for the legal protection of battered women.
Included is information on what laws have been passed and what laws
are pending. Useful as a quick guide for the helping professions and
for drafters of legislation.

946 Lesse, Stanley. "The Status of Violence Against Women: Past,
         Present and Future Factors." American Journal of Psycho-
         therapy 33 (April 1979): 190-200.
     Lesse, Editor-in-Chief of this journal, believes that wife
beating and rape, as well as other types of violence against women,
will increase in frequency over the next two decades and then decline.
This is based on his view of the world and the evolution of the relationship between men and women from the dawn of history to the present.
The next generation of men will have assumed a greater psychosocial
status and will have become the equals of women.

947 Lesser, Bobbie Zuckerman. "Factors Influencing Battered Wom-
         en's Return to Their Mates Following a Shelter Program--
         Attachment and Situational Variables." Ph.D. dissertation,
         California School of Professional Psychology, Los Angeles,
         1981. 211 p. Abstract in Dissertation Abstracts International
         42B (July 1981): 379.

948 Lester, David. "A Cross-culture Study of Wife Abuse." Aggres-
         sive Behavior 6 (1980): 361-4.
     Using the data from 71 societies in the Human Relations
Area File it was found that in societies in which cruelty and aggression are more common, wife beating will be, too. It was also found
that wife beating was more common in societies in which women had
inferior status to men. Societies with high divorce rates also had
high rates of spouse abuse.

949 LeValley, Joseph D. "Safe-house Network for Rural Victims."
         MS 11 (October 1982): 19.
     A news note regarding Door Opener's Crisis Intervention
Program, a resource center for battered women in Mason City, Iowa.
A network of volunteer private "safe houses" has been established.
Battered women who call on the hot line are referred to a safe refuge
until the danger passes.

950 Levens, Bruce R. "Domestic Crisis Intervention--A Literature
         Review of Domestic Dispute Intervention Training Programs,
         Parts 1 and 2." Canadian Police College Journal 2, no. 2
         (1978): 215-47; 2, no. 3 (1978): 299-328.

951 Levens, Bruce. "Domestic Crisis Intervention: Domestic Dis-
         putes, Police Response and Social Agency Referral." Ca-
         nadian Police College Journal 2, no. 4 (1978): 356-81.
     This study, a continuation of the author's earlier ones, sug-

gests the adoption by police departments of a clear policy of police
intervention; effective family crisis intervention requires cooperation
between social service agencies and the police.   Dispatchers often
have inadequate information, and alcohol consumption by disturbers
makes officer assistance difficult.   Trained officers tend to refer
abuse victims to social services more frequently than the nontrained
officers.

952   Levens, Bruce, and Donald Dutton.   "Domestic Crisis Interven-
             tion: Citizens' Requests for Services and the Vancouver
             Police Department Response."   Canadian Police College
             Journal 1 (Summer 1977): 29-50.
      Police responses to citizen complaints or requests for as-
sistance account for about 80 percent of their mobilizations and many
of these are family disputes.   This study analyzes this activity of the
Vancouver Police Department.   Results indicate that a considerable
amount of police time is spent on family disputes.   Police involvement
occurs when one of the disputants, usually the wife, calls for help.

953   Levens, Bruce R. , and Donald G. Dutton.   The Social Service
             Role of Police: Domestic Crisis Intervention.   Ottawa,
             Ont. : Ministry of the Solicitor General of Canada, 1980.
             240 p.

954   Lever, Ann B.   "Domestic Violence Legislation for Missouri:
             A Proposal. "   St. Louis University Law Journal 22 (1978):
             151-96.
      This article discusses the current legal situation in Missouri
regarding domestic abuse.   The present laws, if pursued vigorously,
could provide relief when the violence results in physical injury.   Peace
bonds are noted as possible deterrents, but their constitutionality is in
question.   Lever believes that legal remedies are necessary and that
better administration of those laws can provide protection to victims.
Proposed legislation is appended.

955   Levin, Marj Jackson.   "The Wife Beaters. "   McCall's 102 (June
             1975): 37.
      General discussion for the lay reader based on the research
of Sue Eisenberg and Pat Micklow, two University of Michigan law
students.

956   Levine, David N.   "Marital Cruelty: New Wine in Old Bottles. "
             Family Law Quarterly 2 (1968): 296-321.
      The question of marital cruelty which includes physical and
mental cruelty as grounds for divorce is discussed.   Not concerned
especially with battered spouses, the author does criticize the state
(in the late 1960's) of the divorce law which was not responsive to the
reality of married life.

957   Levine, Montague B.   "Interparental Violence and Its Effect on
             the Children: A Study of 50 Families in General Practice. "
             Medicine, Science and the Law 15, no. 3 (1975): 172-6.
      Fifty victims of wife abuse were questioned regarding the
number and activities of children in their families.   The purpose was

to determine the effects of family violence on the children. Were they battered too, truant from school, or did they show aggressive behavior, anxiety disorders, insomnia, etc.? The conclusion was that interparental violence does have such effects on the children. The general practitioner has a unique opportunity for discovering this violence since he or she is often in the position of being the first professional involved.

958 Levinger, George. "Physical Abuse Among Applicants for Divorce." In Violence in the Family. Eds. Suzanne K. Steinmetz and Murray A. Straus. New York: Dodd, Mead, 1974, pp. 85-8.
This is an excerpt from the author's article "Sources of Marital Dissatisfaction Among Applicants for Divorce," American Journal of Orthopsychiatry. Among other facts, the author found that 37 percent of wives who applied for divorce gave "physical abuse" as one of the complaints.

959 Levinger, George. "Sources of Marital Dissatisfaction Among Applicants for Divorce." American Journal of Orthopsychiatry 36 (October 1966): 803-7.
Levinger, Department of Psychology, University of Massachusetts, studied the divorce applications of 600 couples in greater Cleveland, Ohio. The complaints fell into 12 categories, including financial problems, neglect, mental cruelty, verbal abuse, and physical abuse. Comparisons of complaints of husbands and wives as well as the difference in middle-class and lower-class complaints are analyzed. Findings indicate a large amount of physical abuse and a tendency for lower-class applicants to mention it more frequently than middle-class. Women are also eleven times more likely to mention it than men. Although not directly concerned with abuse, useful information was discovered in this early study.

960 Levinson, David. "Physical Punishment of Children and Wife-beating in Cross-cultural Perspective." In International Perspectives on Family Violence. Eds. Richard J. Gelles and Claire Pedrick Cornell. Lexington, Mass.: Lexington Books, D.C. Heath and Company, 1983, pp. 73-7. Also in Child Abuse and Neglect 5, no. 2 (1981): 193-5.
A sample consisting of 60 small-scale and folk societies was analyzed to determine the relationship between physical punishment of children and spouse abuse. The Human Relations Area Files were used for the study. Results show wife beating to be more common than physical punishment of children and infants. In fact, it appears "at a societal level that rare or infrequent physical punishment of children is associated with rare or infrequent wife beating, while frequent or common wifebeating is unrelated to the frequency with which physical punishment is used as a socialization technique."

961 Lewin, Tamar. "Battered Women and the Doctrine of Self-defense: A Reevaluation of the Meaning of Deadly Force." Student Lawyer 8 (May 1980): 10-2.
This is a profile of Elizabeth Schneider, staff attorney with

the Women's Self-defense Law Project.   The Wanrow case, handled
by Schneider, in which the plea of self-defense was seen as successful
justification for killing an abusing husband, evoked much interest from
lawyers around the country who were involved in similar cases.   The
old notion of deadly force and self-defense must be viewed differently
when applied in this type of case than when defendant and victim are
both men.   The author is Washington Bureau Chief of the National
Law Journal, where this article first appeared.

962   Lewis, Elissa.   "The Group Treatment of Battered Women."
        Women and Therapy 2 (Spring 1983): 51-8.
        A woman caught in a battering marital relationship needs
counseling and therapy.   This can best be provided in group therapy
since she will be more aware that her condition is not uncommon and
the group will help reduce the social isolation she suffers.   The author teaches psychology at Southwest Missouri State University.

963   Lewis, Linda Ann.   "Internal-External Locus of Control in Bat-
        tered Women."   Ph. D. dissertation, Fielding Institute, 1982.
        154 p.   Abstract in Dissertation Abstracts International 43B
        (February 1983): 2711.

964   Li, K. C.   "Issues on Family Violence, As Observed in the Chi-
        nese Community of Vancouver."   In Domestic Violence: Is-
        sues and Dynamics.   Ed. Vincent D'Oyley.   Toronto: On-
        tario Institute for Studies in Education, 1978, pp. 195-201.
        Several examples of wife abuse, child battering and parental
and sibling abuse among Chinese families in Vancouver, B. C. , are
given.   Increased public concern, improved liaison between legal and
helping professionals, and improvement in life-styles for recent immi-
grants will reduce the magnitude in the problem.

965   Lichtenstein, Violet Ramonaitis.   "The Battered Women: Guide-
        line for Effective Nursing Intervention."   Issues in Mental
        Health Nursing 3 (July/September 1981): 237-50.
        This article provides a good overview of the problem of
abuse, why they leave and why they stay, etc.   Most important is
what the nurse can do to identify a case of abuse and what can be done
to help the victim.   Nurses must be active case finders and work to
stimulate change in societal attitudes toward abuse, if it is to be prevented.

966   Lidkea, Mary Rabb.   "Counseling as a Factor in the Later Inci-
        dence of Wife Abuse: A Follow Up Study of the Clients of
        Brevard Family Aid Society, Inc."   Ph. D. dissertation,
        Florida Institute of Technology, 1982.   109 p.   Abstract in
        Dissertation Abstracts International 43B (June 1983): 4153.

967   Lieberknecht, Kay.   "Helping the Battered Wife."   American
        Journal of Nursing 78 (April 1978): 654-6.
        How a nurse should treat an abuse victim she encounters is
the topic of this article including attitudes to avoid and questions to ask
to encourage the abused to feel at ease and discuss the problem openly.

968 Liebman, Donald A. , and Jeffrey A. Schwartz. "Police Programs
        in Domestic Crisis Intervention: A Review. " In The Urban
        Policeman in Transition. Eds. John R. Snibbe and Homa M.
        Snibbe. Springfield, Ill. : Charles C. Thomas, 1973, pp.
        421-72.
        In 1966, no law enforcement agency in the U.S. had a do-
mestic crisis intervention program. By 1971, 14 law enforcement
agencies had such programs. Police do not view domestic disputes
as real police work and prefer not to be involved in it. However,
the police are the only agency that can effectively deal with the problem. The 14 training programs are reviewed and suggestions for the
development of future programs are included. Has historical and contemporary significance.

969 Lion, John R. "Clinical Aspects of Wife Battering. " In Battered
        Women: A Psychosociological Study of Domestic Violence.
        Ed. Maria Roy. New York: Van Nostrand Reinhold, 1977,
        pp. 126-136.
        Lion, Director of the Clinical Research Program for Violent
Behavior, University of Maryland School of Medicine, maintains that
"the phenomenology of wife battering involves the victim playing a major role. Recognition of this is mandatory, and should not be con-
strued as pejorative. " Wife abuse involves the ambivalence and
pathologies of both partners. To end the abuse, both must be treated.
If only one can be treated, it must be the victim. Their consciousness
must be raised and self-esteem must be improved.

970 Lippi, Laura. "Battered Wives: Jersey Asks: Are You a Wom-
        an or a Spouse?" Majority Report 7 (January 7-20, 1978):
        5.
        Discussion of recent events in New Jersey including the
passage of two new domestic violence laws.

971 Livneh, Ernst. "On Rape and the Sanctity of Marriage. " Israel
        Law Review 2, no. 3 (1967): 415-22.
        Livneh commends the Israel courts for interpreting the law
that marital rape is illegal and not to be allowed. To insure illegal-
ity he recommends that the legislature take action in that vein. He
also surveys the laws in other countries, including the British Commonwealth, the U. S. , France, Germany, the Communist Bloc, and
Scandinavia.

972 Lobsenz, Norman M. "If and When You Fight with Your Hus-
        band. " Woman's Day (October 1975): 26, 179-80.
        The therapeutic aggression theories of Bach and Wyden (The
Intimate Enemy) are discussed and found to be lacking on the grounds
that verbal abuse tends to lead to physical abuse. The thoughts of
Murray Straus on this topic are used to argue against such aggressive
leveling.

973 Loeb, Roger C. "A Program of Community Education for Deal-
        ing with Spouse Abuse. " Journal of Community Psychology
        11 (July 1983): 241-52.

Loeb, University of Michigan, Dearborn, developed a two-
phase program to educate helping professionals, to understand and deal
with spouse abuse.   The first was compilation of a booklet, and the
second was the institution of training programs for the police, the
legal profession including legislators, family counselors and the clergy.
Advice and recommendations for similar programs are provided.

974   London, Julia.   "Images of Violence Against Women."   Victim-
      ology: An International Journal 2, nos. 3-4 (1977-78): 510-
      24.
        This article is a pictorial essay showing the prevalence of
violence against women in advertising.   The author, from Women
Against Violence Against Women, Los Angeles, believes the public
should be sensitive to this issue and pressure offending companies to
stop because such advertising promotes an unsafe environment.

975   Long, Carolyn Jackson.   "An Investigation of the History, Serv-
      ices and Future Development of Shelters for Battered Women
      in Texas."   Ed. D. dissertation, East Texas State University,
      1981.   249 p.   Abstract in Dissertation Abstracts Interna-
      tional 42A (December 1981): 2504.

976   Longtain, Melinda.   Family Violence: The Well-Kept Secret.
      Austin: University of Texas Press, 1979.   35 p.

977   Lootens, Tricia.   "Pulling Together: Being with Children in
      Shelter."   Off Our Backs 12 (March 1982): 16-7, 23, 30.

978   Loraine, Kaye.   "Battered Women: The Ways You Can Help."
      RN 44 (October 1981): 22-8, 102.
        This is a good discussion of what emergency department
nurses can and should do if a patient is a suspected victim of spouse
abuse.

979   Loraine, Kaye.   "Establishing a Task Force for Battered Wom-
      en."   American Journal of Nursing 78 (April 1978): 653.
        General tips on setting up a task force by the coordinator
of one in Waukesha, Wisconsin.

980   Loseke, Donileen.   "Social Movement Theory in Practice: A
      Shelter for Battered Women."   Ph. D. dissertation, Univer-
      sity of California, Santa Barbara, 1982.   267 p.   Abstract
      in Dissertation Abstracts International 44A (July 1983): 298.

981   Loseke, Donileen R. , and Sarah F. Berk.   "The Work of Shel-
      ters: Battered Women and Initial Calls for Help."   Victim-
      ology: An International Journal 7, nos. 1-4 (1982): 35-48.

982   "The Love That Kills."   Human Behavior 6 (September 1977): 7.
        This is a long letter to the editor by an abused wife who
describes what it feels like to be battered and raped by a husband.
Her reasons for staying center largely around fear.

983 Lovejoy, Frances H. , and Emily S. Steet. "Staying Together for
     the Sake of the Children: Spouse Beating and Its Effect on
     the Children. " In Violence in the Family: A Collection of
     Conference Papers. Ed. Jocelynne A. Scutt. Canberra:
     Australian Institute of Criminology, 1980, pp. 41-7.

984 Loving, Nancy. "Developing Operational Procedures for Police
     Use. " In The Abusive Partner: An Analysis of Domestic
     Battering. Ed. Maria Roy. New York: Van Nostrand
     Reinhold, 1982, pp. 277-305.

985 Loving, Nancy. Responding to Spouse Abuse and Wife Beating:
     A Guide for Police. [Washington, D. C.]: Police Executive
     Research Forum, 1980. 219 p.
     This study addresses the question of what police officers
should do in domestic disputes involving use of violence or threat of
violence.   It is designed to help police administrators formulate policy and guidelines for officers called to the scene of the disturbance.
Large numbers of repeat calls indicate that past practices have been
quite ineffective.   This more assertive action by the police may help.

986 Loving, Nancy. Spouse Abuse: A Curriculum Guide for Police
     Trainers. Washington, D. C. : Police Executive Research
     Forum, 1981. 164 p.
     Loving has designed this curriculum guide to help officers
understand the nature and causes of spouse abuse and to teach them
new methods of handling the cases effectively and with increased personal safety.   Traditional methods which emphasize reconciliation and
the avoidance of arrest are inappropriate for violence cases.   In nonviolent cases the traditional practices may be adequate however.   A
20-hour curriculum, this can be used for new and veteran officers.
Recommendations for discussions and readings are included.

987 Loving, Nancy. Working with Police: A Practical Guide for
     Battered Women's Advocates. [Washington, D. C.]: Police
     Executive Research Forum, 1982. 32 p.
     The purpose of this booklet is to aid battered women's advo-
cates plan and execute realistic and effective pgorams in conjunction
with the police.   Understanding the traditional police role, the perspective of the police in these cases, ways to gain police support and cooperation, plus other advice is provided.

988 Loving, Nancy, and Lynn Olson. National Conference on Women
     and Crime: Proceeding. Washington, D. C. : National
     League of Cities and U. S. Conference of Mayors, February
     26-27, 1976. 163 p.
     In this general conference on women and crime, one session
was devoted to wife-beating.   The panel included Bobbie Sterne, Mayor
of Cincinnati; Roberta Sabban, victim; Clare Crawford, NBC News and
Time; Darrel Stephen, Kansas City Police Department; and Susan Jackson, California Rural Legal Assistance.   Suggestions for improving
the situation included more shelters, demanding police protection,
educating boys and girls to act more humanely, bringing the problem

into the open, urging passage of spouse abuse laws, and including
more women on the police forces.

989 Lowenberg, David A. "Conjugal Assaults: The Incarcerated or
        Liberated Woman." Federal Probation 41 (June 1977): 10-3.
        Lowenberg, Program Coordinator, Witness Advocate Pro-
gram, Tucson, Arizona, describes a one-year grant to the Pima
County Attorney's Office to establish a program to aid victims of
spouse abuse. The various supports needed by the victim, such as
counseling, a job, housing, and legal advice, are discussed. This
report was written at the beginning of the project so the outcome and
results are not described.

990 Lowenberg, David A. "Pima County Services for Battered Women."
        Response to Intrafamily Violence and Sexual Assault 1 (De-
        cember 1976): 3-4.

991 Lurie, Abraham, and Elizabeth B. Quitkin, eds. Identification
        and Treatment of Spouse Abuse: Health and Mental Health
        Agency Roles, Proceedings of a Conference, November 21,
        1980, New York. New York: Editors, 1981. 177 p.

992 Lynch, Catherine G. "Women as Victims--Rape, Battering, In-
        cest, and Muggings--Victim Advocacy and Victims Within
        the System." Paper presented at the annual meeting of the
        Sociologists for Women in Society Section of the American
        Sociological Association, Chicago, 1977.

993 Lynch, Catherine G. , and Thomas L. Norris. "Services for
        Battered Women: Looking for a Perspective." Victimology:
        An International Journal 2, nos. 3-4 (1977-78): 553-62.
        Drawing from their experience with Dade County victims
of abuse, these authors discuss the most formidable problems facing
a service program for abused wives. The needs of the victim and
her characteristics, the victim/abuser relationship, what a service
program must consist of, and the personnel requirements are all dealt
with. Some concern is expressed that public interest in spouse abuse
should not be a passing fad. To insure that battered women are not
forgotten, it is best if relevant services are incorporated into the mainstream of the assistance provided by other helping programs, such as
the police, hospital, courts, and social service agencies.

994 Lynn, Nancy. "Middle Class Violence: Spouse Abuse in the Sub-
        urbs." Paper presented at the annual meeting of the Sociol-
        ogists for Women in Society Section of the American Sociol-
        ogical Association, Chicago, 1977.

995 Lystad, Mary Hanemann. "Sexual Abuse in the Home: A Re-
        view of the Literature." International Journal of Family
        Psychiatry 3, no. 1 (1982): 3-31.
        Includes a discussion of incest, both parent-child and sibling,
and marital rape. Characteristics of the individuals and situations,
consequences of the activity, prevention and intervention strategies are

reviewed. More research is needed so better prevention methods can
be instituted.

996 Lystad, Mary Hanemann. "Violence at Home: A Review of the
      Literature." American Journal of Orthopsychiatry 45
      (April 1975): 328-45.
      A scholarly overview of family violence with some attention
devoted to spouse abuse. The various studies have been analyzed from
sociological, psychological, and cultural perspectives with the results
indicating that the theories are not contradictory. A good bibliography
is included.

997 Lystad, Mary. Violence at Home: An Annotated Bibliography.
      Rockville, Md. : National Institute of Mental Health, Di-
      vision of Special Mental Health Programs, 1974. 95 p.
      This well-annotated bilbiography contains 190 items dealing
with family violence. Child abuse, sibling violence, and spousal violence are all discussed. Of limited value because it is now dated,
one may still wish to consult it for the early materials.

998 Lystad, Mary. "Violence in the Home: A Major Public Prob-
      lem." Urban and Social Change Review 15, no. 2 (1982):
      21-5.
      The problem of family violence is reviewed with emphasis
on child and spouse abuse. Various perspectives as described in the
literature, including psychological, social, and cultural interpretations,
are discussed. Lystad also includes an overview of intervention and
prevention methods which should be implemented to end family violence and prevent its being passed on to each succeeding generation.

999 Lythcott, Stephen. Powers and Duties of Family Court Commis-
      sioners. Madison: Wisconsin Legislative Council, 1978.
      9 p.

1000 MacDonald-Bradley, Katie. "Violence in Middle Class Homes."
       Health Visitor 56 (April 1983): 118-9.
       Contrary to the impression left by Jan Pahl's article
[1207], the middle class also has much family violence. Health visitors must be aware of the way various classes will react to such violence and their willingness to seek outside aid. Such aid-seeking
makes the violence public, something middle-class women are less
willing to do.

1001 MacKenzie, Brian. "Battered Women and the Law." Police
       Review 83 (1975): 555.
       The author, Detective Sargeant, Durham, England, takes
exception to an earlier article in Police Review (issue no. 4288) which
suggests that the police do not give sufficient assistance to battered
women. He believes the greatest problem is the women themselves
who refuse to carry through and prosecute their assaulters.

1002 MacLeod, Flora, ed. Family Violence: Report of the Task
      Force on Family Violence. Vancouver, B.C. : United
      Way of the Lower Mainland, 1979.

1003 MacLeod, Flora. Transition House: How to Establish a Refuge
      for Battered Women. Vancouver, B.C. : United Way of
      the Lower Mainland, 1982. 122 p.

1004 MacLeod, Linda, and Andree Cadieux. Wife Battering in Can-
      ada: The Vicious Circle. Hull, Que. : Canadian Govern-
      ment Publishing Centre, 1980. 72 p.
         The information for this study was provided by some 73
      transition houses and hostels that provide shelter to battered women
      in Canada. General information and statistics, common beliefs, why
      she stays, legal remedies and police intervention, shelters, and what
      still needs to be done are all discussed. A list of shelters is in-
      cluded. A serious and thoughtful study.

1005 Mahon, Lisa. "Common Characteristics of Abused Women."
      Issues in Mental Health Nursing 3 (January/June, 1981):
      137-57.
         The author, a psychiatric nurse at Southern Arizona Men-
      tal Health Center, Tucson, conducted this study to determine person-
      ality characteristics common to abused women. She also attempted
      to determine if those characteristics contributed to that abuse. Eleven
      participants completed the Cattell 16 PF questionnaire. The five traits
      shared by these women were 'sizothymia,' lower scholastic mental
      capacity, 'desurgency,' stronger superego strength (self-sufficiency),
      and substantive trend to lower ego strength. The author concedes the
      sample is too small to be conclusive, but nurses should keep these
      elements in mind when offering assistance to abuse victims. Greater
      knowledge of the patient will improve the treatment. A good survey of
      the literature and personality of abused wives is included.

1006 Maidment, Susan. "Laws for Battered Women--Are They an
      Improvement?" Family Law 7 (1977): 50-2.
         General discussion of the legal climate in England. She
      included details on the Domestic Violence and Matrimonial Proceedings
      Act of 1976 and the Law Commission Report on Matrimonial Proceed-
      ings in Magistrates' Court. Other legal needs relative to spouse
      abuse are discussed also.

1007 Maidment, Susan. "The Law's Response to Marital Violence:
      A Comparison Between England and the U.S.A." In Family
      Violence; An International and Interdisciplinary Study.
      Eds. John M. Eekelaar and Sanford N. Katz. Toronto:
      Butterworths, 1978, pp. 110-40. Also in International and
      Comparative Law Quarterly 26 (April 1977): 403-44.
         A member of the Department of Law, University of Keele,
      England, the author analyzes U.S. and British legal response to spouse
      abuse. Unwillingness of the police to interfere is discussed as well
      as the ineffectiveness of the courts to provide protection to the abused.
      The better aspects of the U.S. and English systems are noted with
      recommendations for changes in laws and attitudes.

1008   Maidment, Susan. "The Legal Response to Marital Violence."
       Family Law 7, no. 7 (1977): 201-4.
       The author is Lecturer in Law at Keele University. Her
article points up several areas of English law enforcement which could
be patterned after those in the U. S. This article is an edited version
of a paper presented at the Second World Conference of the International Society of Family Law, Montreal, Quebec, 1977. The ideas of
the article are elaborated further in her article in the International
Comparative Law Quarterly [1007].

1009   Maidment, Susan. "Solicitors and Marital Violence." New Law
       Journal 133 (July 15, 1983): 634.

1010   Makepeace, James M. "Courtship Violence Among College Stu-
       dents." Family Relations 30 (January 1981): 97-102.
       The author, Assistant Professor, Department of Sociology,
College of St. Benedict/St. John's University, reports that the courtship period sees much violence between the couples. Twenty percent
of those in his survey had direct experience and a majority knew of
others who had. Popular and professional perceptions of courtship are
apparently idealized. Further research on this topic is urged.

1011   Makman, Richard S. "Some Clinical Aspects of Interspousal
       Violence." In Family Violence; An International and Inter-
       disciplinary Study. Eds. John M. Eekelaar and Sanford N.
       Katz. Toronto: Butterworths, 1978, pp. 50-7.
       The Director of Quincy Court Clinic, Massachusetts De-
partment of Mental Health, claims that two concepts are important
to understanding spousal violence. The first is attachment, a natural
biologically innate process whereby strong affectionate bonds are made
with others. This helps explain why abused spouses are reluctant to
leave. The other is projection of one's own feelings on others. These
factors increase the possibility of danger. At times of marital stress
and separation, protection for the spouse is important and the courts
should recognize that need. This article explains the dangers and
needs from a perspective not noted elsewhere in such detail. Includes
case studies.

1012   Malhotra, Ajay Kumar. "The Relationship of Attributions for
       Physical Abuse to Learned Helplessness in Battered Wom-
       en." Ph. D. dissertation, California School of Professional
       Psychology, 1983. 172 p. Abstract in Dissertation Ab-
       stracts International 44B (May 1984): 3533.

1013   Mandel, Jane Barclay, and David M. Marcotte. "Teaching Fam-
       ily Practice Residents to Identify and Treat Battered Wom-
       en." Journal of Family Practice 17 (October 1983): 708,
       712, 715-6.
       Seminars were offered to family practice residents using
the learned helplessness model. Simulated patients were used several
months later to test effectiveness of the program. The results show
that attendance at the seminars did not increase the discovery of abuse,
but it did provide a more complete and specific plan for the victim than
when the resident had not attended. Fewer unnecessary prescriptions

were given and thoroughness of the interview and personal history records keeping improved.   This method of educating physicians proved
successful.

1014   Manley, Norma J.   "Battered Women: The Victims' Perceptions."
         M. A. thesis, California State University, Sacramento, 1982.
         113 p.   Abstract in Masters Abstracts 21 (March 1983): 110.

1015   Maracek, Mary.   Say "No" to Violence.   Somerville, Mass. :
         Respond, Inc. , 1983.   50 p.
         A handbook of advice for women abused by their mates.
Rights the women should have--including freedom from physical, emotional, and psychological abuse--are discussed.

1016   Marcovitch, Anne.   "Refuges for Battered Women."   Social Work
         Today 7, no. 2 (1976): 34-5.
         The author draws from her experience with the Acton Wom-
en's Aid Shelter (England).   She details several case histories and
stresses the need for social workers to recognize the urgency of need
in violent spouse-abuse situations.   Rather than social workers concerning themselves with saving the marriage, they should realize that
the immediate need is for safety of the spouse.

1017   Marcovitch, Anne.   "Wife Battering."   British Medical Journal
         1, no. 5958 (March 15, 1975): 629.
         Reference is made to J. J. Gayford's article in this journal.
A plea for more support for shelters and support from the medical
community.

1018   Marcus, Maria L.   "Conjugal Violence: The Law of Force and
         the Force of Law."   California Law Review 69 (December
         1981): 1657-733.
         A long and detailed analysis of the legal aspects of marital
violence.   The questions of self-defense and insanity pleas by wives
who have killed abusing husbands are examined.   Since a major goal
of criminal law prosecution is deterrence of others, refusal of the
jury, judge or law enforcement agencies to view spouse abuse as illegal
assault will only encourage victims to take law into their own hands
as well as fail to deter abusers from their activities.   An excellent
overview.

1019   Marcus, Ruth.   "Virginia Jury in Novel Verdict Awards $65,000
         to Woman Beaten by Her Husband."   National Law Journal
         2 (June 9, 1980): 3, 19.
         While Virginia accepts the principal of interspousal immu-
nity for most situations, in this case a battered ex-wife received a
settlement for medical bills and for pain and suffering.

1020   Margolin, Gayla.   "Conjoint Marital Therapy to Enhance Anger
         Management and Reduce Spouse Abuse."   American Journal
         of Family Therapy 7 (Summer 1979): 13-23.
         Mismanagement of anger is disruptive to the marital rela-
tionship.   If the marriage is to be preserved (not always good) new

methods of expressing anger are needed. This therapy is based on
the beliefs that abusiveness is learned, that it is a mutual problem,
and that it is related to poor problem-solving skills. A case history
and a treatment strategy are provided to show what can be done in
those relationships where resolution is really desired.

1021   Marin County Human Rights Commission. Violence Toward
       Marin Women: Commendations and Recommendations.
       San Rafael, Cal.: The Commission, 1979. 1 v.

1022   "The Marital Rape Exemption." New York University Law Re-
       view 52 (May 1977): 306-23.
       Various justifications for the immunity are detailed, in-
cluding the Hale doctrine, which asserts that the wife is the husband's
property; the implied consent of marriage vows; the problem of prov-
ing rape by the husband; the notion that a conviction for marital rape
would make reconciliation of the couple difficult, if not impossible;
and the idea that the assault and battery laws will take care of marital
rape charges. Recent laws like those of South Dakota and Delaware
would grant married women the protection they currently lack.

1023   "Marital Violence in Rural America." Response to Violence
       and Sexual Abuse in the Family 2 (February 1979): 1-2.

1024   Marquardt, Jane A. , and Cathie Cox. "Violence Against Wives:
       Expected Effects of Utah's Spouse Abuse Act. Journal of
       Contemporary Law 5 (Spring 1979): 277-92.
       Basically a description of Utah's 1979 Spouse Abuse Law.
A long and excellent explanation of the theory of "learned helplessness"
and how this perpetuates wife beating in a family. This new law does
not solve all the problems, but it does indicate institutional recognition
that wife beating is not acceptable behavior. It also puts more teeth
in the protective order and increases the responsiblities that policemen
have at the scene of a domestic dispute. This law is viewed as a
good beginning.

1025   Marsden, Dennis, and David Owens. "The Jekyll and Hyde Mar-
       riage." New Society 32 (May 8, 1975): 333-5.
       This study was conducted by two English sociology lecturers.
Nineteen women were interviewed. Information here basically confirmed other research. Most wives did not want to end the marriage,
which was for the most part acceptable. They only wanted to eliminate
the Mr. Hyde part.

1026   Martin, Del. Battered Wives. San Francisco: Glide, 1976.
       269 p.
       This is one of the best popular accounts of the problem
of wife beating. Written with a feminist perspective, this monograph
discusses patriarchy, what creates the abuser, why the wife stays,
how the legal system and social services fail and recommended legal
changes. A chapter on how the wife can survive the experience contains much practical advice and another includes valuable information
on shelters.

1027   Martin, Del. "Battered Women: Scope of the Problem." In
          Perspectives on Crime Victims. Eds. Burt Galaway and
          Joe Hudson. St. Louis, Mo. : C. V. Mosby, 1981, pp.
          190-201. Also in Battered Women: Issues of Public Pol-
          icy. U. S. Commission on Civil Rights. Washington, D. C. :
          The Commission, 1978, pp. 205-27.
          This article is a good overview of the problem. The prob-
lem cannot be resolved without changes in societal attitudes regarding
male and female roles and the traditional family economic situation.

1028   Martin, Del. "Battered Women: Society's Problem." In The
          Victimization of Women. Eds. Jane Chapman and Margaret
          Gates. Beverly Hills, Cal. : Sage, 1978, pp. 111-41.
          A good overview of wife abuse including an historical per-
spective. Police and social services are seen as ineffective, even
when sympathetic. Social attitudes must be changed. Improving the
legal and social services are only stopgap and should not be viewed
as real solutions. Marriage must be seen as a truly egalitarian
partnership or relationship.

1029   Martin, Del. "The Economics of Wife-beating." Paper pre-
          sented at the annual meeting of the American Sociological
          Association, New York, 1976.

1030   Martin, Del. "Lives on the Rocks: The Phoenix Solution."
          Ms (August 1976): 97. Also in Domestic Violence. U. S.
          Congress. House. Committee on Education and Labor,
          Subcommittee on Select Education. 95th Cong. 2nd Sess.
          Hearings on H. R. 7927 and H. R. 8948, March 16 and 17,
          1978. Washington, D. C. : Government Printing Office, 1978,
          p. 377.
          A short description of Rainbow Retreat Shelter in Phoenix,
Arizona. This refuge is reserved for abused families of husbands
with drinking problems. One sign of the program's effectiveness is
that 64 percent of the husbands do get treatment.

1031   Martin, Del. "Society's Vindication of the Wife Batterer." Bul-
          letin of the American Academy of Psychiatry and the Law
          5 (1977): 391-401.
          A number of ways by which the batterer is vindicated, or
at least the complaints of the victim are not taken seriously, are described. Overall there is a desire by society to preserve the family
so any violent behavior by the husband tends to be ignored. The police,
attorneys, courts, and others all remain uncommitted to strong action.

1032   Martin, Del. "What Keeps a Woman Captive in a Violent Rela-
          tionship? The Social Context of Battering." In Battered
          Women. Ed. Donna M. Moore. Beverly Hills, Cal. :
          Sage, 1979, pp. 33-57.
          The socialization of males and females, the effects of mar-
riage on the woman's rights, the criminal justice system and the social
service system are all discussed and how each helps keep the wife captive to her situation is made obvious. Since wife beating is a crime,

the legal system must accept its responsibility and arrest and prosecute the assaulters.   Currently the shelter network provides the only
real protection the victim has.

1033 Martin, Del.   "Wife-beating and the Marriage Contract."   Nurs-
         ing Dimensions 7 (Spring 1979): 42-4.
      This article was reprinted from her book Battered Wives.
She draws from a variety of sources and cultures throughout history,
painting a graphic picture of how monogamy has not served women well.

1034 Martin, J. P. , ed.   Violence and the Family.   New York: John
         Wiley and Sons, 1978.   369 p.
      The purpose of this volume is to provide an overview of
family violence, to put that knowledge in a psychological and sociological perspective, and to contribute to the process of educating social
workers, other professionals, and the general public about the problem.   J.J. Gayford, R.J. Gelles, D. Marsden, J. Melville and others
all contribute to the volume.   Among the lessons in this book are 1)
the legitimacy of using force in family disputes is primarily socially
determined, not legally, and 2) there is a close correlation between
the amount of force used in society as a whole and the amount found
in the family.   It may not be possible to eliminate family violence, but
it can be limited.   More attention in this book is devoted to spouse
abuse than child abuse.   The author is in the Department of Sociology
and Social Administration at the University of Southampton.

1035 Maryland State Police.   Maryland Battered Spouse Report.   Pikes-
         ville, Md. : Author, 1979.

1036 Mascia, Cynthia A.   "A Study of the Treatment of Battered Wom-
         en in Emergency Room Settings."   Ph. D. dissertation, Kent
         State University, 1983.   190 p.   Abstract in Dissertation
         Abstracts International 44B (November 1983): 1580.

1037 Massachusetts Coalition of Battered Women Service Groups.   In-
         Service Training Committee.   For Shelter and Beyond: An
         Educational Manual for Working with Women Who Are Bat-
         tered.   Boston: The Coalition, 1981.   75 p.

1038 Masson, Judith M.   "Domestic Violence and Matrimonial Pro-
         ceedings Act 1976."   Family Law 7 (1977): 29-31.
      This act amends the English Matrimonial Homes Act of 1967
and gives the court the discretion to attach a power of police arrest
for breach of an injunction in some cases of domestic violence.   The
fine points of the law are described and the implications detailed.
The law provides a simplified procedure for those already protected,
but left cohabitants and divorcees in the same legally vulnerable position as before.

1039 Masumura, Wilfred T.   "Wife Abuse and Other Forms of Ag-
         gression."   Victimology: An International Journal 4, no. 1
         (1979): 46-59.
      The author, with the JWK International Corporation, studied

86 primitive cultures to determine the relationship between wife abuse
and other forms of aggression in each society.   The results indicate
there is a strong correlation between wife beating and homicide, suicide, feuding and other forms of violence.   Sexual jealousy and the
society's general tendency toward violence may well be important factors affecting the rate of wife abuse.

1040 Matthews, Paul.   "Marital Rape."   Family Law 10 (August
          1980): 221-4.
          The author argues the ridiculousness of the notion that a
woman cannot retract her consent to sex after marriage thereby making marital rape legally impossible.   Using the 1954 Miller case in
England as the backdrop, he argues against the Hale doctrine, claiming
that even if Hale interpreted common law accurately in 1736, which is
doubtful, and though the man and wife may be "one" in civil matters,
it certainly does not follow that they are one in criminal matters.   It
is suggested that the matter be submitted to the Court of Appeals for
a new opinion.   This would obviate the need for a statute or the wait
for a new incident of marital rape to test the old doctrine.

1041 Mattingly, Judith Ann.   "Wife Abuse: Correlates and Societal
          Response."   M. S. thesis, Arizona State University, 1981.
          122 p.
          Seventy women who had been abused by their partners and
sought shelter were studied.   Much of this study confirms previous
published research on the topic.   The majority of men and women
came from violent, alcoholic, or broken homes.   Stress is a significant force in these marriages and there is decided inequality in the
distribution of power, with the husband having most.   Economic dependency seems to be the major reason why women stay.

1042 Mauch, Pamela Arlene.   "The Effects of Training on Attitudes
          of Counselors About Battered Women."   Ph. D. dissertation,
          University of Missouri, Columbia, 1982.   236 p.   Abstract
          in Dissertation Abstracts International 43A (June 1983):
          3814.

1043 Mawby, R. I.   "A Note on Domestic Disputes Reported to the
          Police."   Howard Journal of Penology and Crime Preven-
          tion 7 (1978): 160-8.
          Mawby, Lecturer in Social Work, University of Bradford,
analyzes police reports of "domestic disputes" in Sheffield, England,
from March to December 1974.   He found that of 170 cases, 72 (42. 4
percent) involved spouses and of these a very low number (2. 8 percent)
involved injury.   From this, Mawby believes it difficult to justify the
view that injury is common in domestic disputes.   He also concluded
that "environmental" factors of the area also have no relationship to
cases of domestic disturbance.   There is a strong relationship between
the disputants, however.   They are rarely strangers.   There is also
little evidence that the police provide anything more than temporary relief.   More could be done.

1044 Maynard, Ann E.   "Portrait of a Battered Wife: Regaining

Freedom and Dignity." <u>Professional Medical Assistant</u> 13
(March/April 1980): 13-6.
Interview with an abused woman who left her husband. Discusses the decision to leave and her current lack of regrets over the
decision.

1045   McAnally, Mary.   <u>Family Violence: Poems on the Pathology.</u>
         La Jolla, Cal.:   Moonlight Publications, 1982.   102 p.

1046   McCabe, Sarah.   "Unfinished Business: A Note on the Reports
         of the Select Committees on Violence in Marriage and Vio-
         lence in the Family."   <u>British Journal of Criminology</u> 17
         (July 1977):   280-5.
         The reports of the first British Select Committees of 1974-
76 are analyzed and discussed with the problems delineated.   Assault
is a crime which must be dealt with.   If domestic violence is to be
dealt with outside the criminal justice system there must be a system
of justice made available because now there is none.

1047   McClung, Curtis E.   "Discussion" [of Bard's article in the same
         volume] In <u>Violence and the Family.</u>   Ed. Maruice R.
         Green.   (AAAS Selected Symposium, 47.)   Boulder, Colo.:
         Westview Press, 1980, pp. 121-2.
         McClung expresses support for Bard's training program.
The method was tried in Columbus, Georgia, in 1974, but not without
some initial resistance from the rank and file.   In the end the program proved successful.

1048   McConaghy, J. F.   "Police Crisis Intervention in Domestic Dis-
         putes."   <u>Australian Police Journal</u> 30 (July 1976):   142-58.
         The author, Lecturer in Social Psychology and Criminology
at the Queensland Police Academy, provides a general discussion of
police intervention in domestic disputes with emphasis on Australian
society.   He believes that a specially trained corps of policemen would
be a more effective force for enhancing good public relations and increasing social stability.

1049   McCormick, Andrew J.   "Men Helping Men Stop Woman Abuse."
         <u>State and Mind</u> (Summer 1980):   46-50.
         McCormick, a social worker and a founding member of
EMERGE, presents the major objectives and philosophy of this organization, whose purpose it is to help abusing men end their violence.
Male supremacy is at the heart of the problem and violence is used
to maintain power.   At the core is the belief that men have a right
to beat women and that violence is a legitimate way of settling disputes.   Using group and individual counseling, the first goal is to
stop the abuse and then deepen the man's awareness of his own emotional life.

1050   McCreary, Phyllis Groom.   "National Coalition Against Domes-
         tic Violence: A Skill Building Conference."   <u>Response to</u>
         <u>Violence in the Family</u> 3 (March 1980):   1.

1051 McDanal, Clarence E. , Jr. , and Bobbie L. Siegel. "An Abused
        Wife Before and After Filicide and Suicide by Her Husband."
        Hawaii Medical Journal 40 (February 1981): 48.
        This is a short case history of an abusing husband who
killed himself and his 9-year-old daughter when the wife, after a stay
at an abuse shelter, decided to cut all ties with him. The grieving
process, especially over loss of the daughter, was aided by her access to support by friends and relatives and her having realistic career goals.

1052 McDanal, Clarence E. , et al. "Child and Spouse Abuse Resi-
        dential Center." American Journal of Psychiatry 135
        (February 1978): 256-7.
        This letter to the editor tells of a shelter for a mother and
her children (either may be abused) in Honolulu. The shelter is a
five-bedroom house in a residential district and its function is to provide "a warm setting for a parent and child to remain safely together
during a crisis without financial burden." A successful program.

1053 McEvoy, Alan W. , and Jeff B. Brookings. Helping Battered
        Women: A Volunteer's Handbook for Assisting Victims of
        Marital Violence. Holmes Beach, Fl. : Learning Publica-
        tions, 1982. 26 p.
        Shelters often have difficulty attaining the funding levels
needed to provide adequate services. They must therefore rely on
volunteers to provide some of the services that abuse victims and their
families need. This booklet is written for volunteers who are told what
to expect, the personal qualities volunteers should have, how to establish effective communication and tips on telephone crisis counseling.

1054 McEvoy, Alan; Jeff B. Brookings; and Clifford E. Brown. "Re-
        sponses to Battered Women: Problems and Strategies."
        Social Casework 64 (February 1983): 92-6.
        A nonprofit organization designed to help battered women
was studied to determine what would be needed to improve services.
The agency's records, interviews with other cooperating agencies and
a random survey of the adult women of the community supplied the
data. Results indicate that a primary concern for such service agencies should be the continued education and improvement of the staff.
Burn-out can be avoided by not overcommitting staff without opportunities for informal socializing. Public information campaigns are recommended to prevent underutilization of the services, and the agency
should be aware of the negative public reaction that too strong a commitment to feminist politics may have.

1055 McFadyen, Joanna. "Inter-Spousal Rape: The Need for Law
        Reform." In Family Violence; An International and Inter-
        disciplinary Study. Eds. John M. Eekelaar and Sanford N.
        Katz. Toronto: Butterworths, 1978, pp. 193-8.
        The author is a research consultant of the Law Reform
Commission of Canada. In this article she is concerned primarily
with the problem of wife abuse in Canada. The marital exemption for
rape is criticized and new reform laws demanded. Various justifica-

tions for the exemption are discussed.   Full application of rape laws
in marital settings is not asked for in all cases.   Such reform would,
however, affirm the equality of women in marriages.   The current
law does not.

1056 McGlinchey, Anne.   "Woman Battering and the Church's Re-
      sponse." In Sheltering Battered Women.   Ed. Albert R.
      Roberts. New York: Springer, 1981, pp. 133-140.
        A former nun and currently coordinator of Women's Sur-
vival Space, a shelter in New York City, the author believes the church
has an important role to play in aiding battered women.   Instead of
feeding the guilt that these victims already have, more humane and
sensitive counseling and advocacy are recommended.   Too often the
clergy have sent the women back to their violent homes with the admo-
nition to be better wives or to learn to cope since nothing can be done.

1057 McGrath, Colleen.   "The Crisis of Domestic Order." Socialist
      Review 43 (January/February, 1979): 11-30.
        This essay is concerned with the question of wife beating
and explores interpretations of the social significance of family violence,
its causes, and strategies for dealing with it.   The author believes that
capitalist development has undermined the efficiency and legitimacy of
patriarchal family forms.   Feminist activities and the encouragement
of women to work outside the home have further weakened the social
authority of husbands.   Confronted with the erosion of this authority
men attempt to uphold their control the best they can.   This they do
through abuse and battering.   Sheltering is also discussed and seen as
a temporary measure.   McGrath believes that while feminists were
instrumental in founding many shelters, their ideology all too often
threatens their continuance.

1058 McGrath, Patricia E.; Phyllis Stine Schultz; and Diana B. Frank-
      lin.   The Development and Implementation of a Hospital Pro-
      tocol for the Identification and Treatment of Battered Women.
      (Domestic Violence Monograph Series, no. 5.) Rockville,
      Md.: National Clearing House on Domestic Violence, 1980.
      32 p.

1059 McKenzie, Thomas.   "Sticks and Stones Break More Than Bones."
      U. S. Catholic 44 (October 1979): 34-8.
        A general discussion of spouse abuse and the Catholic shel-
ter, Center for Victims of Family Violence.   The author believes two
causes for abuse stand out: alcoholism and the resentment husbands
have for "the new opportunities afforded to women."   Religion and spir-
itualism are viewed as important for women involved in or recently ex-
tricated from abusive marriages.

1060 McKinnie, Karen.   "The Use of Expert Testimony in the Defense
      of Battered Women."   University of Colorado Law Review
      52 (Summer 1981): 587-99.
        The author argues that traditional pleas of self-defense do
not adequately portray the situation as it relates to abused women who
kill their spouses.   Psychological autopsies can be used to reconstruct

the personality of the abuser and give the jury a better picture of the fear and imminent danger he represented.   Psychological autopsies have recently been allowed in Arizona and Colorado court cases.

1061   McLaughlin, Kenneth. "Criminal Law--Sexual Battery--No Inter-
         spousal Exception from Prosecution Under Florida Sexual
         Battery Statute--Smith v. Smith."   Florida State University
         Law Review 10 (Spring 1982): 326-37.
         McLaughlin discusses the question of marital rape as it
applies to the new (1974) Florida Sexual Battery Law.   In the case
of Smith v. Smith, the defense claimed the special exception when he
was accused of violently raping his estranged wife.   He was convicted
and the Court of Appeals recognized that the purpose of the law was
to prevent and punish crimes of violence.   The question that marriage
carries with it an implied consent to submit to sexual intercourse was
not dealt with.   The Smith case does seem to provide wives with the
same protection from sexual violence from their husbands that women
generally can expect when experiencing sexual violence from nonspouses.

1062   McLeod, Maureen C. "The Nature of Spouse Abuse and the
         Victim's Decision to Prosecute." Ph. D. dissertation, State
         University of New York, Albany, 1982.   294 p.   Abstract
         in Dissertation Abstracts International 43A (May 1983): 3713.

1063   McLeod, Maureen. "Victim Noncooperation in the Prosecution
         of Domestic Assault."   Criminology 21 (August 1983): 395-
         416.
         McLeod, Assistant Professor of Criminal Justice, Stockton
State College, N. J. , studied 6,200 cases of domestic assault to determine a relationship between the low rate of prosecution and the level
of victim cooperation.   As much as 78 percent of the wives refused to
cooperate.   There is little difference in frequency whether the victim
leaves or divorces the abuser, or if she stays.   The complexities of
the problem are discussed.

1064   McNeely, R. L. , and Joan M. Jones.   "Refuge from Violence:
         Establishing Shelter Services for Battered Women."   Ad-
         ministration in Social Work 4 (Winter 1980): 71-82.
         The authors describe the patterns of administering a battered-
wife shelter that they believe to be the most effective.   The philosophy
of administration is supported by the experiences of Sojourner Truth
House of Milwaukee, Wisconsin.   Experience also indicates that abuse
is more widespread and common than originally believed and that while
temporary shelters are useful, more long-range provisions must be
made to provide the women with child-rearing and coping skills.   Dr.
McNeely is Associate Professor and Director of the Center for Adult
Development.   Dr. Jones is Assistant Professor, School of Social Welfare, University of Wisconsin-Milwaukee.

1065   McNulty, Faith. The Burning Bed. New York: Harcourt Brace
         Jovanovich, 1980.   275 p.
         This is an account of the case of Francine Hughes who killed
her abusing husband as he slept by setting his bed on fire in 1977.   The

story details the chronic marital violence to which she was subjected, the fatal incident, and the trial. Highly readable and sympathetic.

1066 McShane, Claudette. Annotated Bibliography on Woman Batter-
            ing. Milwaukee: School of Social Welfare, University of
            Wisconsin-Milwaukee, 1977. 25 p.

1067 McShane, Claudette. "Community Services for Battered Women."
            Social Work 24 (January 1979): 34-9.
            The legal, medical, and social services available to bat-
tered women are explained, but experience has proven them to be inadequate. A three-part strategy for improving service is outlined.
The first step is to raise the consciousness of the helping professionals
providing the services. The second is to establish coordinated link-
ages between the various services. This would make each more ac-
cessible. The third is case integration, which involves the coordination of the services for each woman in accordance with her needs.
This strategy will provide a pragmatic workable approach to assisting
abused wives.

1068 Meade, Marion. "The Battered Wife: Now There's Help."
            Sexology 43 (May 1977): 46-51, 80-1.
            A general article describing the problem, the personal char-
acteristics of the abuser and victim, why the victim stays with the
abuser, role of the police and the inadequacy of law enforcement. The
problem stems from the inequality of the sexes in our society and probably will continue as long as the inequality does.

1069 Mechau, Dorik V. Final Evaluation Report on Shelter for Abused
            and Battered Women and Their Children Operated by Abused
            Women's Aid in Crisis (AWAIC), Anchorage, Alaska. Haines,
            Ore.: Author, 1978. 30 p.

1070 Melling, Louise. "Canadian Programs for Men Who Batter."
            Response to Violence in the Family and Sexual Assault 6
            (January/February 1983): 7-8.

1071 Melling, Louise. "Employment Training for Battered Women."
            Response to Violence in the Family and Sexual Assault 6
            (November/December 1983): 1-2.

1072 Melville, Joy. "Hitting at Home." New Society 40 (May 26,
            1977): 397.
            This article is a brief overview of the English Domestic
Violence and Matrimonial Proceedings Act, 1976. The act has good
and bad features, but overall no new real benefits are anticipated.

1073 Melville, Joy. "In Search of a Refuge." New Society 41 (1977):
            389-90.
            Melville tells of the trials and roadblocks Hastings (England)
Refuge Group faced when attempting to establish and operate a shelter
in 1976 and 1977. The opposition encountered from government agencies and social workers was especially disappointing.

1074 Melville, Joy. "Wife Batterers." New Society 37 (August 19,
        1976): 400-1.
        The author describes a new program by the Chiswick Wom-
en's Aid for the husbands who batter.   The men come together weekly
for group therapy.   Most have a wife at the Chiswick Shelter and become involved in therapy to get their wife back.   No radical changes
in behavior are expected, but the hope is that the husband will gain
better control of himself.

1075 Menzies, Ken S. "The Road to Independence: The Role of a
        Refuge." Victimology: An International Journal 3, nos.
        1-2 (1978): 141-8.
        Menzies, University of Guelph, focuses on the entire victim-
offender relationship and how shelters and refuges can help abused
wives.   Thirty-five women from a southern Ontario shelter were surveyed between January 1976 and July 1977.   The abusive situation, why
the abuse was tolerated so long, and the effects of refuge residence
are analyzed.   The results indicate that the shelter experience helped
the victim develop a sense of personal worth and autonomy.   It also
helped her to realize that nothing she did within the relationship would
stop the violence.

1076 Meredith, Eileen. "Some Possibilities and Problems in the Pro-
        ceedings Used in Cases of Abuse of Women in the Family."
        In Battered Women and Abused Children. (Issues occa-
        sional papers, no. 4.) [Bradford, Eng.]: University of
        Bradford, 1979, pp. 16-41.
        A good descriptive overview of the practical problem and
realities of the British legal situation as it applies to spouse abuse.
Many examples are used to illustrate the points.   Of special concern
is the question of property rights and who is being deprived of a home
by the legal action or lack thereof.

1077 Meriweather, Lee. "Is Divorce a Remedy?" Westminster Re-
        view 131 (June 1889): 676-85.
        Arguments regarding easier divorce because of cruelty are
advanced.   A listing of 22 cases of men and 53 women asking for divorce shows much cruelty, beating, and violence is directed at both
men and women.

1078 Mesch, Beverly. "Why Women Stay with Men Who Beat Them."
        Essence 13 (April 1983): 85-7, 147, 149, 151.
        In this article the founder and president of the Family Cri-
sis Shelter in Hilo, Hawaii, discusses why abused women stay with
their assaulters.   She indicates that being Black will sometimes have
an influence in that Black women may feel that the Black family must
stay together at all costs.   Other racially based rationalizations may
have an influence, but most reasons cross such lines.   A list of signs
for recognizing a batterer and advice to battered women are included.

1079 Mettger, Zak. "A Case of Rape: Forced Sex in Marriage."
        Response to Family Violence and Sexual Assault 5 (March/
        April 1982): 1-2, 13-15.

1080 Mettger, Zak. "Help for Men Who Batter: An Overview of Issues and Programs." Response to Family Violence and Sexual Assault 5 (November/December 1982): 1-2, 7-8, 23.

1081 Mettger, Zak. "More Than a Shoestring Budget: Survival and Growth for Family Violence Programs." Response to Family Violence and Sexual Assault 5 (May/June 1982): 1-2, 15, 17-20.

1082 Mexican American Legal Defense Education Fund. The Legal Rights of Battered Women. San Francisco: La Casa de las Madres (197?). 25 p.
This handbook outlines resources available to California women, especially in San Francisco, who are involved in violent home situations. Legal and economic resources are included. This handbook is useful to the general public interested in the problem, not just the abused.

1083 Meyers-Abell, Judith E., and Mary A. Jansen. "Assertive Therapy for Battered Women: A Case Illustration." Journal of Behavior Therapy and Experimental Psychiatry 11 (1980): 301-5.
Assertiveness training is recommended for women who live in abusive relationships. A case history illustrates how women in shelters can begin the training, but more support and reinforcement may be necessary if she returns to her husband. Use of such techniques should not begin abruptly since the new behavior may prompt more violence from the abuser.

1084 Meyers, Laura. "Battered Wives, Dead Husbands." Student Lawyer 6 (March 1978): 46-51.
Many cases of husband-killing terminate a long-standing abusive relationship. There is concern by some over these women "taking the law into their own hands." If the laws were more responsive to the needs of battered women, the killings might not occur in the first place.

1085 "Miami Shelter and Agencies Coordinate Services." Response to Violence and Sexual Abuse in the Family 2 (May/June 1979): 3-4.

1086 Mill, John Stuart. On the Subjection of Women. Greenwich, Conn.: Fawcett Publications, 1971. 127 p.
Often considered one of Mill's "minor" essays, this one does condemn the cruel treatment that far too many women receive at the hands of husbands and other men. Some attention is devoted to wife beating.

1087 Miller, David M. "Domestic Violence." M.A. thesis, California State University, 1982. 67 p.

1088 Miller, Donna. "Innovative Program Development for Battered Women and Their Families." Victimology: An International

Journal 5, nos. 2-4, (1980): 335-46.
Miller discusses the development and philosophy of Hiatus
House, a shelter in Windsor, Ontario. Such elements of the program
as funding, community resources and responses, admission policies,
the program, staffing, and public relations are detailed. To be successful, programs must be involved with research, law reform, prevention programming, and public education. "We must move domestic
violence out of the sphere of a woman's issue to an issue relevant to
all of society."

1089 Miller, J. G. "The Domestic Violence and Matrimonial Proceed-
         ings Act 1976." Conveyancer and Property Lawyer 41
         (September/October 1977): 330-40.
      Miller provides here an analysis of the English Domestic
Violence and Matrimonial Proceedings Act of 1976 as it pertains to
property rights. The new law allows the courts to decide who in the
abused family is to remain in the house and who must find quarters
elsewhere. This action is possible, however, only after papers of
divorce or separation are actually filed. The question of injunctions
and their enforcement, who stays in sole-owner homes and joint-owner
homes, and other concerns are discussed.

1090 Miller, Jeanne Clarissa. "An Application of Learned Helpless-
         ness Theory to Battered Women." Ph.D. dissertation,
         California School of Professional Psychology, San Diego,
         1981. 79 p. Abstract in Dissertation Abstracts International
         42B (November 1981): 2071.

1091 Miller, Mark, and Judith Miller. "The Plague of Domestic Vio-
         lence in the U.S." USA Today 108 (January 1980): 26-8.
      A general overview of domestic violence with attention to
child and wife abuse. National attention must be turned to this problem with funds and resources used comparable to that used for national
defense. Straus, Steinmetz, Gil, Fields, and other researchers are
quoted.

1092 Miller, Nick. Battered Spouses. (Occasional Papers on Social
         Administration, no. 57.) London: G. Bell, 1975. 69 p.
      An early study of spouse abuse, this volume is an expanded
version of the author's master's paper in social administration at the
London School of Economics. Improvements in the official attitudes toward abuse, educating the public regarding the problem, providing
"Family Courts," financial support and shelters, encouraging voluntary
organizations to assist these victims, and other suggestions are advanced by Miller. Overall, a useful study, although some changes have
occurred since publication.

1093 Milligan, N., and Milne Anderson. "Conjugal Disharmony: A
         Hitherto Unrecognized Cause of Strokes." British Medical
         Journal 281 (August 9, 1980): 421-2.
      Two British neurologists from the Midland Centre for Neu-
rosurgery and Neurology report on two cases of stroke in women of
childbearing age. Such occurrences are rare and the authors were

puzzled regarding the cause until it was learned that each had suffered attempted strangulation by their husbands. Doctors are urged to be aware of other such possibilities.

1094 Mills, Joan. Abused Women: Victims of Family Preservation. Congressional Clearing House on Women's Rights. May 23, 1977. 5 p.
Discusses the preservation of the family as an ideal which sometimes conflicts with individual rights and liberties. Care should be taken in this regard.

1095 Mills, Trudy Lorena. "Violence and the Self: A Multi-method Study." Ph. D. dissertation, University of North Carolina, Chapel Hill, 1982. 182 p. Abstract in Dissertation Abstracts International 43A (May 1983): 3722.

1096 Milwaukee Task Force on Battered Women. Battered Women: Handbook for Survival. Revised edition. Milwaukee, Wis.: Author, 1978. 16 p.
A useful pamphlet aimed at abused women in Milwaukee, Wisconsin. Sage and practical advice is offered to those needing relief from domestic violence.

1097 Minnesota Crime Control Planning Board. Family Violence. [St. Paul?]: Author, 1978. 38 p.
This is a study of family violence in Minnesota with emphasis on child and adolescent abuse and spouse battering. A general discussion of the problem is supported with statistics on frequency of incidents, who the abusers are, and legal implications.

1098 Minnesota Department of Corrections. Minnesota Data Collection on Battered Women: System Design and Data Analysis. St. Paul: Author, 1979. 26 p. Also in Domestic Violence: Prevention and Services. U. S. Congress. House. Committee on Education and Labor. Hearing. 96th Cong. 1st Sess. July 10 and 11, 1979. Washington, D. C.: Government Printing Office, 1979, pp. 287-313.
This is an excerpt of the report made to the state legislature regarding programs and services for battered women. Purpose of the data collection is to accumulate information so better policy decisions and laws will result. Number of incidents, location, frequency, length of time violence has been occurring, race of the victim, age, number of children and relationship to the abuser are included, along with many other useful statistics.

1099 Minnesota Department of Corrections. Minnesota Programs for Battered Women, 1981 Update. St. Paul: Author, 1981. 64 p.
Collection of spouse-abuse data was mandated by the state in 1977. The result is many data on the sex, race, frequency, duration, etc. of family violence in Minnesota. Forms were to be completed by physicians, hospitals, public health agencies, and others. A model which other states might wish to consider. Copies of the forms and a list of resources are included.

1100   Minnesota Department of Corrections.   Programs and Services
          for Battered Women.   Battered Women: An Effective Re-
          sponse.   (Loose-leaf for updating.)   Compiled and edited
          by Susan M. Aumer.   St. Paul: The Department, 1978.
          1 v.

1101   Mishkin, Barry.   Domestic Violence.   Dayton, Ohio: P. P. I.
          Publishing, 1981.   74 p.

1102   Mitchell, Alexander R. K.   Violence in the Family.   Hove, Eng. :
          Wayland Publishers, 1978.   144 p.
          Various aspects of family violence are reviewed with some
attention to child abuse and wife battering.   Man is naturally aggressive and violence occurs when this aggression is curbed.   Society must
allow for the natural self-assertion humans desire.   People must be
taught to recognize when their expectations are unrealistic because frustrated expectations result in violent behavior.

1103   Mitchell, Marilyn Hall.   "Does Wife Abuse Justify Homicide?"
          Wayne Law Review 24 (September 1978): 1705-31.
          In response to her question in the title, the author's an-
swer is no.   While the legal profession must accept part of the responsibility for why wife abuse is not treated seriously enough, it cannot accept homicide as legitimate self-defense.   Wife abuse must be
recognized as a crime and prosecuted.   Battered-wife syndrome cannot
be used as a method of avoiding prosecution.   To include it as self-
defense "would not only validate a kind of vigilante justice the law is
supposed to preclude, but would also establish a virtual sex discrimination classification. . . . "

1104   Mitchell, Roger E. , and Christine A. Hodson.   "Coping with
          Domestic Violence: Social Support and Psychological Health
          Among Battered Women."   American Journal of Community
          Psychology 11 (December 1983): 629-54.
          The authors studied sixty women from spouse-abuse shel-
ters and found a relationship between levels of violence, inability to
cope, lack of support from friends and social services, and the victims' low self-esteem and depression.   Of interest is the finding that
victims with few friends, independent from their husbands', received
less support from those friends.

1105   Mitra, Charlotte L.   ". . . For She Has No Right or Power to
          Refuse Her Consent. "   Criminal Law Review (September
          1979): 558-65.
          The author challenges Hale's doctrine that a husband cannot
rape his wife.   The law should protect the victim, but it is obvious
that rape laws are intended to protect a man's property, in this case
his woman.   He, however, can use his property as he wishes.   The
problem, she says, is not of a legal nature, but one of social attitudes
toward and expectations of male and female sexuality.   The first principle that will have to be accepted is that the marriage contract does
not allow sex without the wife's consent.   Secondly, it should be a
legal presumption that consent is required for each sexual act as is
the case for unmarried persons.

1106 Monagan, Marilee. Battered Women. Sacramento: California
        Legislative Assembly Office of Research, 1976. 17 p.
        An attempt to discover how many counties in California had
services and resources available for physically and/or emotionally
abused women. Provided here is a county-by-county listing. One interesting note is that when the 25 agencies were asked if Santa Barbara
needed an emergency shelter only three said there was no need. Two
of these were the Sheriff's Department and the Police Department.

1107 Monagan, Marilee. "California Legislature Considers Pilot
        Centers for Domestic Violence Centers." Response to In-
        trafamily Violence and Sexual Assault 1 (April/June 1977):
        1-2.

1108 Monfalcone, Wesley R. Coping with Abuse in the Family. Phil-
        adelphia: Westminster Press, 1980. 120 p.
        Various forms of family abuse--physical, verbal, and psy-
chological--directed at any of the family's members are this author's
concern. Adhering to Christian principles and living the good life
should be the aim of the abuser and the abused. How to handle abuse
and how to recognize one's own abusive action are discussed.

1109 Moore, Donna M., ed. Battered Women. Beverly Hills, Cal.:
        Sage, 1979. 232 p.
        This collection of essays provides an overview of the prob-
lem of battered women, why it is difficult for women to extricate themselves from such relationships and how the legal system aids and/or
hinders relief. Articles by D. Martin [1032], L. Walker [1667], E. J.
Paterson [1236], S. Blair [145], and others are annotated elsewhere in
this bibliography. The handbook by La Casa de las Madres, Legal
Rights of Battered Women, is reproduced here.

1110 Moore, Donna M., and Fran Pepitone-Rockwell. "Experiences
        With and Views About Battered Women? A Research Note."
        In Battered Women. Ed. Donna M. Moore. Beverly Hills,
        Cal.: Sage, 1979, pp. 119-43.
        In 1978 a conference entitled "Battered Women" was held
at the University of California, Davis. Persons attending were given
a questionnaire regarding any personal experiences with battering and
their attitudes toward battering and violence; 110 women and 10 men
responded. Among the findings was that most participants had not experienced battering, but that most women feared physical violence at
the hands of men. Most also believed that battering was a result of
socialization and that it is a public problem, not a family one. Solving
alcohol abuse will not solve spouse abuse. The authors feel the survey
raised more questions than it resolved.

1111 Moore, Janet Hill. "Sex-role Stereotyping in Battered Women:
        Responses to the BEM Sex-role Inventory." Ph.D. disser-
        tation, Virginia Commonwealth University, 1983. 83 p.
        Abstract in Dissertation Abstracts International 43B (Novem-
        ber 1982): 1663.

1112 Moore, Jean G. "Yo-yo Children." Nursing Times 70 (December 1974): 1888-9.
        Moore, senior tutor in charge of training, NSPCC, describes the effects on children caused by spouse abuse. Health visitors must be alert to the symptoms of this problem if they are to provide any help.

1113 Moore, J. G. "Yo Yo Children: Victims of Matrimonial Violence." Child Welfare 54 (1975): 557-66.
        This article restates the findings of a study done by the British National Society for the Prevention of Cruelty to Children regarding the effects spousal violence has on children. In over 80 percent of the cases, they were adversely affected. Children were too tired or nervous to do good school work, were often pawns in the parents' conflicts, and often turned their aggression inward. Helping these children is very difficult and sometimes all that can be done is to let the child know that someone cares. Much more research is recommended.

1114 Moore, Jean G. "The Yo-Yo Syndrome: A Matter for Interdisciplinary Concern." Medicine, Science, and the Law 15, no. 4 (1975): 234-6.
        Twenty-three cases of violent marital situations were studied to determine the effects of the violence and frequent moving and changing of residence on the children. The offspring were often used as pawns in the conflict, were victims of scapegoating, and had school and other social problems. The long-term effects are not known, but the short-term effects are highly visible.

1115 Moore, Sally. "In Her Own Words: The Battered Wife an Expert Says Can Be Found in Millions of American Homes, Rich and Poor." People 5 (May 3, 1976): 35-8.
        The author interviews Steward Omeglia, a Washington, D. C., attorney who specializes in domestic relations law. Presents a general review of the problem, including who are the abused and the abuser, why it happens, whether it's a crime, whether it occurs before marriage, and other aspects for a popular readership.

1116 Morgan, Karen. Administration and Funding of Domestic Violence Programs in Selected States. Madison: Wisconsin Legislative Council, 1978. 11 p.

1117 Morgan, Patricia A. "Constructing Images of Deviance: A Look at State Intervention in the Problem of Wife Battery." Paper presented at the annual meeting of the American Sociological Association, Toronto, Canada, August 24-28, 1981.

1118 Morgan, Patricia. "From Battered Wife to Program Client. The State's Shaping of Social Problems." Kapitalistate 9 (1981): 17-39.
        Morgan discusses how shelters for battered women begin as feminist, progressive collectivist programs and too often evolve into

professional, bureaucratic agencies. This happens when the capitalist state provides funding. The state seems to feel it necessary to view political problems as social problems and then moves in to "correct" them. The political feminist philosophy behind the original movement is defused as the feminist founders are gradually replaced by the professionals and bureaucrats. It should be understood that the capitalist state does this to all political movements, of which the shelter movement is but one example.

1119 Morgan, P. A. , and L. Wermuth. "Alcohol and Family Violence: An Overview of Information and Resources." Paper presented to the National Institute on Alcohol Abuse and Alcoholism, March 1980.

1120 Morgan, Steven M. Conjugal Terrorism: A Psychological and Community Treatment Model of Wife Abuse. Palo Alto, Cal. : R and E Research Association, Inc. , 1982. 102 p.
    "Conjugal terrorism is the use or threatened use of violence in order to break down the resistance of the victim to the will of the terrorist." The violent husband has a neurotic idealized self-image and feels justified in his need to dominate and control the wife's behavior. He usually has a narrow definition of what is right and proper and relies heavily on inner cues when making these judgments. In many ways the conjugal terrorist is much like the political terrorist. The community has the power to break the cycle of abuse because it has the psychological and financial resources. Two programs, the first being the provision of physical safety (shelters) and the second being job training programs and peer support groups, are seen as the answers. Useful.

1121 Morgan, Steven Michael. "Conjugal Terrorism: A Psychological and Community Treatment Model of Wife Abuse." Ph. D. dissertation, California School of Professional Psychology, Fresno, 1979. 127 p. Abstract in Dissertation Abstracts International 41B (July 1980): 361.

1122 Mott-McDonald Associates, Inc. The Report from the Conference on Intervention Programs for Men Who Batter. Washington, D. C. : U. S. Department of Justice, Law Enforcement Assistance Administration, 1980. 51 p.
    The punishment or counseling of the batterer is often overlooked with most resources being directed at the victim. Since this does little or nothing to stop the activity, a conference on the problem of the abuser was held in Belmont, Maryland, in May 1979 sponsored by LEAA. The purpose was to provide guidance to LEAA in developing intervention programs for batterers. The conference discusses the general problem, the characteristics of batterers and various intervention techniques. The hope is that alternatives to incarceration can be found and the methods outlined here seem to have some promise.

1123 Muldary, Patricia Spezeski. "Attributions of Causality of Spouse Assault." Ph. D. dissertation, United States International University, 1983. 133 p. Abstract in Dissertation Abstracts International 44B (October 1983): 1249.

1124 Mullen, R. "Learned Helplessness and the Sex Role Socializa-
      tion of Battered Women." Master's thesis, Fairfield Uni-
      versity, 1981.

1125 Munson, Paul J. "Protecting Battered Wives: The Availability
      of Legal Remedies." Journal of Sociology and Social Wel-
      fare 7 (July 1980): 586-600.
      Munson, University of Denver, provides an overview of
domestic violence with attention to spouse abuse. English and American legal traditions are examined. The problem currently seems to
be lack of enforcement of present laws. At the same time divorce
laws should be loosened, and the police should see family violence as
their domain and should be trained to handle such problems. The
medical profession must cooperate more fully with the police, more
shelters are needed, and several other remedies are recommended.

1126 Murphy, Robert B. , et al. "Training Patrolmen to Become
      Crisis Intervention Specialists." Police Chief 42 (Decem-
      ber 1975): 44-5.
      The San Jose Police Department, recognizing the need for
special training in dealing with family disturbances, arranged to have
a small number of sworn officers trained to teach others and hold in-
service training and periodic workshops for the rest. The experiment
is viewed as successful and can act as a model for others. All officers would be trained to handle domestic disturbances, but only a few
would be teaching the others. The program was seen as economical
and self-perpetuating with little, if any, need for outside consultants
after the first year.

1127 Murray, Linda. "Battered Women." Playgirl (April 1976):
      28-30.
      A general discussion of wife abuse. This article includes
the ideas of Natalie Shainess, Carol Victer, and others. Case histories and references to the book Looking for Mr. Goodbar are also found
here. Aimed at a popular readership.

1128 Mushanga, Tibamanya Mwene. "Wife Victimization in East and
      Central Africa." Victimology: An International Journal 2,
      nos. 3-4 (1977-78): 479-85. Also in International Perspec-
      tives on Family Violence. Eds. Richard J. Gelles and
      Claire Pedrick Cornell. Lexington, Mass. : Lexington
      Books, D. C. Heath, 1983, pp. 139-45.
      The author, from the University of Nairobi, examines
spouse abuse in East and Central Africa and the cultural values that
legitimize it. Provocation and victim precipitation are discussed.
Beatings and murder occur most frequently when the woman refuses
to be subservient, a situation not uncommonly found when western men
attempt to maintain patriarchy.

1129 Nation, Anne, and Barbara Burkey. Alternatives: A Resource
      Guide for Battered Spouses. Lincoln: Nebraska Commission

on the Status of Women, 1978. 62 p.
This guide provides excellent advice to the Nebraska abused wife regarding medical attention, legal alternatives available, where and how to obtain counseling, and what to do about the children. The information is presented in one way for the woman who stays and another for the woman who leaves. Other states or regions may wish to adopt this format.

1130 National Center for Women and Family Law. Model Handbook for Advocates for Battered Women [Chicago: The Center, 1980]. 271 p.

1131 National Center on Women and Family Law. Legal Advocacy for Battered Women. New York: The Center, 1982. 259 p.

1132 National Center on Women and Family Law. Marital Rape Exemption Packet. New York: The Center, 1982. 30 p.

1133 National Council of Jewish Women. Domestic Violence: A NCJW Response. New York: Author, 1981. 59 p.
This is a useful manual aimed at helping interested persons set up local awareness groups. General facts regarding spouse abuse are given along with details on setting up meetings. Next come sections on community needs assessment, volunteering time and services, etc. A practical aid.

1134 National Society for the Prevention of Cruelty to Children. School of Social Work. "Yo Yo Children: A Study of 23 Violent Matrimonial Cases." London: The Society, 1974. 8 p. Also in Battered Women: A Psychosociological Study of Domestic Violence. Ed. Maria Roy. New York: Van Nostrand Reinhold, 1977, pp. 149-63.
This is a study of children in families with a high level of violence between the parents. The yo-yo syndrome is the constant moving of the children who frequently see several "homes" over a few months. They may be with the mother a few days, then the grandmother, then the father, then the two parents together and then it begins all over. The lack of a stable home situation, plus how this affects the well-being of the children is the primary problem. This study is useful in that in most studies the children are not taken into account. The National Society for the Prevention of Cruelty to Children, School of Social Work, in London, conducted this study in 1973.

1135 National Woman's Aid Federation. Battered Women Need Refuges: A Report. London, The Federation, [1977?]. 50 p.

1136 National Woman's Aid Federation. Battered Women, Refuges, and Women's Aid: A Report. [London: The Federation, 1978]. 54 p.

1137 "Needs of Battered Women Receive Special Attention from Milwaukee DA's Office." Response to Intrafamily Violence and Sexual Assault 1 (February 1977): 1-2.

1138 Neidig, Peter, and Dale H. Friedman. The Domestic Conflict
      Containment Program: Trainers Manual. Beaufort, S. C. :
      Behavioral Science Associates, 1983. 267 p.
      This ten-week program aims to end the violence, not the
relationship of the couple. The abuser is encouraged to accept responsibility for the violence.

1139 "Neighborhood Justice Centers: An Option for Battered Women?"
      Response to Intrafamily Violence and Sexual Assault 1
      (June/August 1978): 3.

1140 Nelson, Joanne C. ; Aviva Breen; and Bev Balos. Domestic
      Abuse Act: Order for Protection; The 'How to' Packet.
      [St. Paul: Minnesota Department of Corrections, Programs
      and Services for Battered Women, 1979]. 50 p.

1141 Nelson, Susan. "How Battered Women Can Get Help." Reader's
      Digest 110 (May 1977): 21-3, 26, 28.
      A general discussion of wife abuse, why men do it and why
women stay. Wives who are abused must seek help through counselors,
hot lines, shelters, and other forms.

1142 Nelson, Wendy. "Family Violence: Is Husband Abuse as Rare
      as It Seems?" Unpublished paper, St. Anselm's College,
      Manchester, New Hampshire, 1980. 11 p.
      This is a brief student paper which argues that since hus-
band abuse is as prevalent as wife abuse, similar resources should be
made available. Nurses and other health professionals should be prepared to give advice and assistance when these victims turn up in hospital emergency rooms.

1143 "New Findings Relate Victims' Problems to Poor Medical Prac-
      tices." Response to Violence and Sexual Abuse in the Fam-
      ily 2 (May/June 1979): 1-2.
      An overview of the Yale medical school study by Flitcraft,
Stark, and Frazier [1496].

1144 New Hampshire Advisory Committee to the U.S. Commission on
      Civil Rights. Battered Women and the New Hampshire Jus-
      tice System; A Consultation. Washington, D. C. : U. S.
      Commission on Civil Rights, 1980. 35 p.
      While interested in the problem as it relates to all of New
Hampshire, this advisory committee was particularly concerned with
abuse as it affected rural residents. The general problem, police responsiveness, the judicial system, social service agencies and shelters,
and 1979 New Hampshire legal reforms are all discussed. Relief is
recommended in the form of shelters and improved social, medical,
and legal services. Although some may believe the government has no
role in these domestic issues, the committee thinks it does.

1145 New Jersey Advisory Committee to the U. S. Commission on
      Civil Rights. Battered Women in New Jersey. Washington,
      D. C. : U. S. Commission on Civil Rights, 1981. 33 p.

Though concerned with all of New Jersey, most of the data
come from Trenton and Ewing Township in Mercer County and Hack-
ensack in Bergen County.   Examined are the criminal justice procedures, including police departments and the courts, and those of public and private social service agencies, such as hospitals, shelters,
and welfare agencies.   At least 30 witnesses and battered women were
interviewed.   The results indicate that New Jersey is in the forefront
of the shelter movement, but there is much that needs to be done.
More funding of necessary services is required.   Abuse exists only
because it is tolerated.   It will cease only when society decides that
such behavior is unacceptable and is, in fact, a criminal act.

1146 "New Training Project for Pennsylvania Shelters." Response to
      Violence and Sexual Abuse in the Family 2 (November/De-
      cember 1978): 1-2.

1147 New York.   Governor's Task Force on Domestic Violence.   Do-
      mestic Violence: Report to the Governor and the Legisla-
      ture.   Karen Burstein and Marjory Fields, Co-Chairpersons.
      [Albany]: The Task Force, 1981.   62 p.
      The New York Task Force was established in May 1979 to
study the traumatic effects of domestic violence and how social and
legal systems can better deal with such violence and its causes.   Domestic violence, including child abuse, elder abuse and spouse abuse,
is life threatening and no one should be forced by social or economic
pressure to live under such conditions.   Long-term measures must
include raising the status of children, the elderly and women in society.
A total of twenty-one recommendations are suggested for ending abuse,
including legal reform, judicial reform, education of the public and
professionals, and use of toll-free hotlines.   Copies of proposed New
York laws are appended.

1148 New York.   State Department of Social Services.   Special Care
      Homes: A New Beginning; A Program Planning Guide.
      Albany: Author, 1980.   18 p.

1149 NiCarthy, Ginny.   Getting Free: A Handbook for Women in
      Abusive Relationships.   Seattle, Wash.: Seal Press, 1982.
      272 p.
      The author was founder and director of the Abused Women's
Network in Seattle and is currently a counselor with the Seattle Women's
Counseling Group.   This book is a practical guide for assisting women
to free themselves from abusive relationships and marriages.   The
handbook is also of value to counselors and professionals providing assistance to abused wives.   Basically a self-help guide, this book will
give the reader many insights into their situations.   Questions and concerns such as "Is it right to break up a family?" "But I still love him,"
and "How to get professional help" are all dealt with.

1150 Nichols, Beverly B.   "The Abused Wife Problem." Social Case-
      work 57 (January 1976): 27-32.
      Nichols is a caseworker for Family Counseling Services,
Waltham, Massachusetts.   She considers such factors as patriarchy,

male aggressiveness and female masochism as influencing abusive behavior. Several approaches to treatment, such as group therapy, assertiveness training, and individual counseling, are suggested. Social workers should be more assertive in abuse intervention.

1151 Nichols, Claudia. "The Military Installation: How the Company
      Town Deals With Rape, Spouse Abuse and Child Abuse."
      Victimology: An International Journal 7, nos. 1-4 (1982):
      242-51.

1152 Nichols, Margaret Elizabeth. "Reclaimed Lives: Experiences
      of Women and Feminist Counseling." Ph.D. dissertation,
      Columbia University, 1981. Abstract in Dissertation Abstracts International 44B (June 1984): 3940.

1153 Nichols, William C. "Wife Abuse: A Widespread Problem in
      Family Life Today." Parents Magazine 53 (January 1978):
      26.
      A general note on spouse abuse. Nichols observes that
humiliation is a major feature of the violence. Various efforts are
being made to end abuse, but more must be done.

1154 Nielsen, J., et al. "Why Women Stay in Battering Relationships."
      Paper presented at the annual meeting of the American Sociological Association, Boston, 1979.

1155 Niera, David J. "Wife-Killing in Medieval Hispanic Letters: A
      Prelude to the Calderon-Honor-Vengeance Trilogy." Paper
      presented at the Tennessee Philological Association, March
      1975.

1156 Nisonoff, Linda, and Irving Bitman. "Spouse Abuse: Incidence
      and Relationship to Selected Demographic Variables." Victimology: An International Journal 4 (1978): 131-40.
      Middle-class, suburban residents of Suffolk County, N.Y.
were surveyed by telephone between May and mid-June 1977. The
purpose was to determine if divorced or separated respondents would
be more apt to report spouse abuse than others, whether more persons
under forty than over would report knowing of cases of abuse, and the
relationship of occupational status and economic and job factors on
abuse. Information regarding this was found, as well as the fact that
spouse abuse in Suffolk County is not uncommon, that husbands and
wives engage in spouse abuse with equal frequency, and that such violence and some demographic factors are related.

1157 Nordby, Virginia Blomer. "Reforming Rape Laws: The Michigan Experience." In Rape Law Reform. Ed. Jocelynne A.
      Scutt. Canberra: Australian Institute of Criminology, 1980,
      pp. 3-34.
      Some attention is devoted to marital rape.

1158 Novak, Deborah Gayle. "Life Styles and Social Interest Ratings
      of Battered Women." Ph.D. dissertation, University of

Texas, Austin, 1979. 312 p. Abstract in Dissertation
Abstracts International 40B (September 1979): 1429.

1159 Novak, Deborah G. , and Deborah Tucker Meismer. "A Plea
      for Help: One Community's Response." Victimology: An
      International Journal 2, nos. 3-4 (1977-78): 647-53.
The motivation behind the establishment of the Austin Center for Battered Women in Texas and the problems encountered are
described. Information about the goals, the program, the funding grant,
the target population and the response to the program are all included.

1160 Oberg, Shirley, and Ellen Pence. "Responding to Battered Wom-
      en." In Perspectives on Crime Victims. Eds. Burt Gala-
      way and Joe Hudson. St. Louis, Mo.: C.V. Mosby, 1981,
      pp. 385-91.
The author discusses the Minnesota experience with spouse
abuse shelters. In 1977 the Minnesota legislature provided funding for
four shelters in a pilot experiment. By June 1980 the number had
grown to 15. An education program was also begun for the public and
professionals who were most likely to encounter cases of abuse. The
programs in Minnesota have not reduced the incidence of abuse, but
they have provided a much needed service. In that regard they are
quite successful.

1161 O'Brien, John E. "Violence in Divorce-prone Families." Journal
      of Marriage and the Family 33 (November 1971): 692-8.
      Also in Violence in the Family. Eds. Suzanne K. Stein-
      metz and Murray A. Straus. New York: Dodd, Mead,
      1974, pp. 65-75.
This study of 150 spouses involved in divorce action revealed a significant incidence of family violence. This behavior was
found to be most common when the husband was not achieving well in
the worker/earner role and where he demonstrated certain status characteristics lower than those of his wife.

1162 O'Donnell, Carol, and Heather Saville. "Sex and Class Inequality
      and Domestic Violence." In Violence in the Family: A
      Collection of Conference Papers. Ed. Jocelynne A. Scutt.
      Canberra: Australian Institute of Criminology, 1980, pp.
      79-83.
O'Donnell, Lecturer, Department of Education, Macquarie
University, and Saville, Tutor, Department of Sociology, University of
New South Wales, argue that constant battering is closely associated
with the vulnerability that accompanies the role of housewife and mother.
Emphasis on the individual psychology of the abuser or victim is mis-
leading. Information was gained from questionnaires from 145 battered
women.

1163 O'Donnell, William J. "Consensual Marital Sodomy and Marital
      Rape--The Role of the Law and the Role of the Victim."
      Paper presented at the annual meeting of the Academy of
      Criminal Justice Sciences, 1980.

1164   Ohio.   Attorney General's Task Force on Domestic Violence.
          Report.   Columbus: The Task Force, 1978.   68 p.
          This report deals with spouse abuse as well as child abuse
and parent abuse.   Few data were available on the family violence
situation in Ohio.   A lack of understanding of the problem was found
in many sectors, including law enforcement.   Recommendations were
made that the police be better trained to handle domestic situations,
certain legal forms be changed, hotlines be established, and shelters
be granted more and better financial support.

1165   Ohrenstein, Manfred.   Battered Women.   2 parts.   Albany: New
          York State Senate, Office of the Minority Leader, [1977?].
          This is New York's first statewide study of battered women,
the purpose of which was to determine how many there are, where they
are, and whether their needs are being met by current service systems.   Part one contains a general discussion of the problem plus the
results of an extensive survey of social service agencies, hospitals,
the police and court systems and shelters, to determine what each
knew about spouse abuse, what statistics were kept, and what services
were offered.   Part two is a county-by-county profile of the attitudes
of the several helping agencies and how many persons helped, if known.
A list of recommendations is included in this report.   Among them are
a statewide reporting requirement for police and health related service
agencies, the opening of more shelters, hot lines, and better coordination of services.

1166   Okun, Lewis Edward.   "A Study of Woman Abuse: 300 Battered
          Women Taking Shelter, 119 Woman-batterers in Counseling."
          Ph. D. dissertation, University of Michigan, 1983.   502 p.
          Abstract in Dissertation Abstracts International 44B (Decem-
          ber 1983): 1972.

1167   Olsen, Albert J.   Volunteers as Family Counselors: Paper
          Presented to the National Conference on Social Welfare.
          New York: Home Advisory and Service Council, 1972.
          10 p.

1168   Olson, Esther Lee, and Kenneth Petersen.   No Place to Hide:
          Wife Abuse, Anatomy of a Private Crime.   Wheaton, Ill.:
          Tyndale House, 1982.   144 p.
          This is the personal story of Charles and Claire and their
twenty-year violent marriage.   The authors point out that some Christian teachings taken to extremes can produce very dangerous situations
for Christian women.   For example, Claire's faith, her view of wom-
en's roles and traditional marriage and her interpretation of biblical
teaching nearly cost her her life.   This account is presented from a
staunch born-again Christian perspective.

1169   O'Neil, Michael J.   "A Little Help from Our Friends: Citizen
          Predisposition to Intervene in Spouse Abuse."   Law and
          Policy Quarterly 1 (April 1979): 177-206.
          O'Neil believes that more citizen participation would help
the police in their efforts to deal with spouse abuse.   A telephone survey

of 1,208 Chicago housewives was conducted to determine who was inclined to intervene personally or call the police if they suspected wife beating of a neighbor. The older citizens and the poor were most apt to call the police. A program for involving more citizens in crime intervention is described.

1170 Opel, Robert. "Due Process and Vermont's Abuse Prevention Statute." Vermont Law Review 7 (Spring 1982): 185-204.
After a brief discussion of spouse abuse, the author describes the Vermont Abuse Prevention Statute. Under it an order may be obtained to restrain the batterer from future acts of violence, to award the victim exclusive possession of the home, and award her sole custody of the children. The second element is what concerns the author most since it may be an unconstitutional deprivation of property without due process. This is argued at length with the conclusion that family violence is not to be allowed, but ex parte deprivations may cause even more frustration and in fact exacerbate the problem.

1171 Open University Course Team. Conflict in the Family: A Continuing Education Course. Milton Keynes, England: Open University, 1980. 6 v.

1172 Oppenlander, Nancy. Coping or Copping Out: Police Service Delivery in Domestic Arguments and Assaults. Bloomington: Indiana University Workshop in Political Theory and Policy Analysis, 1981. 31 p. Also in Criminology: An Interdisciplinary Journal 20 (November 1982): 449-65.
This paper describes the actions of investigating officers with family or intimately related persons during police encounters of arguments and assaults. It compares these with like investigations of nonrelated disputants. The findings illustrate important differences in police service for domestic disputes. Dispatches of patrol units tend to underreport the nature of domestic disputes. Thus, backup assistance and the primary officers' expectations do not fit the reality. Rather than an assault situation, they expect only a domestic argument.

1173 Oppenlander, Nan. "The Evolution of Law and Wife Abuse." Law and Policy Quarterly 3 (October 1981): 382-405.
The rights of American husbands regarding the beating of wives is traced to English and Roman law. Special attention is devoted to the last two hundred years and the gradual lessening of that right. The author notes that the right still exists in fact since law provides little protection to assaulted spouses, especially wives. The survival of marriage as a legal institution depends upon the policies pursued by the courts in the coming decades.

1174 Oppenlander, Nancy. Private Control, Public Problem: Legal Remedies to Violence in Marriage. Bloomington: Indiana University Workshop in Political Theory and Policy Analysis, 1981. 25 p.
To this author wife assault is simply the outcome of power struggles within the marriage. Couples implicitly or explicitly allocate responsibilities to maintain the household, a process called negotiating

the private marital contract. Wife abuse is a result of conflict over
its rules. This private contract is not the same as the legal/social
one and it is this one that has changed over the past 150 years.
These changes have not yet been fully sanctioned by or reflected in
the law.

1175 "Orders of Protection in Family Court Disputes." Columbia
       Journal of Law and Social Problems 2 (June 1966): 164-75.
       The New York Family Court provides a valuable service
and its orders of protection are practical aids in handling situations
of marital discord. Its limitations and strengths are evaluated. The
belief is that despite its drawbacks the order of protection constitutes
a flexible and effective tool.

1176 O'Reilly, Jane. "Wife Beating: The Silent Crime." Time 122
       (September 5, 1983): 23-4, 26.

1177 Organizing and Implementing Services for Men Who Batter.
       Boston: EMERGE, 1980. 122 p.

1178 Ostrowski, Margaret V. Legal Process for Battered Women.
       Vancouver, B. C. : United Way of the Lower Mainland,
       1979. 50 p.
       This handbook is of particular interest to battered women
of British Columbia, especially those who hope to invoke the legal
process to protect themselves from abusive husbands. The various
court procedures and remedies are described along with the Family
Relations Act (1978), assault, peace bonds, self-defense, and other
legal questions. A model handbook for other states.

1179 Ottenberg, Perry. "Violence in the Family: Abused Wives and
       Children." American Academy of Psychiatry and Law Bul-
       letin 5 (1977): 380-90.
       The author, Senior Attending Psychiatrist at the Institute
of the Pennsylvania Hospital, Philadelphia, and Professor of Clinical
Psychiatry, University of Pennsylvania, provides an overview of child
and spouse abuse. Various interpretations of the abuse are considered
with the conclusion that all wife-beating is not necessarily mental illness. Nor should all wife-beating necessarily lead to a legal confron-
tation. Crisis centers and shelters can help heal the family's wounds,
physical, and psychological.

1180 "Our Home Was a Battlefield." Good Housekeeping 175 (Octo-
       ber 1972): 78, 80-1, 83, 85-6.
       A personal account of wife beating. When the victim could
take no more she involved the police and the couple went to a family
counselor. There they learned how to resolve conflict without physical abuse.

1181 Owens, David. "Battered Wives: Some Social and Legal Prob-
       lems." British Journal of Law and Society 2 (Winter
       1975): 201-11.
       Owens, of the Department of Sociology, University College,

Cardiff, reviews some of the legal and social problems associated with spouse abuse. Interestingly, most of his suggestions were also quite independently made in the Report of the Select Committee on Violence in Marriage by the English House of Commons. Refuges are seen as important, but only as temporary measures. Since many women in abuse situations will end up in one-parent families, aid, advice, and assistance in that vein should be given more routinely. Aid to women who wish to remain in marriages without the violence should also be easier to acquire.

1182 Owens, David J., and Murray A. Straus, "The Social Structure of Violence in Childhood and Approval of Violence as an Adult." Aggressive Behavior 1 (1975): 193-211.
Based on a master's thesis by Owens, this paper details the results of a survey to determine whether violence observed by or inflicted on children affects their attitude toward it as adults. "We conclude that the culture of violence characterizing American society is, at least in part, attributable to the high level of violence experienced during the formative years of childhood." As such, the witnessing of violence between the parents, including wife beating, would have an effect. An interesting study supporting the notion that violent behavior is learned and passed from one generation to another.

1183 Ozzanna, Susan. "The Battered Woman's Only Solution." Majority Report 5 (February 7-21, 1976): 4.
This is the first of a five-part series regarding spouse abuse in Minnesota and the Women's Advocates of St. Paul. The following four articles [1184-1187] constitute the rest of the series.

1184 Ozzanna, Susan. "Life in a Feminist Crisis Center." Majority Report 5 (January 24/February 7, 1976): 1, 14.

1185 Ozzanna, S. Harmony. "A Refuge Is Where Women Can 'Grow Together.'" Majority Report 5 (March 5/March 20, 1976): 15.

1186 Ozzanna, S. Harmony. "What's Red and Black and Harbors Women in Crisis?" Majority Report 5 (February 21/March 6, 1976): 10.

1187 Ozzanna, S. Harmony. "Women's Crisis Housing Is for Pioneers." Majority Report 5 (March 20/April 3, 1976): 12.

1188 Paddington Neighbourhood Law Centre. Injunctions for Battered Wives: A Do-It-Yourself Kit. London: The Centre, [1975]. 6 p.

1189 Page, Barbara. "Marital Rape Banned: Sex Crime Reforms in South Australia." Ms 6 (August 1977): 19.

1190 Pagelow, Mildred Daley. "Battered Women: A New Perspective."

In Domestic Violence, 1978. U. S. Congress. Senate.
Committee on Human Resources, Subcommittee on Child
and Human Development. Hearings. 95th Cong. 2nd
Sess. On Domestic Violence and Legislation with Respect
to Domestic Violence, March 4 and 8, 1978. Washington,
D. C. : Government Printing Office, 1978, pp. 521-54.
Pagelow believes that to understand why wife abuse occurs,
one must see it in terms of the tripartite theoretical perspective she
outlines. Discussed in detail are the theory of causation, which describes the sociohistorical background of battering and the role tradition plays; the primary battering incident and how the personality of
the participants and their upbringing relate to it; and the secondary
battering, or the reoccurrence of incidents after the first one. She
fears some will view her approach as reductionist, but she believes
that understanding the interacting couple is the best way to analyze
the problem. This paper was also presented at the International Sociological Association, Dublin, August 1977.

1191 Pagelow, Mildred Daley. "Battered Women: Class and Race
        Differences and Similarities and Their Implications for Fu-
        ture Social Policy. " Paper presented at the annual meet-
        ing of the American Sociological Association, New York,
        August 1980.

1192 Pagelow, Mildred Daley. "Blaming the Victim: Parallels in
        Crimes Against Women--Rape and Battering. " In Domes-
        tic Violence, 1978. U. S. Congress. Senate. Committee
        on Human Resources, Subcommittee on Child and Human
        Development. Hearings. 95th Cong. 2nd Sess. On Do-
        mestic Violence and Legislation with Respect to Domestic
        Violence, March 4 and 8, 1978. Washington, D. C. : Gov-
        ernment Printing Office, 1978, pp. 608-39.
The crimes of rape and wife battering have much in common. Both are committed primarily by men against women, with wom-
en often being blamed for provoking it, not carrying through with prosecution, or being considered pathological. In both cases the crimes
are often seen as occurring primarily in the lower classes. All of
these concepts are discussed in detail and, in the last analysis, the
author says both crimes must be seen as hostile assaults on women intended to humiliate, degrade, and subjugate the victim. The purpose
is social control of women by men in an attempt to keep them "in
their places. "

1193 Pagelow, Mildred Daley. "Blaming the Victim: Parallels in
        Crime Against Women--Rape and Battery. " Presented at
        the annual meeting of the Society for the Study of Social
        Problems, Chicago, September 1977. 34 p. Also Wash-
        ington, D. C. : U. S. Department of Justice, LEAA, Na-
        tional Criminal Justice Service, 1978. 1 microfiche.

1194 Pagelow, Mildred Daley. "Does the Law Help Battered Women:
        Some Research Notes. " Paper presented at the annual
        meeting of the Law and Society Association Meetings, 1980.

1195 Pagelow, Mildred Daley. "Double Victimization of Battered
        Women: Victimized by Spouses and the Legal System."
        Paper presented at the annual meeting of the American
        Society of Criminology, 1980.

1196 Pagelow, Mildred Daley. "Factors Affecting Women's Decisions
        to Leave Violent Relationships." Journal of Family Issues
        2 (December 1981): 391-414.
            Pagelow challenges Gelles' opinions that severity and fre-
quency of abuse, and the amount of abuse suffered as a child are
among the factors that influence how much abuse a woman takes before she leaves her husband. She studied 350 battered women, mostly
from California and Florida, and found no support for the severity and
frequency hypothesis. In fact, just the opposite could be proven. Wom-
en in long-standing battering relationships are battered more frequently
and more severely. Thus, some stay regardless. The second theory
was not supported either. In fact it appears that the more violence
one has experienced as a child, the less one will tolerate as an adult.

1197 Pagelow, Mildred Daley. "Needs Assessment of Victims of
        Domestic Violence." In Research into Violent Behavior:
        Domestic Violence. U.S. Congress. House. Committee
        on Science and Technology. Hearings. 95th Cong. 2nd
        Sess. February 14, 15, 16, 1978. Washington, D.C.:
        Government Printing Office, 1978, pp. 1010-37.

1198 Pagelow, Mildred Daley. "Personal and Material Resources of
        Battered Women." Paper presented at the annual meeting
        of the Pacific Sociological Association, Anaheim, California,
        1979.

1199 Pagelow, Mildred Daley. "Preliminary Report on Battered Wom-
        en." Paper presented at the Second International Symposi-
        um on Victimology, Boston, 5-11 September, 1976. Also
        in Domestic Violence, 1978. U.S. Congress. Senate.
        Committee on Human Resources, Subcommittee on Child
        and Human Development. Hearings. 95th Cong. 2nd Sess.
        On Domestic Violence and Legislation with Respect to Do-
        mestic Violence, March 4 and 8, 1978. Washington, D.C.:
        Government Printing Office, 1978, pp. 555-607.

1200 Pagelow, Mildred Daley. "Secondary Battering and Alternatives
        of Female Victims to Spouse Abuse." In Women and Crime
        in America. Ed. Lee H. Bowker. New York: Macmillan,
        1981, pp. 277-300.
            In this article Pagelow examines the alternatives that are
open to female victims of repeated beatings by spouses. Secondary
battering refers to progression into the second stage of repeated beatings that escalate in frequency and intensity after the first or primary
battering. The concern here is with the question of why the victims
do not leave the abusive environment. Victim blaming and the ramifications this has for social policy are detailed. The majority of victims try to change themselves or the abusers in an attempt to end the

violence.   When this fails, they sometimes seek aid outside the family.   It is here that the helping professions can render aid, if, in fact, they will.

1201   Pagelow, Mildred Daley.   "Secondary Battering: Breaking the Cycle of Domestic Violence."   Paper presented at the Sociologists for Women in Society, American Sociological Association, University of California, September 5-9, 1977.   Also in Domestic Violence, 1978.   U. S. Congress. Senate.   Committee on Human Resources, Subcommittee on Child and Human Development.   Hearings.   95th Cong. 2nd Sess.   On Domestic Violence and Legislation with Respect to Domestic Violence, March 4 and 8, 1978.   Washington, D. C. :   Government Printing Office, 1978, pp. 484-520.

1202   Pagelow, Mildred Daley.   "Sex Roles, Power, and Women Battering."   In Women and Crime in America.   Ed. Lee H. Bowker.   New York: Macmillan, 1981, pp. 239-77.
          Several questions are raised and attempts are made regarding the male need to dominate females.   Male fear, hatred and envy of women are discussed.   Men's need to prove fatherhood of offspring, the physical limitations on male sexual activity relative to females' unlimited capability, the male's need-dependency of women, the transmission of the anti-women phobias through literature, religion, mythology, films and television, and other topics are included.   The differences between men and women are genetic, but attitudes such as fear and envy can be changed.

1203   Pagelow, Mildred Daley.   "Social Learning Theory and Sex Roles: Violence Begins in the Home."   Paper presented at the Ninth World Congress of Sociology, Uppsala, Sweden, 1978.

1204   Pagelow, Mildred Daley.   Women-Battering; Victims and Their Experiences.   (Sage Library of Social Research, v. 129.) Beverly Hills, Cal. :   Sage Publications, 1981.   288 p.
          This solid sociological study focuses on the victims themselves, to learn how they perceived the violence, their attempts to avoid it, and how their efforts to obtain outside assistance were received.   An overview of the problems, why it occurs, characteristics of abusers and victims, why the abused person stays in the situation, possible solutions to the problem, etc. are considered in detail.   A copy of the survey instrument is included.

1205   Pagelow, Mildred Daley.   "Woman Battering: Victims of Spouse Abuse and their Perceptions of Violent Relationships."   Ph. D. dissertation, University of California, Riverside, 1980.   305 p.   Abstract in Dissertation Abstracts International 41A (December 1980): 2790.

1206   Pahl, Jan.   "The General Practitioner and the Problems of Battered Women."   Journal of Medical Ethics 5 (1979): 117-23.

Pahl, Research Fellow, Center of Research in the Social Sciences, University of Kent, interviewed 50 women in a shelter in South East England. Among the questions were several regarding the helpfulness of physicians. Fifty-six percent felt he had been "very helpful" or "quite helpful," whereas 44 percent thought the physican was "unhelpful." The "unhelpful" ones also tended to prescribe anti-depressants and tranquilizers, such as Valium. The question still remains, Is the physician responsible for healing cuts and bruises or the overall health of the individual?

1207 Pahl, Jan. "Men Who Assault Their Wives--What Can Health Visitors Do to Help?" Health Visitor 55 (October 1982): 528-31.

1208 Pahl, Jan. "Police Response to Battered Women." Journal of Social Welfare Law (November 1982): 337-43.
A survey of 42 battered women in an English shelter shows general dissatisfaction with police assistance. If married but not living together, or not married but living together, women were assisted more than if married and living together. Concern for invading one's privacy seemed to be what stopped the police from acting. The role of the police is ambiguous and many are not sure if they are "peace keepers" or "law enforcers." The existence of an injunction seems to help reclassify the situation as serious and worthy of police attention in the minds of individual officers.

1209 Pahl, Jan. A Refuge for Battered Women: A Study of the Role of a Women's Centre. London: HMSO, 1978. 81 p.
This study was done at the Canterbury Women's Centre in 1976. The aim of the research, performed for the Department of Health and Social Security, was to monitor the establishment of the center and to evaluate the assistance rendered. Many of the residents had been in contact with social workers, police, doctors, and solicitors, but did not believe they received the help they needed. The center helped the women regain their self-confidence and self-reliance and many experienced feelings of personal change while at the center. Useful study of the effectiveness of shelters. Copies of the questionnaires are included.

1210 Pahl, Jan. "Refuges for Battered Women: Social Provision or Social Movement?" Journal of Voluntary Action Research 8 (Winter/Spring 1979): 25-35.
Pahl, in this article, studies the early shelter movement. Her purpose was to discover what sustained the commitment of the founders and investigate the ambiguities and contradictions within the movement for refuges. Two groups were responsible. The first viewed the immediate concerns of battered women as the important problem and therefore stressed spouse abuse shelters. The second viewed the problems of battered women only as one part of the larger problem of sex inequality in society. Important study.

1211 Palmer, Stuart. "Family Members as Murder Victims." In Violence in the Family. Eds. Suzanne K. Steinmetz and

Murray A. Straus. New York: Dodd, Mead, 1974, pp.
91-7.
Emphasis is placed on how often murder victims are family
members. The author sees victim-precipitation as an important element. Included is a graphic case example of escalating husband-wife
violence which ends in murder. This article is taken from the author's
The Violent Society.

1212 "The Paralysis of the Battered Wife." Human Behavior 6 (May
        1977): 47-8.
        A short news note taken from the research of Richard J.
Gelles. Women who have grown up seeing abuse or being abused
themselves were more likely to accept the abuse of their husbands
than those who had no violence in their childhood.

1213 Park Slope Safe Homes Project. How to Set up Community
        Based Services for Battered Women and Their Families.
        Brooklyn, N.Y.: The Project, 1984. 150 p.

1214 "The Park Slope Safe Homes Project Services." In Fight Back:
        Feminist Resistance to Male Violence. Eds. Frederique
        Delacoste and Felice Newman. Minneapolis: Cleis Press,
        1981, pp. 123-4.
        A short description of the project and the services it pro-
vides.

1215 Parker, Barbara. "Battered Women." Paper presented to the
        Seminar on Violence, District 3, Maryland Nurses Associa-
        tion, Annapolis, Maryland, 10 May, 1978.

1216 Parker, Barbara. "Communicating with Battered Women."
        Topics in Clinical Nursing 1 (October 1979): 49-53.
        The importance of communication is stressed in this article.
Nurses have an opportunity as well as a duty to convey information and
hope to abused women.

1217 Parker, Barbara. "The Relationship of Violence in the Nuclear
        Family of Origin and the Battered Wife Syndrome." M.S.
        thesis, University of Maryland, 1976. 86 p.

1218 Parker, Barbara, and Dale N. Schumacher. "The Battered Wife
        Syndrome and Violence in the Nuclear Family of Origin:
        A Controlled Pilot Study." American Journal of Public
        Health 67 (August 1977): 760-1.
        An interesting study of 50 women of which 30 were nonbat-
tered and 20 were battered. The results indicated that if the mother
in the wife's family of origin was a victim of abuse, there was a sta-
tistically significant probability that the wife would be battered by her
husband. There was no significant relationship to her own abuse as a
child. Another significant finding was that husbands of battered women
had less education than those of nonbattered women.

1219 Parker, Jan Reese. "The Battered Women: An Empirical

Assessment of the Effects of Demographic and Social Psychological Variables on the Post-pummel Response." M. A. thesis, University of Texas at Arlington, 1981. 151 p.

The author interviewed 258 battered women from two Texas shelters in Tarrant and Dallas counties to determine the relationship between external factors (demographic and socioeconomic characteristics) and recidivism. Of interest, too, was the relationship of the victim's sociopsychological variables and recidivism. The results indicate that external factors have greater influence that the social-psychological factors. The best indicators of whether a woman will leave her abuser is if she has a job and post high school education.

1220 Parker, S. "The Need for Protection from Violence: The Legal Background." Paper presented at the DHSS Seminar on Violence in the Family--Recent Research on Services for Battered Women and Their Children, University of Kent at Canterbury, 1981.

1221 Parkin, M. W. "Domestic Violence Against Women: The Role of Health Professionals." Australian Nurses Journal 12 (October 1982): 41-4.

1222 Parnas, Raymond I. "Judicial Response to Intra-family Violence." Minnesota Law Review 54 (January 1970): 585-644.

This article describes the actual response to some courts and their related agencies when faced with requests for relief from intrafamily violence. The Chicago Court of Domestic Relations, peace bonds, referrals to other agencies, New York's Family Court, and other legal remedies are discussed. The courts cannot effectively deal with unhappy marriages without cooperation with social workers, psychologists, counselors, and others. In fact, the best solution is in not looking to the courts for this type of relief.

1223 Parnas, Raymond. "Police Discretion and Diversion of Incidents of Intra-Family Violence." Law and Contemporary Problems 36 (Autumn 1971): 539-65. Also in The Criminal in the Arms of the Law. Eds. Leon Radzinowicz and Marvin E. Wolfgang. (Crime and Justice, v. 2.) New York: Basic Books, 1971, pp. 206-36.

Traditional methods of dealing with intrafamily violence are inadequate. Development of Family Crisis Intervention units may prove helpful but may only give the illusion of change. Collaboration between the police and mental health professions as used in the New York model is essential. Conciliation courts and, of course, a commitment to prevention are needed.

1224 Parnas, Raymond I. "The Police Response to the Domestic Disturbance." Wisconsin Law Review 1967 (Fall 1967): 914-60.

An early analysis of the problem of domestic disturbances and the police response to it. The police spend much time at this activity but little if any attention has been directed at formulating more effective preventative control and correctional measures. Poor and

inadequate training is characteristic of the preparation officers receive
for dealing with these disputes. The discretion allotted to the dis-
patcher in referring calls and the discretion of the officers in making
arrests is noted. The police make the first contacts with assaults and
potential homicides in domestic disputes. They should be better trained
to accept the responsibility for dealing with it. The courts and social
agencies must also recognize their roles in this regard.

1225 Parnas, Raymond I. "Prosecutorial and Judicial Handling of
          Family Violence." Criminal Law Bulletin 9 (November
          1973): 733-69.
          This early study by Parnas, Professor of Law, University
of California, Davis, is concerned with family violence in general,
but does include discussions germane to spouse abuse. Much needs
to be done to relieve the conditions of poverty, discrimination, and
other societal inequities which encourage family violence. Judicial,
legal, and social services provide some assistance, but it is inadequate.

1226 Parnas, Raymond. "The Relevance of Criminal Law to Inter-
          spousal Violence." In Family Violence; An International
          and Interdisciplinary Study. Eds. John M. Eekelaar and
          Sanford N. Katz. Toronto: Butterworths, 1978, pp. 188-
          92.
          Interspousal violence in the U. S. has been traditionally pro-
hibited by the general provisions of the penal codes, but in actual practice there has been little enforcement. The idea that spouse abuse
should be decriminalized is absolutely rejected. Only the law has the
power to control undesired violence. Arbitration and lay neighborhood
courts may be useful, but only as adjuncts to the criminal process.
Parnas is on the faculty of the School of Law, University of California, Davis.

1227 Parnas, Raymond I. "The Response of Some Relevant Commu-
          nity Resources to Intra-Family Violence." Indiana Law
          Journal 44 (1968-69): 159-81.
          Parnas, Assistant Professor of Law, University of Arkan-
sas, provided one of the early studies of domestic violence and the
role the police could play in improving the situation. He comments on
the several services available, including settlement houses, neighborhood churches, family service agencies, legal aid societies, alcoholism
services, and others. The police can play an important role in referring disturbed families to the appropriate agencies.

1228 Parnell, Laurel Ann. "Fusion, Differentiation of Self and Inter-
          personal Perception in Battering Couples." Ph. D. disser-
          tation, 1983. 245 p. Abstract in Dissertation Abstracts
          International 44B (January 1984): 2256.

1229 Parthum, Mary Lassance, and Gloria Hart. "Domestic-Violence
          Intervention: A Generic Service Model." Canadian Woman
          Studies 4 (Summer 1983): 73-4.
          The Catholic Family Services of Toronto developed a
domestic-violence program that is integrated into the total agency

program.   Each social worker is expected to handle abuse cases in order to prevent burn-out of a few case workers doing them all.   The philosophy of the program/ is influenced by feminist consciousness with a Catholic value base and supported by staff experience.   Cooperation is encouraged with other agencies, such as the police and the medical and legal professions, and with the community as a whole.

1230 Pascal, Harold J.   The Secret Scandal: Battered Wives.   Canfield, Ohio: Alba Books, 1977.   133 p.
      Fr. Harold Pascal, Assistant Professor of Psychology at St. John's University in New York, has produced a highly readable overview of the problem of spouse abuse.   The book is a synthesis of the research efforts of others and his major contribution is popularization of the problem.   As an active participant in the National Marriage Encounter Movement he believes in this approach, basically a crash course in communication, where married couples learn to share their love, feelings, and fears. Inability to handle anger often precipitates beating episodes.   The encounter experience helps the couple deal with the anger.

1231 Pascoe, Elizabeth Jean.   "Shelters for Battered Wives."   McCall's 104 (October 1976): 51.
      A short general news discussion of battered women shelters, including Women's Advocates of St. Paul, Minnesota, and La Casa de las Madres of San Francisco.   The value and purposes of the shelters are given.

1232 Pascoe, Elizabeth Jean.   "Wife Beating: A Community to the Rescue."   McCall's 105 (November 1977): 81.
      This short note explains how a five-part series on social problems with a special report on spouse abuse by TV station KYW raised the consciousness of Philadelphia.   Within weeks, hundreds of battered women called requesting assistance, demonstrating the need for services.   Several examples of state and local relief are briefly described.

1233 "Pat Ford-Roegner Panel on Battered Wives."   American Academy of Psychiatry and the Law Bulletin 5 (1977): 402-7.
      This panel discussion includes Pat Ford-Roegner, a nurse and social worker; Stephanie Kerns, a lawyer; and Margaret Nichols, a psychologist.   Each makes a short presentation, seeing through the eyes of their profession problems that must be dealt with.   A safe house, more rigorous prosecution of assaulters, perhaps publishing the abusers' names in newspapers, and more publicity and public awareness of the problem are seen as means of dealing with the problem.

1234 Patai, Frances.   "Pornography and Woman Battering: Dynamic Similarities."   In The Abusive Partner: An Analysis of Domestic Battering.   Ed. Maria Roy.   New York: Van Nostrand Reinhold, 1982, pp. 91-9.

1235 Paterson, Andrew, "Crisis Intervention."   In Violence in the

Family: A Collection of Conference Papers. Ed. Jocelynne
A. Scutt.   Canberra: Australian Institute of Criminology,
1980, pp. 173-81.

1236 Paterson, Eva Jefferson.   "How the Legal System Responds to
Battered Women." In Battered Women. Ed. Donna M.
Moore. Beverly Hills, Cal. : Sage, 1979, pp. 79-99.
This article concerns itself with how the legal system does
and does not respond to battered women.   A historical overview, the
effectiveness of temporary restraining orders, why police do not act,
attitudes of judges and district attorneys, and the needed changes in
the legal system are all discussed.   The author is Assistant Director
of the San Francisco Lawyers' Committee for Urban Affairs and active
in battered-wife legal action.

1237 Patterson, G. R. , and H. Hops.   "Coercion, a Game for Two:
Intervention Techniques for Marital Conflict." In The Experimental Analysis of Social Behavior. Eds. Roger E.
Ulrich and Paul T. Mountjoy. New York: Appleton-Century-
Crofts, 1972, pp. 424-40.
"Coercion is a special form of dyad interchange in which
both persons provide aversive stimuli which control the behavior of
the other.   The negative reinforcement resulting from the termination
of the aversive stimuli serves to strengthen the behavior of both parties." The purpose of this article is to provide a program whereby
that coercion can be lessened or ended.   May be useful in dealing
with couples and in preventing or changing abusive marriages.   Couples
need to be trained to pinpoint behaviors which they want changed in
their partners.   The pilot project reported here indicated that these
problem-solving skills may reduce marital conflict.

1238 Payne, Celine Margaret.   "Battered Women and Attributions of
Responsibility." M. A. thesis, Georgia State University,
1977. 37 p.
Two scenarios were given to twenty males and twenty females who were asked to attribute blame or responsibility for the
beating of the wife that occurs.   In one case a verbal disagreement
precedes the violence and in the second case there is no apparent
cause.   The attribution theory of Heider is used to assign responsibility for the violence.   Results indicate that in neither case do most
respondents blame the wife.   Therefore it seems she should not be
viewed negatively when seeking protection or separation.   Copies of
the scenarios are included.

1239 Peacock, Geraldine, et al.   "Intervention." In Conflict in the
Family: A Continuing Education Course (Block 4, Units
9-12). Open University. Milton Keynes, England: Open
University Press, 1980. 83 p.

1240 Pelling, Mark, and Robert Purdie. Matrimonial and Domestic
Injunctions: Practice and Precedents. London: Butterworths, 1982. 190 p.

1241 Peltoniemi, Teuvo. "Family Violence: Police House Calls in
        Helsinki, Finland in 1977." Victimology: An International
        Journal 5, nos. 2-4 (1980): 213-24.
        Over a two-week period in 1977, 264 police house calls
were recorded, of which most were family disputes. Verbal abuse
was most common, but one fourth of the cases involved physical violence. Alcohol is thought to be a factor in domestic disputes, but
this author finds the empirical evidence does not support the claim.
Family violence must be better defined.

1242 Penfold, P. Susan. "Children of Battered Women." International
        Journal of Mental Health 11 (Spring/Summer 1982): 108-14.
        Penfold, Associate Professor, Division of Child Psychiatry,
Children's Hospital, Vancouver, B. C. , found that 17 out of 117 children
referred to her over a six-month period had a parent who was battered
by the other. (Sixteen were battered wives, one was a battered husband.) The effects of spouse abuse on the children have been widely
reported and this study of 17 children indicates that professionals
dealing with disturbed children should consider the possibility of spouse
abuse as a contributing factor. Identifying abused parents is not done
easily and this research points up the unwillingness of the victim to
come forward. This paper was originally presented at the annual
meeting of the Canadian Psychiatric Association, Winnipeg, 23 September 1981.

1243 Penland, Michelle E. "Self-esteem, Locus of Control and Sex-
        role Attitudes in Battered Women." M. A. Thesis, University
        of North Dakota, Grand Forks, 1981. 132 p.
        This study attempts to validate the model proposed by
Lenore Walker which says that battered women have a traditional view
of being female, a predominantly external locus of control, and low
self-esteem. Three groups were studied: 20 battered women, 16 nonbattered women in therapy, and 20 who were neither battered nor in
therapy. No difference among the three groups was found regarding
attitudes toward being female. Those in therapy had a more external
locus of control, with the battered group slightly more so. The question of self-esteem did not show that the battered women scored significantly lower. More study is recommended using more standard
measurements.

1244 Pepe, Helene. "Wife Abuse: Does the American Legal System
        Offer Adequate Protection to the Abused Wife?" Paper pre-
        sented at the annual meeting of the American Sociological
        Association, New York, August 1976.

1245 Peretti, Peter O. , and Mavis Buchanan. "Psycho-socio-behavioral
        Variables of Enduring Chronic and Acute Battered Wife
        Roles." Psychologia 21 (June 1978): 63-9.
        The authors, Department of Psychology, Kennedy-King Col-
lege, Chicago, interviewed 184 battered women to determine which
psycho-socio-behavioral variables were present and to what degree
they helped abused women endure their victimization. Two types,
chronically abused and acutely battered women were analyzed. Results

show that love, dependency, anxiety, and children were the variables associated with the chronic battered wife, whereas factors such as humiliation, loss of a sex partner, fear that the husband might lose his job, masochism, and no money were associated with the acute battered wife. Much of this results from the socialization of boys and girls in American society.

1246   "Persistent Cruelty to a Wife." Justice of the Peace 65 (June 1, 1901): 339.

1247   Peterson, Julie, and Lib Hutchison. "Informal Support Networks: Help for Battered Women." Response to Family Violence and Sexual Assault 5 (January/February 1982): 8-9.

1248   Petersen, Kenneth W. "Wife Abuse: The Silent Crime, the Silent Church." Christianity Today 27 (November 25, 1983): 22-6.
        Approaching from a "Christian" perspective the author shows how the church has not always been supportive of abused wives, and in fact may have even contributed to the occurrence. Ministers are urged to learn the facts of abuse; women are urged to avoid the salvation syndrome, and church members are urged to set up "shepherding homes" (temporary sanctuaries in a Christian family's home) or support other shelter programs. Biblical concerns with a wife's submission and proscription against divorce are discussed.

1249   Peterson, Roger. "Social Class, Social Learning and Wife Abuse." Social Service Review 54 (September 1980): 390-406.
        A random telephone survey of 602 Maryland married or cohabiting women was conducted to determine if it is the sexist structure and traditions of society or the social stress and behavior learned in childhood that are most closely related to use of violence against wives. A modification of Gelles' theories is suggested. The author believes the violence is a response to either private or structural stresses and that is a learned behavior. A lower-class environment can also socialize a person to believe violence is legitimate, not just living in a violent family environment. Because of the high amount of wife abuse in the lower classes, social services to aid the victims and prevent its recurrence should be aimed at the stress which that group faces.

1250   Pethick, Jane. Battered Wives: A Select Bibliography. Toronto: Centre of Criminology, University of Toronto, 1979. 114 p.
        This is a well-annotated listing of spouse abuse materials through 1978. The annotations are those of a person who knows the subject. One of the best early bibliographies on the problem.

1251   Petro, Jane A.; Patricia L. Quann; and William P. Graham III. "Wife Abuse, the Diagnosis and Its Implications." American Medical Association Journal 240 (July 21, 1978): 240-1.
        It is difficult for physicians to recognize abuse, but frequently

there are circumstances that should arouse the doctor's suspicion.
Five case examples are provided which show common findings.   Often
the victim shows up for medical treatment a day or two after the injury, not immediately.   The injuries are often to the face and head,
and a history of abuse may be uncovered.   Physicians should be aware
that abuse exists and that there are services available to the victim.

1252   Peurye-Hissong, Celene; Candace Davis; and Hedy Weinberg.
          Illinois Domestic Violence Act: A Victim Advocates Man-
          ual.   Springfield: Illinois Coalition Against Domestic Vio-
          lence, [1983].   129 p.

1253   Pfouts, Jane H.   "Violent Families: Coping Responses of Abused
          Wives."   Child Welfare 57 (February 1978): 101-11.
          The author is Associate Professor in the School of Social
Work, University of North Carolina, Chapel Hill.   She believes that
social workers must be able to recognize the coping behavior of battered women if help is to be successful.   The wife must view the rewards of marriage to the abuser higher than leaving, or the rewards
of leaving to be higher.   Whichever provides the greatest reward will
determine her action.   The role of the social worker is to help her
see which has the true advantage.   It is often difficult for the victim
to see this at the time of a battering incident.

1254   Pfouts, Jane H. , and Connie Renz.   "The Future of Wife Abuse
          Programs."   Social Work 26 (November 1981): 451-5.
          After centuries of neglect, abused wives are receiving some
much needed service.   The question is raised of how to maintain the
service if feminists and the socially concerned move on to other issues.   Alliances with firmly established community agencies, professional standards with a feminist orientation, and changes to a multi-
focus on family violence should be sought.   Care must be taken so the
recent progress is not lost.

1255   Phelps, Lourn G. ; Jeffrey A. Schwartz; and Donald A. Liebman.
          "Training an Entire Patrol Division in Domestic Crisis
          Intervention Techniques."   The Police Chief 38 (July 1971):
          18-9.
          Rather than training of a special group for handling domes-
tic disturbances the whole Richmond, California, police department
was taught the necessary skills.   The reactions of most of the force
were favorable, even though most were initially skeptical or openly
hostile.   After training, only about 15 percent remained negative.
The advantage of training the whole force is that elitism is avoided.

1256   Phillips, Angela.   "Battered Women: How to Use the Law."
          Spare Rib no. 17(1973): 32.
          A report on the current legal remedies available to bat-
tered women.   Finding a solicitor, preparing the case, and describing
what happens when one goes to court are all dealt with.   The report
"Battered Women and the Law" was issued on behalf of Chiswick Wom-
en's Aid.

1257   Pibus, Christopher J.   "Civil Remedies for Interspousal Vio-
          lence in England and Ontario: A Comparative Study."
          University of Toronto Faculty Law Review 38 (1980): 33-51.
          Although the solution to the societal problem of spouse
abuse cannot be found only in the legal arena, there is much that
needs to be done there.   The English laws and those of Ontario are
compared and while the former are found to be insufficient, the latter
are even less useful.   The best parts of the English law should be
used as a model for Ontario in order to provide the most help to
victims of interspousal conflict.

1258   Pierce, Marianne McIntire.   "Community Services for Battered
          Women."   M. A. thesis, Pacific Lutheran University, 1978.
          37 p.   Abstract in Masters Abstracts 18 (March 1980): 56.

1259   Pines, Burt.   Los Angeles City Attorney Domestic Violence
          Program.   Los Angeles, California: [City Attorney's Of-
          fice?], 1978.   32 p.   Also in Domestic Violence: Preven-
          tion and Services.   U. S. Congress.   House.   Committee
          on Education and Labor.   Hearings.   96th Cong. 1st Sess.
          July 10 and 11, 1979.   Washington, D. C.: Government
          Printing Office, 1979, pp. 367-401.
          This is a description by the L. A. city attorney of Los
Angeles' program, its objectives, goals, personnel, and duties.   The
process used to handle cases, the guidelines for filing charges and
numerous other pertinent elements of the program are described.

1260   Pirro, Jeanine Ferris.   "Domestic Violence: The Criminal
          Court Response."   New York State Bar Journal 54 (Octo-
          ber 1982): 352-7.

1261   Pittman, David J. , and William Handy.   "Patterns in Criminal
          Aggravated Assault."   Journal of Criminal Law, Criminol-
          ogy and Police Science 55 (December 1964): 462-70.
          The authors, both from the University of Washington (Pitt-
man, Professor of Sociology, and Handy, Research Assistant with the
Crime Research Center) studied the crime reports of the St. Louis
Metropolitan Police Department.   They analyzed 25 percent of the
965 aggravated assault reports for the period January 1, 1961, through
December 31, 1961.   Particular attention was paid to variables of time,
location, season of the year, weapon, injury, alcohol involvement,
victim-offender relationship, and arrest records.   The findings are
not restricted to marital conflict and are not concerned with it in particular, but useful findings in that regard are found here.

1262   "Pizzey Comments on American Tour."   Response to Violence
          and Sexual Abuse in the Family 2 (May/June 1979): 2-3.

1263   Pizzey, Erin.   "Chiswick Women's Aid--A Refuge from Vio-
          lence."   Royal Society of Health Journal 95 (December
          1975): 297-8, 308.
          Pizzey describes what it is like to stay at Chiswick Wom-
en's Aid.   A major advantage of her assistance relates to the fact

that women with children and on their own, without financial security
and lonely, tend to accept the first male who will offer security.
The shelter allows the women to take more time and not feel pres-
sured to do that.

1264 Pizzey, Erin. Infernal Child; A Memoir. London: Victor
        Gollancz, 1978. 128 p.
        In this memoir, Pizzey describes her childhood and early
years in China, the Near East, and elsewhere. Her relationships
with her sister and parents are frankly detailed. Provides valuable
insights into the personality of one of the first modern proponents of
relief for battered women.

1265 Pizzey, Erin. Scream Quietly or the Neighbors Will Hear.
        Short Hills, N.J.: Ridley Enslow, 1977, 1974. 154 p.
        This is the classic discussion of Chiswick Women's Aid,
which began to raise the consciousness of many regarding the plight
of battered women. Numerous heart-rending cases are related along
with the callous indifference of the public and government service
agencies. A horrifying and depressing book, but one that was necessary.

1266 Pizzey, Erin. "Violence Begins at Home." The Spectator 233
        (November 23, 1974): 658.
        A general discussion of wife battering and violence with
emphasis on the batterer. There is much concern for violence in
the streets, but the answer is stopping it in the home where it begins.

1267 Pizzey, Erin, and Jeff Shapiro. "Choosing a Violent Relation-
        ship." New Society 56 (April 23, 1981): 133-5.
        The authors believe there are at least two types of women
who are battered and show up at shelters for help. The first are those
who truly want assistance, whereas the second, which Pizzey and
Shapiro call violence-prone, merely use the shelter to their own ends
and have no serious intentions of leaving their violent partner. Unfortunately, the latter seem to be most well known in the popular
mind. The authors speculate that this violence-prone condition may
stem from an "addiction" to noradrenaline which the body releases
during times of excitement, extreme activity, and stress. Persons
working with battered women should be aware of those two types, because they must be treated differently.

1268 Pizzey, Erin, and John Gayford. "Battered Wives 2." Nursing
        Mirror 143 (July 22, 1976): 58-61.
        This illustrated article continues one called "Battered
Wives 1" by John Gayford and focuses on the Chiswick Women's Aid
Shelter in London. Day-to-day operation of the shelter and the occu-
pants' routines are described. This report is part of the film by
Camera Talks Productions of London.

1269 Pizzey, Erin, and Roger Blades. "Violence in the Family."
        Medico-Legal Journal 45, no. 3 (1977): 65-81.
        The authors, both of Chiswick Women's Aid, in a talk

before the Royal Society of Medicine describe how the shelter was
established and the day-to-day activities of the residents and the staff.
Blades spoke especially about the children at the shelter and effects
of family violence on them.   Good inside view of the first British
shelter.

1270   Pleck, Elizabeth.   "Is Family Violence Increasing?   An Histori-
           cal Perspective."   Paper presented at the National Confer-
           ence for Family Violence Researchers, New Hampshire,
           July 1981.

1271   Pleck, Elizabeth.   "Wife-beating in Nineteenth-century America."
           Victimology: An International Journal 4, no. 1 (1979):
           60-74.
           Contrary to the impression given in many articles, by
about 1870 wife beating was illegal in most states and was so considered by most men and women.   However, the sanctions were more
from neighbors and churches than from the law.   If women fit the
Victorian ideal of the weak and helpless female, protection was more
likely.   In the long run, that system probably was no more effective
than the current one.   An interesting and enlightening study on a historical basis.   Originally presented at the annual meeting of the American Studies Association, Chicago, October 1977.

1272   Pleck, Elizabeth; Joseph Pleck; Marilyn Grossman; and Pauline
           Bart.   "The Battered Data Syndrome: A Reply to Steinmetz."
           Victimology: An International Journal 2, nos. 3-4 (1977-
           1978): 680-3.
           A scathing criticism of S. K. Steinmetz's "Battered Husband
Syndrome" [1502].   Twelve examples of how data and/or the research
and conclusions of others were misinterpreted.   Especially disconcert-
ing is that her conclusions are used by the popular press and others
to obscure the needs of abused wives.

1273   Pogrebin, Letty Cottin.   "Do Women Make Men Violent?"   Ms
           3 (November 1974): 49-52, 55, 80.
           Pogrebin takes issue with an article by Dotson Rader in
the New York Times which suggests that if men are violent it is because women encourage and expect it of males.   Since women are
often the victims of male violence and aggression, it would be self-
defeating and ridiculous of women to promote such behavior.   In fact,
masochism is the fault of men.   It is men who encourage men to violence.

1274   "Police May Be Able to Head Off Family Violence."   Criminal
           Justice Newsletter 7 (July 19, 1976): 3.
           This is a news announcement of a National Institute of
Mental Health grant to the Kansas City, Missouri, Police Department
to study abuse.   An earlier study in Kansas City indicated that domestic violence is predictable.   This study would be aimed at prevention
and intervention.

1275   "Police Training Keys."   Response to Intrafamily Violence and
           Sexual Assault 1 (February 1977): 4-5.

1276 Polis, Nikki S. "Battered Women: Factors Influencing Them
         to Stay with Abusive Mates." M. S. thesis, Ohio State Uni-
         versity, 1979. 100 p.
         In this study of twenty-four self-identified formerly battered
women, the author formulated a Likert-type scale to study the factors
that influence women to stay in an abusive relationship. The Rotter
Internal-External Scale (1966) and the AWAIC intake questionnaire were
also used. The results of the study suggest that the battered women
do not believe they can influence the violence and therefore are powerless. Little will be accomplished until the woman sees this difficulty.
Health professionals have a role in sensitively pointing out options to
the victims. The author's sample included only those who had left
their situations, but she suggests comparative studies with women who
stayed with their abusers. Copies of the survey instruments are included.

1277 Ponzetti, James J.; Rodney M. Cate; and James E. Koval.
         "Violence Between Couples: Profiling The Male Abuser."
         Personnel and Guidance Journal 61 (December 1982): 222-4.
         The literature of abuse as it relates to the husband is re-
viewed in the hope that methods of effective intervention will be the
result. Internal factors such as learned predisposition toward violence,
alcohol and drug dependancy, emotional dependence, inability to express
oneself and assertiveness, and external factors including economic
stress, isolation and cultural norms are detailed. Counselors should
concentrate on the reduction of stereotypic role expectations of the
abusers and the improvement of communication skills.

1278 Porter, Beatrice and K. Daniel O'Leary. "Marital Discord
         and Childhood Behavior Problems." Journal of Abnormal
         Child Psychology 8, no. 3 (1980): 287-95.
         The authors, both from the Department of Psychology,
State University of New York at Stony Brook, found that in families
with open hostility between the parents, the male children have more
behavior problems than the daughters. The hostility may or may not
include spouse abuse.

1279 Porter, Carol Anne. "Blame, Depression and Coping in Bat-
         tered Women." Ph. D. dissertation, University of British
         Columbia, 1983. Abstract in Dissertation Abstracts Inter-
         national 44 (November 1983): 1641.

1280 Porter, Shirley J. "An Overview of Violence in the Family:
         Incidence and Causal Variables." Paper presented to the
         Illinois Sociological Association, 1983.

1281 Post, Robin Dee, et al. "Childhood Exposure to Violence Among
         Victims and Perpetrators of Spouse Battering." Victimology:
         An International Journal 6, nos. 1-4 (1981): 156-66.

1282 Post, Robin Dee, et al. "A Preliminary Report on the Preva-
         lence of Domestic Violence Among Psychiatric Inpatients."
         American Journal of Psychiatry 137 (August 1980): 974-5.

All patients admitted to the inpatient units of the Colorado
Psychiatric Hospital between August and mid-December 1979 were
interviewed regarding abuse.   Results showed that of the 60 people
studied (38 women, 22 men), 48 percent had a history of battering in
an intimate relationship.   The study showed abuse to be a major problem in this population; patients do not usually volunteer the abuse information, but will discuss it freely when asked.

1283   Potter, Joan.   "Police and the Battered Wife: The Search for
          Understanding."   Police Magazine 1 (September 1978): 41-
          50.
          The situations in Minneapolis, Phoenix, Portland, and
Monmouth County, N.J., are discussed.   The relations between wom-
en's groups and shelters and the police are detailed.   New laws and
open communication between the police and women's groups indicates
growing understanding of each other's perceptions of the problem of
spouse abuse.

1284   Powers, Robert J., and Irwin L. Kutash.   "Alcohol, Drugs and
          Partner Abuse."   In The Abusive Partner: An Analysis of
          Domestic Battering.   Ed. Maria Roy.   New York: Van
          Nostrand Reinhold, 1982, pp. 39-75.

1285   Pracher, Maria.   "The Marital Rape Exemption: A Violation
          of a Woman's Right to Privacy."   Golden Gate University
          Law Review 11 (Summer 1981): 717-57.
          Pracher, third-year law student, Golden Gate University
reviews the statutory status of the marital rape exemption and its
historical origins, and then critically examines the legal justifications
for its continuance.   The contract theory, consent theory, proof problems, the fear of false accusations, and the constitutional aspects of
marital rape are discussed in detail.   The right of privacy is seen as
a valid justification for dismissing the exemption.   Wives are not the
property of their husbands and the exemption contradicts this notion.
Legal justifications are based on factual and legally suspect assumptions.

1286   Preller, Gordon H.   "Evidence: Admitting Expert Testimony
          on the Battered Woman Syndrome."   Washburn Law Journal
          21 (Spring 1982): 689-97.
          The author discusses expert testimony as it relates to
spouse abuse.   The Georgia case, Smith v. State, allowed use of such
testimony because it helped the jury understand the condition known
as battered-wife syndrome.

1287   Prescott, Suzanne, and Carolyn Letko.   "Battered Women: A
          Social Psychological Perspective."   In Battered Women; A
          Psychological Study of Domestic Violence.   Ed. Maria Roy.
          New York: Van Nostrand Reinhold, 1977, pp. 72-96.
          This study is based on the reports of forty women who an-
swered a 53-question survey.   The results indicate how social and
economic stress, limits in resources, and sex roles affect the victims,
their children, marriages, and help-seeking behavior.

1288 Prescott, Suzanne, and Carolyn Letko. "Spouse Violence: Factors Affecting Women, Children and Marriage. " Paper presented at the annual meeting of the Western Social Science Association, Denver, April 1977.

1289 Price, John, and Jean Armstrong. "Battered Wives: A Controlled Study of Predisposition." Australian and New Zealand Journal of Psychiatry 12 (March 1978): 43-8.
The authors, both of the University of Queensland, conducted research with sixty women, thirty battered and a control group of thirty. Results indicate that battered women more often witnessed violence by their husbands toward others prior to marriage. The fathers of their group had more mental illness, were more violent generally, and tended to be more strict. Use of alcohol by the husband seemed to be similar in both groups, but problems arose over how the wife tolerated the drinking, not how much there was. The battered wife frequently comes from a very disturbed background. There is often a connection between a poor relationship between father and daughter and a greater predisposition to abuse from the husband in later life.

1290 Price, John; Ngairetta Brennan; and Gail Williams. "Hostility Scores in Australian Women with Special Reference to the Battered Wife." Australian Psychologist 15 (July 1980): 189-97.
The author sought to discover whether women who were battered had greater hostility than those who were not. The Hostility and Direction Hostility Questionnaire (HDHQ) was administered to 177 Australian women. These were compared to a standardized English sample and the Austrlians were found to be more hostile. Several reasons were cited to explain the difference including the different class makeup of the two groups and the historical cultural difference in the Australian experience.

1291 Priem, Teresa. Marital Rape: What Happens When Women Fight Back. Berkeley. Cal.: Women's History Research Center, 1981. 8 p.

1292 Prinz, Lucie. "Powerless in the Suburbs: The Battered Wife." McCall's 106 (November 1978): 63.
This is a short discussion of the situation in Natick, Massachusetts. Interesting observations are noted regarding the differences between the suburban and city women's circumstances.

1293 "Prosecutors Discourage Battered Women from Dropping Charges. " Response to Violence in the Family 3 (December 1979): 1-2.

1294 Prosecutor's Responsibility in Spouse Abuse Cases. Washington, D. C.: Law Enforcement Assistance Administration, U. S. Department of Justice, 1980. 40 p.
Two essays are published in this booklet, one by Diane Hamlin [699] and one by Terry Fromson [563]. Annotations are given for each in this bibliography under the respective authors.

1295 "Prosecutor's Role in Spouse Abuse Cases." Response to Vio-
       lence and Sexual Abuse in the Family 2 (November/Decem-
       ber 1978): 3, 6.

1296 "Psychologists Treat Batterers in Residential Program." Re-
       sponse to Violence and Sexual Abuse in the Family 2
       (July 1979): 1-2.
       An overview of recent research by Ganley and Harris [574].

1297 Pugh, R. J. "The Battered Fetus." British Medical Journal
       1, no. 6116 (April 1, 1978): 858.
       The author questions why there is no outcry over the bat-
tered fetus, the result of beatings given to pregnant women.

1298 Quarm, Daisy, and Martin D. Schwartz. "Legal Reform and
       the Criminal Court: The Case of Domestic Violence."
       Northern Kentucky Law Review 10, no. 2 (1983): 199-225.
       The Ohio Domestic Violence legislation of 1979 specifically
made such violence a criminal matter. The authors studied the court
records for 1980 in Hamilton County, Ohio, to assess the effects and
to see if such cases were being prosecuted. Results indicate that 81
percent were dismissed before a verdict was reached and of those convicted 64 percent received no time in jail and 27 percent received
neither jail time nor probation. Thus, the 1980 data suggest a very
high dismissal rate and little punishment. The very existence of the
law, however, does provide support for the fact that wife beating is
unacceptable behavior, thereby putting abusers on notice. If the values
of the community do not encourage prosecution of batterers, the courts
can at least adopt programs of mandated counseling. The wife must
be provided with protection. If it is difficult for her to follow through
with the charges, court mandated counseling might increase her willingness to involve the legal process.

1299 Quinn, Kathleen M. Domestic Violence Order of Protection:
       Prose Handbook. Springfield: Illinois Coalition Against
       Domestic Violence, [1983]. 8 p.

1300 Rae-Grant, Quentin. "Family Violence--Myths, Measures and
       Mandates." Canadian Journal of Psychiatry 28 (November
       1983): 505-12.
       This is the presidential address to the 33rd annual meeting
of the Canadian Psychiatric Association in Ottawa, September 1983.
Spouse abuse is discussed along with child abuse and other forms of
family violence. General comments regarding the problem and suggestions for research are made.

1301 Raiha, Nancy. "I Can't Go Home Tonight: One Hospital's Ex-
       perience in Sheltering the Battered Spouse." Paper pre-

sented at the Biennial Social Work Symposium, San Antonio, Texas, March 1980.

1302 Raiha, Nancy K. "Spouse Abuse in the Military Community: Factors Influencing Incidence and Treatment." In The Abusive Partner: An Analysis of Domestic Battering. Ed. Maria Roy. New York: Van Nostrand Reinhold, 1982, pp. 103-25.

1303 "Rape and Battery Between Husband and Wife." Stanford Law Review 6 (July 1954): 719-28.
A relatively early standard discussion of marital rape. Urges that prosecution for this offense not be encouraged. If reconciliation of separated couples is to be encouraged it would be best not to allow the husband to be prosecuted for rape until divorce is absolute and final. Serious cases of battery can be best resolved in divorce court rather than criminal court.

1304 Raske, Gabriella. "The Victim of the Female Killer." Victimology: An International Journal 1 (Fall 1976): 396-402.
Hungarian women who had killed were studied. Results show a high percentage of victims were husbands, and many of these had engaged in provocative behavior, including cruelty. Female murderers are not often motivated by material gain. Long-lasting emotional conflict situations are at the root of the killing. This paper was originally presented at the Second International Symposium on Victimology, Boston, 1976.

1305 Reamey, Gerald S. "Legal Remedial Alternatives for Spouse Abuse in Texas." Houston Law Review 20 (October 1983): 1279-1320.

1306 Reed, David, et al. All They Can Do ... Police Response to Battered Women's Complaints. Chicago: Chicago Law Enforcement Study Group, 1983. 111 p.

1307 "Refuge for Battered Wives." Intellect 106 (March 1978): 353.
This is a short, general article about spouse abuse. Most of the information is provided by Marya Grambs for the San Francisco shelter La Casa de las Madres. Typical characteristics of the abuser and the victim are discussed.

1308 "A Refuge for Women." Royal Society of Health Journal 98 (August 1978): 149.
A short note with supportive comments on Jan Pahl's [1209] A Refuge for Battered Women: A Study of the Role of a Women's Centre, HMSO, 1978.

1309 Rehwaldt, Nancy. "Program for Battered Women." Corrections Perspective 3, no. 3 (1977): 5.
The author, a staff writer for the Minnesota Department of Corrections, explains the new bill enacted by the Minnesota Legislature (1977) establishing pilot programs for battered women.

1310 Reinshagen, Kendra. Employment Law Handbook for Domestic
          Violence Programs: A Draft. Springfield: Illinois Coali-
          tion Against Domestic Violence, 1982. 24 p.

1311 Reitz, Willard E. "Evaluation of Police Family Crisis Training
          and Consultation." Canadian Police Chief 63 (July 1974):
          29-32.
          The author, clinical psychologist and member of the De-
partment of Psychology, University of Western Ontario, proposes and
evaluates a model for training police officers used in London, Ontario.
He says that police have always been involved in sociology whether
they want to admit it or not. This program can serve as a model
for communities experiencing the purist approach, that is, police wanting to do only "police work" and "law enforcement" and not wishing to
become involved in family crisis work.

1312 Remsberg, Bonnie, and Charles Remsberg. "The Case of Pa-
          tricia Gross." Family Circle (April 24, 1979): 58, 60, 152,
          155.
          Patricia Gross killed her abusing husband in May 1978 after
years of being mistreated. Self-defense was the verdict. This article
details her experiences.

1313 Renvoize, Jean. Web of Violence: A Study of Family Violence.
          London: Routledge and Kegan Paul, 1978. 240 p.
          The author discusses several facets of family violence, in-
cluding child abuse, incest, elder abuse, and spouse abuse. Violence
breeds violence and the family provides an important breeding ground
and perpetuates the web of violence. The section on battered wives
draws heavily on English research, such as that of Gayford, Moore,
and Faulk and American studies by Gelles and Levinger. General
overview which argues current family violence must be ended for its
own sake as well as the sake of future generations.

1314 The Report from the Conference on Intervention Programs for
          Men Who Batter. Washington, D.C.: Law Enforcement
          Assistance Administration, U.S. Department of Justice,
          1981. 51 p.
          A general discussion of the problem of abuse with attention
devoted to programs to help the abuser. Much aid, relatively speak-
ing, is given the victim, but little is done to rehabilitate the batterer.
This report from a two-day conference gives numerous suggestions for
such programs. Use of behavior modification, cognitive restructuring,
biofeedback techniques, stress reduction, improvement of communication skills and others are suggested as aids and techniques to reduce
or end violent behavior.

1315 Resnik, Mindy. Wife Beating; Counselor Training Manual, #1.
          Ann Arbor, Mich.: N.O.W., Washetnaw County Chapter
          Wife Assault Project, 1976. 38 p.
          This author, Volunteer Counselor Coordinator of the project,
prepared the handbook for its counselors. The purpose is to train peer
counselors in the proper ways of assisting battered women with the legal

system. The techniques of interviewing, information collecting, and helping the client get in touch with her feelings are detailed.   The crime of spouse abuse is explained along with step-by-step instructions on what the client must do to free herself from the abuse and/or achieve legal justice.

1316   Reynolds, Lynn. "Power and Inequality: A Case Study of
          Abused Women. " Ph. D. dissertation, Fordham University,
          1981.   136 p.   Abstract in Dissertation Abstracts Interna-
          tional 42A (November 1981): 2308-9.

1317   Reynolds, Rosemary, and Else Siegle. "A Study of Casework
          with Sado-masochistic Marriage Partners. " Social Case-
          work 40 (December 1959): 545-51.
          This study of nine "sado-masochistic" marriages indicates
that no fundamental change in the relationship can be brought about by
the casework method.   It can, however, be modified.   In this study
over half of the husbands were the more masochistic of the couple.
Frequent verbal and physical fighting characterized the marriage.
Husband and wife abuse was evident (but not called that by the author).

1318   Rhode Island Feminist Theatre.   Internal Injury.   Providence:
          Author, 1978.
          This is a play in which three battered women tell their
stories from their different perspectives.

1319   Richardson, Deborah Capasso, and Jennifer L. Campbell.
          "Alcohol and Wife Abuse: The Effect of Alcohol on Attri-
          butions of Blame for Wife Abuse. " Personality and Social
          Psychology Bulletin 6 (March 1980): 51-6.
          The purpose of this study was to determine what effect alco-
hol use by the husband or the wife would have on attribution of blame
for the violence between them.   Undergraduate students at the University of Georgia read two accounts of a beating incident, in one the
husband had been drinking, in the other the wife had been.   Results
indicate that while the husband was given the most blame there was
a tendency to blame situational factors when he had been drinking, and
a greater tendency to blame the woman when she had been drinking,
too much.   The authors attribute this to female drunkenness being a
violation of social norms.

1320   Richette, Lisa A. "Support Services: Long-term Needs for
          Battered Women--Underpinnings to Decay or Foundations
          for New Structures?" In Battered Women: Issues of Public
          Policy.   U. S. Commission on Civil Rights.   Washington,
          D. C. :   The Commission, 1978, pp. 409-40.

1321   The Rideout Pamphlet.   Berkeley, Cal. : Women's History Re-
          search Center, n. d.   9 p.
          Overview of the Rideout trial for marital rape.

1322   Ridington, Jillian. "The Transition Process: A Feminist En-
          vironment as Reconstitutive Milieu. " Victimology: An

International Journal 2, nos. 3-4 (1977-78): 563-75.
      The establishment of the Vancouver Transition House and
the philosophy behind it are detailed by staff member Ridington.   Three
years of observing the effects of their work showed her the value of
an environment managed by women for helping battered women overcome the guilt and anxiety caused by leaving a violent marriage.   Receiving support and assistance in formulating their new life plans from
other women helps to decrease dependence on men and prepares them
to head their own households.

1323   Riley, John.   "Spouse-abuse Victim Jailed After No-drop Policy
            Invoked. "   National Law Journal 5 (August 22, 1983): 4.

1324   Riordan, Annette L.   "Internal-External Locus of Control in
            Battered and Non Battered Women. "   M. A. thesis, Kean
            College of New Jersey, 1980.   55 p.
      Testing the hypothesis that the battered woman's expecta-
tion for control of events is significantly more external than that of
the nonbattered woman's, the author studied 54 New Jersey women
(29 nonbattered and 25 battered).   Each completed Rotter's Internal-
External Locus of Control Scale.   The original hypothesis was confirmed.
She also found that battered women who do not use shelters have significantly higher external scores than those who do.

1325   Rittenmeyer, Steven D.   "Of Battered Wives, Self-defense and
            Double Standards of Justice. "   Journal of Criminal Justice
            9, no. 5 (1981): 389-95.
      The author, Assistant Professor of Law, Western Illinois
University, takes issue with the notion that killing an abusive husband
should be seen as self-defense.   There is some question as to the
constitutionality of such claims and that pleas of self-defense will make
the legal problems involved in battered-wife syndrome worse.   Spouse
abuse should not be tolerated by law or society and existing laws should
be enforced.   If this was done there would be no need for the homicide.

1326   Roark, Mary L. , and Stella Vlaltos.   "An Analysis of the Ego
            States of Battered Women. "   Transactional Analysis Journal
            13 (July 1983): 164-7.
      Previous research suggests that the ego states of battered
women is different from adults in general.   This author administered
the N. R. Heyer Ego State Profile Questionnaire to 40 battered women
who had sought refuge in an abuse shelter.   Results show they suffer
lower adult ego states that the norm, which supports their inability to
make decisions in their own behalf.   They also score high on the adapted
child ego scale, thus confirming their need to please or be submissive
to those in authority.   This study indicates that transactional analysis
would help in the treatment and counseling of these victims.

1327   Roberts, Albert R.   "A National Survey of Services to Batterers. "
            In The Abusive Partner: An Analysis of Domestic Battering.
            Ed. Maria Roy.   New York: Van Nostrand Reinhold, 1982,
            pp. 230-43.
      Most programs are aimed at victims of abuse, but this study

suggests more is in the offing for the abuser.   Roberts reports on
current services for batterers which include telephone hotlines, and
the problems encountered, staffing patterns and referral sources.

1328   Roberts, Albert R.   Sheltering Battered Women: A National
           Study and Service Guide.   (Springer Series, Focus on
           Women, vol. 3.)   New York: Springer, 1981.   227 p.
           Written by a professor of sociology and social welfare at
the University of New Haven, this book reports the results of the
first national survey of the institutional structure of 89 intervention
services for battered women.   It also provides practical advice and
techniques for program planning and development.   Included in the
appendix is a listing of the respondents with addresses and services
available.   Useful for learning how shelters actually operate in the
community.   As it turns out, the local environment is often hostile.

1329   Roberts, Bill, et al.   "Abuse."   In Conflict in the Family: A
           Continuing Education Course.   (Block 3, Units 5-8.)   Open
           University, Milton Keynes, England: Open University
           Press, 1980.   59 p.

1330   Roberts, J.   "Wife-beating."   Paper presented to a conference
           on Women's Health in a Changing Society at University of
           Queensland, St. Lucia, 1975.

1331   Robinson, David C.   "Domestic Violence--Practitioner's View-
           point."   New Law Journal 129 (March 8, 1979): 251-4.
           The author discusses the Domestic Violence and Matrimo-
nial Proceedings Act 1976 and finds its motivation commendable, but
its application difficult.   He takes issue with S. Maidment's "The
Legal Response to Marital Violence" [1008], which says the problem
of enforcement resides in the inefficiency of private practice lawyers.
Robinson points out what he sees to be the real problems with en-
forcement--the way the law is written and ambivalence of the victims
to their own plight.   The new law, he fears, actually does little to
improve the situation.

1332   Robinson, Jeffery.   "Defense Strategies for Battered Women
           Who Assault Their Mates: State v. Curry."   Harvard
           Women's Law Journal 4 (Spring 1981): 161-75.
           The author, a Harvard law student, worked for the Seattle
Public Defender and assisted in this case during the summer of 1980.
He discusses the possible uses of battered-wife syndrome in support
of a self-defense plea, the thorough knowledge of battering behavior
that is required of the attorney, pre-trial investigations, jury selection, and defense strategy.   The question of imminence of danger
may be the crucial one for a jury when battered-wife syndrome is
used as a basis for a self-defense plea.

1333   Robinson, Karen Meier.   "Working with a Community Action
           Group."   Journal of Psychiatric Nursing and Mental Health
           Services 16 (August 1978): 38-42.
           Robinson, Assistant Professor, University of Louisville,

Division of Nursing, provides a step-by-step analysis of a community action group. The experiences are analyzed and compared to Yalom's three stages of group development and presented so readers can use it as a guide to their own groups' development. This group was interested in the establishment of a shelter for physically abused women.

1334   Robitscher, Jonas. "Battered Wives and Battered Children."
       American Academy of Psychiatry and the Law Bulletin. 5
       (1977): 374-9.
       This introduction to other papers in this issue makes a few
comparisons between battered children and battered women. He observes that such family violence is a sign of a deeper illness in society. He notes also some scholarly observation that society has overreacted legally to child abuse, but underreacted legally to wife abuse.

1335   Rock, Maxine. "How Could This Happen to My Friend?"
       McCall's 110 (April 1983): 54-8.
       This article, directed at a popular audience, provides advice for helping friends and neighbors living in a battering situation.
The author tells of her experience helping a friend.

1336   Rockwood, Marcia. "Battered Wives: Help for the Victim Next
       Door." Ms 5 (August 1976): 95. Also in Domestic Vio-
       lence, 1978. U. S. Congress. Senate Committee on Human
       Resources, Subcommittee on Child and Human Development.
       Hearings. 95th Cong. 2nd Sess. On Domestic Violence and
       Legislation with Respect to Domestic Violence, March 4
       and 8, 1978. Washington, D. C.: Government Printing
       Office, 1978, p. 656; Domestic Violence. U. S. Congress.
       House. Committee on Education and Labor, Subcommittee
       on Select Education. 95th Cong. 2nd Sess. Hearings on
       H. R. 7927 and H. R. 8948, March 16 and 17, 1978. Wash-
       ington, D. C.: Government Printing Office, 1978, p. 379.
       A short note commenting on James Bannon's (Detroit Police
Commander) call for spouse abuse to be viewed as a public issue
rather than private problem. Developments in crisis intervention and
women police trainees are noted.

1337   Rockwood, Marcia. "Courts and Cops: Enemies of Battered
       Wives?" Ms 5 (April 1977): 19.
       Comments on the class action suit claiming the New York
City Police and Family Court System do not adequately protect victims
of spouse abuse.

1338   Rockwood, Marcia. "How to Tell It to the Judge." Ms (August
       1976): 96. Also in Domestic Violence. U. S. Congress.
       House. Committee on Education and Labor, Subcommittee
       on Select Education. 95th Cong. 2nd Sess. Hearings on
       H. R. 7927 and H. R. 8948, March 16 and 17, 1978. Wash-
       ington, D. C.: Government Printing Office, 1978, p. 378;
       Domestic Violence, 1978. U. S. Congress. Senate. Com-
       mittee on Child and Human Development. Hearings. 95th
       Cong. 2nd Sess. On Domestic Violence and Legislation

with Respect to Domestic Violence, March 4 and 8, 1978.
Washington, D. C. : Government Printing Office, 1978,
p. 673.
Although recognizing legal remedies vary from state to state,
this short article defines civil and criminal proceedings, citizen's arrest,
criminal complaint, protective orders and other legal processing.

1339 Rod, Tess. "Marital Murder." In Violence in the Family: A
         Collection of Conference Papers. Ed. Jocelynne A. Scutt.
         Canberra: Australian Institute of Criminology, 1980, pp.
         95-105.
         The author, a postgraduate student at Macquarie University,
Ryde, New South Wales, claims murder is typically a family affair
since in New South Wales around half of all victims are killed by
spouses or other relatives. In many cases of spouse killing there is
a long history of abuse and violence. Spouse murders are extreme
outcomes of domestic violence.

1340 Rodrigues, JoAnn V. "Battered Women: A Study of Learned
         Helplessness and Sex Role Stereotyping." M. S. thesis,
         California State University, Hayward, 1981. 56 p.
         Twenty battered women and twenty nonbattered women were
tested for "learned helplessness" as measured by the Beck Depression
Inventory (BDI) and sex role stereotyping as measured by the BEM
Sex Role Inventory (BSRI). The results show significant differences
in the groups with regard to learned helplessness, with battered wom-
en more often victims of that phenomenon. The sex role tests show
nonvictims to be more androgynous than battered women. Strong femi-
ninity was not the most common characteristic of battered women.
Rather they tended to score higher in masculinity. It was also noted
that there was no significant relationship between learned helplessness
and length of stay in the shelter.

1341 Rogovin, Sheila Anne. "The Violent Marriage: Investigation of
         the Battered Woman, Her Parent-Child Relationship and
         Family Background." Ph. D. dissertation, American Uni-
         versity, 1979. 90 p. Abstract in Dissertation Abstracts
         International 40B (August 1979): 932.

1342 Rolph, C. H. "Battered Wives." New Statesman 90 (December
         26, 1975): 811-2.
         A general discussion of spouse abuse in England. Special
notice is paid to Erin Pizzey's opinion and her study Scream Quietly
or the Neighbors Will Hear [1268].

1343 Romeike, Henry. The Wife-beaters' Manual: A Guide to Hus-
         bands' Connubial Corrections, with a List of Prices At-
         tached. Edited by Charles W. Barker. London: The Ar-
         tistic and Literary Correspondence, 1884. 32 p.

1344 Rosenbaum, Alan. "Wife Abuse: Characteristics of the Partic-
         ipants and Etiological Considerations." Ph. D. dissertation,
         State University of New York, 1979. 312 p.

The author studied 52 physically abused wives and compared them with 20 others with dysfunctional marriages and no abuse, and 20 others with satisfactory marriages. Results indicate that the differences between the wives in the abusive and the dysfunctional marriages were minimal, but the differences between husbands were significant. Abusive husbands were less assertive with their wives, had been abused as children and had witnessed parental spouse abuse as children. The long-term effect of abuse, that it is passed to future generations, found support in this study.

1345 Rosenbaum, A.; D. Goldstein; and K. D. O'Leary. "An Evaluation of the Self-esteem of Spouse Abusive Men." Paper presented at the annual meeting of the American Psychological Association, Montreal, September 1980.

1346 Rosenbaum, Alan, and K. Daniel O'Leary. "Children: The Unintended Victims of Marital Violence." American Journal of Orthopsychiatry 51 (October 1981): 692-9.
       The authors, both professors of psychology (Rosenbaum at Syracuse University, and O'Leary at State University of New York, Stony Brook), studied the effects of marital violence on the children in the family. Three groups of women completed the Personal Data Questionnaire and the Peterson-Quay Behavior Problem Checklist. It appears that children in abusive families have an increased risk of developing conduct or personality disorders. The risk seems to be higher for male than female children. Male children are more apt to be abusive, but females are not particularly more accepting of abuse, when they witnessed wife beating in their family of origin. A strong relationship between spouse abuse and child abuse was evident. More research on the topic is recommended. This is an abbreviated version of a paper which received a New York State Psychological Association research award.

1347 Rosenbaum, Alan, and K. Daniel O'Leary. "Marital Violence: Characteristics of Abusive Couples." Journal of Consulting and Clinical Psychology 49 (February 1981): 63-71.
       This article is based on Rosenbaum's doctoral dissertation [1344] which studied 52 abused wives and 20 abusive husbands. Questionnaires completed by these were compared to others completed by 20 couples with satisfactory marriages and 20 marginally dysfunctional nonviolent marriages. The results indicate that abusive husbands tend to be less assertive with their wives, were often abused as children and witnessed more abuse between their parents than men in the other two groups. Based on a paper presented to the annual meeting of the American Psychological Association, New York, 1979.

1348 Rosenthal, A. M. Thirty-eight Witnesses. New York: McGraw-Hill, 1964. 87 p.
       An account of the murder of Catherine Genovese in 1964 in Queens, New York. Thirty-eight witnesses saw or heard the assault and only one called the police and that was after it was too late to help. The question of apathy is discussed with no particular insights other than people have an unwillingness to get involved. Spouse abuse is

not discussed but there are some interesting implications for male-female conflicts when the two appear not to be strangers. Onlookers just will not render assistance. The author is Metropolitan Editor for the New York Times.

1349 Rosewater, L. "When Battered Women Kill: M. M. P. I. Data." Paper presented at the Symposium 'When Battered Women Kill: Psychologists as Expert Witnesses,' American Psychological Association Annual Meeting, Los Angeles, August, 1981.

1350 Rounsaville, Bruce J. "Battered Wives: Barriers to Identification and Treatment." American Journal of Orthopsychiatry 48 (July 1978): 487-94.
    The author, from the Department of Psychiatry, Yale University School of Medicine, studied 37 abused women seeking emergency treatment at the Yale Emergency Room and Hospital over a one-month period; 75 percent agreed to emergency psychiatric treatment, but only 35 percent of those kept a follow-up appointment. Social resourcefulness was viewed as a major problem for treatment. Either many women are not aware of the services available, or they do not use them. Providing more services and widely publicizing them will help those battered women who want relief. Police training and welfare reform will also help.

1351 Rounsaville, Bruce. "Battered Women: Very Common but Difficult to Reach." Paper presented at the annual meeting of the American Psychiatric Association, Toronto, Canada, 2-6 May 1977.

1352 Rounsaville, Bruce J. "Theories in Marital Violence: Evidence from a Study of Battered Women." Victimology: An International Journal 3, nos. 1-2 (1978): 11-31.
    The author explains and analyzes several sociological and psychological theories of spouse abuse. He argues that there is evidence to support any and all of the theories. It appears then that it merely becomes a matter of emphasis as to the correctness of any particular theory. In order to provide support and treatment, it is necessary to determine which theory is more applicable in a particular case. An excellent overview of the theories and one of the more important articles for students of the problem. The theories analyzed include masochism, learned helplessness, lack of resources, mental illness, ability to tolerate intimacy, modeling and childhood exposure to violence, stress and others.

1353 Rounsaville, Bruce, and Myrna M. Weissman. "Battered Women: A Medical Problem Requiring Detection." International Journal of Psychiatry in Medicine 8, no. 2 (1977-1978): 191-202.
    For one month in 1976, emergency room (E. R.) clinicians at the Yale-New Haven Hospital were instructed to identify spouse abuse victims; 33 from the surgical and 4 from the psychiatric E. R. were found. They represented 3. 8 and 3. 4 percent of admissions, respectively. The nature and history of abuse were recorded along with other

information.   Among the results was the recommendation that E. R.
physicians be alert to possible abuse victims.   Especially in emergency situations, medical personnel can play an important role.   Useful
study.

1354   Rounsaville, Bruce; Norman Lifton; and Margo Bieber.   "The
         Natural History of a Psychotherapy Group for Battered
         Women."   Psychiatry 42 (February 1979): 63-78.
         The authors detail a strategy for treating battered women
referred to them from the Yale-New Haven Hospital emergency room
and the Connecticut Mental Health Center.   Of 75 identified patients,
only 31 came for the first follow-up session.   Of these only ten became involved in treatment and of these only six did so on a regular
basis.   This poor response indicates the problems with making psychiatric treatment attractive to battered women.   The conclusion is
that group therapy is very helpful to the abused, but few initially saw
this as worthwhile enough to attend.   This article provides many insights for treating the abused, but no attention is devoted to the
abuser.

1355   Roy, Maria, ed.   The Abusive Partner: An Analysis of Domes-
         tic Battering.   New York: Van Nostrand Reinhold, 1982.
         319 p.
         Most studies have been aimed at the victim, but this col-
lection of original essays focuses on the perpetrator of the violence.
The concerns included are biological predisposition, alcohol and drug
use, pornography, environmental factors, nutrition, and others.   Special populations are discussed, such as prisoners and military personnel.   Various treatment programs are analyzed.   A major work for
those wishing to study the abuser.

1356   Roy, Maria, ed.   Battered Women: A Psychosociological Study
         of Domestic Violence.   New York: Van Nostrand Reinhold,
         1977.   334 p.
         This is a collection of essays, most of which have not been
published previously.   Experts in psychiatry, sociology, law enforcement, neurology, and many other areas have contributed.   Wife abuse
is seen as having many facets with no simple causes or solutions.
Violence is also cyclic and can be passed from generation to generation.   A good selection which provides documentation of the problem
and proposals for solutions.

1357   Roy, Maria.   "A Current Survey of 150 Cases."   In her Battered
         Women: A Psychosociological Study of Domestic Violence.
         New York: Van Nostrand Reinhold, 1977, pp. 25-44.
         This is a survey of 150 American women who had attempted
to extricate themselves from violent homes numerous times, but could
find no viable alternatives to their home situations.   The problem has
no easy solutions and no simple causes.   Most notable was the finding
of the presence of violence in the background of the overwhelming
number of husbands.   Husbands do not reform spontaneously and violence does not lessen over time.   Society has a responsibility to find
a solution.

1358   Roy, Maria. "Early Warning Checklist." Reader's Digest 110
          (May 1977): 26.
          A short note itemizing the five points that signal a poten-
tially abusive marriage. Abuse during the honeymoon and heavy drinking are among the clues.

1359   Roy, Maria. "Four Thousand Partners in Violence: A Trend
          Analysis." In her The Abusive Partner: An Analysis of
          Domestic Battering. New York: Van Nostrand Reinhold,
          1982, pp. 17-35.
          Roy studied 4,000 cases of abuse in the New York City
area and provides many data regarding abusers. Age of victims and
children in the relationship, financial status of the family, criminal
record of the abuser, nature and frequency of the abuse, catalysts
of the abuse, and many other factors are analyzed.

1360   Roy, Maria. "The Nature of Abusive Behavior." In her The
          Abusive Partner: An Analysis of Domestic Battering. New
          York: Van Nostrand Reinhold, 1982, pp. 3-16.

1361   Roy, Maria. "The Unmaking of the Abusive Partner." In her
          The Abusive Partner: An Analysis of Domestic Battering.
          New York: Van Nostrand Reinhold, 1982, pp. 145-7.

1362   Roy, Maria, and Marcia Wooding Caro. Up from Battering.
          New York: Abused Women's Aid in Crisis, 1981. 133 p.
          Roy and Caro have reproduced seven important interviews
typifying various aspects of the struggle of battered women to free
themselves from their victimization. Several common threads run
through the stories. Most women marry because it is the thing to
do, because their friends are, or because they need to leave an intolerable home life. Most are romantics who believe that bad marriages
can be turned into good ones. They assume responsibility for their
husbands' behavior and believe if they change their own habits the husband will change. Support from others was usually necessary to extricate themselves from the battering relationship. The danger to the
children or fear of the effects of the violence on them, prompted many
to leave.

1363   Royal College of Psychiatrists. Memorandum on Battered Wives.
          London: The Royal College, 1974. 22 p.

1364   Rozovsky, Lorne E. "A Husband's Consent to His Wife's Abor-
          tion." Dimensions in Health Service 57 (January 1980):
          34, 36.
          A battered pregnant wife leaves her husband and considers
an abortion. Doctors agree that another child would threaten the
woman's life or health. The husband then threatens a court injunction
against the doctor or hospital. Under Canadian law would that attempt
be successful? The author, a Halifax lawyer, provides his opinion on
the case.

1365   Ruether, Rosemary R. "Is God a Wifebeater? The Western

Religious Tradition and Violence Against Women in the
Home." Movement: The Journal of Christian Action and
Ideas, no. 31 (Augumn 1977): 11-4.
Western religious tradition has accepted and promoted patriarchal assumptions regarding women's inferior status. Catholic
and Protestant alike subscribed to that notion. Christianity has within
itself the theory of liberation, equality, and dignity for all persons,
but it has seldom been applied to women.

1366   Russell, Diana E. H.   "The Prevalence and Impact of Marital
         Rape in San Francisco." Paper presented at the American
         Sociological Association Meeting, New York, August 1980.

1367   Russell, Diana E. H.   Rape in Marriage. New York: Macmillan,
         1982.   412 p.
         Rape in marriage has received relatively little attention
until recently. This is the first English language book on the topic.
It is also the first study of marital rape in the U. S. to be based on
a random sample. The results indicate that 14 percent of the 930
women interviewed had been raped at least once by their husband or
ex-husband. This means that one out of seven of all women who are
or have been married have been raped by their spouse. While concerned primarily with rape, the book also shows that physical abuse
and beating often accompanied it. Since marital rape is usually not
illegal, the author urges legal reform. Economic independence for
women is also necessary since many women do not feel free to leave
violent husbands for lack of financial support. The book is written
in a readable style with many case studies and exerpts from the interviews. An appendix gives a state-by-state listing of the legality
of marital rape.

1368   Russell, Diana E. H.   "Rape in Marriage: A Case Against Le-
         galized Crime." Paper presented at the annual meeting
         of the American Society of Criminology, San Francisco,
         November 1980.

1369   Rutherford, Margaret.   "Domestic Violence and Cohabitees."
         New Law Journal 128 (April 20, 1978): 379-80.
         Rutherford discusses the British Domestic Violence and
Matrimonial Proceedings Act of 1976 and explains its effect on unmarried couples. The purpose of the act was to provide protection to
these women, not to deprive the men of their property rights. In
cases of abuse, property rights are merely suspended when the abuser
is ordered away from the home by the courts.

1370   Rypstat, Meredith R.   "Wife Battering: Casual Factors, Rea-
         sons Women Stay and Programs for Battered Women in
         West Central Wisconsin Shelter and in Wausau, Wisconsin."
         M. S. thesis, University of Wisconsin-Stout, 1981.   43 p.

1371   Sacco, Lynn A.   "Wife Abuse: The Failure of Legal Remedies."

John Marshall Journal of Practice and Procedure 11 (Spring 1978): 549-77.
Several legal remedies for the abused spouse are discussed. They include divorce, criminal prosecution, family court and civil action. All are found wanting, although some relief can be found. The legal community must come to terms with the problem and "must admit that a bone broken from an intentional beating is a bone broken no matter who struck the damaging blow."

1372 Sagarin, Edward. "Rape of One's Wife." Medical Aspects of Human Sexuality 12 (February 1978): 153.
To the question of whether one can legally rape one's wife, the author says that because rape is illegal one cannot legally rape anyone. One can, however, sexually assault an unwilling spouse, but conviction would be difficult without witnesses.

1373 Sallmann, Peter. "Rape in Marriage in South Australia." Victimology: An International Journal 1 (Winter 1976): 600-5.
The author, from the Legal Studies Department, La Trobe University, presents some background and discussion of the Criminal Law Consolidation Act, Amendment Act, a sexual law reform bill passed in 1976. Included was the controversial rape-in-marriage clause which made sexual assault by a husband illegal. Various pros and cons raised by Australian special interest groups are noted. The clause was not deleted as had been feared.

1374 Sallmann, Peter A. "Rape in Marriage and the South Australian Law." In Rape Law Reform. Ed. Jocelynne A. Scutt. Canberra: Australian Institute of Criminology, 1980, pp. 79-86.
A strong call is made for the elimination of the immunity from marital rape which husbands have. Rape is only one type of assault which occurs in marriage frequently. Such assaults should be treated as criminal acts, but the general social, economic and political conditions of our times create the greater barriers to justice, not the law itself.

1375 Sammons, Lucy Newmark. "Battered and Pregnant." MCN: American Journal of Maternal Child Nursing 6 (July/August 1981): 246-50.
The author, an ob/gyn nurse practitioner in Walnut Creek, California, points out the special vulnerability pregnant women suffer and the danger to the unborn child. Nurses dealing with pregnant women should be especially alert to the signs of battering. Why abuse occurs during pregnancy, how to identify it, and what steps should be taken to provide assistance to such victims are described.

1376 Sanchez-Dirks, Ruth. "Reflections on Family Violence." Alcohol Health and Research World 4 (Fall 1979): 12-6.
This author points out how both the violence and alcoholism are passed to the next generation, and how both the spouse and the child are apt to be abused and the abuser. It seems that the alcoholic and the children of alcoholics all have low self-esteem, immaturity,

problems with role reversal, severe depression, impulsivity, and other problems. Experience indicates that treatment of the alcoholic will help end the violence. Suggestions for future action are given.

1377   SANENEWS: A National Newsletter on Battered Women. Middletown, Conn.: Community Health Center. 1982-present.
A new organ for disseminating information regarding spouse abuse, this publication is a gold mine for current activities and news. The title stands for Spouse Abuse North East Newsletter.

1378   Sansalone, Vicki. "A Community Responds to Wife Assault: A Look at London, Ontario." Response to Family Violence and Sexual Assault 5 (November/December 1982): 4-6.

1379   Sanson, Barbara E. "Spouse Abuse: A Novel Remedy for a Historic Problem." Dickenson Law Review 84 (Fall 1979): 147-70.
The author reviews the legal problem associated with spouse abuse and believes it requires a national solution. The Pennsylvania law of 1976 and its amendments are analyzed with the strengths and weaknesses highlighted. Because the legal system is reluctant to prosecute husbands under assault laws, Sanson argues that laws should proscribe spouse abuse specifically and that both state and federal governments should fund shelters. A civil scheme similar to that of Pennsylvania protective orders should prove useful.

1380   Saravanapavananthan, N. "Wife Battering: A Study of Sixty Cases." Forensic Science International 20 (September/October 1982): 163-6.
The author, from the University of Jaffna, studied sixty abused women referred to him by the police between August 1978 and August 1981 to determine the types of weapons used, the nature and locations of the injuries and the patterns of assaults. Results indicate that common items such as sticks, firewood and knives are the most frequently used weapons, with head and upper limbs receiving greatest injury. Most of the women are illiterate, none had a university education, and most were economically dependant upon the husband. Alcohol was frequently involved, with violence occurring in 70 percent of the cases when the husband was drunk. Of special interest is that in 60 percent of the cases, the wife resorted to calling the police for the first time only after ten years of marriage. Social and cultural factors would account for such reluctance to involve outsiders.

1381   Saunders, Daniel G. "Marital Violence: Dimensions of the Problem and Modes of Intervention." Journal of Marriage and Family Counseling 3 (January 1977): 43-52.
The author, a social worker for Family Services, Madison, Wisconsin, originally delivered this paper at the Spring Social Work Symposium, Madison, in April 1976. He reviews the problem of marital violence, offering intervention techniques and several cases as examples. He is especially critical of the catharsis hypothesis in explaining and treating spouse abuse.

1382 Saunders, Daniel. "The Police Response to Battered Women:
       Predictors of Officer's Use of Arrest, Counseling or Minimal
       Action." Ph.D. dissertation, University of Wisconsin-
       Madison, 1979. 267 p. Abstract in Dissertation Abstracts
       International 40A (June 1980): 6446.
       The data for this study were collected by questionnaire
from a sample of 116 police officers from three city and seven small-
town police departments in Wisconsin. The study shows police action,
either arrest of the husband or informal counseling, to be a result of
many factors, not just a sexist or nonsexist attitude. Rather, it was
done largely on a professional stance although a personal bias did en-
ter in. More research is recommended.

1383 Saunders, Daniel G. , and Patricia Barrett Size. Marital Vio-
       lence and the Police: A Survey of Officers Victims and
       Victim Advocates. Madison, Wis. : Family Service, 1980.
       52 p.

1384 Saunders, Sheila. A Study of Domestic Violence: Battered
       Women in Israel. London: Anglo-Israel Association,
       [1982]. 22 p.

1385 Saville, N. , et al. "Sex Roles, Inequality and Spouse Abuse. "
       The Australian and New Zealand Journal of Sociology 17
       (March 1981): 83-8.
       The authors asked a sample of 145 battered women to com-
plete questionnaires regarding their experiences. Results show that
sexual inequality best explains what makes women vulnerable to abuse.
Non-mothers with adequate employment are least likely to be beaten,
while mothers who are unemployed appear most susceptible. Of special
interest is the suggestion that the wife should not be assumed to be in
the same economic class as her husband. This would depend upon her
employment situation.

1386 "Scarred Lives of Battered Women." Glamour 78 (October
       1980): 56.
       General discussion of wife abuse encouraging long-term
solutions. This editorial states that at least a third of all women
seeking asylum are turned away from shelters because of lack of
space.

1387 Schapp, William. "The Military Legal System." Response to
       Violence in the Family 4 (July/ August 1981): 3-5.
       This article answers questions about military justice deal-
ing with a wife beater.

1388 Schauss, Alexander G. "Effects of Environmental and Nutritional
       Factors on Potential and Actual Batterers." In The Abusive
       Partner: An Analysis of Domestic Battering. Ed. Maria
       Roy. New York: Van Nostrand Reinhold, 1982, pp. 76-90.

1389 Schechter, Lowell F. "The Violent Family and the Ambivalent
       State: Developing a Coherent Policy for State Aid to

Victims of Family Violence." Journal of Family Law 20,
no. 1 (1981-82): 1-42.
The author discusses family violence generally believing
special attention to either child abuse, spouse abuse, or the abuse
of elders to miss the point.   All must be studied together, not in isolation.   Past policies and legislative action of the U.S. and the individual states are surveyed wherein the ambivalence of government
officials toward victims is revealed.   The Reagan programs have resulted in a reduction of financial support for needed relief.   Some
professionals have begun to question the wisdom of government intervention in child abuse.   In the past it has been most common not to
violate "family privacy" on the behalf of battered wives.   Now both
problems lack the aid they should have.   A new commitment must
be made to all victims of family violence, not only a particular group.

1390 Schechter, Susan.   "The Future of the Battered Women's Move-
              ment." In Fight Back! Feminist Resistance to Male Vio-
              lence.   Eds. Frederique Delacoste and Felice Newman.
              Minneapolis: Cleis Press, 1981, pp. 93-103.
This was originally a keynote speech presented at the conference "Addressing Woman Abuse: Visions and Actions" at Lake
Geneva, Wisconsin, November 12-14, 1980.   The need for planning
for future action is stressed.   Consolidation and expansion of aims
and actions are needed.

1391 Schechter, Susan.   Psychic Battering; The Institutional Response
              to Battered Women.   A revised version of a speech at the
              Midwest Conference on Abuse of Women, May 1978, St.
              Louis University Medical Center (unpublished paper).
A social worker with the Family Abuse Project in New York
City, the author believes that service institutions and their staffs not
only sanction spouse abuse, but create it.   This is because service
agencies and the courts do not provide the protection the women deserve as crime victims.

1392 Schechter, Susan.   Women and Male Violence: The Visions
              and Struggles of the Battered Women's Movement.   Boston:
              South End Press, 1982.   367 p.
"This story is told from the perspective of a socialist
feminist who is trying to show the striking accomplishments of a movement and at the same time detail the similarities, differences, and
tensions within it."   A social worker activist, the author is concerned
that the many grass-roots women--feminists, activists, and battered
alike--will not receive their rightful place of recognition when the
story of the early days of the battered-women's movement is told.
This book hopes to set the record straight.   The first eight chapters
provide an overview of the roots of the movement, chapter nine gives
a theory of violence against women in the family, and the remaining
chapters explore current dilemmas and problems that the feminist part
of the movement faces.   The movement to end spouse abuse cannot be
fully understood without being aware of this perspective.

1393 Schechter, S.   "The Future of the Battered Women's Movement."

Paper presented at the Women's Abuse Conference, Lake
Geneva, Wisconsin, November 1980.

1394 Scheurell, Robert P. , and Irwin D. Rinder. "Social Networks
      and Deviance: A Study of Lower Class Incest, Wife-beating
      and Non-support Offenders. " Wisconsin Sociologist 10
      (Spring/ Summer 1973): 56-73.
      The authors sought to discover the relationship between a
man having a loose-knit or close-knit system of personal social relationships with friends and family and the tendency toward deviance in
the form of incest, wife beating, and nonsupport. The expectation
was that all three groups of lower-class offenders would have a close-
knit social network and a segregated pattern of conjugal role perform-
ance. This was not found to be true, at least for the incest offender.
More research is necessary.

1395 Schickling, Barbara H. "Relief for Victims of Intra-family As-
      saults--The Pennsylvania Protection from Abuse Act. "
      Dickinson Law Review 81 (Summer 1977): 815-22.
      In October 1976, the Pennsylvania Legislature passed a
Protection from Abuse Act aimed at providing family members legal
recourse when they are being physically abused by others. Relief
includes protective orders to refrain from abuse, but most importantly
power to order the offending party to vacate the home for a period up
to one year. Unlike the New York law, this one also covers cohabiting couples, not just those legally married. The advantages and problems with the law are discussed along with comparisons with similar
laws in other states. The author believes this is not the ultimate solution, and suggestions for amendments are proposed.

1396 Schiff, Arthur Frederick. "The New Florida 'Rape' Law."
      Florida Medical Association Journal 62, no. 9 (1975): 40-2.
      Dr. Schiff, Deputy Medical Examiner for Dade County, has
written a descriptive discussion of the new (1974) Florida rape law.
Although seen as an improvement over the old law, marital rape, incest, and female rape of males are inadequately dealt with by the new
legislation.

1397 Schiff, Arthur Frederick. "Rape: Wife vs Husband. " The
      Forensic Science Society Journal 22 (1982): 235-40.
      Discusses the general law on rape with some attention to
historical attitudes. Recent changes in U. S. state legislation regarding marital rape are detailed.

1398 Schiff, Arthur Frederick. "State of Oregon vs. Rideout--Can
      Husband Rape Wife?" Medical Trial Technique Quarterly
      26 (Summer 1979): 49-56.
      A general discussion of marital rape with particular em-
phasis on the Rideout case. The major results of that case are that
men are now on notice that such conduct will no longer be tolerated,
and that it will not be the last case of its kind.

1399 Schlachet, Barbara Cohn. "Rapid Intervention with Families in

Crisis in a Court Setting." In Family Violence: An International and Interdisciplinary Study. Eds. John M. Eekelaar and Sanford N. Katz. Toronto: Butterworths, 1972, pp. 224-30.

In 1972, the Rapid Intervention Project (RIP) was established as an emergency room of the Family Court in New York City. Spouse abuse was only one of its concerns. RIP gave advice on which agency a troubled family needed to consult. The RIP team consisted of a psychiatrist or psychologist, social worker, and mental health worker to give the best recommendations. Unfortunately, RIP ceased in 1974 due to lack of funds. The pros and cons of the service are discussed.

1400   Schlesinger, Benjamin. "Abused Wives: Canada's Silent Screamers." Canada's Mental Health 28 (June 1980): 17-20.
The author, Professor of Social Work, University of Toronto, reviews the facts of abuse, including Canadian statistics, why the wife stays, the characteristics of the husband, recommendations regarding the abuse, and other facets of the problem. A good brief overview based on the research of others.

1401   Schlesinger, Louis B.; Mark Benson; and Michael Zornitzer. "Classification of Violent Behavior for Purposes of Treatment Planning: A Three-pronged Approach." In The Abusive Partner: An Analysis of Domestic Battering. Ed. Maria Roy. New York: Van Nostrand Reinhold, 1982, pp. 148-69.

1402   Schneider, Elizabeth M. "Equal Rights to Trial for Women: Sex Bias in the Law of Self-defense." Harvard Civil Rights-Civil Liberties Law Review 15 (Winter 1980): 623-47.
"This article examines how the several stereotypes of women and the male orientation built into the law prevent judges and jurors from appreciating the circumstance of battered women and their perceptions." The general problem is discussed along with the law of self-defense, the equal force rule, the imminent danger rule, the reasonable man standard, etc. Individualization, that is, consideration of the battering situation and the victim's perceptions, is preferred by this author.

1403   Schneider, Elizabeth; Susan B. Jordan; and Christina A. Arquedas. "Representation of Women Who Defend Themselves in Response to Physical or Sexual Assault." National Journal of Criminal Defense 4 (1978): 141-69. Also in Women's Rights Law Reporter 4 (Spring 1978): 149-163; Women's Self-defense Cases: Theory and Practice. Ed. Elizabeth Bochnak. Charlottesville, Va.: Michie Company, 1981, pp. 1-39.
The authors intend this article to act as an aid to attorneys defending women who have committed homicides after they or their children have been physically or sexually assaulted. Their interest is in developing a legal analysis which incorporates women's experiences and perspectives into existing concepts of criminal law. While not arguing for a separate legal standard for women, they do believe that

present law has a male orientation which works against women. The question of self-defense, impaired mental state, various trial tactics, and education of the judge and jury are all considered.

1404 Schneider, James. Selected Deferred Prosecution Programs in
      Wisconsin and Other States. Madison: Wisconsin Legis-
      lative Council, 1978. 27 p.

1405 Schonborn, Karl L. "Interpersonal Violence and Family Crisis
      Peacekeeping." In his Dealing With Violence: The Chal-
      lenge Faced by Police and Other Peacekeepers. Spring-
      field, Ill.: Charles C. Thomas, 1975. Chapter 2, pp.
      15-46.
      In New York City the frequency and causes of violence be-
tween spouses, intimates, and friends are examined along with a variety of techniques for dealing with the problem. Crisis police, those
schooled in family psychology, were contrasted with regular police re-
lying on conventional procedures. Some of these latter techniques
were found to be inadequate for coping fully with family conflicts.
Crisis police were more successful in these dangerous situations.

1406 Schreiber, Fiora Rheta, and Melvin Herman. "When Did You
      Stop Beating Your Wife?" Science Digest 57 (March 1965):
      20.
      A popularization of the Snell, Rosenwald, and Robey re-
search published in the Archives of General Psychiatry [1464].

1407 Schudson, Charles B. "Needs of Battered Women Receive Spe-
      cial Attention from Milwaukee DA's Office." Response to
      Intrafamily Violence and Sexual Assault 1 (February 1977):
      1-2. Also in Domestic Violence. U. S. Congress. House.
      Committee on Education and Labor, Subcommittee on Select
      Education. 95th Cong. 2nd Sess. Hearings on H. R. 7927
      and H. R. 8948, March 16 and 17, 1978. Washington,
      D. C.: Government Printing Office, 1978, pp. 424-5.
      During 1975 and 1976 the Milwaukee District Attorney's
office was funded by LEAA for the Battered Women Project of the
Citizen Complaint Unit. Battered women came directly to the unit
and were advised by lawyers or social workers regarding the course
of action that could be taken. Some women wanted legal action taken,
others wanted divorce or separation, and others wanted the husbands
officially "warned." The project is seen as successful since it provided assistance in numerous ways. When funding ran out at the end
of 1976, the project was incorporated directly into the Citizen Victim
Complaint Unit. Several lessons of value to other D. A. offices are
detailed.

1408 Schulman, Joanne. "Battered Women Score Major Victories in
      New Jersey and Massachusetts Marital Rape Cases."
      Clearing House Review 15 (August/September 1981): 342-5.
      In two state supreme court cases, State of New Jersey v.
Smith and Commonwealth v. Chretien, Massachusetts and New Jersey
ruled that no common-law marital rape exemptions existed in their

respective rape statutes. They both rejected the Hale doctrine, but neither challenged that doctrine as part of common law. These two decisions make clear that regardless of whether such an exemption ever existed in common law, there is no place in today's society for such a concept.

1409   Schulman, Joanne. "Expansion of the Marital Rape Exemption." Women's Advocate Newsletter 1, no. 2 (1980): 3-4.
   This news note lists thirteen states in which the marital rape exemption was extended to cohabitants. In five states the extension included those who had had a sexual relationship, but currently were not cohabiting.

1410   Schulman, Joanne. "The Marital Rape Exemption." Women's Advocate Newsletter 1, no. 1 (1980): 6-8.
   The current status of the marital rape exemption in each state is given.

1411   Schulman, Joanne. "The Marital Rape Exemption in the Criminal Law." Clearing House Review 14 (October 1980): 538-40.
   The author discusses the current status of marital rape exemption showing how most states do not make such sexual activity a crime. Worse, the exemption is, in some states, being extended to cohabiting couples. Ironically in many of these same states the "advantages" of marriage are not extended to the woman. For example, "palimony," division of the couple's property, and civil orders of protection are often denied. When they are granted, the courts, in some cases, have required an express or implied agreement between the parties. Interestingly, no such agreement is needed in regard to marital rape. In any case the extensions, like the original concept, are not grounded in common law, and such claims must not be made.

1412   Schulman, Mark A. A Survey of Spousal Violence Against Women in Kentucky. (Study no. 792701 conducted for Kentucky Commission on Women.) Washington, D. C.: U. S. Department of Justice, 1979. 80 p.
   This study was conducted by Louis Harris Associates and shows the extent of spouse abuse in Kentucky. About 10 percent of women had been abused within the past 12 months and 21 percent had been at some time or other. Interestingly, the profile of the violence-prone family is hardly distinguishable from the average family. Violent families also seem to beget violent families. Victimized spouses seem to have few services available to them Numerous other findings are found in this detailed study.

1413   Schultz, LeRoy G. "The Victim-offender Relationship." Crime and Delinquency 14 (April 1968): 135-41.
   In many cases, the victim has been party to the act, intentionally or nonintentionally, so it is often useful to determine the role of the victim if justice is to prevail. Among other crimes, this also applies to rape and spouse assault when wives play the masochistic role. The author is Instructor of Social Work, University of Missouri.

1414 Schultz, LeRoy G. "The Wife Assaulter." Corrective Psychi-
        atry and Journal of Social Therapy 6 (1960): 103-112.
        Also in Deviancy and the Family. Eds. Clifton D. Bry-
        ant and J. Gipson Wells. Arlington Heights, Ill.: AHM
        Publishing Corp. , 1973, pp. 257-65.
          Schultz, Probation and Parole Officer, St. Louis, Missouri,
        analyzed four cases of husbands convicted of assaulting their wives
        with the intent to kill. He says the victims in spouse assaults can
        always be assumed to have played a crucial role in the offense and
        may have directly or indirectly brought about or precipitated their
        own victimization. The personalities and interpersonal dynamics are
        discussed along with treatment. An early study with some obvious
        limitations, such as size of sample.

1415 Schultz, LeRoy G. , and Billy Bair. Wife Battering in the Small
        Community: A Social Policy Analysis, 1976. Morgantown:
        School of Social Work, West Virginia University, 1976.
        38 p.

1416 Schultz, Sandra L. "The Marital Exception to Rape: Past,
        Present and Future." Detroit College of Law Review 1978
        (Summer 1978): 261-76.
          The legal background to the court's attitude toward marital
        rape is explained. Even though most states are reexamining their
        rape laws, there is little interest, says the author, on the part of
        legislators to tamper with the marital exception clauses. The ques-
        tion has not been resolved, but for the time being only ignored.

1417 Schuyler, Marcella. "Battered Wives: An Emerging Social
        Problem." Social Work 21 (November 1976): 488-91.
          Situations in society are not viewed as problems needing
        resolution until important or powerful groups believe them to be.
        If the problem of wife beating is to be resolved it will have to be
        recognized for the crime it is. Social workers can help this process
        by educating their colleagues and the public. The profession must
        help establish such programs as shelters, hot lines, and advocacy,
        as well as encourage more research into the problem.

1418 Schwartz, Jeffrey A. "Domestic Crisis Intervention: Evaluation
        of a Police Training Program." Crime Prevention Review
        2, no. 4 (1975): 9-16.
          The author discusses several early programs to train po-
        lice officers in dealing with the domestic disputes. The 1967 New York
        experiment and 1969 Oakland, California, program are analyzed and
        faults examined. Several more successful programs (including the
        one in Richmond, California, in the early 1970's) are described with
        the conclusion being that special training is needed and the time and
        energy spent will be advantageous to the department and community.

1419 Schwartz, Martin D. "The Spousal Exemption for Criminal Rape
        Prosecution." Vermont Law Review 7 (Spring 1982): 33-57.
          The author, Assistant Professor of Criminal Justice and
        Women's Studies, University of Cincinnati, discusses the current

legality of spousal rape. As of this writing, in only ten states could
a married woman living in the same house as her spouse be protected
from forcible rape by him. He says the arguments against it include
the idea that it is not a serious problem, that criminal law is not an
appropriate forum for dealing with it, and that it is difficult to prove
it was actually rape. Other objections to making marital rape a
crime is the fear that vindictive women will file false charges, and it
is claimed that other remedies are available to victims. Since it is
one of the last vestiges of truly unequal treatment of women embodied
in statutes, the author believes this exemption needs to be eliminated.

1420 Scott, Morgan E. "The Battered Spouse Syndrome." Virginia
        Medical 107 (January 1980): 41-3.
            Scott, a Radford, Virginia, M. D. , provides four case his-
tories, two of wife abuse and two of husband abuse. He argues that
regardless of which spouse is doing the abusing, there is a strong
relationship between the conditions of one's family of origin and how
much abuse will be tolerated. Scott concludes that his experience
shows conjoint therapy to be the most successful approach. He believes
such marriages are inherently sadomasochistic relationships. Unless
the sadistic and masochistic traits are resolved, the abuse will not end.

1421 Scott, P. D. "Battered Wives." British Journal of Psychiatry
        125 (November 1974): 433-41.
            Battering is seen as the failure of social adaptation on the
part of the abuser. Cultural and psychological factors, jealousy, drug
and alcohol abuse, mental illness, the relationship between wife abuse
and baby-battering and other factors are discussed. In this early
study, Scott rejects masochism as the reason for couples staying together. The problem is multifaceted and needs a variety of agencies
as well as much education of the public to effectively deal with it.
Scott is with Maudsley Hospital, London.

1422 Scottish Women's Aid. Battered Women in Scotland: Your
        Rights and Where to Turn for Help. Prepared by Margaret
        Gimblett, et al. Edinburgh: Scottish Women's Aid, 1978.
        36 p.

1423 Scottish Women's Aid. The Housing Needs of Battered Women
        in Scotland. [Edinburgh: Scottish Women's Aid, 1980].
        16 p.

1424 Scottish Women's Aid. Information Kit for Agencies. [Edinburgh:
        Scottish Women's Aid, 1981?]. 1 portfolio.

1425 Scottish Women's Aid. Women's Aid: A Manual for Local Au-
        thorities. Edinburgh: Scottish Women's Aid, [1982?].
        21 p.

1426 Scratton, Joan. "Violence in the Family." In Rage, Hate,
        Assault and Other Forms of Violence. Eds. Denis J. Mad-
        den and John R. Lion. New York: Spectrum, 1976, pp.
        17-32.

Scratton is concerned with family violence in general, but she does address the problem of spousal assault. Her primary conclusion is that the state of knowledge of family violence at this time precludes any simple or singular explanations. Useful as an overview of violence theory.

1427 Scutt, Jocelynne. "The Alcoholic Imperative: The Sexist Rationalization of Rape and Domestic Violence." Hecate 7, no. 1 (1981): 88-105.

An interesting study of and challenge to those who attempt to excuse violence toward women as caused by alcohol. "Rather than concentrating upon alcohol as the culprit, if the aim is to eliminate domestic violence and rape from our society, clearly what must be concentrated upon are the methods by which we socialize men and women, boys and girls into patterns promoting violence as a way of life. "

1428 Scutt, Jocelynne A. "Consent in Rape: The Problem of the Marriage Contract." Monash University Law Review 3 (June 1977): 255-88.

The author takes the new (1976) South Australian Legislation regarding marital rape to task. She says, "There is no legal justification for a rule that a husband cannot be prosecuted for the rape of his wife. The law cannot be taken as rendering a husband immune from a serious criminal charge, simply by way of the marital contract." A long discussion of the case history of the concept, with reasoned arguments against it.

1429 Scutt, Jocelynne A. "Debunking the Theory of the Female Masked Criminal." Australian and New Zealand Journal of Criminology 11 (March 1978): 23-42.

The author contests the beliefs of Pollak (The Criminality of Women, New York: Barnes, 1961) that official crime rates distort the amount of crime women commit. Because of the types of offenses they engage in, favorable treatment by the law and chivalrous treatment by law enforcement agencies, it appears that women commit fewer crimes than they actually do. A variety of criminal areas are analyzed to test that theory including wife beating and domestic violence. The author's research results indicate that any changes in reporting crime statistics will still show men commit more crime than women.

1430 Scutt, Jocelynne A. "In Support of Domestic Violence: The Legal Basis." Family Law Review 3 (Spring 1980): 23-32.

Scutt points out that rather than being concerned with halting violence, the law is framed to protect the family unit in spite of any violence from within. Her analysis reveals four ways this happens. Some legal backing of violence is given because there is sometimes no recourse against the attacker husband or father. Some laws, especially made for certain crimes, such as incest, are rarely applied due to the "specialness" of the problem. Other laws which apply to violence in the family, just like violence outside the family, are not enforced. Many times, also, a special court is established to handle family problems thereby endorsing the notion that domestic violence is different from other forms of violence.

1431   Scutt, Jocelynne A. , ed.   Rape Law Reform: A Collection of
       Conference Papers. Canberra: Australian Institute of
       Criminology, 1980. 304 p.
       These are the proceedings of a national conference on rape
law reform held in Hobart, Tasmania, May 28-30, 1980. Among the
various concerns is that of marital rape. Articles by V. B. Nordby
[1157], W. J. E. Cox [303], and Peter Sallmann [1374] are included
and are cited separately in this bibliography.

1432   Scutt, Jocelynne A.   "Spouse Assault: Closing the Door on
       Criminal Acts. "   Australian Law Journal 54 (December
       1980): 720-31.
       A general account of spouse abuse with emphasis on the
legal situation in Australia. Her basic suggestion is that all assault
is a crime and the fact that it occurs in the home should not make it
less so. Legal and social changes are necessary if abuse is to end.
The government has an important role to play and must accept its
responsibility.

1433   Scutt, Jocelynne A.   "To Love, Honour and Rape with Impunity:
       Wife as Victim of Rape and the Criminal Law. " Paper
       presented to the Third International Symposium on Victim-
       ology, 2-8 September, 1979.

1434   Scutt, Jocelynne A. , ed.   Violence in the Family: A Collection
       of Conference Papers. Canberra: Australian Institute of
       Criminology, 1980. 222 p.
       These papers delivered at the Australian Institute of Crimi-
nology Conference are concerned with child abuse, incest, and spousal
violence. Papers presented by Lovejoy and Steet [983], Rod [1339],
O'Donnell and Saville [1162], and Stratmann [1526] are listed elsewhere
in this bibliography by author. This collection represents an overview
of the current state of Australian research into domestic violence, the
inadequacy of the law in dealing with domestic violence and a view of
government services.

1435   Search, Gay. "London: Battered Wives. " Ms 2 (June 1974):
       24-6.
       A general discussion of wife beating in London with empha-
sis on the Chiswick Women's Aid. Shelters provide much needed relief
but are viewed as "putting a bandaid on a cancer. " Legal and social
reforms are needed.

1436   Search, Gay. "Scream Quietly. " Ms 5 (August 1976): 96-7.
       Discusses the changes and progress in England since her
Ms June 1974 article [1435]. Many new shelters have been established.

1437   Sebastian, Richard J. "Social Psychological Determinants. " In
       The Dark Side of Families: Current Family Violence Re-
       search. Eds. David Finkelhor, et al. Beverly Hills, Cal. :
       Sage, 1983, pp. 182-92.
       The author, Assistant Professor of Organizational Behavior,
University of New Hampshire, argues that physical aggression against

family members is common because the inhibitions against it are weak
and because intimates can arouse each other to violence more easily
than nonintimates. The weakness of the victim, as well as the lack
of legal or social proscriptions, also contributes to its occurrence.
This general discussion applies to spouse abuse along with other types
of family violence.

1438   Sedge, Suzanne. "Spouse Abuse." In The Battered Elder Syn-
          drome: An Exploratory Study. Eds. Marilyn R. Block
          and Jan D. Sinnott. College Park: University of Mary-
          land, Center on Aging, 1979, pp. 33-48.
       A general discussion of spouse abuse with some attention
to husband abuse. The public is still not aware of the extent of this
abuse. More shelters and other resources are needed, as well as
better protection for the victim and rehabilitation for the abuser.
She believes violence is learned behavior so changes in the way society views abuse must be made to eliminate it.

1439   Segal, Julius. "Violent Men--Embattled Women." Cosmopolitan
          180 (May 1976): 238-41.
       An article for a general audience, this one deals with per-
sonal characteristics of the abuser and the victim, why women stay,
how the abuser and abused interact and what a woman can do to get
out from under the situation. Strong psychological overtones in this
essay.

1440   "Seminar Gives Guidelines on How to Handle Family Abuse
          Cases." RNABC News 10 (June/July 1978): 26-8.
       This article provides general advice to nurses and medical
staff for handling suspected cases of child and spouse abuse. It is
important to establish rapport and ask questions to determine if abuse
is actually taking place. If it is, it should be reported or appropriate
advice given to the victim.

1441   Sesan, Robin Sue. "The Development of an Instrument to Study
          Sex Bias in Psychotherapy with Women Clients." Ph. D.
          dissertation, Michigan State University, 1983.

1442   Shainess, Natalie. "Psychological Aspects of Wife-battering."
          In Battered Women: A Psychosociological Study of Dom-
          estic Violence. Ed. Maria Roy. New York: Van Nos-
          trand Reinhold, 1977, pp. 111-19.
       This article concentrates on the personality and interaction
of the couple involved in the abusive situation. Masochism is discussed since it plays a role. That is not to say the victim enjoys
the abuse, however. Various avoidance strategies are described and
advocated. Court action and counseling are urged.

1443   Shainess, Natalie. "Vulnerability to Violence--Masochism as
          Process." American Journal of Psychotherapy 33 (April
          1979): 174-89.
       The author, Lecturer in Psychiatry, Columbia University
College of Physicians and Surgeons, reexamines the Freudian concept

of female masochism. She translates it into a more or less universal
culturally determined process which women use in certain circumstances.
This submissive and self-destructive style increases the vulnerability
to violence.   This tendency can be observed in many everyday interchanges in which a fear of men, especially authority figures, leads to
difficulty.   If those offering aid to assaulted women understand this
process, more effective assistance and relief will be forthcoming.

1444   Shapiro, Rodney J. "Alcohol and Family Violence." Family
        Therapy Collections.   Vol. 3.   Clinical Approaches to
        Family Violence.   Rockville, Md.: Aspen Systems, 1982,
        pp. 69-89.

1445   Shaw, Bill.   "She Killed Her Husband, But Supporters Like
        Valerie Harper Say Joyce Devillez Was The Real Victim."
        People Weekly 14 (August 4, 1980): 66-7.
        A brief account of the plight of Joyce Devillez who con-
tracted to have her abusive husband murdered in Indiana in 1974.

1446   The Shelter Experience; A Guide to Shelter Organization and
        Management for Groups Working Against Domestic Violence.
        (Domestic Violence Monograph Series, no. 4.) Rockville,
        Md.: National Clearinghouse on Domestic Violence, 1980.
        124 p.
        This is a manual on how to set up a community crisis cen-
ter.   Although not directly concerned with spouse abuse, many of the
same principles apply.   Based on the experiences of those who set up
a center in Elgin, Illinois.   Definitely useful.

1447   Sheridan, Daniel J.   "Nursing Care for Battered Women...."
        American Journal of Nursing 81 (May 1981): 956.
        This letter to the editor states that a survey of shelters in
Illinois and bordering states indicates that in-shelter nursing care is
not usually provided.

1448   Sherman, Adrian C.   "Domestic Violence: Perceived Likelihood
        of Violence as a Function of Situation and Sex of Aggressor."
        M. A. thesis, Appalachian State University, 1982.   41 p.
        In this study 344 undergraduate introductory psychology
students were asked to complete a questionnaire after reading five vignettes and assess likelihood of violence from the arguments that en-
sued in the stories.   The situational factors used were alcohol, jealousy, personality conflict, finances, and childhood observation of spouse
abuse.   Results indicate that in most situations female aggression is
seen as inappropriate and therefore less likely than male violence.
This method of researching opinions was found to be sound and therefore should be used more often.   Additional research is needed since
violence cannot be ended if it is not clear what causes it.

1449   Sherman, K. O.   "The Battered Woman." Dimensions in Critical
        Care Nursing 2 (January/February 1983): 30-5.

1450   Sherman, Lawrence W. , and Richard A. Berk.   Police Responses to Domestic Assault: Preliminary Findings. Washington, D.C.: Police Foundation, n.d. 13 p.

Minneapolis police officers participated in a study to determine the best method of handling domestic violence cases. The options were arrest, informal mediation, and an order for the abuser to leave for eight hours. The results, albeit inconclusive, indicate that arrest may be the best action to take if domestic violence is to be reduced. Recidivism is less if the husband is arrested rather than advised or ordered to leave the home for eight hours. More research is necessary.

1451   Shields, Nancy M., and Christine R. Hanneke. "Battered Wives' Reactions to Marital Rape." In The Dark Side of Families: Current Family Violence Research. Eds. David Finkelhor, et al. Beverly Hills, Cal.: Sage, 1983, pp. 131-48.

Ninety-two wives of violent men participated in standardized, in-depth interviews to determine the effects of marital rape on their lives and attitudes. Results indicate that marital rape and nonsexual violence produce two distinct reactions on the part of the victim. Other researchers of battered women must take the question of marital rape into account when observing conclusions from their studies. One finding here is that sexual violence seems to co-occur with battering and as the severity of each increases the greater the reaction of the victim. "Marital rape seems to have the greatest impact on victims' feelings and emotions (especially self-esteem and feelings about sex), while severe battering seems more likely to produce an action response-for example, extramarital sex."

1452   Shields, Nancy M., and Christine R. Hanneke. "Violent Husbands and Their Wives' Reactions." Law and Policy Quarterly 3 (July 1981): 371-5.

The authors are research associates at the Policy Research and Planning Group of St. Louis, Missouri. This article is a preliminary analysis of a two-year study funded by the National Institute of Mental Health, Center for Studies in Crime and Delinquency. Three violence patterns were studied: men who were involved in family only violence; men who were involved in nonfamily violence; and men who were generally violent, that is, they engaged in violence with both family and nonfamily. The study produced information on the best way to conduct such a study again. It also indicated that family-only violence tended to be done by a middle-class, otherwise "loving" husband. The other two groups had a more violent attitudinal behavioral orientation.

1453   Shipley, Susan B., and Donna C. Sylvester. "Professionals' Attitudes Toward Violence in Close Relationships." JEN: Journal of Emergency Nursing 8 (March/April 1982): 88-91.

The purpose of this study was to gather data on the attitudes of health professionals toward spouse abuse. Low returns of the questionnaire mean that only limited inferences could be made. Results show that the health care professionals in this survey closely paralleled the current thoughts on violence presented in the professional literature.

Education programs should be aimed at workers in the emergency
department and ambulatory clinics.

1454   Shotland, R. Lance, and Margaret K. Straw.   "Bystander Re-
       sponse to an Assault When a Man Attacks a Women."
       Journal of Personality and Social Psychology 34 (November
       1976): 990-9.

1455   Showalter, C. Robert; Richard J. Bonnie; and Virginia Reddy.
       "The Spousal-homicide Syndrome."   International Journal
       of Law and Psychiatry 3, no. 2 (1980): 117-41.

1456   Silverman, Phyllis R.   "The Grief of the Battered Woman."
       In her Helping Women Cope with Grief.   (Sage Human Serv-
       ices Guide, 25.)   Beverly Hills, Cal.:   Sage, 1981, pp.
       81-99.
          Written as a guide for professionals in social service agen-
cies, mental health clinics and other human service organizations, this
chapter on battered women provides an overview of the problem.   The
doubts, anxiety, low self-esteem and other characteristics of these
victims are detailed and illustrated with short vignettes and actual experiences of abused wives.   The needs of victims are described, as
are aids for grief counseling.

1457   Silver(wo)man, Sandy.   "Rape in Marriage: Is It Legal?"   Do
       It Now 9 (June 1976): 10.

1458   Simon, Roger.   "I Killed My Husband ... and I Have Some Ad-
       vice...."   Quarterly Journal of Corrections 1 (Fall 1977):
       41-2.
          This short article originally appeared in the Los Angeles
Times, May 9, 1977.   A battered wife phoned the author and told how
and why she killed her abusing husband.   The advice is not to have a
gun in the house.

1459   Slot-Anderson, Ingerlise.   "A Dutch Refuge for Battered Women:
       Who Comes?"   Paper presented at the annual meeting of
       the American Sociological Association, New York, August
       1976.

1460   Slovenko, Ralph.   "The Marital Rape Exemption."   Victimology:
       An International Journal 4, no. 1 (1979): 178-81.
          Slovenko, School of Law, Wayne State University, discusses
the concept of marital rape.   Hale's doctrine, common law on the subject, and the New Jersey case State v. Smith are analyzed.   The author supports the exemption, believing the "crime" difficult to prove
and too easily invoked by a spiteful wife.

1461   Smith, Andrew C.   "Violence."   British Journal of Psychiatry
       134 (May 1979): 528-9.
          Three papers presented at the autumn quarterly meeting
of the Royal College of Psychiatrists are discussed.   Of interest to
Smith is J. J. Gayford's characteristics of battered women as described
in his article in the British Medical Journal [592].

1462 Smith, Barbara E. Non-stranger Violence: The Criminal
         Court's Response. Washington, D. C. : National Institute
         of Justice, U. S. Department of Justice, 1983.   197 p.
         The criminal court responses to domestic violence in Char-
lotte (North Carolina), Los Angeles, and Minneapolis are studied.
Numerous similarities and differences were noted between the victims'
perceptions of the handling of their cases. Comparisons are made between the cities regarding the police response, the prosecutor's role
and how the judge treated the case and victim satisfaction with each.

1463 Smith, Teresa S. "Abused Wives: Communication and Person-
         ality Factors. " M. S. thesis, University of Delaware,
         1982.   93 p.
         The author studied two groups of abused women. Those in
the first group (12 women) were currently living with their abusers and
the second group (16 women) had separated or divorced the abuser.
Both groups completed demographic and communication behavior questionnaires and Cattell's 16 Personality Factor Inventory. Length of
marriage, severity of abuse, number of children, and jobs outside of
the home did not prove to be significant. However, the abuse being
extended to the children, calling the police, high communication behavior
related to the abuse, and a warm, outgoing, tradition-valuing personality were all factors related to a woman leaving the violent home.

1464 Snell, John E. ; Richard J. Rosenwald; and Ames Robey. "The
         Wifebeater's Wife: A Study of Family Interaction. " Ar-
         chives of General Psychiatry 11 (August 1964): 107-12.
         Also in Deviancy and the Family. Eds. Clifton D. Bryant
         and J. Gipson Wells. Arlington Heights, Ill. : AHM Pub-
         lishing Corp. , 1973, pp. 87-95.
         An early study of wife beating, this one characterizes the
husband as passive, sexually inadequate and indecisive, whereas the
wife is aggressive, masculine, frigid and masochistic. The violence
satisfies the wife's masochism while giving the husband a temporary
feeling of adequacy. More study is necessary.

1465 Snyder, Douglas K. , and Lisa A. Fruchtman. "Differential Pat-
         terns of Wife Abuse: A Data-based Typology. " Journal of
         Consulting and Clinical Psychology 49 (December 1981):
         878-85.
         This study divides 119 battered women into five groups
which experienced abuse in different intensities and frequency. It is
believed that different forms of intervention would be more effective in
each case. Only a relatively small group (9 percent) have resigned
themselves to violence as a way of life. For the rest, attempts at
change may be more successful. More attention must be paid to the
abusers. Only then will any real progress against abuse be made.

1466 Snyder, Douglas K. , and Nancy S. Scheer. "Predicting Dispo-
         sition Following Brief Residence at a Shelter for Battered
         Women. " American Journal of Community Psychology 9
         (October 1981): 559-66.
         The authors studied 74 women who stayed for at least four

days at the Detroit Shelter, Women-in-Transition.   They were surveyed
six to ten weeks following discharge from the shelter and 41 (55 percent) were again living with the assailant. Only 14 percent admitted a
preference for returning to the abuser when they were admitted to the
shelter. By the time of discharge it was already 33 percent.   Results
show it is inappropriate to base counseling and service for battered
women on the statements they make at the time of entry.

1467   Social Work Services Group.   Scottish Education Department.
       Violence in the Family: Theory and Practice in Social
       Work. Edinburgh: HMSO, 1982.   70 p.

1468   Soler, Esta, and Sue Martin. "Domestic Violence Is a Crime."
       San Francisco, Cal. : Family Violence Project, [1982?].
       [48 p.] Also in Domestic Violence.   U. S. Congress.
       House. Committee on Education and Labor, Subcommittee
       on Select Education.   Hearing, 98th Cong. 1st Sess.   23
       June 1983. Washington, D. C. : Government Printing Of-
       fice, 1983, pp. 209-57.
       The San Francisco Family Violence Project is detailed.
General facts regarding abuse are given along with fact sheets describing the procedures and protocols of the police and criminal justice system.

1469   Somsel, Anne E.   "Relationship Between Battered Women's Mas-
       culine and Feminine Characteristics of Self-esteem."   M. S.
       thesis, Arizona State University, Tempe, 1981.   58 p.
       The purpose of this study was to investigate the relation-
ship between sex-role characteristics of battered women and their self-
esteem.   The sample consisted of thirty-one American women who had
temporarily resided in a spouse abuse shelter.   The BEM Sex-role Inventory and the Texas Social Behavior Inventory were used to measure
the masculine and feminine characteristics.   The study found a relationship between high self-esteem and masculine characteristics.   When
providing assistance to battered women, development of her masculine
traits should be emphasized.

1470   Sonkin, David Jay, and Michael Durphy.   Learning to Live With-
       out Violence: A Handbook for Men.   San Francisco: Vol-
       cano Press, 1982.   110 p.
       This workbook is aimed at men who use or fear they will
use violence in their interactions with spouses.   It is not meant to re-
place counseling, but instead to be an adjunct to individual, group, or
couples counseling, or as an immediate tool to bring the violence under
control while seeking professional help.   Geared to take about fourteen
weeks, it contains readings and homework exercises to reinforce the
lessons.   Recognizing and controlling anger, learning to listen and com-
municate needs, the value of stress reduction and the relationship of
violence to alcohol and drugs are all among the weekly lessons.

1471   Sorrel, Lorraine. "Neglecting Abused Women."   Off Our Backs
       11 (June 1981): 23.
       News regarding spouse abuse in Washington, D. C. , with
emphasis on "My Sisters Place," a local shelter.

1472 South Carolina Commission on Women. <u>Spouse Abuse.</u> Colum-
         bia: Author, 1981. 8 p.
         A brief brochure with an overview of spouse abuse, who
is abused, who is the abuser, what can be done and what the South
Carolina law says on the subject. A list of services with addresses
and phone numbers is included.

1473 Southern California Coalition on Battered Women. <u>Shelter
         Directory of Services in California.</u> Santa Monica, Cal. :
         The Coalition, 1983. 47 p.

1474 Spencer, Margaret. "The Domestic Proceedings and Magistrates'
         Courts Act 1978, Part I." <u>New Law Journal</u> 128 (July 27,
         1978): 727-9; Part II, (August 3, 1978): 750-2.
         A general discussion of the new British law with some
reference to how the husband can be barred from the matrimonial home
if he threatens or uses violence on the wife or children.

1475 Spiegel, John P. "Ethnopsychiatric Dimensions in Family Vio-
         lence." In <u>Violence and the Family.</u> Ed. Maurice R. Green.
         (AAS Selected Symposium 47) Boulder, Colo. : Westview
         Press, 1980, pp. 79-89.
         There is no universal, monolithic, unvarying and easily un-
derstood unit called the American Family. All families differ and ethnic subculture is one cause for the difference. This author contrasts
Italian-American, Irish-American and mainstream Wasp middle-class
families with respect to their acceptance of family violence. All three
are then contrasted with the Tahitian family style. No particular concern with child or spouse abuse, but relevant.

1476 Spieker, Gisela. "Family Violence and Alcohol Abuse." <u>Toxic-
         omanies</u> 13 (1980): 13-42.
         The relationship of alcohol abuse to child and spouse abuse
is studied by this author, Professor of Social Work, University of Arkansas, Little Rock. Demographics regarding age, number of children,
employment, education and marital status are provided. The actual
cause of the violence is difficult to pinpoint, but there is no question
that alcohol use is a contributing factor. More research is necessary.

1477 Spitzner, Joseph H. , and Donald H. McGee. "Family Crisis In-
         tervention Training, Diversion and the Prevention of Crimes
         of Violence." <u>The Police Chief</u> 42 (October 1975): 252-3.
         The Columbus, Ohio, Patrol Division Officers were given
a training course in family crisis intervention by the Family Crisis
Unit of the Columbus Area Mental Health Center. The program emphasized two conflict resolution techniques, mediation and referral.
Officers found the training successful and reports from citizens confirmed these methods were more satisfactory than the traditional methods of advising them to separate voluntarily for a cooling off period
or of informing them of legal options available.

1478 "Spouse Abuse Cases Top One Million." <u>Public Administration
         Times</u> 1 (March 1978): 6.

This news note uses data from Deirdre Gaquin article in Victimology [576] reporting on cases between 1973 and 1975.

1479 Spouse Assault: An Initial Glimpse at the Problem and Possible
        Solutions in San Diego. Edited and compiled by Pat Spez-
        eski and Carmen Germaine Warner. San Diego, Cal.:
        County Department of Human Resources/City Advisory
        Board on Women, [1977]. 70 p.
        This booklet contains the results of a San Diego research
project 1) to determine the extent of spouse abuse, the impact of the
problem on the community, and the nature of the services provided;
and 2) to provide recommendations for relief. The study consists of
a review of the literature, an analysis of the data collected from 223
community agencies, and a recommendation intended for city and county
action. Many charts display the data and statistics regarding frequency
and its personal and community impact. The appendix includes the
questionnaire and letters used for data collection.

1480 Stacey, William, and Anson Shupe. The Family Secret: Domes-
        tic Violence in America. Boston: Beacon Press, 1983.
        237 p.
        The authors, professors of sociology, University of Texas,
Arlington, compiled data on battered women from a variety of sources,
the most important of which being two shelters, Friends of the Family
in Denton, Texas, and Family Place in Dallas. Most of the information
was collected between 1979 and 1982. History of the problem, effects
on the family, backgrounds of the batterers, options available to the
victims, legal and police responses to abuse, and proposed solutions
make up the major elements of the book. Some concern is expressed
regarding the spreading "cult of violence" which seems to be occurring.
The authors are not pessimistic, however, and believe that while violence may be increasing it is man-made and therefore can be controlled.

1481 Stachura, James S., and Raymond C. Teske, Jr. A Special Re-
        port on Spouse Abuse in Texas. Huntsville, Tex.: Sam
        Houston State University, Criminal Justice Center, Survey
        Research Program, 1979. 18 p.
        Based on survey responses of 682 Texans, the authors have
what they view to be an accurate idea of the extent of spouse abuse
(husband and wife) in Texas. Many facts are revealed, such as 12.2
percent of Texas women and 2.2 percent of Texas men have been
abused by their spouses. No fewer than 87,000 adult Texans are subject to spouse abuse weekly. Very enlightening report.

1482 Stachura, James S. "Spouse Abuse in Texas: Its Scope and
        Nature as Determined by a Statewide Public Mail Survey."
        M.A. thesis, Sam Houston State University, 1979. 185 p.
        The purpose of this study was to establish the extent of
spouse abuse in Texas and to ascertain the nature of the phenomenon.
A statewide sample of 682 was used to determine that nearly a half
million women over 18 in Texas have been abused and 43 percent of
these within the past 18 months. Also, 88,000 male Texans over 18
years of age have been abused by a spouse. Use of alcohol, the cycle

of violence, involvement of the police, divorce action taken, etc. are
all discussed. An especially good master's paper.

1483 Stafford, J. "Battered Women and the National Women's Aid
        Federation." Paper presented at the annual meeting of
        the American Sociological Association, New York, 1976.

1484 Stahly, Geraldine Butts. "A Review of Select Literature of
        Spousal Abuse." Victimology: An International Journal 2,
        nos. 3-4 (1977-78): 591-607.
    The research into the phenomenon of spouse abuse is ana-
lyzed by Stahly. Among the conclusions is the realization that while
there have been numerous studies, few have been empirical. To date
most have been theoretical. More empirical research is necessary.

1485 Stahly, Geraldine Butts. "Victim Derogation of the Battered
        Woman, the Just World and the Observer's Past History of
        Victimization." Ph. D. dissertation, University of Califor-
        nia, Riverside, 1983. 259 p. Abstract in Dissertation
        Abstracts International 44B (January 1984): 2285-6.

1486 Stamm, Linda J. "Children of Battered Women: Their Reactions
        and Perceptions of the Conjugal Violence Experience." Psy.
        D. dissertation, Rutgers University, 1983. 246 p. Abstract
        in Dissertation Abstracts International 44B (December 1983):
        1979.

1487 Star, Barbara. "Characteristics of Family Violence." In The
        Many Faces of Family Violence. Ed. Jerry P. Flanzer.
        Springfield, Ill.: Charles C. Thomas, 1982, pp. 14-23.
    This article is concerned with family violence in general
including wife abuse. Several characteristics of abuse include 1) violent behavior accelerates over time, increasing in frequency and severity; 2) there is no need for prolonged argument to provoke the violence;
3) gradually the abuser is more dependent upon external factors (than
internal ones) to bring the assaultive behavior under control; 4) use of
alcohol increases risk of injury; and 5) there is a self-propelling quality to the abuse; that is, it seems to take on a life of its own. Assaulters
share characteristics such as having seen their own parents use violence, having experienced or seen little affection when young, and ex-
hibiting a tendency to externalize the blame for the outbreak. They
are also highly possessive of the victims and expect them to meet a
wide range of deep and unfulfilled needs. Victims were often raised
in emotionally restricted home environments and were encouraged to
be passive. They are also socially isolated and often internalize the
blame, believing they caused the violence. Victims also rarely fight
back and are often loyal to the assaulter. The most common reactions
to the violence are depression, fear, and impaired trust. A highly
readable overview of the basic characteristics associated with family
violence by a professor of social work at the University of Southern California, Los Angeles.

1488 Star, Barbara. "Comparing Battered and Non-battered Women."

Victimology: An International Journal 3, nos. 1-2 (1978):
32-44.
Star, in this study, compared psychosocial aspects of 57
battered and nonbattered women at Haven House, a Los Angeles area
shelter. The findings are not seen as conclusive, but there are a
few points deserving further study. Battered women showed no signs
of being submissive, but were instead within the normal range of submissive assertive. They also were not masochistic. They did appear to be more passive, however. They tended to believe that any
action would only make matters worse. Lack of education and conservative religious beliefs tended to reinforce the passivity.

1489 Star, Barbara. Helping the Abuser: Intervening Effectively in
        Family Violence. New York: Family Service Association
        of America, 1983. 262 p.

1490 Star, Barbara. "Patterns in Family Violence." Social Case-
        work 61 (June 1980): 339-46.
        A general discussion of family violence, this article pro-
vides details on the characteristics of the assaulter and the victim.
Use of force is viewed as legitimate and there are often inappropriate
expectations of the other spouse to satisfy personal needs. A limited
knowledge of parenting, an inability to relate to others or to tolerate
stress are also factors. The social worker must be sensitive to the
problems of family violence, obtain freely and openly the necessary
information from the client and be aware of other community services
to which the client can be referred.

1491 Star, Barbara, et al. "Psychosocial Aspects of Wife Battering."
        Social Casework 60 (October 1979): 479-87.
        Battered women from shelters in California and Arizona
were given questionnaires and batteries of personality inventories in
early 1977 in an attempt to determine the personality characteristics
of battered women. The wife's previous exposure to violence, the
quality of her marital relationship and her personality are discussed.
Treatment by the social worker must take all these factors into consideration and guidelines for doing so are detailed. Treatment must
continue after the shelter experience.

1492 Star, Barbara. "Treating the Battered Woman." In Toward
        Human Dignity: Social Work in Practice. Ed. John W.
        Hanks. Washington, D. C. : National Association of Social
        Workers, 1978, pp. 217-25.
        Star examines the psychosocial dynamics of abused women
and their marital situations, highlighting aspects of spouse abuse that
social workers encounter. Social workers must confront the victim
about the existence of violence (the wife tends to downplay its importance), her emotional emptiness her social isolation, the pent-up anger, her depression, and other problems. Treatment progress is not
speedy, but unless the situation is faced squarely no progress will be
made at all.

1493 Stark, Evan. "Psychiatric Perspectives on the Abuse of Women:

A Critical Approach. " In Identification and Treatment of
Spouse Abuse: Health and Mental Health Agency Roles,
Proceedings of a Conference. Eds. Abraham Lurie and
Elizabeth B. Quitkin. New York: Editors, 1981, pp.
9-33.

1494 Stark, Evan, and Anne Flitcraft. "Social Knowledge, Social
        Policy, and the Abuse of Women; The Case Against Patri-
        archal Benevolence." In The Dark Side of Families; Cur-
        rent Family Violence Research. Eds. David Finkelhor,
        et al. Beverly Hills, Cal. : Sage Publications, 1983, pp.
        330-48.
        The authors point out how the research by social scientists
in England and the U.S. forms the image and conceptualization of the
abused wife which in turn affects how society and government treat
the problem. In the case of spouse abuse it is the convergence of
the social research with political authority that makes the intervention
appear to be an effective portrayal of a serious social issue. The
new knowledge gives the aura that wife abuse is inevitable and genetic,
not social-historical.

1495 Stark, Evan; Anne Flitcraft; and William Frazier. "Medicine
        and Patriarchal Violence: The Social Construction of a
        'Private' Event." International Journal of Health Services
        9, no. 3 (1979): 461-93.
        The authors describe the patterns of spouse abuse and dis-
cuss it in the context of the contribution the medical profession and the
other helping professions make to its continuance. Prior to capitalism,
the economic system supported partiarchal family organization, but the
instability of capitalism weakened it. Spouse abuse may have occurred
under the old system, but it then became a means of maintaining male
control. A good discussion of the literature is included.

1496 Stark, Evan, et al. Wife Abuse in the Medical Setting: An In-
        troduction for Health Personnel. (Domestic Violence,
        Monograph Series, no. 7, April 1981.) Rockville, Md. :
        National Clearinghouse on Domestic Violence, 1981. 54 p.
        Must reading for health professionals and others interested
in spouse abuse. Emphasis is on the need for medical practitioners
to be aware of the problem and what they can do to help. For too
long health professionals have treated the bruises, but inadvertently
helped reinforce the sexist biases of society and have done nothing to
try to change that. An overview of the problem, what to look for in
suspected abuse cases, and how to render assistance are all detailed.
A fine study from staff of the School of Medicine and the Center for
Health Studies, Yale University.

1497 Stark, Rodney, and James McEvoy III. "Middle Class Violence."
        Psychology Today 4 (November 1970): 52-4, 110-2. Also
        in Change: Readings in Society and Human Behavior. Del
        Mar, Cal. : Communications Research, 1972, pp. 272-7.
        The results of a poll by Louis Harris and Associates of 1,176
Americans for the National Commission on the Causes and Prevention

of Violence in October 1968. Along with many opinions regarding violence is the belief by one fifth of all Americans that slapping one's
spouse is appropriate on occasions. This opinion increases with income and education.

1498 Stark-Adamec. Cannie, and Robert E. Adamec. "Aggression
         by Men Against Women: Adaption or Aberration?" Inter-
         national Journal of Women's Studies 5 (January-February
         1982): 1-21.
      These Canadian authors have analyzed the literature of
male aggression against females and place it in the context of rape
and wife beating. Because this aggression crosses cultural lines,
some researchers want to attribute a biological basis, but these authors believe a more multicausal approach is required. The root
cause is probably fear of women (gynaephobia).

1499 Stedman, Beirne. "Right of Husband to Chastise Wife." Vir-
         ginia Law Register 3 (August 1917): 241-8.
      After a brief history of this "right" in Roman times and
English common law, Stedman discusses the concept in American law.
He says, "The right of the husband to chastise his wife has generally
met with disapproval in the United States and at this late date is entirely obsolete even in those states which formerly acquiesced in the
practice. And it is now as unlawful for a husband to beat his wife as
for another to do so, and he is amendable to the criminal law for
such offense." Useful historical perspective.

1500 Steinem, Gloria. Women Alive! A License for Violence. The
         Tragedy of Battered Wives. Chiswick Women's Aid, 1977.
         13 p. Also in Domestic Violence. U. S. Congress. House.
         Committee on Education and Labor, Subcommittee on Select
         Education. 95th Cong. 2nd Sess. Hearings on HR 7927 and
         HR 8748, March 16 and 17, 1978. Washington, D. C.: Gov-
         ernment Printing Office, 1978, pp. 385-97; Domestic Vio-
         lence, 1978. U. S. Congress. Senate. Committee on Hu-
         man Resources, Subcommittee on Child and Human Develop-
         ment. Hearings. 95th Cong. 2nd Sess. On Domestic Vio-
         lence and Legislation with Respect to Domestic Violence,
         March 4 and 8, 1978. Washington, D. C.: Government
         Printing Office, 1978, pp. 660-72.
      Steinem provides an introduction and analysis and commen-
tary of the battered-woman problem as portrayed in this film which
first was broadcast on public television April 25, 1977. The need for
shelters and hot lines is seen as immediate but temporary. Legal reform and police training are among the more permanent solutions.

1501 Steinmetz, Robert L. "Spouse Abuse-Adult Abuse Act Allowing
         Trial.... Journal of Family Law 21 (November 1982): 163-7.
      "...court to issue ex parte order excluding husband from
his home or from contact with his children upon finding that he presented immediate and present danger of abuse to his wife upheld as
constitutional." State ex rel. Williams v Marsh, 626 S. W. 2d 223
(Mo. 1982).

1502 Steinmetz, Suzanne K. "The Battered Husband Syndrome." Vic-
         timology: An International Journal 2, nos. 3-4 (1977-78):
         499-509. Also in Perspectives on Crime Victims. Eds.
         Burt Galaway and Joe Hudson. St. Louis, Mo.: C. V.
         Mosby, 1981, pp. 201-8.
              The author discusses an even more unreported crime than
    wife beating--husband abuse. Some historical information, comic
    strips, and more recent studies are analyzed. Husband abuse is more
    common than many will admit. While concern for it should not detract
    from wife abuse, husbands also need aid. Her purpose is to show the
    pervasiveness of family violence and its many forms. Society's atti-
    tudes toward all forms of violence must change. Controversial article.

1503 Steinmetz, Suzanne K. "A Cross-cultural Comparison of Marital
         Abuse." Journal of Sociology and Social Welfare 8 (July
         1981): 404-14.
              The statistics regarding wife abuse were analyzed for six
    countries: United States, Canada, Finland, Israel, Puerto Rico, and
    Belize. The preliminary results indicate that the percentage of abus-
    ers in a society does not predict the severity or the frequency. Areas
    where more people used it did not have the most frequent or severe forms.
    More research is recommended to determine the relationship of marital
    violence to economic conditions, level of technology in society, social
    and political philosophies, and other influences.

1504 Steinmetz, Suzanne K. "A Cross-cultural Comparison of Sibling
         Violence." International Journal of Family Psychiatry 2,
         nos. 3-4 (1981): 337-51.

1505 Steinmetz, Suzanne K. ed. The Cycle of Violence: Assertive,
         Aggressive, and Abusive Family Interaction. New York:
         Praeger Publishers, 1977. 191 p.
              This study deals with 57 families, their sources of intrafamil-
    ial conflict and the various methods they utilize to resolve those conflicts.
    Each family is consistent in the resolution method it uses, with parents
    using the same method of solving problems with their children as they
    do with each other. These methods are also passed on through each
    generation. Thus those families that resolve conflict with violence
    pass that method on to their children who then pass it on to theirs
    when they become parents. They in effect are passing on the idea that
    physical force is an acceptable way of dealing with conflict, thereby per-
    petuating the "cycle of violence."

1506 Steinmetz, Suzanne. "Intra-familial Patterns of Conflict Resolu-
         tion: Husband/Wife; Parent/Child; Sibling/Sibling." Ph. D.
         dissertation, Case Western Reserve University. 1975.
         338 p. Abstract in Dissertation Abstracts International
         36A (February 1976): 5586-7.
              Steinmetz studied 57 randomly selected families from New
    Castle County, Delaware to determine intrafamily conflict resolution.
    Almost all families used discussion and verbal aggression to resolve
    conflict. Interestingly, siblings used physical aggression in 95 percent
    of families, parent and child in 70 percent of families, and spouses

in 60 percent of the couples.   She notes that while all of the aggression cannot be considered abuse, its frequency does seem to raise the tolerance level toward violence and abuse in family interaction.

1507   Steinmetz, Suzanne K.   "Investigating Family Violence."   Journal of Home Economics 72 (Summer 1980): 32-6.
This article is concerned with the extensiveness of different types of family violence, including sibling violence, child and spouse abuse, and child to parent violence, causes of violence, intervention strategies and the implications for home economists.   Because of their educational role home economists could promote a critical link for public awareness and future teachers and service professionals.   Those who are teaching family-related classes have a unique opportunity.

1508   Steinmetz, Suzanne K.   "Reply to Pleck, Pleck, Grossman and Bart."   Victimology: An International Journal 2, nos. 3-4 (1977-78): 683-4.
Steinmetz defends her research and conclusions from the charges made by Pleck et al. in their earlier article "The Battered Data Syndrome" [1272].   She suggests they may have their own biases and their comments are suspiciously similar to those raised by many regarding the existence of wife battering a few years earlier.

1509   Steinmetz, Suzanne K. , ed.   Resource Booklet for Battered Spouses.   Wilmington, Delaware: Governor's Commission on the Status of Women, 1977.   41 p.
An outgrowth of the three-seminar forum in Delaware "The Battered Partner: The Law and Family Violence," this pamphlet provides an overview essay by Steinmetz, and the laws, resources and services of Delaware, Pennsylvania, and Maryland.

1510   Steinmetz, Suzanne K. , ed.   Resource Booklet for Families in Crisis.   3rd ed. Wilmington, Del. :   Governor's Commission on the Status of Women, 1978.   52 p.
This booklet begins with an essay by Steinmetz which provides an overview of the problem of family violence.   The laws of Delaware, Maryland, and Pennsylvania are included along with a list of the services and shelters available in these states.   This is a revision of her Resource Booklet for Battered Spouses [1509].

1511   Steinmetz, Suzanne K.   "Secondary Analysis of Data from a United States-Canadian Comparison of Intra-family Conflict."   Canadian Conference on Family Violence, Simon Fraser University, Burnaby, Canada,March 12, 1977.

1512   Steinmetz, Suzanne K.   "Services to Battered Women: Our Greatest Need.   A Reply to Fields and Kirchner."   Victimology: An International Journal 3, nos. 1-2 (1978): 222-6.
In this article the author responds to citicism [490] of her article "The Battered Husband Syndrome."   After justifying her data, she urges more effort on battering research, not professional infighting.

1513   Steinmetz, Suzanne K.   "Spousal Abuse: An Interdisciplinary

Perspective." Paper presented at the meeting of the American Psychological Association, New York, September 1979.

1514 Steinmetz, Suzanne K. "The Use of Force for Resolving Family Conflict: The Training Ground for Abuse." The Family Coordinator 26 (January 1977): 19-26.
This article studied the questionnaires of 78 people between the ages of 18 and 30 to determine the relationship between use of violence by parents on each other, on the children or between the children to resolve conflict. The premise is that families do use force and that the family setting is where use of force is legitimized. Results indicate that there is a relationship between method of conflict resolution between parents and between parents and children. Siblings tend to use similar methods among themselves. The lessons are also carried to the next generation.

1515 Steinmetz, Suzanne K. "Violence Between Family Members: A Review of the Recent Literature." Marriage and Family Review 1 (May/June 1978): 1-16.
An excellent review of the literature, research and studies of family violence including spouse abuse. Along with a discussion of family violence in general, the author includes an analysis of the factors which contribute to it, theories of violence, and programs for prevention and intervention.

1516 Steinmetz, Suzanne K. "Violence-prone Families." In Forensic Psychology and Psychiatry. Eds. Fred Wright, Charles Bahn and Robert W. Rieber. (Annals of the New York Academy of Sciences, v. 347.) New York: N. Y. Academy of Sciences, 1980, pp. 251-65.
Here Steinmetz provides an overview of the characteristics of violence-prone families. Factors such as class, income, education, employment status, length of marriage, age, sex differences, and isolation are dealt with. Many data have been gathered over the past decade, but more are necessary. Of special interest is that violence patterns occur in many generations. Is this learned or is there a chromosomal/hormonal influence?

1517 Steinmetz, Suzanne K. "Wife Beating: A Critique and Reformulation of Existing Theory." American Academy of Psychiatry and The Law Bulletin 6, no. 3 (1978): 322-34.
Steinmetz challenges several theories of wife abuse stating that new research shows some discrepancy between previously held assumptions and recent findings. Emphasis is given to the need to distinguish between the "Saturday Night Brawl" and the "Chronic Battered Syndrome." The former is typified by reciprocal, escalating, violent interactions, with either spouse likely to be the victim in a given fight. Battered wives do not precipitate the event and in fact go out of their way to avoid it and will not retaliate because they fear escalation. Most often they remain passive, protect themselves, or escape. The author devotes much attention to the brainwashing which is part of the dynamics of the syndrome. An important study and critique.

1518 Steinmetz, Suzanne K. "Wifebeating, Husbandbeating--A Com-

parison of the Use of Physical Violence Between Spouses
to Resolve Marital Fights. " In Battered Women: A Psychosociological Study of Domestic Violence.   Ed. Maria
Roy.   New York: Van Nostrand Reinhold, 1977, pp. 63-72.
Steinmetz argues that while wife abuse is far more prevalent than husband abuse, the latter is not unknown.   In fact, it is
probably even less reported than wife abuse.   She says, "The myth of
women receiving socialization for greater impulse control appears to
have little support in reality--at least as far as marital fights are
concerned. "   Men, however, do more damage than women.

1519 Steinmetz, Suzanne K.   "Women and Violence: Victims and Per-
        petrators. "   American Journal of Psychotherapy 34, no. 3
        (1980): 334-50.
      A review of the historical roots of violence is followed by
a discussion of how women are victims of abuse, but also how they
are often abusers.   Husband abuse is more underreported than wife
abuse.   Several "myths" need reevaluation.   They include the marriage
license as a hitting license, blaming the victim, violence in the home
of origin increases tolerance, and greater resources facilitate leaving
the abuser.   None of these are necessarily true, and deserve rethinking.
This paper was presented at the Twentieth Emil A. Gutheil Conference
of the Association for the Advancement of Psychotherapy, New York,
November 18, 1979.

1520 Steinmetz, Suzanne K. , and Murray A. Straus.   "The Family as
        a Cradle of Violence. "   Society 10 (September/October 1973):
        50-6.   Also in Readings in Criminology.   Eds. Peter
        Wickman and Phillip Whitten.   Lexington, Mass. : D. C.
        Heath, 1978, pp. 59-65; Sociological Realities, II.   Irving
        L. Horowitz.   New York: Harper and Row, 1975; Social
        Problems in Corporate America.   Eds. Helen Icken Safa
        and Gloria Levitas.   New York: Harper and Row, 1975,
        pp. 217-23; Readings in Marriage and the Family 79/80.
        Guilford, Conn. : Annual Editions Publishing Co. , 1979,
        pp. 125-31.
      Family violence is discussed with some special attention
to violence between spouses.   Corporal punishment of children has good
intentions, but it also legitimizes the use of violence and is therefore
seen by children as an appropriate means to an end.   Several myths
are exposed, such as abusers are psychopathological, are lower class,
have no other resources so they must use violence to dominate others,
there is a connection between sex and violence, and the catharsis myth
that aggression should not be bottled up, but instead should be vented
through "normal" violence.   Many of these myths have a kernel of truth,
but care must be taken not to exaggerate it.

1521 Steinmetz, Suzanne K. , and Murray A. Straus, eds.   Violence in
        the Family.   New York: Dodd, Mead, 1974.   337 p.
      This volume is a collection of articles relating to family
violence.   Articles by Levinger [958], Calvert [225], Palmer [1211],
and others concerned with spousal conflict are included.   Much of the
material has been published elsewhere.   Individual articles are listed
by author and annotated elsewhere in this bibliography.

1522 Stencel, Sandra. "Violence in the Family." Editorial Research
        Reports 1 (April 1979): 307-24.   Also in Changing American
        Family. Washington, D. C. : Congressional Quarterly, 1979,
        pp. 21-40.
             An overview of violent family behavior, this article discusses
child abuse and wife beating. Some attention is devoted to husband
abuse, marital rape, the transgenerational theory of violence and efforts made to help the abuser and victims change their communication
patterns.

1523 Stephens, Darrel W. "Domestic Assault: The Police Response."
        In Battered Women: A Psychosociological Study of Domestic
        Violence. Ed. Maria Roy. New York: Van Nostrand
        Reinhold, 1977, pp. 164-72.
             Stephens, Assistant Chief of Police, Lawrence, Kansas, re-
views the general practice of police intervention, and the research experiments of Morton Bard in New York and Kansas City. Training
similar to that proposed by Bard should be standard to all police departments, shelters should be available and volunteer organizations
should be established to aid abuse victims.

1524 Stewart, Mark A. , and C. Susan DeBlois. "Is Alcoholism Re-
        lated to Physical Abuse of Wives and Children?" Paper
        presented at the annual meeting of the National Council on
        Alcoholism, St. Louis, 1978.

1525 Stewart, Mark A. , and C. Susan DeBlois. "Wife Abuse Among
        Families Attending a Child Psychiatry Clinic." American
        Academy of Child Psychiatry Journal 20 (Autumn 1981):
        845-62.
             The parents of 122 boys from a child psychiatric clinic
were interviewed to determine the relationship of the parents' violent
background (if any) and that of the child. Results indicate that 41 percent of the mothers were abused by the husbands. Causes included
antisocial personality and alcoholism of the father and neurotic disorders of the mother. Child abuse tended to occur more frequently in
homes with wife abuse. Women who had conduct or neurotic disorders
tended to marry men more predisposed to abusiveness. Overall it
appeared that wife abuse was common in these families and had much
to do with the child's behavior. To treat the child properly one must
be cognizant of the total family problem.

1526 Stratmann, Penelope M. "Law Reform and the U. K. Domestic
        Violence and Matrimonial Proceedings Act, 1976." In Vio-
        lence in the Family: A Collection of Conference Papers.
        Ed. Jocelynne A. Scutt. Canberra: Australian Institute
        of Criminology, 1980, pp. 121-35.

1527 Straus, Murray A. "Cultural and Social Organizational Influences
        on Violence Between Family Members." In Configurations:
        Biological and Cultural Factors in Sexuality and Family Life.
        Eds. Raymond Prince and Dorothy Barrier. Lexington,
        Mass. : D. C. Heath, Lexington Books, 1974, pp. 53-69.

Also in Research into Violent Behavior: Domestic Violence.
U. S. Congress. House. Committee on Science and Technology. Hearings. 95th Cong. 2nd Sess. February 14,
15, 16, 1978. Washington, D. C. : Government Printing
Office, 1978, pp. 806-22.

Violence between family members is as typical as love.
These acts of violence by one family member against another are the
result of socially learned and socially patterned behavior.   Cultural
norms, the social organization of the family, and personality characteristics of the individuals all combine to encourage and justify violence.

1528 Straus, Murray A. "Cultural Approval and Structural Necessity
        or Intra-family Assaults in Sexist Societies. " Paper pre-
        sented at the International Institute of Victimology, Bellagio,
        Italy, July 1975.

1529 Straus, Murray A. "A General Systems Theory Approach to a
        Theory of Violence Between Family Members. " Social
        Science Information 12, no. 3 (1973): 105-25.

        This article discusses family violence in general, but
husband-wife violence is its particular concern.   Straus believes that
the continuing violence in an abusive relationship is "a systemic product
rather than a product of individual behavior pathology. " This theory
specifies the positive feedback and the negative feedback which serves
to maintain the level of violence in the family.   A final section outlines
the implications of a systemic approach for research design and research technology.

1530 Straus, Murray A. "Husbands and Wives as Victims and Aggres-
        sors in Marital Violence. " Paper presented at the annual
        meetings of the American Association for the Advancement
        of Science, San Francisco, January 1980.

1531 Straus, Murray A. "Leveling, Civility, and Violence in the
        Family. " In Confronting the Issues; Sex Roles, Marriage,
        and the Family. Ed. Kenneth C.W. Kammeyer. Boston:
        Allyn and Bacon, 1975, pp. 321-30. Also in Dynamics of
        Marital Interaction. Eds. Richard W. Cantrell and David
        F. Schrader. Kendall/Hunt, 1974; Journal of Marriage and
        the Family 36 (February 1974): 13-29 (addendum in August
        1974 issue).

        The author takes issue with the notions of Bach and Wyden,
The Intimate Enemy, which urge "therapeutic aggression" between
couples.   He believes this is dangerous if done in the home without
the supervision of a therapist.   They propose leveling, that is, honesty
and "having it out" as the best way to relieve conflict.   Straus describes
and criticizes this "leveling" or "catharsis" approach.   Bach and Wyden
would argue that the verbal aggression drains off physical aggression.
Straus shows that this is not true.   In fact verbal aggression increases
the likelihood of physical aggression.   Civility is more likely to be a
better method of intermarital conflict.

1532 Straus, Murray A. "The Marriage License as a Hitting License:

Evidence from Popular Culture, Law, and Social Science."
In The Social Causes of Husband-Wife Violence.   Eds.
Murray A. Straus and Gerald T. Hotaling.   Minneapolis:
University of Minnesota Press, 1980, pp. 39-50.
A number of examples of the common notion that chastising
wives is acceptable are detailed.   Laws granting spousal immunity, fail-
ure of the police and prosecutors to act, and several surveys express-
ing popular attitudes are included.   The idea of marriage license as
hitting license is deeply embedded in American and English cultures.
Part of this article is reprinted from the author's "Sexual Inequality,
Cultural Norms and Wife Beating" [1538].

1533   Straus, Murray A.   "Measuring Intrafamily Conflict and Violence:
       The CT Scales."   Paper presented at the annual meeting of
       the National Council on Family Relations, 1976.

1534   Straus, Murray A.   "Measuring Intrafamily Conflict and Violence:
       The Conflict Tactics (CT) Scales."   Journal of Marriage
       and the Family 41 (February 1979): 75-88.
       Conflict is an unavoidable part of human association, includ-
ing the family.   The Conflict Tactics Scales is a means of measuring
how some families attempt to deal with the conflict.

1535   Straus, Murray A.   "Ordinary Violence, Child Abuse, and Wife
       Beating: What Do They Have in Common?"   In The Dark
       Side of Families: Current Family Violence Research.   Eds.
       David Finkelhor et al.   Beverly Hills, Cal.:   Sage, 1983,
       pp. 213-34.
       A study of 2,143 American families shows how intercon-
nected and pervasive violence is.   Over 97 percent of American children have experienced physical punishment.   The more violent parents
are toward their children the more violent the children are to siblings.
The more violent the husband is toward the wife, the more violent she
is to the children.   Children who experience violence tend to use it
with their own children and spouses later.   Violence is used to discipline, but too often the lesson of how much is too much is not clearly
understood by the abuser.   This will have to be understood and dealt
with if the child and spouse abuse is to end.

1536   Straus, Murray A.   "Re-evaluation of the Conflict Tactic Scale."
       Paper presented at the National Conference for Family Vio-
       lence Researchers, University of New Hampshire, July 1981.

1537   Straus, Murray A.   "Sexual Inequality and Wife Beating."   In The
       Social Causes of Husband-Wife Violence.   Eds. Murray A.
       Straus and Gerald T. Hotaling.   Minneapolis: University
       of Minnesota Press, 1980, pp. 86-93.
       Sexist organization of the family and of society in general
is the major reason for male violence toward women.   With increased
equality between the sexes this might be changing.   There are no guar-
antees, however.   In the meantime violence may just increase during
this social transition.   Parts of this article were reprinted from "Sexual Inequality, Cultural Norms and Wife Beating" [1538].

1538   Straus, Murray A. "Sexual Inequality, Cultural Norms, and
           Wife Beating." Victims and Society. Ed. Emilo Viano.
           Washington, D.C.: Visage Press, 1976, pp. 543-59.
           Also reprinted in Victimology: An International Journal
           1 (Spring 1976): 54-76; and in Women Into Wives; The
           Legal and Economic Impact of Marriage. Eds. Jane R.
           Chapman and Margaret Gates. Beverly Hills, Cal.: Sage,
           1977, pp. 59-77.
           In Euro-American societies, the marriage license becomes,
in effect, a hitting license. Culture legitimizes this activity in literature, the legal system, etc. Sexual inequality and male/female role
differentiation helps to keep women subjugated. Changes in these conditions along with male and female liberation will go far to reduce
spouse abuse. This paper was also presented at the International
Institute on Victimology, Bellagio, Italy, July 1975.

1539   Straus, Murray A. "Social Stress and Marital Violence in a
           National Sample of American Families." In Forensic Psy-
           chology and Psychiatry. Eds. Fred Wright, Charles Bahn,
           and Robert W. Rieber. (Annals of the New York Academy
           of Sciences, v. 347.) New York: N.Y. Academy of Sci-
           ences, 1980, pp. 229-50.
           Straus observes that the family is the most violent institu-
tion, group or setting that a typical citizen is likely to encounter.
The typical citizen has a high probability of being violently assaulted
only in his or her own home. Many see the home as a place where
one can escape the stresses of the world, but the family poses its
own high level of conflict and stress. A stress-measuring instrument
was administered to 2,143 American couples. There appears to be a
strong relationship between stress and family violence, but such is not
proved.

1540   Straus, Murray A. "Societal Morphogenesis and Intrafamily
           Violence in Cross-cultural Perspective." In International
           Perspectives on Family Violence. Eds. Richard J. Gelles
           and Claire Pedrick Cornell. Lexington, Mass.: Lexington
           Books, D.C. Heath, 1983, pp. 27-43. Also in Issues in
           Cross-cultural Research. Ed. Leonore Loeb Adler. New
           York: N.Y. Academy of Sciences, 1977, pp. 717-30.
           Research conducted with various societies indicates that the
level of violence found in the family is a reflection of the level of violence found in that society in general. Straus also suggests "that the
level in intrafamily violence is related to the ecological conditions in
which a society is operating and the society's 'technico-economic' adap-
tion to these ecological realities and to changes in the subsistence is
the basis of the society." The tendency of societal violence to be reflected in family violence is further compounded by the tendency of
violence in one family role to be found in others. The violence must
be seen in a general systems theory approach if true understanding is
to be achieved.

1541   Straus, Murray A. "Societal Morphogenesis and Intrafamily
           Violence in Cross-cultural Perspectives." Paper presented

to the New York Academy of Science Conference on Issues in Cross-cultural Research, New York, 1975.

1542   Straus, Murray A. "A Sociological Perspective on the Causes of Family Violence." In Violence and the Family. Ed. Maurice R. Green. (AAAS Selected Symposium, 47.) Boulder, Colo.: Westview Press, 1980, pp. 7-31.
Straus rejects the notion that family violence is caused by some psychopathology on the part of the aggressor. Instead most violence reflects a combination of normal social processes and situations. Children are taught violence by their parents who use it to discipline them, from their siblings, and by watching parents use it on each other. The "right" of families to "correct" their members, or the man to be head of the house, and stress levels in the family are all discussed as contributing to the widespread view that a certain amount of violence is justifiable and therefore normal. We are now at a time, historically, when what is "normal violence" and what is "abuse" is gradually seeing an increase in the perception that much "normal violence" is in fact abuse. The number of incidents are not on an increase, only what is considered unacceptable.

1543   Straus, M. "A Sociological Perspective on the Prevention and Treatment of Wifebeating." Paper presented at the Meeting of the American Psychiatric Association, Toronto, Canada, May 2-5, 1977.

1544   Straus, Murray A. "A Sociological Perspective on the Prevention and Treatment of Wife-beating." Nursing Dimensions 7 (Spring 1979): 45-63. Also in Battered Women: A Psychosociological Study of Domestic Violence. Ed. Maria Roy. New York: Van Nostrand Reinhold, 1977, pp. 194-239.
One cannot fully understand the phenomenon of wife beating unless one recognizes that in our society the marriage license becomes in effect a hitting license. Violence permeates society, thereby encouraging individual violence. The family is viewed by Straus as a "training ground" for violence because there is so much of it there. Conflict is normal in the family, but it need not be violent. Sexism in society must be eradicated as well as the encouraging of equality between the sexes. Suggestions are made to wives regarding avenues of escape and/or avoidance of abuse situations. Fundamental to Straus' whole system is that no one can be allowed to hit another person. One of the more important articles on the topic.

1545   Straus, Murray A. "Victims and Aggressors in Marital Violence." American Behavioral Scientist 23 (May-June 1980): 681-704.
This author's research indicates that wives are about as likely to engage in violence as husbands. The damage done by husbands, however, is more severe. Part of the author's concern was why so much violence is committed by women inside the marital relationship and not outside it. Among the reasons are these: 1) the high rate of assault by husbands increases the rate of retaliation by wives; 2) the marriage license as a hitting license is widely accepted by women as well as men; 3) childhood training in the use of violence is almost the

same for women as men; 4) child-care practices use violence which
wives carry over to husbands; 5) the high degree of frustration in
marriage encourages women to lash out violently. Thus society has
similar effects on both men and women when it comes to use of violence.

1546 Straus, Murray. "Violence in the Family: Wife Beating." In
          Encyclopedia of Crime and Justice. Ed. Sanford H. Kadish.
          New York: Free Press, 1983, pp. 1629-34.

1547 Straus, Murray A. "Wife Beating: Causes, Treatment, and
          Research Needs." In Battered Women: Issues of Public
          Policy. U. S. Commission on Civil Rights. Washington,
          D. C.: The Commission, 1978, pp. 463-527.

1548 Straus, Murray A. "Wife Beating: How Common and Why."
          Victimology: An International Journal 2, nos. 3-4 (1977-
          78): 443-58. Also in The Social Causes of Husband-Wife
          Violence. Eds. Murray A. Straus and Gerald T. Hotaling.
          Minneapolis: University of Minnesota Press, 1980, pp.
          23-36; Family Violence: An International and Interdiscipli-
          nary Study. Eds. John M. Eekelaar and Sanford N. Katz.
          Toronto: Butterworths, 1978, pp. 34-49; Research into
          Violent Behavior: Domestic Violence. U. S. Congress.
          House. Committee on Science and Technology. Hearings.
          95th Cong. 2nd Sess. February 14, 15, 16, 1978. Wash-
          ington, D. C.: Government Printing Office, 1978, pp. 823-42.
          Straus, Professor of Sociology, University of New Hamp-
shire, discusses the results of a nationwide survey of over 2,000 American couples. The purpose of this article is to present factual data
regarding abuse and to suggest reasons why violence occurs in an institution like the family which is supposed to provide love and support.
Both husband and wife abuse data are included along with the notion
that sexual inequality contributes to that violence. Because both family
factors and society in general militate to cause conflict, the elimination
of inequality will not end the violence since it is too deeply ingrained.
The results of the study are considered in more detail in the book by
Straus, Gelles, and Steinmetz [1551]. This paper was presented at the
Conference on "Battered Wives: Defining the Issues," Center for Research on Women, Stanford University, May 20, 1977, and at the 2nd
World Congress, International Society on Family Law, Montreal, June
14, 1977. A shorter version appears in Straus and Hotaling.

1549 Straus, Murray A. , and Gerald T. Hotaling, eds. The Social
          Causes of Husband-Wife Violence. Minneapolis: University
          of Minnesota Press, 1980. 268 p.
          This is an interesting collection of essays by various au-
thors which points up the relationship between increased intimacy and
the possibility of increased violence. The aggression which occurs is
not the personality of the actors so much as a reflection of social
structures and cultural norms. Families "are the breeding ground
of both love and hostility, of selfless devotion and of destructive violence." Each of the essays is also included in this bibliography under
the author's name.

1550   Straus, Murray A. , and Richard J. Gelles.   Physical Violence
       in American Families.   Ann Arbor, Mich. :   Inter-University
       Consortium for Political and Social Research, 1980.   300 p.

1551   Straus, Murray A.; Richard J. Gelles; and Suzanne K. Steinmetz.
       Behind Closed Doors; Violence in the American Family.
       Garden City, N. Y. :   Anchor Press/Doubleday, 1980.
       301 p.
         Most aspects of physical violence in the family are dis-
       cussed including child abuse, sibling violence, husband abuse and wife
       abuse.   A total of 2,143 families were studied with the results showing
       that both love and violence are hallmarks of family relationships.   Vio-
       lence begets violence and being raised in a violent situation shows it to
       be "normal."   Social stresses, economic factors, glorification of force
       and violence contribute to its prevalence in the family setting.   A good
       scholarly study written with a popular audience in mind.

1552   Straus, Murray A.; Richard J. Gelles; and Suzanne K. Steinmetz.
       "Normative and Behavioral Aspects of Violence Between
       Spouses.   Preliminary Data on a Nationally Representative
       USA Sample."   Paper presented at the Symposium on Vio-
       lence in Canadian Society, Simon Fraser University, 12
       March 1977.

1553   Straus, Murray A.; Richard J. Gelles; and Suzanne K. Steinmetz.
       "Physical Violence in a Nationally Representative Sample of
       American Families."   In The Family in Change.   Ed. Jan
       Trost.   Vasteras, Sweden: International Library, 1980,
       pp. 149-65.

1554   Straus, Murray A.; Richard J. Gelles; and S. K. Steinmetz.
       "Preliminary Data.   Study of Physical Violence in Ameri-
       can Families."   Report by M. A. Straus to the International
       Society for the Study of Family Law, Montreal, 1977.

1555   Straus, Murray A.; Richard J. Gelles; and Suzanne K. Steinmetz.
       "Theories, Methods and Controversies in the Study of Vio-
       lence Between Family Members."   Paper presented at the
       annual meeting of the American Association for the Advance-
       ment of Science, Boston, February 1976.   Also presented
       at the annual meeting of the American Sociological Associ-
       ation, New York, June 1973.

1556   Straus, Murray A.; Richard J. Gelles; and Suzanne K. Steinmetz.
       "Violence Between Spouses: Preliminary Data on a Nation-
       ally Representative Sample."   Paper presented at the Con-
       ference on Violence, Simon Fraser University, Burnaby,
       British Columbia, 11-13 March, 1977.

1557   Straus, Murray A.; Richard J. Gelles; and Suzanne K. Steinmetz.
       "Violence in the Family: An Assessment of Knowledge and
       Research Needs."   Paper presented at the annual meeting
       of the American Association for the Advancement of Science,

Boston, 23 February, 1976. In Research into Violent Be-
havior: Domestic Violence. U. S. Congress. House.
Committee on Science and Technology. Hearings. 95th
Cong. 2nd Sess. February 14, 15, 16, 1978. Washing-
ton, D. C. : Government Printing Office, 1978, pp. 843-93.
What is known about the causes and frequency of intrafamily
violence is summarized here, with emphasis on child and wife abuse.
Seventeen controversies are identified with more research urged.

1558 "Stroke by Strangulation. " Emergency Medicine 13 (April 30,
      1981): 126-7.
A short synopsis of the article by Milligan and Anderson
in the British Medical Journal [1093]. Stroke is uncommon in younger
women of reproductive age. When it happens, a physician should suspect the possibility of attempted strangulation within the previous several weeks.

1559 Strube, Michael J. , and Linda S. Barbour. "The Decision to
      Leave an Abusive Relationship: Economic Dependence and
      Psychological Commitment. " Journal of Marriage and the
      Family 45 (November 1983): 785-93.
The authors, Strube, Washington University, and Barbour,
University of Utah, studied the relationship between the battered wife's
commitment to saving the marriage and her economic dependence on
her husband and her decision to leave him. Both of these are commonly seen as factors, but there has been no empirical research to
support it. Ninety-eight women were studied with objective and sub-
jective measures. Results show there is a relationship, but they are
not the only ones that influence the wife's decision.

1560 Studer, Marlene Michelle. "Wife Beating as a Social Problem:
      The Process of Definition. " Paper presented at the North
      Central Sociological Association, 1983.

1561 Sullivan, Gail. "Sheltering Battered Women. " Sojourner (March
      1982): 4, 22.
The author met with members of the English Women's Aid
Federation and the Scottish Women's Aid and compared notes on the
shelter movement and housing situation in these countries. The differences and similarities of the local political environments are discussed.

1562 Sullivan, Joan C. "Crime: Havens for Battered Wives. " Trial
      Magazine 12 (January 1976): 72.
A news note stating the problem of wife beating is finally
being recognized for the crime it is. Shelters are being established
and books written.

1563 Sullivan, Ronald. "Violence, Like Charity, Begins at Home. "
      In Police Community Relations; An Anthology and Bibliogra-
      phy. Eds. William H. Hewitt and Charles L. Newman.
      Mineola, N. Y. : Foundation Press, 1970, pp. 108-28.
A detailed account, with many vignettes and examples, the
article tells of the effectiveness of New York City's Family Crisis

Intervention Unit.   The training program and its implementation in
the streets are included.   One police captain said of the program,
"Look at the changes here in the way the community has reacted.
We've got families now who come in here and ask for the family cops.
Last year, they might have come in here looking, instead, for the
civilian complaint review board."

1564   "Survey Examines Police Response to Domestic Disputes."
        Response to Violence in the Family 4 (November/December
        1980): 4-5.

1565   Sutton, Jo.   "The Growth of the British Movement for Battered
        Women."   Victimology: An International Journal 2, nos.
        3-4 (1977-78): 576-84.
        The author was the first coordinator for the National Wom-
en's Aid Federation in England and helped organize numerous refuges
and shelters.   Here she discusses the problems raised by government
officials and others during the early stages of the shelter movement.

1566   Sutton, Jo.   "Modern and Victorian Battered Women: A Look
        at an Old Pattern."   In Battered Women and Abused Chil-
        dren.   (Issues occasional papers, no. 4.) [Bradford,
        Eng.]: University of Bradford, 1979, pp. 9-15.
        Reformers of the nineteenth century believed that legislative
reform would bring an end to abuse.   In the 1970's the necessary laws
have been passed, but they have been inadequately enforced.   The emphasis now is on blaming the victim.   The Women's Aid movement
will help.

1567   Sweeney, Teresa M.   "The Effects of Two Variables, Victim
        Provocation and Defendent Intoxication on Simulated Jurors'
        Perceptions of Guilt in a Case of Wife-battering."   M. A.
        thesis, University of Montana, 1979.   84 p.
        The myth that the victim provoked the assault and the myth
that drunkenness excuses the violence are cultural beliefs that seem to
legitimize spouse abuse.   One hundred seventy-four subjects were asked
to read cases of abuse, some with drinking and some with provocation
to determine a verdict and recommend sentencing.   Results indicate
that jurors who were told of the drinking were no more likely to find
the husband guilty than if there was no drinking and that jurors with
traditional attitudes toward women were not less likely to find the husband guilty.   Female jurors were more likely than males to find defendants guilty if there was provocation.

1568   Sweet, Richard.   Legislation Relating to Domestic Abuse.   Mad-
        ison: Wisconsin Legislative Council, 1979.   12 p.

1569   Sweet, Richard N.   Arrests of Abusers Without Written Com-
        plaints.   Madison: Wisconsin Legislative Council, 1978.
        2 p.

1570   Sweet, Richard N.   State Legislation Relating to Domestic Vio-
        lence.   Madison: Wisconsin Legislative Council, 1977.   7 p.

1571 Symonds, Alexandra. "Violence Against Women: The Myth of
        Masochism." American Journal of Psychotherapy 33
        (April 1979): 161-73.
        The author, Clinical Associate Professor, New York Medi-
cal College, challenges the Freudian theory of female masochism as a
factor in spouse abuse. She believes there are two types of violent
marriages. The first and most common involves a violent man who
brings his violent problem-solving behavior to the marriage. The
second and less common involves the marriage where violence occurs
as a last resort when other forms of communication break down. In
this case the partners are neurotically bound to each other. This type
is more likely to seek psychiatric help and because of their dynamics
give false support to the theory of masochism. This paper was also
presented at the fourteenth National Scientific meeting of the Association for the Advancement of Psychotherapy, Atlanta, Georgia, May 7,
1978.

1572 Symonds, Martin. "The Psychodynamics of Violence-prone Mar-
        riages." American Journal of Psychoanalysis 38 (August
        1978): 213-22.
        Symonds is Associate Clinical Professor of Psychiatry,
New York University Medical Center and Director of the Victimology
Program, Karen Horney Clinic. The purpose of his article is to arrive at an understanding of the personality traits and interpersonal
reactions of couples which produce a violence-prone marriage. His
conclusions are based upon observations made of the patients in his
private practice and the Horney Victimology Program. He concludes
that violence begins when listening stops. Counseling can be helpful in
those marriages where failure in communication is a major problem.
A useful study stressing an individual's personality for the cause of
abuse.

1573 Symonds, Martin. "Violence-prone Marriages." In Identification
        and Treatment of Spouse Abuse; Health and Mental Health
        Agency Roles, Proceedings of a Conference. Eds. Abraham
        Lurie and Elizabeth B. Quitkin. New York: Editors, 1981,
        pp. 35-40.

1574 Szinovacz, Maximiliane E. "Using Couple Data as the Method-
        ological Tool: The Case of Marital Violence." Journal of
        Marriage and the Family 45 (August 1983): 633-44.
        Much study has been done of battering, but most research
utilizes data obtained from only one person of the couple. This author
from Florida State University, Department of Sociology, uses Straus'
Conflict Tactics Scale with 103 Pennsylvania couples randomly selected.
Comparisons of the responses show that both report similar rates of
violence by the husband, but wives report greater frequency of their
own violence toward husbands than the husbands themselves report.
Other differences in the reporting show that in researching sensitive
topics, use of couple data will provide greater accuracy of response.

1575 Tahourdin, Betty. "Battered Wives: 'Only a Domestic Affair.'"
      International Journal of Offender Therapy and Comparative
      Criminology 20, no. 1 (1976): 86-8.
      General discussion of wife beating in England. Says that
abusing husbands are either bullies, drunkards, or psychotics. Shelters like the Chiswick Women's Aid will greatly help since about half
of the women sheltered there have returned home to husbands who no
longer abuse them because they realize the wives now have a place
to go. Legal, financial, and medical aids are necessary to lessen
abuse.

1576 Tahourdin, Betty. "Family Violence." International Journal of
      Offender Therapy and Comparative Criminology 27, no. 1
      (1983): 79-83.

1577 Tanay, Emaneul. "Psychiatric Study of Homicide." American
      Journal of Psychiatry 125 (March 1969): 1252-8.
      This study of 53 homicide cases points up several facts of
interest to the topic. Most offenders had a history of violent child
rearing, most had killed spouses or lovers and most homicides were
preceded by quarreling.

1578 Task Force to Study a Haven for Physically Abused Persons. A
      Report Prepared for the County Council, Montgomery County,
      Maryland. Silver Spring, Md.: The Task Force, 1975.
      25 p.
      The needs of domestic abused victims were studied and
information regarding available resources and services collected. The
task force recommended that a shelter be established in Montgomery
County. Other recommendations are included.

1579 Taub, Nadine. "Equitable Relief in Cases of Adult Domestic
      Violence." Women's Rights Law Reporter 6 (Summer 1980):
      241-70.
      Even in states where there is no domestic abuse legislation,
the victim does have some hope. Equity through the use of injunctive
relief serves as an alternative to criminal proceedings for the victim
of abuse who does not wish to prosecute. It may also provide reflection time for those considering divorce. A long discussion of its advantages by an associate professor of law, Rutgers Law School.

1580 Taub, Nadine. "Ex Parte Proceedings in Domestic Violence
      Situations: Alternative Frameworks for Constitutional Scru-
      tiny." Hofstra Law Review 9 (Fall 1980): 95-128.
      Taub, Associate Professor of Law, Rutgers University,
argues at length the question of ex parte proceedings requiring the
abuser to vacate the home of the couple. The question is one of
whether the individual has been deprived without due process in opposition of the intent of the 14th Amendment. Her conclusion is that if
judged by the ruling in Mathews v. Eldridge, the action can withstand
the test of constitutionality.

1581 Taylor, Betsy. "Victims of Violence." In Family Violence:
      A Cycle of Abuse. Ed. Margaret E. Ankeney. Laramie:
      College of Education, University of Wyoming, 1979, pp.
      64-75.
           Three victims discuss their personal experiences with abu-
      sive husbands after which the author, Director of Education, Women
      in Crisis Program of Lakewood, Colorado, presents information on
      how communities can provide shelter to abuse victims. Statistics for
      the clients served by Women in Crisis are given.

1582 Tellis-Nayak, V., and Gearoid O'Donoghue. "Conjugal Equali-
      tarianism and Violence Across Cultures." Journal of Com-
      parative Family Studies 13 (Autumn 1982): 277-90.
           Tellis-Nayak (Department of Sociology and Anthropology,
      St. Xavier College, Chicago) and O'Donoghue (R. T. College, County
      Kerry, Ireland) concern themselves with the structure of decision-
      making authority among spouses and the use of physical violence be-
      tween them.   High school students in the U. S. , Ireland, and India
      completed questionnaires responding as they saw the situation with
      their parents.   The U. S. has the most marital violence and India the
      least.   It appears that it is the disjuncture between cultural ideals and
      egalitarian behavioral styles that leads to violence.   More study is
      necessary.

1583 Teske, Richard H. C. , Jr. , and Mary L. Parker. Spouse Abuse
      in Texas: A Study of Women's Attitudes and Experiences.
      Huntsville, Tex. : Criminal Justice Center, Sam Houston
      State University, 1983.   32 p.

1584 Texas Department of Human Resources. Directory of Shelter
      Centers in Texas. Austin: The Department, 1982.   36 p.

1585 Thane, Pat. "Cruel Kicks." New Society 33 (September 18,
      1975): 625.
           Short overview of wife abuse which points out that it is an
      age-old problem and receives attention only when women campaign
      against it.   Francis Cobb's essay is mentioned as well as sixteenth-
      century French practices.

1586 Thar, Annie E. "The Admissibility of Expert Testimony on
      Battered Wife Syndrome: An Evidentiary Analysis." North-
      western University Law Review 77 (October 1982): 348-73.
           The various state courts have been inconsistent about al-
      lowing expert testimony in cases of battered women killing their abu-
      sers.   Thar believes expert testimony should be allowed because the
      battered wife syndrome creates special circumstances and a unique
      frame of mind that should be considered if justice is to prevail.   It
      is also "beyond the ken of the average layman."   A clearly written
      overview by one who believes that a legal system that so often fails
      to protect a woman from her abuser should then at least protect her
      right to self-defense.

1587 Thoennes, Nancy Ann. "Social Network Functioning Among

Battered Women: The Consequences of Geographic Mobil-
ity." Ph. D. dissertation, University of Denver, 1981.
202 p. Abstract in Dissertation Abstracts International
42A (May 1982): 4947.

1588 Thome, Maxine Alyce. "An Analysis of Differences Between
Battered and Non-battered Women with Respect to Sex Role
Acceptance, Life Histories, and Personal Adjustment."
Ph. D. dissertation, Michigan State University, 1982.
135 p. Abstract in Dissertation Abstracts International
43B (March 1983): 3047.

1589 Thompson, Frederick D. "Spousal Rape." American Bar Association Journal 66 (December 1980): 1494.
This letter to the editor takes issue with Susan Barry's
"Spousal Rape: The Uncommon Law." ABA Journal (September
1980) [82].

1590 Thompson, Louise. "Beaten Wives Strike Back on Apathy."
Majority Report 6 (December 21, 1976/January 7, 1977): 1.

1591 Thompson, Louise. "Wife Beating: How Wife Beaters Also Beat
the Rap." Majority Report 7 (May 28-June 10, 1977): 1.
This news note continues the earlier one below [1592]. The
hearings are described showing the unwillingness of courts to punish
abusers.

1592 Thompson, Louise. "Wife Beating: What Happens When You
Tell It to the Judge." Majority Report 6 (April 16-29,
1977): 3.
The author describes in a short news note the reaction of
the judges and attorneys during a court appearance on March 11, 1977.
The report clearly shows lack of judicial support for the abused. The
seemingly endless shuffling and red tape are evident.

1593 Thomson, Judge C. M. "Resolution of Domestic Disputes in the
Courtroom." In Domestic Violence: Issues and Dynamics.
Ed. Vincent D'Oyley. Toronto: Ontario Institute for Studies in Education, 1978, pp. 101-8.
Judge Thomson describes the difficulties in attempting to
decide on how such cases should be handled. Often it is impossible to
reach a decision that satisfies both parties. In the last analysis a judge
is the by-product of his environment and is faced with a problem subject to much confusion and uncertainty. No easy answers are available.
More will be gained by attempting remedies that more directly deal
with the personal and practical problems that produce violent marriages.

1594 Thorman, George. Family Violence. Springfield, Ill. : Charles
C. Thomas, 1980. 184 p.
Written by a social worker for social workers, this book
looks at several aspects of family violence with some attention to spouse
abuse. Included is a general overview of violence in the family, characteristics of the abused, methods of intervention and the alternatives and

approaches to preventing family violence. A good balanced approach
to the problem incorporating much of the research of other experts.
Thorman is Associate Professor of Social Work at St. Edward's University, Austin, Texas.

1595   Thyfault, R. "Childhood Sexual Abuse, Marital Rape, and Bat-
             tered Women: Implications for Mental Health Workers."
             Paper presented at the annual meeting of the Colorado
             Mental Health Conference, Keystone, October 1980.

1596   Thyfault, R. "Sexual Abuse in the Battering Relationship."
             Paper presented at the annual meeting of the Rocky Moun-
             tain Psychological Association, Tucson, Arizona, April
             1980.

1597   Tidmarsh, Mannes. "Violence in Marriage: The Relevance of
             Structural Factors." Social Work Today 7, no. 2 (1976):
             36-8.
             The author, a lecturer in psychology at Sheffield Polytech-
nic, discusses the factors found in the family and social structure
which appear to have a bearing on family violence. They include educational and occupational differences between the spouses, the inadequacy of the husband in family roles, social isolation, alcohol, and
age factors. More research is suggested.

1598   Tierney, Kathleen J. "The Battered Women Movement and the
             Creation of the Wife-beating Problem." Social Problems
             29 (February 1982): 207-20.
             Wife beating has received much attention over the past dec-
ade, not because it is increasing, but because social movement organizations have worked hard to make it a public issue. In this they have
been quite successful. The future will see the movement and services
co-opted by official organizations which in turn will change the charac-
ter of the battered-women's movement. Future efforts will be moder-
ate, reformist and traditional, while the self-help, self-defense principles of radical feminism will be less noticeable.

1599   Tierney, Kathleen Jane. "Social Movement Organization, Re-
             source Mobilization, and the Creation of a Social Problem:
             A Case Study of a Movement for Battered Women." Ph.D.
             dissertation, Ohio State University, 1979. 248 p. Abstract
             in Dissertation Abstracts International 40A (February 1980):
             4756.

1600   Titterud, Loretta, and Murray A. Straus. "Resources, Power,
             and Wife-beating: An Empirical Test of the Ultimate Re-
             source Theory." Paper presented at the annual meeting
             of the Eastern Sociological Society, Boston, March 22, 1980.

1601   Toby, Jackson. "Violence and the Masculine Ideal: Some Quali-
             tative Data." In Violence in the Family. Eds. Suzanne K.
             Steinmetz and Murray A. Straus. New York: Dodd, Mead,
             1974, pp. 58-65.

Discusses the concept of compulsive masculinity which not infrequently leads to husband-wife violence. The article is reprinted from Patterns of Violence, edited by Marvin E. Wolfgang, Philadelphia: American Academy of Political and Social Service, 1966.

1602 Tomalin, Caroline. "Refuge for Battered Women." Health and
      Social Science Journal 84, no. 4388 (1974): 1169.
      An early article describing the Chiswick Women's Aid
Center.

1603 Tomes, Nancy. "A 'Torrent of Abuse': Crimes of Violence Be-
      tween Working-class Men and Women in London, 1840-1875."
      Journal of Social History 11 (Spring 1978): 328-45.
      A historical analysis of wife beating during a period of
economic and social upheaval in England. Between the beginning and ending of the period covered here there seems to have been a lessening in the amount of such violence. A rise in the standard of living and a more widespread adoption of middle-class values may have been the cause.

1604 Tracey, Dick. Battered Wives. London: Bow Publications,
      [1974?], (mimeo). 6 p.
      An overview of the problem from a British perspective.
The author makes several recommendations. Shelters must be established with aid provided by psychiatrists who will visit the refuges on a regular basis. Financial, medical, and legal assistance must be provided. Short but thoughtful analysis.

1605 Traicoff, M. Ellen. "Family Interventions from Women's Shel-
      ters." Family Therapy Collections. Vol. 3. Clinical
      Approaches to Family Violence. Rockville, Md.: Aspen
      Systems, 1982, pp. 105-15.

1606 Treloar, Carol. "Politics of Rape: A Politician's Perspective."
      In Rape Law Reform. Ed. Jocelynne A. Scutt. Canberra:
      Australian Institute of Criminology, 1980, pp. 191-8.
      Some attention is devoted to marital rape.

1607 Trent, Delores J. "Wife Beating: A Psycho-legal Analysis."
      Case and Comment 84 (November/December 1979): 14-16,
      18, 20, 22. Also in Woman Lawyers Journal 65 (1974):
      9-15, 21-5.
      General discussion of the remedies for battered women.
The problem is placed in historical perspective. Current inadequacies of police protection, lack of sympathy and understanding by judges and lawyers, and problems related to restraining orders and peace bonds are detailed. Trent believes that the victim's life and liberty will be protected only after explicit legislation is enacted to spell out her rights. The author is a law student at West Virginia University College of Law.

1608 Truninger, Elizabeth. "Marital Violence: The Legal Solutions."
      Hastings Law Journal 23 (November 1971): 259-76.

The author provides an overview of the legal remedies for spouse abuse with emphasis on California law. Though an interesting discussion, it is now dated.

1609 Turner, Willie M. "Levi Strauss Funds Domestic Violence Projects." Response to Violence in the Family 3 (May 1980): 1.
In 1980 this foundation made $1.2 million of its $4.6 available for direct services to local communities. Battered-wife shelters are eligible.

1610 Turner, Willie M., and Barbara Star. "Programs for Men Who Batter; Parts 1 and 2." Response to Violence in the Family 3 (April 1980): 6-7; (May 1980): 6-7.
This is an alphabetical list by state of such programs. Addresses, phone numbers, contact persons, and a brief note regarding the programs are all included.

1611 Turner, Willie M., and Lois A. West. "Violence in Military Families." Response to Violence in the Family 4 (May/June 1981): 1-5.

1612 Ulbrich, Patricia, and Joan Huber. "Observing Parental Violence: Distribution and Effects." Journal of Marriage and the Family 43, no. 3 (1981): 623-31.
Using telephone interviews in 1978, the authors surveyed 1,092 women and 910 men to determine their attitudes toward women's roles and use of violence against women. Seventeen percent of the respondents had witnessed intra-parental hitting. Such witnessing did not affect attitudes toward women's roles, but attitudes regarding rape, and woman-hitting were affected. The response varied with age and sex of the observer, but as a generalization, if a man had witnessed his father hitting the mother, he was more apt to see such violence as legitimate.

1613 Ulbrich, Patricia, and Joan Huber. "The Effects of Observing Parental Hitting on Gender-related Attitudes." Paper presented at the annual meeting of the American Sociological Association, Boston, 1979.

1614 "Unforgettable Letters from Battered Wives." MS 5 (December 1976): 97-100. Also in Domestic Violence, 1978. U.S. Congress. Senate. Committee on Human Resources, Subcommittee on Child and Human Development. Hearings. 95th Cong. 2nd Sess. On Domestic Violence and Legislation with Respect to Domestic Violence, March 4 and 8, 1978. Washington, D.C.: Government Printing Office, 1978, pp. 647-50; Domestic Violence. U.S. Congress. House. Committee on Education and Labor, Subcommittee on Select Education. 95th Cong. 2nd Sess. Hearings on H.R. 7927 and H.R. 8948, March 16 and 17, 1978. Washington, D.C.: Government Printing Office, 1978, pp. 381-4.

In response to the battered spouse articles in the August 1976 issue of MS, numerous women wrote letters describing their personal experiences. A sampling of these letters appears here.

1615 United Community Services of Metropolitan Detroit. Spouse Abuse Project Committee. Spouse Abuse in the Tricounty Area: The Problem and Some Answers. Detroit: Author, 1980. 106 p.

1616-17 United States Catholic Conference. Violence in the Family: A National Concern, a Church Concern. Prepared by Barbara Ann Stolz. Washington, D. C. : Author, 1979. 44 p.

Spouse abuse, child abuse, and elder abuse are all types of family violence which society must address. The Catholic community has a moral obligation to respond to   issue. A general discussion of the causes of violence in the family with its myths and realities are followed by a section on what action should be taken to alleviate abuse and provide relief for the victims. Although directed at Catholics, others will find this pamphlet useful.

1618 U. S. Commission on Civil Rights. Battered Women: Issues of Public Policy. Washington, D. C. : Author, 1978. 706 p.

This consultation was intended both to define the problem relating to spouse abuse and to address potential solutions, including the need for federal legislation. Many noted researchers and activists contributed including Murray Straus, Lenore Walker, Lisa Leghorn, Marjory Fields, James Bannon, and Del Martin. Appendices include a directory of shelters and resources for battered women, and a chart of state legislation on domestic abuses, as well as other pertinent information.

1619 U. S. Commission on Civil Rights. The Federal Response to Domestic Violence. Washington, D. C. : Author, 1982. 173 p.

This report identifies the major needs of abused women and the organizations that provide for those needs. The information of this report was obtained from federal agency program staff and includes a review of the literature and discussions with local service providers. Nineteen federal programs are reviewed; the results indicate that while there is some recent aid, it is sporadic. Another finding is that local medical personnel, law enforcement officers and courts, social service agents, and the public are generally unaware of the depth and magnitude of the problem. The federal agencies will have to be more creative in their handling of the diminishing financial resources.

1620 U. S. Commission on Civil Rights. Under the Rule of Thumb: Battered Women and the Administration of Justice. Washington, D. C. : Author, 1982. 100 p.

This report evaluates the treatment by the criminal and civil justice systems and by various social service agencies of women who are victims of domestic violence. While wife beating is illegal,

the law has often failed to protect the victims.   Police officers, prosecutors, and judges often fail to take appropriate action, treating spouse
abuse as a family matter and not as a crime.   Numerous recommendations are made for local officials to help eradicate the problem.

1621 U. S. Congress.   House.   Committee on Education and Labor.
        Domestic Violence Assistance Act of 1978.   Report.   95th
        Cong.   2nd Sess. to accompany H. R. 12299, 10 May 1978.
        Washington, D. C. : Government Printing Office, 1978.
        The committee recommended amendments to the Act.
Budget recommendations are included.

1622 U. S. Congress.   House.   Committee on Education and Labor,
        Subcommittee on Select Ecuation.   Domestic Violence.
        95th Cong.   2nd Sess.   Hearings on HR 7927 and HR 8948,
        March 16 and 17, 1978.   Washington, D. C. : Government
        Printing Office, 1978.   753 p.
        This committee heard much testimony regarding domestic
violence with attention devoted to spouse abuse.   The purpose of HR
7927 and HR 8948 was to provide a grant program to study the problem, establish shelters, train professionals to deal with the victims
and abusers, and establish a national center for community action
against family violence and a coordinating council on family violence.
The testimony and articles were presented by a number of congress-
men as well as many noted experts, such as J. Fleming, M. Pagelow,
M. D. Fields, and J. Bannon.   Included are many reprints of articles.

1623 U. S. Congress.   House.   Committee on Education and Labor,
        Subcommittee on Select Education.   Domestic Violence.
        Hearing.   98th Cong. 1st Session.   23 June 1983.   Washing-
        ton, D. C. : Government Printing Office, 1983.   268 p.
        In recent years the number of battered women seeking ref-
uge has been increasing.   At the same time funding of shelters and
other family violence relief has been on the decrease.   Personal
statements and printed literature are submitted here for consideration
by the committee.   Statements are given by directors of shelters,
state agencies concerned with abuse, former victims, and law enforcement agencies.

1624 U. S. Congress.   House.   Committee on Education and Labor,
        Subcommittee on Select Education.   Domestic Violence in
        Vermont.   Hearing, 95th Cong. , 2nd Session, 22 June 1978.
        Washington, D. C. : Government Printing Office, 1978.   71 p.
        Held in Montpelier, this hearing sought testimony from wit-
nesses regarding the problem of domestic violence and the types of
services needed by and provided to victims of spouse abuse in Vermont.
Representatives from shelters, Parents Anonymous, government agencies and medical organizations provided information.

1625 U. S. Congress.   House.   Committee on Education and Labor,
        Subcommittee on Select Education.   Domestic Violence:
        Prevention and Services.   Hearing.   96th Cong.   1st Sess.
        10-11 July 1979.   Washington, D. C. : Government Printing

Office, 1979.   550 p.
This includes much testimony from many individuals regarding domestic violence. Statements were made by federal politicians, directors of battered-women shelters and programs, religious organizations and state agency directors. Much literature in the form of newspaper articles, leaflets, written statements, and research reports is appended.

1626   U. S. Congress. Senate. Committee on Human Resources.
         Domestic Violence Prevention and Services Act. Report.
         95th Cong. 2nd Sess. to accompany S. 2759, 15 May 1978.
         Washington, D. C. : Government Printing Office, 1978. 64 p.
This act provides for grants to be provided for domestic violence programs, establishment of a National Center on Domestic Violence, encouragement of research and other activities to provide relief for victims of family abuse.

1627   U. S. Congress. Senate. Committee on Human Resources, Sub-
         committee on Child and Human Development. Domestic
         Violence, 1978. Hearings. 95th Cong. 2nd Sess. On
         Domestic Violence and Legislation with Respect to Domes-
         tic Violence, March 4 and 8, 1978. Washington, D. C. :
         Government Printing Office, 1978. 708 p.
These hearings comprise two days of testimony regarding domestic violence with the intent of determining what the federal government should do to render relief   Physical violence between adults was the major focus, thus child abuse was not considered. Abuse relief was seen by Alan Cranston, Chairman of the subcommittee, to be best handled at the local level, but funding and stimulation of local activity was certainly within the realm of federal involvement. Statements by politicians, professionals working with battered women, victims, shelter administrators, and others are found here. Included also are many reprints of articles, scholarly and popular, and pamphlets from concerned organizations.

1628   U. S. Congress. House. Committee on Science and Technology,
         Subcommittee on Domestic and International Scientific Plan-
         ning, Analysis and Cooperation. Research into Violent Be-
         havior: Domestic Violence. Hearings. 95th Cong. 2nd
         Sess. February 14, 15, 16, 1978. Washington, D. C. :
         Government Printing Office, 1978. 1041 p.
These hearings were held to further inform the committee regarding the problem of domestic violence. Politicians, researchers, and others provided testimony. Among them were Lindy Boggs, M. A. Straus, R. J. Gelles, L. E. Walker, M. D. Fields, and S. K. Steinmetz. Hearings during these days concentrated on battered spouses, abused children, and sexual assault within the home.

1629   U. S. Congress. House. Committee on Science and Technology.
         Subcommittee on Domestic and International Scientific Plan-
         ning, Analysis and Cooperation. Research into Violent Be-
         havior: Domestic Violence. Report. 95th Cong. 2nd Sess.

October 1978. Washington, D. C. : Government Printing
Office, 1978.   47 p.
This report results from the hearings held on February
14, 15, 16, 1978.   The purpose was to review the status of research
being conducted regarding family violence, to identify areas needing
more research and recommend appropriate action.   Spouse and child
abuse are the primary concerns, but some attention is given to sibling
and elder violence.   Changes must be made in the current legal, police, medical, and social responses to this problem.

1630   U. S. Department of Justice. Bureau of Justice Statistics. Intimate Victims: A Study of Violence Among Friends and
Relatives. Washington, D. C. : Government Printing Office, 1980.   52 p.
This report contains information derived from interviews
of 136,000 individuals across the U. S. regarding events occurring
from 1973 to 1976.   The data are organized into three sections which
address the setting of the violence, the victim-offender interaction and
the aftermath.   In this study intimates include relatives, friends, neighbors, and work associates, as contrasted with similar studies concerned
with violence committed by strangers.   Much useful data will be found
here regarding the number of participants, weapons used, injuries inflicted, etc.

1631   U. S. Department of Justice. Law Enforcement Assistance Admin-
istration. Law Enforcement Assistance Administration-
Family Violence Programs. Washington, D. C. : Author,
1978.   11 p. Also in Domestic Violence. U. S. Congress.
House. Committee on Education and Labor, Subcommittee
on Select Education.   95th Cong.   2nd Sess.   Hearings on
HR 7927 and HR 8948, March 16 and 17, 1978.   Washington,
D. C. : Government Printing Office, 1978, pp. 739-50.
The family violence programs of the LEAA are described.
In the fall of 1977, a major offensive against domestic violence and sexual abuse was initiated.   Recognition was given to the need for social
and legal considerations with the underlying belief that intra-familial
violence is a crime.   Violence directed at women and children is of
greatest concern, so funds were granted to projects reflecting such an
interest.

1632   U. S. National Commission on the Observation of International
Women's Year. Workshop Guidelines on Wife Abuse.
Washington, D. C. : Department of State, 1976.   24 p.
This is a useful guide for those wishing to set up a spouse-
abuse consciousness-raising workshop.   Recommendations for what should
be included, factual data regarding the frequency of the problem, a
short list of films and speakers available and a brief bibliography provide practical assistance.

1633   United Way of Minneapolis Area Task Force on Battered Women.
Battered Women: A Study of Physical Abuse of Women.
Minneapolis: Author, 1972.   54 p.
A local study of Minneapolis area women, attempting to

discover the extent of the problem, the background of the victims and
the forms of help sought by them. Data were analyzed by race, education level, family income, marital status, etc. Improvements in
legal, medical, and police resources are urged. Useful statistical
information with some limitations.

1634 University of Wisconsin Extension. Women's Education Resources.
        Problem of Battered Women. Madison: Author, 1978. 15
        pieces in a portfolio.

1635 "Using HUD Funds to Establish Shelters." Response to Violence
        and Sexual Abuse in the Family 2 (August 1979): 1-2.

1636 Vaisrub, Samuel. "Violence Begins at Home." American Med-
        ical Association Journal 245 (May 8, 1981): 1852.
        In this letter to the editor, the author refers to the N. Mil-
ligan and M. Anderson article "Conjugal Disharmony: A Hitherto Unrecognized Cause of Strokes" [1093]. He says that while the causes
of spouse abuse belong in the realm of psychiatry, their recognition is
the concern of the physician. Doctors must be aware of a patient's
medical as well as social history.

1637 Valenti, Carol. "Working with the Physically Abused Woman."
        In Women in Stress: A Nursing Perspective. Eds. Diane
        K. Kjervik and Ida M. Martinson. New York: Appleton-
        Century-Crofts, 1979, pp. 187-96.
        This author provides an in-depth perspective for nurses
who may encounter abused women in their work. Caution against labels, discussion of the dynamics of the unhealthy relationship, and
intervention techniques are all included. The helping professional is
warned of the frustration which often attends working with people who
are not ready for the help.

1638 Van Stolk, Mary. "Beaten Women, Battered Children." Chil-
        dren Today 5 (March/April 1976): 8-12.
        A general overview of the problem with many comparisons
to child abuse. Several case examples of abuse are included. In
some cases spouse abuse appears to be "unborn child" abuse.

1639 Vandenbraak, Sarah Baseden. "Limits on the Use of Defensive
        Force to Prevent Intramarital Assaults." Rutgers-Camden
        Law Journal 10 (Spring 1979): 634-60.
        The author criticizes the limiting of defensive force by the
spouse in the prevention of intramarital abuse. If marital rape or
spouse abuse is not illegal, then use of force to protect oneself becomes illegal. The "imminent harm" and "prior retreat" concepts
are also discussed and found inadequate. The law of self-defense must
be changed to provide for a more equitable response to abused spouses.
Interestingly, she does not advocate that abuse and marital rape be
made illegal.

1640 Vanfossen, Beth. "Cultural Myths About Wife-beating." Paper
        presented to the Association for Humanistic Sociology, New
        York, 1977.

1641 Vanfossen, Beth E. "Intersexual Violence in Monroe County,
        New York." Victimology: An International Journal 4, no.
        2 (1979): 299-304.
        Vanfossen, Associate Professor of Sociology, State Univer-
sity of New York, Brockport, analyzed the assault and domestic disturbance reports of the police and sheriff's department in Monroe
County, N.Y., in 1977. Twenty victims appearing in the Monroe
County Family Court also completed a questionnaire which explored
the emotional consequences of abuse. Results show women were victims in 90 percent of cases and men in 10 percent. Types of weapons, demographic characteristics, causes of the incident, time and
location of event, and the role of the police are all detailed. Victims
would discuss the abuse with relatives, but rarely consulted with the
helping professionals. This may explain why so little is known about
how extensive the problem is.

1642 Varma, Margaret. "Battered Women; Battered Children." In
        Battered Women: A Psychosociological Study of Domestic
        Violence. Ed. Maria Roy. New York: Van Nostrand
        Reinhold, 1977, pp. 263-77.
        Varma believes that child abuse and spouse abuse have sim-
ilar origins; that is, childhood situations with violence or neglect and
insufficient love and caring. People have to be taught how to be good
spouses and parents. It does not come naturally. Parents currently
abusing their children must be treated so that the violence stops, otherwise that method of solving problems will be passed on to the next generation. She is Education Director, Cardinal Spellman Headstart and
Graduate Programs Faculty of the Bank Street College of Education,
New York.

1643 Vaughan, Sharon Rice. "The Last Refuge: Shelter for Battered
        Women." Victimology: An International Journal 4, no. 1
        (1979): 113-9.
        Vaughan is the coordinator for the Harriet Tubman Women's
Shelter in Minneapolis. She discusses that shelter and the Women's
Advocates Shelter, also of Minneapolis. The shelter experience is described with its major importance being a place to feel safe and to
assess one's life and circumstance away from the fear-provoking actions of the abuser. Based on a paper presented at the annual meeting
of the American Psychiatric Association, 1977.

1644 Vaughan, Sharon. "Where It All Began." Do It Now 9 (June
        1976): 5-6.

1645 Verville, Tom. "Bias on Battered Women." Social Work 23
        (March 1978): 179.
        This letter to the editor challenges the conclusions of Bonnie
E. Carlson's "Battered Women and Their Assailants" [232].

1646 Viano, Emilio. "Working with Battered Women: A Conversa-
        tion with Lisa Leghorn." Victimology: An International
        Journal 3, nos. 1-2 (1978): 91-107.
        Viano, editor of Victimology, interviewed Leghorn regard-
ing her views about wife abuse and the operation and philosophy behind Transition House in Cambridge, Mass. The philosophy is that
of self-help and is based on the notion that all women have the strength
they need to free themselves from the abuse. The role of the refuge
is to help find that strength. The rules, regulations and operating
principles are described.

1647 Victims Information Bureau of Suffolk. Spouse Abuse: Couples
        in Conflict. Hauppauge, N. Y.: VIPS Counseling Center,
        n. d. 7 p. Also in Domestic Violence, 1978. U. S. Con-
        gress. Senate. Committee on Human Resources, Subcom-
        mittee on Child and Human Development. Hearings. 95th
        Cong. 2nd Sess. On Domestic Violence and Legislation
        with Respect to Domestic Violence, March 4 and 8, 1978.
        Washington, D. C.: Government Printing Office, 1978,
        pp. 458-64.
        This pamphlet explains the New York laws with a general
discussion of what abuse actually is, including verbal, physical and
sexual abuse. A map showing the location of the VIPS Counseling Center is included along with a description of the services available.

1648 Victor, Jill Blumbers. "He Beat Me: Battered Wife Tells Why
        She Took It for Seven Years." Vogue 168 (January 1978):
        177, 183, 185-6.
        The author gives her account of a seven-year marriage
characterized by frequent abuse. She gives practical advice to others
in similar situations. Seek psychological help, support community
efforts to establish shelters, prepare a survival kit with extra cash
or credit cards in one's own name and investigate a safe place in case
you should need to leave home in a hurry.

1649 Viken, Richard M. "Family Violence: Aids to Recognition."
        Postgraduate Medicine 71 (May 1982): 115-7, 120-2.
        Child abuse, wife abuse, parent abuse, and husband abuse
are all identified and medical professionals are urged to be alert to
suspicious circumstances. Not much can be done to eliminate such
violence if it is not recognized and reported. If the circumstances
are suspicious, there is no substitute for direct inquiry for identifying
victims.

1650 Vincent, Adele. "Divorce Tax Helps Battered Spouses." MS
        9 (October 1980): 23.
        A news note describing an Indiana law adding $10 to the
divorce filing fee. The money generated would be used to fund battered-
spouse shelters.

1651 Violence Against Women: Causes and Prevention: A Literature
        Search and Annotated Bibliography. Prepared by Wisconsin
        Education Resources, University of Wisconsin, Extension,

Carolyn F. Wilson and Kathryn F. Clarenback. 2nd ed.
(Domestic Violence Monograph Series, no. 3, June 1980.)
Rockville, Md.: National Clearing House on Domestic Vio-
lence, 1980. 37 p.

The many faces of violence against women are portrayed
here, including rape, incest, and wife abuse. The bibliography is
selected, but the annotations are good. Much of this publication was
again published, with revisions, by G. K. Hall [1736]. Wilson is listed
as the author of that volume. High quality workmanship.

1652 "Violence Against Women--Women Battering." The New Wom-
      an's Survival Sourcebook. Eds. S. Rennie and K. Grim-
      stad. New York: Knopf, 1975, pp. 214-5.

A short general discussion pointing out the lack of concern
from male dominated police and court systems. The feminist movement did not cause this crime to increase as some contend, but it has
helped bring it to public attention. Progress is beginning to be made,
but the women's movement must continue to take an active role. Several important books are listed and annotated.

1653 "Violence in American Home Topped Only by Riot and War."
      Juvenile Justice Digest 5 (March 4, 1977): 5.
      Quotes study by Gelles, Straus, and Steinmetz.

1654 Virginia. Department of Welfare. Directory of Spouse Abuse
      Programs in Virginia. Richmond, Va.: Author, 1981.
      26 p.

A listing of available resources for victims of spouse abuse
in Virginia. Includes addresses, phone numbers, services available,
staffing, etc.

1655 Visser, Gwen L., and Anne W. Steytler. "Women's Center
      and Shelter of Greater Pittsburgh: A Model for a Shelter-
      ing Community." In Domestic Violence. U. S. Congress.
      House. Committee on Education and Labor, Subcommittee
      on Select Education. 95th Cong. 2nd Sess. Hearings on
      HR 7927 and HR 8948, March 16 and 17, 1978. Washington,
      D. C.: Government Printing Office, 1978, pp. 459-92.

1656 Waaland-Thompson, Pamela K. "The Effects of Situational
      Factors and Officer Characteristics on Police Decision-
      making for Wife Assault." Ph. D. dissertation. Bowling
      Green State University, 1983. 158 p. Abstract in Disser-
      tation Abstracts International 44B (February 1984): 2601.

1657 Wachter, Oralee, and Thomas Boyd. "'Time Out': Description
      of a Film Series Dramatizing the Conflicts and Consequences
      Faced by Men Who Batter." In The Abusive Partner: An
      Analysis of Domestic Battering. Ed. Maria Roy. New
      York: Van Nostrand Reinhold, 1982, pp. 247-66.

1658 Waites, Elizabeth A. "Female Masochism and the Enforced
          Restriction of Choice." Victimology: An International Jour-
          nal 2, nos. 3-4 (1977-78): 535-44.
      Waites, Certified Consulting Psychologist, Ann Arbor,
Michigan, challenges the theory of female masochism. Widely accepted
by psychologists, it has no scientific basis. Sometimes some psychologists point to wife abuse as an example of masochistic interaction, but
if the situation were studied properly, it would be found that abused
wives stay with their husbands because they believe they have no real
choices, not because they like the pain.

1659 Walker, Lenore E. "Battered Women." In Women and Psycho-
          therapy. Eds. Annette M. Brodsky and Rachel T. Hare-
          Mustin. New York: Guilford Press, 1980, pp. 339-63.
      Various theories of spouse abuse are reviewed with her
cycle theory of battering and learned helplessness also being described.
Treatment recommendations, such as individual psychotherapy, group
therapy, and couples counseling are analyzed with the final conclusion
being that psychotherapy results are inconclusive. Paraprofessional
counseling and the crisis-intervention models of shelters have shown
some success. Little is known of the results of counseling abusers
and children. In the future, treatment plans will be more widely
available.

1660 Walker, Lenore E. The Battered Women. New York: Harper
          and Row, 1979. 270 p.
      This monograph is one of the better overall treatments of
the problem and has a psychological orientation. The author's theories
of learned helplessness, the cycle of violence and other perceptions
are detailed and developed at length.

1661 Walker, Lenore E. "Battered Women and Learned Helplessness."
          Victimology: An International Journal 1, nos. 3-4 (1977-
          78): 525-34. Also in Research into Violent Behavior: Do-
          mestic Violence. U. S. Congress. House. Committee on
          Science and Technology. Hearings. 95th Cong. 2nd Sess.
          February 14, 15, 16, 1978. Washington, D. C. : Government
          Printing Office, 1978, pp. 781-97.
      Walker describes the concept of learned helplessness and
applies it to the battered wives' perceptions of their circumstances.
This theory explains why women stay in their marriages to the author's
satisfaction much better than Freudian female masochism. Her interviews with over 100 English and American women confirm the notion.
Learned helplessness combines with social, legal and other psychological factors to keep her from leaving the abuser. It also helps to explain the difficulties various counselors have had treating and advising
the victim. Recognizing the problems will help with the treatment.

1662 Walker, Lenore E. "Battered Women: Hypothesis and Theory
          Building." Paper presented at the annual meeting of the
          American Psychological Association, Washington, D. C. ,
          1976.

1663 Walker, Lenore E. "Battered Women: Sex Roles and Clinical
          Issues." Professional Psychology 12 (February 1981):
          81-91.
      Walker's research suggests that sex role bias contributes
to the origins of spouse battering, compounds its psychological effects
and interferes with effective treatment.   Unfortunately a psychothera-
pist's own sex role biases can have an effect on progress of a battered
wife's treatment.   Nonsexist treatment is required for success.

1664 Walker, Lenore E. "The Battered Woman Syndrome Study."
          In The Dark Side of Families: Current Family Violence
          Research.   Eds. David Finkelhor et al.   Beverly Hills,
          Cal. : Sage, 1983, pp. 31-48.
      Walker studied 403 self-identified battered women to learn
about domestic violence from the victim's perspective.   Key psychological and sociological theories were tested, especially "learned helplessness" and the "cycle theory of violence."   Battering behavior,
Walker says, comes from the abusers learned behavioral responses,
not from the interaction of the couple or the wife's irritating habits.
Data from the current study confirm this belief.   There are no specific
personality traits which would suggest a victim-prone personality for
women, but there are some for predicting violence-prone men.   Results
of the study support the theories of learned helplessness and the Walker
cycle of violence.

1665 Walker, Lenore E. "A Feminist Perspective on Domestic Vio-
          lence." In Violent Behavior: Social Learning Approaches
          to Prediction, Management and Treatment.   Ed. Richard B.
          Stuart.   New York: Brunner/Mazel, 1981, pp. 102-15.
      Walker asserts that sexism is an underlying cause of all vio-
lence against women.   Eliminating such violence is not easy since the
cause is complex.   Based on a paper presented at the 11th annual conference on Behavior Modification, March 1979.

1666 Walker, Lenore E. "Feminist Psychotherapy with Victims of
          Violence." Paper presented at the American Psychological
          Association, Division of Psychotherapy, midwinter meeting,
          March 1975.

1667 Walker, Lenore E. "How Battering Happens and How to Stop It."
          In Battered Women.   Ed. Donna M. Moore.   Beverly Hills,
          Cal. : Sage, 1979, pp. 59-78.
      The author discusses her cycle theory which explains how
completely the wife becomes victimized.   The value of shelters and
psychotherapy in breaking the cycle is detailed.   Unlike some marital
therapists who say that it is the relationship which must be treated,
the author believes it is the individuals.   Each must view himself or
herself as an independent person who can survive without the other.
Only then can their marriage be a healthy relationship between two
individuals.

1668 Walker, Lenore E. "Male Batterers and Their Families: Treat-
          ment Implications." Paper presented at the meeting of the
          American Psychological Association, Toronto, September 1978.

1669 Walker, Lenore E. "Psychotherapy and Counseling with Battered Women." In Research into Violent Behavior: Domestic Violence. U. S. Congress. House. Committee on Sciences and Technology. Hearings. 95th Cong. 2nd Sess. February 14, 15, 16, 1978. Washington, D. C. : Government Printing Office, 1978, pp. 943-80.

1670 Walker, Lenore. "Treatment Alternatives for Battered Women." In Victimization of Women. Eds. Jane Chapman and Margaret Gates. Beverly Hills, Cal. : Sage, 1978, pp. 143-74. Also in Research into Violent Behavior: Domestic Violence. U. S. Congress. House. Committee on Science and Technology. Hearings. 95th Cong. 2nd Sess. February 14, 15, 16, 1978. Washington, D. C. : Government Printing Office, 1978, pp. 896-942.
       An excellent discussion of the cycle theory of battering incidents, detailing the three phases of the cycle. The pros and cons of sheltering are discussed along with the criminal justice system. The value of psychotherapy, individual, group and couple, receives some attention. In the last analysis, it must be realized that the wife is the victim and that possibly only separation or divorce will resolve the problem.

1671 Walker, Lenore E. "Victimology and the Psychological Perspectives of Battered Women." Victimology: An International Journal 8 (Winter/Spring 1983): 82-104.

1672 Walker, L. "When Battered Women Kill: Psychologists as Expert Witnesses." Symposium presented with A. Browne, R. Thyfault, and L. Rosewater at the annual meeting of the American Psychological Association, Los Angeles, August, 1981.

1673 Walker, Lenore E. "Who Are the Battered Women?" Frontiers: A Journal of Women Studies 2 (Spring 1979): 52-7.
       A general discussion of the problem with attention to the cycle of violence which includes the period of happiness and the contriteness which entraps the victim. Women stay because of love, the belief the husband will change, and the feeling that she somehow provoked him to violence. Embarrassment and learned helplessness explain why she does not leave her abuser. For this author the term "battering" includes psychological as well as physical abuse. In fact, the former seems the more long lasting in its effects.

1674 Walker, Lenore; Karen Schreiber; and Morton Flax. "The Battered Woman Syndrome." Symposium presented at the annual meeting of the American Psychological Association, Washington, D. C. , 3 September 1976.

1675 Walker, Lenore E. , and M. L. Flax. "Psychotherapy with Battered Women and Their Partners." Paper presented at the Conference on Violent Crimes Against Women, University of Washington, Seattle, 2 May, 1977.

1676 Walker, L. E.; M. L. Flax; M. J. Fields; and M. W. Leidig.
      "The Battered Woman Syndrome Revisited." Symposium
      presented at the annual meeting of the American Psycho-
      logical Association, San Francisco, 29 August 1977.

1677 Walker, Lenore E.; Roberta K. Thyfault; and Angela Browne.
      "Symposium: Family Violence in America--Part II. Be-
      yond the Juror's Ken: Battered Women." Vermont Law
      Review 7 (Spring 1982): 1-14.
      The authors argue the case for allowing expert testimony
in cases involving women who kill their battering spouses. Too many
myths surround the battered wife phenomenon and a knowledgeable expert is necessary to insure the jury understands the wife's frame of
mind at the time of the killing. Legal concepts of self-defense and
reasonable response as well as psychological theories of cycle of violence and learned helplessness are discussed.

1678 Walker-Hooper, Ashley. "Domestic Violence: Assessing the
      Problem." In Conflict Intervention in Social and Domestic
      Violence. Ed. Carmen Germaine Warner. Bowie, Md.:
      Robert J. Brady, Co., 1981, pp. 47-87.
      This is an excellent overview of the problem drawing from
the research of Straus, L. Walker, M. Elbow, and others. Why men
batter and their characteristics, why victims stay with the abuser and
their traits, the dynamics of the abuse, and the roles of the police,
legal, and medical professions are discussed. The professionals must
provide assistance and support, but in the last analysis it is only the
victim who can solve the problem. Working with battered wives is
extremely frustrating and thankless, and the professionals must see
themselves as "helpers" only and keep their expectations within the
realm of possibility.

1679 Walker-Hooper, Ashley. "Domestic Violence: Responding to
      Victim's Needs." In Conflict Intervention in Social and Do-
      mestic Violence. Ed. Carmen Germaine Warner. Bowie,
      Md.: Robert J. Brady Co., 1981, pp. 185-215.
      Service providers must at least attempt to understand the
dynamics of a battering relationship. Otherwise there is a danger that
they will be imposing their value systems upon the victims. Who
should be counselors, strategies for working with victims, understanding the victim, couple counseling, assertiveness training, and divorce
counseling are given attention by the author. Of special importance is
the counselor playing the proper role. If not, both the client and the
counselor will be frustrated and disappointed.

1680 Wall, Virginia A. "Biographical, Attitudinal and Psychopatho-
      logical Symptom Correlates of Domestic Abuse Reported
      by Women." M. S. thesis, Villanova University, 1979. 55 p.
      A study of sixty-nine women from a variety of sources was
conducted to determine if their exposure to abuse as a child, whether
as victim or as observer, affected their being abused as an adult. The
study reports a relationship between present abuse and abuse as a child.
There was no significance in present abuse and having witnessed it as

a child, but a high significance between abuse and higher level of psychopathological symptoms. A relationship between current abuse and socioeconomic indicators was also apparent.

1681 Wallendorf, Susan. Domestic Violence Project: Report April
      1975-December 1976, a Summary of the Project's Organ-
      ization and Activities. Ann Arbor, Mich.: NOW Domestic
      Violence Project [1977]. 23 p. Also in Domestic Violence,
      1978. U.S. Congress. Senate. Committee on Human Re-
      sources, Subcommittee on Child and Human Development.
      Hearings. 95th Cong. 2nd Sess. On Domestic Violence
      and Legislation with Respect to Domestic Violence, March
      4 and 8, 1978. Washington, D.C.: Government Printing
      Office, 1978, pp. 398-420.

1682 Walsh, James C. "Suffolk County Counsels Victims of Rape and
      Family Violence." Victimology: An International Journal 1
      (Winter 1976): 590-1.
      Walsh, Executive Director of the Victim Information Bureau
of Suffolk County (VIBS) in New York, described the new 24-hour hot
line and counseling program for rape and family violence victims. He
notes that rape victims generally need five to eight weeks of counseling,
whereas family violence victims more often require six months to two
years.

1683 Walsh, Joseph A., and Pamela G. Witte. "Police Training in
      Domestic Crisis: A Suburban Approach." Community Men-
      tal Health Journal 11 (Fall 1975): 301-6.
      A family crisis training program was presented to seven
suburban police departments by the Dupage County, Illinois, Mental
Health Center. The success of this program indicates that suburban
police may need different training than that suggested by Bard and
Berkowitz for urban police in their New York model.

1684 Walter, Paula Donner. "Expert Testimony and Battered Women:
      Conflict Among the Courts and a Proposal." Journal of
      Legal Medicine 3 (June 1982): 267-94.
      Walter, a law student at the Southern Illinois University
School of Law, takes up the question of expert testimony as it applies
in cases when abused wives kill their husbands and then claim self-
defense. Because of the circumstances often surrounding the homicide,
the traditional standards of self-defense do not always apply. Use of
expert testimony to show that the abused spouse's perceptions of imminent harm are different has been attempted with varying degrees of
success. The lack of uniformity in the admissibility of expert testimony
in general has been the major source of conflict over the admissibility
of expert testimony about the battered women's syndrome. This conflict could be resolved by uniform adoption of Federal Rule of Evidence
702, which requires the expert to qualify through knowledge, skill, experience, training, or education, and to assist the jury in understanding
the evidence.

1685 Wardell, Laurie; Dair L. Gillespie; and Ann Leffler. "Science

and Violence Against Wives." In The Dark Side of Families: Current Family Violence Research.   Eds. David
Finkelhor et al.   Beverly Hills, Cal.:   Sage, 1983, pp.
69-84.
    The major thrust of this study is to determine if there is
sexual bias in the current research on spouse abuse.   With the rise
of the feminist movement in the 1960's the hope is that its effects have
reached into social science research methodology.   The final judgment,
however, is that "... despite its genuinely benevolent intentions, the
wife-beating literature is riddled with misogyny.   Its sexist bias may
be seen with respect to its analyses of the causes, solutions, and context of the problem."   The literature professes to be anti-sexist, and
although these claims are sincere, the results are still sexist.

1686 Warner, Carmen Germaine.   Conflict Intervention in Social and
        Domestic Violence.   Bowie, Md.:   Robert J. Brady Co.,
        1981.   283 p.
    Numerous articles by Warner and by others have been
written for this collection.   Directed primarily at the needs of hospital
emergency departments, she stresses the notion that the first responder
to the crisis is the most important as far as the victim's willingness
to accept help is concerned.   Victims in this work include virtually all
family members, but emphasis is placed on the physical and sexual
abuse of children and battered wives.   Important book for those who
are the first, or among the first, to have contact with victims of domestic violence.   Articles of special relevance to spouse abuse are
annotated separately in this bibliography under each author's name.

1687 Warner, Carmen Germaine.   "Techniques in Conflict Intervention."
        In her Conflict Intervention in Social and Domestic Violence.
        Bowie, Md.:   Robert J. Brady Co., 1981, pp. 147-60.
    When health professionals are attempting to provide assist-
ance to persons involved in conflict situations, it must be kept in mind
that the participants are under a great deal of stress.   If not, the violent episode would not have occurred.   Various methods of conflict intervention are itemized for child abuse victims, sexually abused children, spouse abuse victims, and suicidal persons.   Most important is
the belief that it is the first responder to the crisis event that sets the
tone for trust and willingness to accept the assistance offered by helping professionals.   Appropriate intervention is not possible if the first
responder is not an open, nonbiased, empathetic individual.

1688 Warner, Carmen Germaine, and G. Richard Braen.   Management
        of the Physically and Emotionally Abused: Emergency As-
        sessment, Intervention and Counseling.   East Norwalk,
        Conn.:   Appleton-Century-Crofts, 1982.   329 p.

1689 Warren, Mary.   "Battered Husbands."   In Family Violence: A
        Cycle of Abuse.   Ed. Margaret E. Ankeney.   Laramie:
        College of Education, University of Wyoming, 1979, pp.
        76-8.
    When traditional marriage roles are reversed, men too may
be subject to abuse by their spouses.   Often this happens in revenge

for previous wife beatings.   Husband battering is just another facet of
family violence.

1690 Warrior, Betsy. <u>Battered Lives</u>. Pittsburgh: KNOW, 1975.
     24 p.

1691 Warrior, Betsy. <u>Battered Women's Directory</u>.   8th ed.   Cam-
     bridge, Mass. :   Author.   1982.   275 p.
     Previously called <u>Working on Wife Abuse</u>, this is the single
most important guide to shelters and services available in the U. S. and
abroad.   Several essays regarding abuse are included along with discussions of programs such as EMERGE and RAVEN which are aimed at the
abusers.

1692 Warrior, Betsy.   <u>Wifebeating</u>. 2nd ed. Somerville, Mass. : New
     England Free Press, 1976.   21 p.
     This pamphlet provides a succinct but perceptive analysis of
the problem.   Cases are used as illustrations of how society and the
victims view the situation.   Warrior concludes that wife beating exists
and continues because the culture is sexist.   Spouse abuse is just one
method men use to keep women in their "place" and protect the male
supremacist culture.   Psychiatrists see wife beating as an expression
of sick individuals.   Warrior rejects this belief.

1693 Washburn, C. ; I. Frieze; and J. Knoble. "Some Subtle Biases
     of Therapists Toward Women and Violence. "   Paper pre-
     sented at the annual Research Conference of the Association
     for Women in Psychology, Dallas, Texas, 1979.

1694 Wasileski, Maryann; Martha E. Callaghan-Chaffee; and R. Blake
     Chaffee. "Spousal Violence in Military Homes: An Initial
     Survey. "   <u>Military Medicine</u> 147 (September 1982): 761-5.
     The U. S. Navy established the Family Advocacy Program
in order to identify and treat Navy and Marine Corps members and de-
pendents who are victims or perpetrators of abuse, sexual assault, and
rape.   The ultimate purpose is to prevent recurrence of domestic violence.   Claiming to be the first to present spouse abuse data entirely
on a military population, these authors (all Navy officers) studied 60
San Diego abused military spouses from June 1980 to February 1981.
Much detail is presented regarding demographic characteristics, location, time of day, and day of the week the incident occurred, perceived
precipitating facts, type of help sought, etc.   Various recommendations
include the expansion of the Family Advocacy Program, that alcohol rehabilitation and abuse programs should be interfaced, and abuse recognition training be established for emergency room personnel.

1695 Wasoff, F.   "Legal Protection from Wife-beating: The Process-
     ing of Domestic Assaults by Scottish Prosecutors and Crim-
     inal Courts. "   <u>International Journal of the Sociology of Law</u>
     10, no. 2 (1982): 187-204.

1696 Wasoff, F.   "Violence to Women in the Home: A Research
     Strategy. "   Paper presented at the DHSS seminar on Violence

in the Family--Recent Research on Services for Battered
Women and their Children.   University of Kent at Canterbury, September 1981.

1697 Wasoff, Fran; R. Emerson Dobash; and Russell P. Dobash. "The
         Current Evidence and Legal Remedies Regarding Battered
         Women." Law Society of Scotland Journal 25 (May 1979):
         178-83.
         This article criticizes a two-part article by J. Stuart
McNeill in the November and December issues of this journal.   While
McNeill is applauded for sympathizing with the victims, these authors
believe some of his information is outdated and on occasion gives the
wrong impression to the reader.   They go on to present the results of
some recent research on abuse in Scotland and correct several conven-
tionally held misconceptions.

1698 Watchman, Paul Q. "Housing (Homeless Persons) Act 1977--
         Homelessness--Whether a Woman Living in a Battered
         Women's Refuge Can Be Deemed to Be Homeless...." Jour-
         nal of Social Welfare Law (July 1982): 237-9.
         The British case of R. v. Ealing London Borough Council,
ex P. Sidhu clarifies parts of the Housing (Homeless Persons) Act 1977.
Residents of battered women's shelters are considered homeless under
this law, no final custody order is required in these cases, and battered women, at least Mrs. Sidhu, could not be considered intentionally
homeless.   Housing had to be found for her.

1699 Watson, Arthur. "Reform of the Law of the Australian Capital
         Territory Relating to Rape and Other Sexual Offenses."
         In Rape Law Reform: A Collection of Conference Papers.
         Ed. Jocelynne A. Scutt.   Canberra: Australian Institute of
         Criminology, 1980, pp. 67-77.
         Several changes in the law are called for by this attorney-
general for Australia.   One change requested was an end to the husband
immunity from rape prosecution.

1700 Watson, Charles G.; Angela M. Rosenberg; and Norman Petrik.
         "Incidence of Wife-battering in Male Psychiatric Hospital
         Patients: Are Special Treatment Programs Necessary?"
         Psychological Reports 51 (October 1982): 563-6.

1701 Watts, Deborah L., and Christine A. Courtois. "Trends in the
         Treatment of Men Who Commit Violence Against Women."
         Personnel and Guidance Journal 60 (December 1981): 245-9.
         The authors study several methods of treating men who com-
mit incest, rape, or acts of wife battering.   Treatment and counseling
as individuals, couples, and groups are discussed with the goal directed
at ending the behavior.   None of the methods used to date have "demonstrated long term success through experimental outcome studies."
Recognition and prevention of violent behavior is a primary duty of
counselors.

1702 Wayne, Candace J. Illinois Domestic Violence Act: A Law

Enforcement Officers Manual. Springfield: Illinois Coa-
lition Against Domestic Violence [1982?] 24 p. Also in
Domestic Violence. U. S. Congress. House Committee on
Education and Labor, Subcommittee on Select Education.
Hearing. 98th Cong. 1st Sess. 23 June 1983. Washington,
D. C.: Government Printing Office, 1983, pp. 165-208.
This is a comprehensive explanation of police and court
responsibilities under the Illinois laws. A general discussion of the
problem of domestic violence is followed by a description of the Act,
orders of protection, and copies of the various forms.

1703 Webb, P. R. H.   "Matrimonial Cruelty: A Lawyer's Guide for
        the Medical Profession."   Medicine, Science and the Law
        7 (1967): 110-6.
        Webb (Reader in Conflict of Laws, University of Nottingham,
and Professor of Law, University of Auckland, New Zealand) discusses
various types of cruelty that could be used to obtain a divorce in England. Since the medical profession is often called upon to testify in
such cases, this article is designed to acquaint them with some of the
legal aspects of the concept. Some discussion of wife beating is included but not adequately dealt with.

1704 Weingourt, Rita. "Battered Women: The Grieving Process."
        Journal of Psychiatric Nursing and Mental Health Services
        17 (April 1979): 40-7.
        Using the five stages of grief described by Kubler-Ross, this
author, Assistant Professor, Intercollegiate Center for Nursing Education, Spokane, shows the similarities of grieving for the loss of a significant other and the battered woman's attitude toward leaving her
abusing husband. This process will often begin while at a shelter.
Assistance is needed to help the victim through the stages and to see
them as temporary.

1705 Weir, Angela.   "Battered Women: Some Perspectives and Prob-
        lems."   In Women in the Community.   Ed. Marjorie Mayo.
        London: Routledge and Kegan Paul, 1977, pp. 109-20.
        Much attention has been devoted to spouse abuse lately and
the purpose of this article is to examine the causes of the sudden concern. The women's movement, along with the realization women have
a common oppression regardless of class, and a recognition that bliss-
ful family relations are not normal are all discussed. Refuges are
important for battered women, but victims need more long-term assistance. Primarily British in orientation.

1706 Weitzman, Jack, and Karen Dreen.   "Wifebeating: A View of the
        Marital Dyad."   Social Casework 63 (May 1982): 259-65.
        If counselors are to be successful with abusing families they
cannot treat the wife and the husband separately since it is their method
of interacting which causes the violence to erupt. The issue which pre-
cipitates the violence rarely has anything to do with the argument at
hand. More often the issue at stake is who is in control of the situation. Neither may be aware that it is a question of power, not the

matter under discussion. Counselors must be aware of this and work
with the couple if treatment is to work. Several example cases are
used.

1707 Wermuth, Laurie. "Domestic Violence Reforms: Policing the
        Private?" Berkeley Journal of Sociology 27 (1982): 27-49.
        It is sometimes argued that the state too often interferes
in the private lives of individuals. This author examined that notion
as it is applied to spouse abuse. She looks at the new police training
for crisis intervention and at the newly focused multiagency treatment
programs. She concludes that "despite appearances, the reforms did
not substantially enhance the state's mediation in private relationships."
Wholesale criminalization of wife beating probably would not serve the
wishes of the victim or the needs of society, but routinely sidestepping
punitive measures probably would not either. Alternative support agencies inspired by the women's movement should be expanded with energy,
persistence and money.

1708 Wermuth, Laurie Ann. "Wife Beating: The Crime Without Pun-
        ishment." Ph. D. dissertation, University of California,
        Berkeley, 1983. 217 p.

1709 Wessel, Peter. "Jurisdiction over Family Offenses in New York:
        A Reconsideration of the Provisions for Choice of Forum."
        Syracuse Law Review 31 (Spring 1980): 601-30.
        New York law allows for a choice between pursuing relief
in cases of spouse abuse through the criminal courts or the family
courts. This note traces the development of this choice of forum. The
intent of the legislature is examined, along with the actual consequences,
and new revisions are recommended. Questions of double jeopardy,
due process, equitable relief and constitutionality are discussed. While
somewhat improved, several changes would be helpful. Victims must
be ensured adequate access to the police and the courts, legal counsel
must be guaranteed, and the language of the statute must be clarified,
diminishing the likelihood that the laws will be declared unconstitutional.

1710 West, Lois A. "Air Force Personnel Attend Spouse Abuse Work-
        shop." Response to Violence in the Family 3 (July 1980): 2.

1711 West, Lois A. "U. N. Conference Participants Discuss Wife
        Abuse." Response to Violence in the Family 4 (November/
        December 1980): 2.

1712 West, Lois A.; William M. Turner; and Ellen Dunwoody. Wife
        Abuse in the Armed Forces. Washington, D. C. : Center
        for Woman Policy Studies, 1981. 186 p.
        This report "investigates the nature of wife abuse in the
military community, and the development, availability, and delivery of
services to violent couples. Information was gathered from battered
wives of servicemen, Armed Forces and civilian service providers who
work with violent military families, and Armed Forces policy makers."
Problems that are unique to the military and common with civilian battering are discussed.

1713   Western States Shelter Network. <u>Directory of Shelter Programs</u>
        <u>and Shelter Referrals.</u>   San Francisco: The Network, 1982.
        <u>24</u> p.

1714   Westra, Bonita L. "Battered Women and Child Development."
        M. S. thesis, University of Colorado, 1979.   131 p.
        The purpose of this study was to assess the development
of children from homes where the mothers were abused by the father.
Some studies trace retarded motor skill and cognitive and verbal ability development to aggressive behavior between parents.   Twenty children between the ages of 2-1/2 and 8 years were tested.   Results
indicate that the level of aggression in this group was higher than for
peers, and motor, verbal, and cognitive skills were lower.

1715   Westra, Bonnie, and Harold P. Martin.   "Children of Battered
        Women."   <u>Maternal-Child Nursing Journal</u> 10 (Spring 1981):
        41-54.
        This study was motivated by concern for the effects of wife
beating on the children.   Twenty children ages 2-1/2 to 8 from shelters in Denver were studied.   Results indicate they had significantly
poorer cognitive, verbal, motor, and quantitative abilities than should
be expected in a normal population.   There were also personality
problems, including hostile-aggressive behavior as well as hearing
and articulation deficits.   All of this is compounded by the inability
of recently battered mothers to respond to the emotional needs of the
children.   More research in this area is needed.

1716   Wetzel, Laura, and Mary A. Ross.   "Psychological and Social
        Ramifications of Battering: Observations Leading to a
        Counseling Methodology for Victims of Domestic Violence."
        <u>Personnel and Guidance Journal</u> 61 (March 1983): 423-8.
        Personality characteristics of the batterers and the victims
are described along with a counseling methodology, and indices for
assessing the victim's readiness to change her life situation.   The
counselor's goal is to stop the battering and since this is done in
stages, it is imperative that the counselor be able to assess the progress of the victim so appropriate assistance can be given.

1717   Wharton, Carol S. "Redefining Woman Battering: The Construc-
        tion of a Social Problem." Ph. D. dissertation, Michigan
        State University, 1982.   297 p.   Abstract in <u>Dissertation</u>
        <u>Abstracts International</u> 43A (August 1982): 563.

1718   Wharton, Carol S. "Shelters for Battered Women: Creating
        New Families."   Paper presented to the American Sociolog-
        ical Association, 1983.

1719   Whelan, Pat. "Funding for Transition Houses in Canada: National
        Survey Results." <u>Response to Violence in the Family and</u>
        <u>Sexual Assault</u> 6 (November/December 1983): 5-6.

1720   "Where to Get Help for Battered Women." <u>Emergency Medicine</u>
        11 (April 15, 1979): 28-9, 33-4, 39-42.

A partial state-by-state listing of shelters with addresses and phone numbers. Compiled for physicians who wish to refer patients involved in spouse abuse situations.

1721 White, Joyce. "Women Speak!" Essence 10 (June 1979): 75, 129, 131.
     Personal accounts of abuse by a number of women. The answer is not in continued silence. Instead the police and legal systems must be called upon to provide aid and relief. Domestic violence must be made a public issue.

1722 White, Shelley. "Legal Help for Battered Women." The Women's Yellow Pages: Original Sourcebook for Women. Eds. Carol Edry and Rosalyn Gerstein. New England Edition. Boston: The Public Works, 1978, pp. 322-4.
     This is a general discussion of the legal system and advice on how New England battered women can make it work to their advantage. Acquiring a lawyer is urged, but how to deal with the police, filing a criminal complaint, protective orders, going to court and other matters are explained.

1723 White, Susan O., and Murray A. Straus. "The Implications of Family Violence for Rehabilitation Strategies." In New Directions in the Rehabilitation of Criminal Offenders. Eds. Susan E. Martin, Lee R. Sechrest, and Robin Redner. Washington, D.C.: National Academy Press, 1981, pp. 255-88.

1724 Whitehurst, Robert N. "Violence in Husband-Wife Interaction." In Violence in the Family. Eds. Suzanne K. Steinmetz and Murray A. Straus. New York: Dodd, Mead, 1974, pp. 75-82.
     Whitehurst believes that since the idea of male supremacy is dominant in our society, interspousal violence is not likely to subside in the short run. However, egalitarian conditions will in the long run reduce violent encounters between husband and wife.

1725 Whitehurst, Robert N. "Violence Potential in Extramarital Sexual Responses." Journal of Marriage and the Family 33 (November 1971): 683-91.
     Courtroom cases, survey data, and clinical cases were investigated to determine in what ways extramarital sexual activity provoked marital problems. Whitehurst found violence to be a more common factor in family relations than previously thought. He believes that because males are socialized in instrumental and aggressive ways they tend to use violence to retain or regain control of the marital relationship. Extramarital sex by the wife is seen by him as a loss of control over her.

1726 Whitehurst, Robert N. "Violently Jealous Husbands." Sexual Behavior 1 (July 1971): 32-41.
     The author, Associate Professor of Sociology, University of Windsor, Ontario, believes men resort to violent behavior with their

wives because of their inability to control a specific situation to their
satisfaction in any other way. Biological and social factors account
for the propensity of men to use violence to resolve conflict. The influence of women's liberation, the difference between lower- and
middle-class male violence and jealousy are all discussed. The author emphasizes the importance of the sexual relationship in male-
female interaction. Male violence is not expected to subside soon.
How can it when "men are not programmed to be other than aggressive"?

1727 "The Wife Beater and His Wife." Time 84 (September 25, 1964):
        81-2.
        This is a journalistic recounting of the article in Archives
of General Psychiatry by Snell, Rosenwald, and Robey [1464]. Wife
beating is a by-product of alcoholism. The beater is a hard worker,
but ineffectual mother's boy, whereas the wife is aggressive, masculine,
and sexually frigid. This interaction causes the conflict, especially
after the husband has been drinking.

1728 "Wife-beating as an American Pastime." Behavior Today 8
        (February 21, 1977): 5.
        A note regarding the research of Marya Grambs with a
synopsis of the results. Frequency of abuse and abuser characteristics
are provided.

1729 "Wife Beating: It Happens in the Best of Families--I Realized
        That He Might Kill Me." Family Circle (November 15,
        1977): 62, 68.
        Personal reminiscences and the decision to leave her abu-
sive husband.

1730 "Wife-beating Should Be Considered a Crime: Forum." Jet 59
        (December 11, 1980): 37.

1731 Wilkerson, Cheryl A. "Spouse Abuse: Proposal for a New Rule
        of Thumb." University of Richmond Law Review 17 (Spring
        1983): 633-60.
        Wilkerson discusses the incidence of abuse in the U.S. and
Virginia, reviews that state's response to the problem and the legal
remedies available, and then suggests legislation reforms. Of special
interest is the successful use of civil protection orders elsewhere. The
Virginia legislature should enact the same.

1732 Williams, James E. "An Empirical Phenomenological Study of
        Witnessing Spouse Abuse as a Preadolescent." Ph.D. dis-
        sertation, University of Pittsburgh, 1983. 242 p. Abstract
        in Dissertation Abstracts International 44B (February 1984):
        2573.

1733 Williams, Roger. "The Right Not to Be Beaten." Psychology
        Today 11 (June 1977): 36.
        The Appalachian Women's Rights Organization has been
pushing for better treatment of women and now has added the demand

that men end the wholesale physical and mental abuse of wives.   A news note.

1734 Willis, J. E. "Compensation for Victims of Domestic Violence."
      In Violence in the Family: A Collection of Conference
      Papers. Ed. Jocelynne A. Scutt. Canberra, Australian
      Institute of Criminology, 1980, p. 145-55.
      Victims of domestic violence, including battered women
and children, should be eligible for compensation.   It would reduce
the violence and provide the victim with increased financial independence.   The current attitude is clearly anachronistic.

1735 Willis, Lillian B. "Clear Cassandra Peter."   Union WAGE,
      no. 49 (September/October 1978): 5.
      This news article is, in essence, a plea for funds to help
Cassandra Peter in her court battle.   An abused wife, she was accused
of attempted murder.

1736 Wilson, Carolyn F.   Violence Against Women: An Annotated
      Bibliography.   Boston: G. K. Hall, 1981.   111 p.
      An enlargement of her 1978 pamphlet by the same title
[1651], Wilson has one of the best selected, annotated bibliographies,
The book is divided into several topics and includes a general overview, battered spouses, rape, sexual abuse of children, and pornography.   Scholarly and popular items are found here.

1737 Wilson, E.   "Battered Wives: A Social Worker's Viewpoint."
      Royal Society of Health Journal 95, no. 6 (1975): 294-7.
      Wilson, Lecturer in Social Work, North London Polytech-
nic, explains why English social workers have been less than enthusi-
astic about recognizing and aiding abused women.   Trained to view the
family relationship as important, they are not inclined to encourage
its breakup.   Such breakups also require more housing, a scarce com-
modity in England.   The attitude of social workers will be slow to
change.

1738 Wilt, G. Marie, et al.   Domestic Violence and the Police:
      Studies in Detroit and Kansas City.   Washington, D. C. :
      Police Foundation, 1977.   47 p.
      Domestic violence was studied in both cities and several
major conclusions were noted: 1) the participants were young; 2) the
couple has a history of conflict, often with arrest records; 3) presence of firearms is a high predictor of violence; 4) background and
attitude of the victim are as important to the final outcome as those
of the offender; and 5) threats should not be taken lightly.   The whole
category of domestic disturbances must be reevaluated so that poten-
tially violent ones can be handled differently by the police.   Adequate
and proper training is also a must.

1739 Wilt, G. Marie, and James D. Bannon.   Screening and Dispatch-
      ing Processes of the Detroit Police Department in Response
      to Social Conflict Calls.   [Detroit: n. p.], 1975.   93 p.

1740 Winstead, Elizabeth. Marital Violence: An Assessment of
         Client Outcomes. Ph. D. dissertation, Florida State Uni-
         versity, 1981. 177 p.
         The most common model of treatment for marital violence
is temporary sheltering and counseling. While this is assumed to be
effective, no real research has been done to test it. The Hubbard
House program in Jacksonville, Florida, served as the basis of this
study. Reduction of severity and frequency of the violence, elimination of the violence or changes in the relationship, such as divorce or
separation, were all felt to be possible effects of the program and
were tested for. Of interest too was what characterized the situations
of women with positive outcomes compared with negative outcomes.
Results indicate that the majority did reduce the severity and frequency
of the violence. Those that reduced the violence also in fact had ter-
minated the relationship rather than revise the dynamics. Employment,
education, and age of the youngest child are related to positive outcomes.

1741 Wisconsin Department of Health and Social Services. Domestic
         Abuse Report. Madison: The Department, 1983. 20 p.
         In February 1980, the Wisconsin Domestic Abuse program
was established to be administered by the Department of Health and
Social Services. As of this report there were 50 programs and task
forces throughout the state, with 19 state-funded shelters. This report is a review of the many services being provided.

1742 Wisconsin Legislative Council Staff. Special Committee on Do-
         mestic Violence. Issues Relating to Domestic Violence.
         Madison, Wis. : The Staff, 1977. 23 p.

1743 Wisconsin. University Extension. Women's Education Resources.
         The Problem of Battered Women. Madison: Author, 1978.
         A collection of pertinent articles and other materials useful
for public awareness and education. Includes the articles by Joan
Mills, Judith Gingold, Ann Geracimos, and others. This was compiled as part of a University of Wisconsin-Extension class.

1744 "Witness: Expert Testimony; Battered Woman Syndrome. "
         IACP Law Enforcement Legal Review no. 117 (March
         1982): 13.

1745 Wolfe, Nancy. "Victim Provocation: The Battered Wife and
         Legal Definition of Self Defense. " Sociological Symposium
         25 (Winter 1979): 98-118.
         A number of cases where the wife has killed her abusing
husband are analyzed along with the evolving concept of self-defense.
Of concern, too, is the issue of how the husband had provoked the
final actions of the wife. Wolfe notes that there has been some concern that more women will resort to homicide if the plea of self-
defense works. No such upsurge has occurred as yet, however.

1746 Wolfgang, Marvin E. "Family Violence and Criminal Behavior. "
         American Academy of Psychiatry and the Law Bulletin 4,

no. 4 (1976): 316-27.
Wolfgang discusses family violence, including child abuse
and spousal homicide, but not specifically wife beating.   Most of his
intraspousal homicide statistics are duplicated in another article.
His overall view is that family violence is partly a reflection of violence in society, but serious crimes in the family are most commonly
related to subcultural values that encourage or at least do not inhibit
such behavior.   By restricting violence in society and by giving individuals positive reinforcement, praise, rewards, and other pleasures,
violence will be lessened.   Since we cannot experience pleasure and
be violent at the same time, the provision of pleasure will reduce
violent behavior.

1747 Wolfgang, Marvin E.   "Husband-Wife Homicides."   Journal of
         Social Therapy 2, no. 4 (1956): 263-71.
         In his analysis of 588 consecutive criminal homicides in
Philadelphia from January 1, 1948, to December 31, 1952, the author
found 100 to be husband-wife homicides.   The findings include the revelation that when a man is killed by a woman, the woman is most likely
his wife, and when a woman commits homicide, she is more likely than
a man to kill her mate.   He also notes that husband-wife homicides
were more violent than homicides in general; most slayings occurred
in the bedroom; and wives tended to use knives more than guns, while
husbands used either equally.   He believes many murders are victim
precipitated and "husbands more often than wives are the major precipitating factors in their own homicidal deaths."

1748 Wolfgang, Marvin E.   "Victim Precipitated Criminal Homicide."
         Journal of Criminal Law, Criminology and Police Science
         48 (May-June 1957): 1-11.
         This is an early study, not directly interested in wife abuse.
There is, however, some data of value regarding wives killing abusive
mates.

1749 Wolfgang, Marvin E.   "Who Kills Whom."   Psychology Today 3
         (October 1969): 54-6, 72, 74-5.   Also in Change: Readings
         in Society and Human Behavior.   Del Mar, Cal. :   Commu-
         nications Research, 1972, pp. 256-60.
         This is a popularized account of the study Wolfgang did of
588 homicides in Philadelphia.   The amount of intrafamily, especially
husband-wife homicide, is striking.   The original study was published
in the Journal of Social Therapy [1747].

1750 Wolfgang, Marvin E. , and F. Ferracuti.   "Emergency Domestic
         Police Service."   In The Criminal in the Arms of the Law.
         Eds. Leon Radzinowicz and Marvin E. Wolfgang, Vol. 2
         of Crime and Justice, (New York: Basic Books, 1971),
         pp. 236-8.

1751 Woman, Lois M. Hake.   "Diary of a Battered Housewife."   Do
         It Now 9 (March 1976): 4.
         A letter to the editor describing her feelings and urging
open discussion of the battered-wife problem.   Hiding the problem, or
denying it exists, will not end it.

1752 Women Helping Women: A State-by-State Directory of Services.
         New York: Women's Action Alliance, 1981. 179 p.
         This directory, with an alphabetical state-by-state arrange-
ment, categorizes eight types of services for women, including career
counseling, health centers and others.   The first category under each
state is "Battered Women and Rape Victim Services" with each entry
listed alphabetically by city.   Addresses and phone numbers are included.

1753 Women's Advocates; The Story of A Shelter.   St. Paul, Minn. :
         Women's Advocates, 1980. 98 p.
         This booklet tells how the Women's Advocates Shelter of
St. Paul began in 1974 and developed and evolved over the years.   Relations with the local police, education of the community, fund raising,
legislation, and details of the operation of the house itself, including
the program and policies, are described.   In the last analysis it is
felt that while the shelter did not change society or bring an end to
family violence, it has helped many individual women.   A good history
of one of the first shelters in the U. S.

1754 Women's Center and Shelter of Greater Pittsburgh.   Women Shel-
         tering Women: A Grassroots Response to Battered Wives.
         Pittsburgh: Author, 1978.   4 p.   Also in Domestic Vio-
         lence.   U. S. Congress. House. Committee on Education
         and Labor, Subcommittee on Select Education.   95th Cong.
         2nd Sess. Hearings on HR 7927 and HR 8948.   March 16
         and 17, 1978. Washington, D. C. : Government Printing
         Office, 1978, pp. 455-8.

1755 Wood, Beth. "Navaho Battered Women. "   Off Our Backs 8
         (August/ September 1978): 5.
         This news note discusses the activities of the Navaho women
of Shiprock, New Mexico.   Cultural changes and the increase of family
violence were topics of an abuse workshop.

1756 Woods, Frances Burton.   "A Community Approach to Working
         with Battering Women. "   Ph. D. dissertation, University
         of Arkansas, 1979.   354 p.   Abstract in Dissertation Ab-
         stracts International 40B (September 1979): 1435.

1757 Woods, Frances Burton.   Living Without Violence: A Community
         Approach to Working With Battered Women and Their Chil-
         dren.   Fayetteville, Ark. : Project for Victims of Family
         Violence, 1981.   333 p.

1758 Woods, Joan. "Wife Battering: A Theoretical Model and Treat-
         ment Approaches. "   M. A. thesis, Western Michigan Uni-
         versity, 1980.   250 p.   Abstract in Masters Abstracts 19
         (September 1981): 270.

1759 Woods, Laurie. "Challenges to Legislation Enacted on Behalf
         of Battered Women. "   Clearinghouse Review 14 (August/
         September 1980): 426-7.

Over 30 states had enacted legislation regarding spouse
abuse between 1975 and 1980. This author comments on four challenges
to some of the legislation, Boyle v. Boyle in Pennsylvania, Ohio v.
Heyl, LeBlanc v. Florida and People v. Cameron in California. Eviction of the abuser, temporary protection orders as a condition of bail,
police arrest powers, and classifying wife assault as a felony were
the issues under contention. The conclusion reached by the author is
that much of the legislation seems to be holding up. Battered-wife
advocates should continue pressing their position.

1760 Woods, Laurie. "Litigation on Behalf of Battered Women."
       Women's Rights Law Reporter 5 (Fall 1978): 7-33.
       In December 1976 a class action suit was filed against the
New York City police, the New York City Department of Probation,
and the clerks of the Family Court, alleging that these agencies "...
engaged in a pervasive pattern and practice of denying to abused wives
the legal protection and assistance to which they were entitled under
state law." The case of Bruno v. Codd was the focus. The article
discusses the problem of abuse generally and then specifically as the
legal structure of New York applied, or failed to be applied. The details of the class action are included and would be useful for others
considering similar action.

1761 Woods, Laurie. "Litigation on Behalf of Battered Women."
       Women's Rights Law Reporter 7 (Fall 1981): 39-45.
       This essay reviews and updates the author's earlier article
by the same name. In the three years since Bruno v. Codd much education work has been done by the plaintiffs. Overall it appears that
there has been some improvement, but much yet needs to be done.

1762 Woods, Laurie. "Update: Litigation on Behalf of Battered Wom-
       en." Clearinghouse Review 15 (July 1981): 261-3.
       Woods discusses the effects of several class action suits
on behalf of battered women including Scott v. Hart in Oakland, California, and Bruno v. Codd in New York City. Experience shows that the
police, district attorneys, judges, and others welcome the efforts of
battered-women advocates so long as they are restricted to mediation
and referral. When it comes to changes in their actual policies and
practices these agencies are less agreeable. Although drastic, it
appears that litigation may be required. Thus far it has been successful.

1763 Woolley, Sabra F. Battered Women: A Summary. 2nd ed.
       Washington, D.C.: Women's Equity Action League, 1980.
       27 p.
       This fine booklet provides a general introduction to the
problem, including its history, the social context in which wife abuse
appears, theories of why it happens and why many women do not leave
their abusers. The author, Assistant Professor of Anthropology,
University of Hawaii, Hilo College, makes recommendations for both
prevention and treatment.

1764 Woon, T.H., and Shirley George. "Battered Wife." Medical

Journal of Malaysia 34 (March 1980): 281-4.
Woon (Associate Professor and head of the Department of
Psychological Medicine, University of Malaysia) and George (psychiatrist, General Hospital, Seremban) detail a case history of a middle-
aged Indian woman who had visited numerous doctors for assorted
ailments and injuries over many years.   The hope is that readers
and other medical professionals will take steps to recognize the work
of abusive husbands and draw upon local resources to help the victim.
Kuala Lumpur has no shelter, but if it had, maybe this woman would
not have suffered for so many years.

1765 Wrathall, Leila.   "Discarded Workers Take Violence Home."
        Union WAGE, no. 66 (July-August 1981): 8.
        In a number of Oregon mill towns, unemployment had in-
creased dramatically.   Along with other demands on local social services, calls for assistance in abuse cases have increased.   This news
item shows the relation between economic stress and family violence.

1766 Wright, Alisa Deborah.   "Locus of Control in Battered Women."
        M. A. thesis, Southern Methodist University, 1980.   76 p.
        Three groups of women were studied.   The first were
abused who had recently left the violent home, the second were abused
who had been removed for a longer period, and the third were nonabused.   The results show a relationship between the frequency of
abuse and an external locus of control and Machiavellianism.   Abused
women may be more inclined to be manipulative rather than use open
communication.   The husband, feeling his loss of control, may resort
then to violence more frequently.   This may add to the cycle of violence.   To counter abuse, battered women must increase their sense
of shared control and their skill at communicating love.   Self-esteem
will be improved and abuse lessened.

1767 Wright, Connie.   "Police Action on Wife Beaters: Make More
        Arrests." Nation's Cities Weekly 3 (October 6, 1980): 3.

1768 Wright, Moira.   "The DVMPA 1976: An Evaluation."   New Law
        Journal 130 (February 7, 1980): 127-30.
        The author, Lecturer in Law, Birmingham University,
discusses the effects of the new Domestic Violence and Matrimonial
Proceedings Act two years after passage.   Various legal cases are
examined with the overall view that the basic intentions of the Parliament are being met, but that the law fell short of the needs.   The
much touted injunction is a limited remedy for relieving battered wom-
en, even with the power of arrest attached.   More must be done by
the legal system and Parliament.

1769 Yahraes, Herbert.   "Physical Violence in Families."   In his
        Families Today; A Research Sample on Families and Chil-
        dren.   (National Institute of Mental Health, Science Mono-
        graphs no. 1.) Washington, D. C.: DHEW, 1979, pp. 553-
        76.

The author synthesizes recent research by Murray Straus
and Richard J. Gelles. General discussion of various types of family
violence, with some attention to spouse abuse. This violence is
viewed as learned behavior and if parents would stop using physical
violence on each other and the children, and stress to the offspring
that violence is not an acceptable method of resolving conflict, family
violence would disappear.

1770   Yllo, Kersti. "Sexual Equality and Violence Against Wives in
       American States." Journal of Comparative Family Studies
       14 (Spring 1983): 67-86.
       The relative status of women to men in each of the fifty
states is studied to determine if a relationship exists between it and
domestic violence. Results show that in states in which women have
low status the incidence is higher and as status increases, violence
decreases, but only to a point. Then violence increases again. Of
interest, too, is the finding that in states where women enjoy the
higher status, the violence by wives toward husbands is also much
higher. Distinctions between the short-run and the long-run effects
of sexual equality are important and no state currently can be considered equalitarian. There is a complicated web of factors that affect
wife abuse. Any attempt to explain the abuse with unicausal assumptions will be inaccurate.

1771   Yllo, Kersti. "The Status of Women and Wife-beating in the
       U.S.: A Multi-level Analysis." Ph.D. dissertation, Uni-
       versity of New Hampshire, 1980. 192 p. Abstract in
       Dissertation Abstracts International 41A (May 1981): 4853.

1772   Yllo, Kersti. "Types of Marital Rape: Three Case Studies."
       Paper presented at the National Conference for Family
       Violence Researchers, Durham, New Hampshire, July 1981.

1773   Yllo, Kersti. "Using a Feminist Approach in Quantitative Re-
       search: A Case Study." In The Dark Side of Families:
       Current Family Violence Research. Eds. David Finkelhor
       et al. Beverly Hills, Cal.: Sage, 1983, pp. 277-88.
       Yllo, in this study, provides quantitative data which support
feminist theories of spouse abuse. Feminists argue that wife beating
is one element of patriarchy and the desire for male domination of
women. In response to those who say feminist theory has not produced supporting data the "Status of Women Index" was developed.
This scale examines the economic, educational, political, and legal
dimensions of female participation in each state of the U.S. to determine which are the most equalitarian. It seems that none are completely so.

1774   Yllo, Kersti, and Murray A. Straus. "Interpersonal Violence
       Among Married and Cohabiting Couples." Family Rela-
       tions 30 (July 1981): 339-47.
       There has been some assumption that legal marriages are
more likely to contain violence than cohabiting relationships. On the
contrary it appears that cohabiting women are four times more likely

to be subjected to violent behavior by their mates.   Age and income
have a strong relationship to the violence with lower incomes and
younger persons having higher rates of violence.   However, cohabita-
tors over 30, divorced women, those with high incomes and relationships of over ten years have less violence than married counterparts.
Based on a paper presented at the annual meeting of the National
Council on Family Relations, 1978.

1775   Yllo, Kersti, and Murray A. Straus.   "Patriarchy and Violence
          Against Wives: The Impact of Structural and Normative
          Factors."   Paper presented at the Johns Hopkins Symposium
          on Feminism and the Critique of Capitalism, Baltimore,
          Maryland, April 25, 1981.

1776   Young, Gregory.   "Legal Consequences of Wife-beating."   Sepia
          27 (April 1978): 12+.
          Popular treatment of spouse abuse with several cases for
illustration.   Little real discussion of the legal consequences.   One of
the less important articles.

1777   Young, Jim.   "Wife-beating in Britain: A Socio-historical Anal-
          ysis, 1850-1914."   Paper presented at the annual meeting
          of the American Sociological Association, New York, 1976.

1778   Younger, Eric.   "Crime Victims: An Agenda for the 1980's.
          In Anatomy of Criminal Justice, A System Overview, 1980.
          Eds. Cleon H. Foust and D. Robert Webster.   Lexington,
          Mass. :   Lexington Books, D. C. Heath, 1980, pp. 173-82.
          Concern for victims seems to be more apparent than in
past years.   Among these are victims of family violence.   During the
next decade (1980's) there will be "a good deal of change in this area."
Government, including the legal system, can help victims, but the
real victory will come by way of the best American tradition--citizens
helping other citizens.   A commentary to this article is provided by
Edith Flynn on pages 183-6 of the same book.

1779   Zahn, Margaret A.   "The Female Homicide Victim."   Crimi-
          nology 13 (November 1975): 400-15.
          Essentially a discussion of the relationship between drug
abuse and female homicide, this study reaffirms that women are frequently slain by spouses or friends.

1780   Zeegers, Michael.   "Violence Between Intimate Partners: Case-
          histories and Commentary."   International Journal of Law
          and Psychiatry 5, nos. 3-4 (1983): 431-8.
          The author, Professor of Forensic Psychology, Leyden Uni-
versity, relates several cases of assault against or murder of wives
or lovers.   The reason for the behavior lies in human deficiency.   We
are all essentially lonely, and violence between intimates confronts us
with the theme of failed human communication.

1781   Ziegler, Linda Kay. "Wife Abuse: A Social Service Needs
       Assessment." M. S. W. thesis, Ohio State University, 1978.
       109 p.

1782   Zimmerman, Martin W. "Wife Battering: An Investigation of
       Alienation and Method of Conflict Resolution." M. S. the-
       sis, University of Maryland, 1979. 83 p.

1783   Zullo, Allen A. , and Ricki Fullman. "Wife Beating in 'Nice'
       Homes." New Woman (March-April 1976): 68-9.
              General discussion of abuse. Much quoting of Maria Roy,
       Executive Director of Abused Women's Aid in Crisis (AWAIC), who
       stresses that it is not a lower-class problem. It is not uncommon
       among the socially advantaged in the suburbs.

552, 563, 679, 1009, 1259,
1293, 1294, 1331, 1407
Attorney's manual   703, 938
Attribution Theory see Blame,
  attribution of
Austin, Texas 11, 12, 1159
Austin Center for Battered
  Women (Texas) 1159
Australia 87, 252, 288, 426,
  497, 596, 691, 844, 866,
  867, 1048, 1189, 1290, 1373,
  1374, 1428, 1432, 1699
Australian Family Law Act
  (1975) 87
AWAIC see Abused Women's
  Aid in Crisis
Awareness groups, establish-
  ment of 1133

Battered Baby Syndrome 464
Battered Wives 1033
Batterers Anonymous 636
Beck Depression Inventory
  1340
Behind Closed Doors 608, 612
Belize 1503
BEM Sex-role Inventory 1111,
  1340, 1469
Bibliographies 3, 135, 234,
  245, 246, 297, 595, 651,
  772, 825, 864, 996, 997,
  1066, 1250, 1651, 1736
Biological factors contributing
  to abuse 439, 440, 613,
  1355, 1726
Black families 1078
Blame, attribution of 72, 276,
  278, 294, 300, 329, 352,
  518, 533, 557, 570, 729,
  760, 761, 808, 846, 883,
  1123, 1192, 1193, 1238,
  1279, 1319, 1519, 1566,
  1567
Boggs-Steers bill 837
Bowen Family Systems Theory
  620
Boyle v. Boyle 5, 1759
Brevard Family Aid Society,
  Inc. 966
Brigham and Women's Hospital 70
British Association of Social

Workers 40
British Columbia 1178
Bruno v. Codd (New York) 208,
  1760, 1761, 1762
Buchrle v. State (Wyoming) 313
Bystander response to violence
  1348, 1454

Calgary, Alberta 342
California 151, 224, 905, 1082,
  1106, 1107, 1473, 1608
Canada 229, 230, 342, 375,
  397, 401, 568, 650, 671, 672,
  738, 815, 1004, 1055, 1070,
  1400, 1503, 1511, 1719
Capgras' Syndrome 114
Capitalism 723, 884, 1118
Career assistance for victims
  171, 274, 856, 1071, 1310
CASA 239
La Casa de las Madres (San
  Francisco) 904, 1231, 1307
Catharsis Hypothesis 1381, 1531
Catholics 1616
Cedar Grove, New Jersey 10
Center for Victims of Family
  Violence 1059
Ceylon 1380
Charivari 370
Charlotte, North Carolina 873,
  1462
Chastisement rights of husbands
  16, 203, 225, 364, 473, 1499,
  1532
Chicago, Illinois 1169
Chicago Court of Domestic Re-
  lations 1222
Child abuse 31, 34, 74, 76,
  122, 132, 184, 189, 206,
  302, 383, 425, 456, 457,
  462, 516, 535, 548, 603,
  614, 619, 627, 658, 671,
  687, 698, 745, 754, 888,
  893, 997, 998, 1034, 1097,
  1102, 1147, 1151, 1164, 1179,
  1300, 1313, 1334, 1434, 1507,
  1535, 1551, 1616, 1629, 1642,
  1649, 1686, 1746
Child molesting 595, 885, 1736
Childrearing, non-sexist 777
Children, effects of witnessing
  spouse abuse on 207, 325,